PRACTICAL PROJECT MANAGEMENT

R. G. GHATTAS
DeVry Institute of Technology—Atlanta

SANDRA L. MCKEE
DeVry Institute of Technology—Atlanta

Upper Saddle River, New Jersey
Columbus, Ohio

Library of Congress Cataloging-in-Publication Data
Ghattas, R. G.
Practical project management/R. G. Ghattas, Sandra McKee.
p. cm.
Includes bibliographical references and index.
ISBN 0–13–095309–1
1. Industrial project management. I. McKee, Sandra L.
TA190.G45 2001
658.5–dc21 00–032645

Vice President and Publisher: Dave Garza
Editor in Chief: Stephen Helba
Executive Editor: Debbie Yarnell
Associate Editor: Katie Bradford
Production Editor: Tricia Huhn
Photo Coordinator: Ryan Lamb
Design Coordinators: Robin G. Chukes, Karrie Converse-Jones
Text Designer: Rebecca Bobb
Cover art/photo: FPG
Cover Designer: Tom Mack
Production Manager: Brian Fox
Electronic Text Management: Karen L. Bretz
Illustrations: Lithokraft II
Marketing Manager: Jimmy Stephens

This book was set in Times New Roman by Lithokraft II and was printed and bound by Phoenix Color Corp. The cover was printed by Phoenix Color Corp.

10 9 8 7 6 5 4
ISBN: 0-13-095309-1

To all of you who may one day, or already, have the designation of project manager assigned to you without the benefit of guidance or training.

PREFACE

With the complex demands project managers are expected to meet, the last thing they need is an even more complex and difficult learning aid. During our many years of consulting, training, and teaching, we repeatedly ran into students and industry professionals who had no background in project management experience or practices. Wading through encyclopedic volumes was not an option for these people. To help them, we developed our own materials as handouts, overheads, etc., to provide new project managers with the basic techniques and skills needed to successfully handle projects. These materials eventually grew into this text.

Unlike other texts, the reader of this book is not expected to have extensive prior experience in project management, engineering, or elaborate statistical models. The concepts and principles found here are accessible to all and are presented in a lively and engaging manner.

Reviewed by industry professionals and students and teachers in the field of project management, this text has been developed to be a useful tool. Where other books focus primarily on computer and statistical techniques for planning and controlling projects, *Practical Project Management* gives equal attention to the critical people issues that can determine the success or failure of projects.

The particular project management techniques explored were selected for practicality, ease of use, and applicability to a wide variety of projects. They will enable project teams to meet project constraints of money, time, and resources, along with problems that can and generally do occur, without undue risk or stress.

THE PEOPLE CHAPTERS

Chapter 1 provides readers with an overview of project management, including the role of people in a project. Because change is a way of life for the project manager, Chapter 2 emphasizes the role of **change** in the project process and methods of fostering a constructive change environment. **Leadership** skills and methods of motivating people are introduced in Chapter 3. **Communication** skills and approaches, covered in Chapter 4, will help the project manager to convey ideas effectively. These skills are further reinforced in Chapter 5, with an introduction to **teams** and the problem-solving nature of these groups. In addition, all of these issues enter into the increasingly significant area of **cultural diversity** in the employee mix, which is covered in Chapter 6.

The "people" section of this text is designed to help the project manager adroitly guide the project team through the challenges of the work at hand and ensure highest productivity from open and committed employees.

The Process Chapters

The process fundamentals in the text are arranged into conceptual groupings that build upon each other and follow the typical flow of a project:

Goal Setting ➤ Scheduling ➤ Resource Management ➤ Monitoring and Problem Solving

The text focuses on practical, pre-emptive strategies to avoid and eliminate stress in project implementation. The three critical constraints of **goal setting** are explained in Chapter 7, as well as how to lay the foundation for commitment from all stakeholders in the project. **Scheduling concepts** start in Chapter 8, with **Work Breakdown Structure.** This ensures comprehensive exploration of all elements of the project so that later surprises are mimimized.

Chapter 9 continues with scheduling by simplifying the use of networks and timelines, to allow the creation of visual images of the project schedule that can be understood and used by the multiple disciplines involved in the project. **Critical path** and other **time/cost tradeoff techniques** are introduced to focus the project manager's efforts on the vital elements of the project, as well as to enable meeting imposed deadlines with minimal cost and stress. **Resource management,** outlined in Chapter 10, concludes the planning phase. Here the reader learns to finalize an optimum project plan, which meets the project's goals and constraints and secures the commitment of all project participants.

In Chapter 11, monitoring ensures that the project manager can spot trouble before problems get out of hand. Chapter 12 offers specific **problem solving techniques** as well as **conventions of reporting progress. Cost control techniques,** also presented in this chapter, allow proactive, preventive control rather than the typical after-the-fact corrective control, with its attendant difficulties.

Software Applications

In those chapters where process concepts are presented, computer activities using **Microsoft Project** or other project management software are found at the end of the problem or applications sections. A free full-product 120-day evaluation version of Microsoft Project 2000 software is provided on a CD-ROM at the back of the text. Readers have an opportunity to practice using Microsoft Project with chapter exercises, enabling them to become conversant with this powerful project management software tool.

Other Chapter Features

- **Project Management Seminar.** This book follows a training seminar given to six management professionals. Led by a two-person team, the facilitator and the content area specialist, the seminar chronicles the experiences of a group of trainees who are studying project management, just as the reader of the text is. Through a unique dialogue feature, the trainees offer their experiences, questions, concerns, and even arguments regarding the material they, like the reader, are learning for the first time in a formalized way. The dialogue feature engages the reader and helps present a variety of concerns and points of view from several different industries and backgrounds while interjecting a critical thinking element plus real-world examples into the text's conceptual content.

- **Chapter Summary.** The summary pulls together the main ideas for reinforcement.
- **Chapter Questions.** The questions feature both recall and analysis type questions.
- **Interview with an Expert.** These interviews feature practicing project managers from a variety of industries and further apply project management concepts.
- **Project Challenge: Applying What You Know.** These problems and cases are drawn directly from the authors' experiences or represent composites of client situations the authors have handled.
- **Tool Box Tips.** Interspersed throughout the text and noted with a special toolbox icon, these tips provide users with operational suggestions for applying recommendations from the text.
- **Key Terms and Definitions.** These are highlighted in the chapter margins for students to easily find and review.
- **Appendices.** The appendices include project management organizations and suggested reading.

INSTRUCTOR RESOURCES

- **Instructor's Manual.** Includes solutions to textbook exercises and a chapter-by-chapter testbank.
- **Companion Website.** Located at *http://www.prenhall.com/ghattas,* this site features additional practice questions for each chapter, links to resource websites, and tutorials on the various phases of a project, with instructions on the use of some commonly available tools.

ACKNOWLEDGEMENTS

The authors wish to acknowledge all those who reviewed or class-tested this material on its way to its final form, including the many students of ours who offered suggestions and invaluable help, especially Frank Torres and Brandon Davis. Those who reviewed and offered helpful feedback in the manuscript stage include:

Donald T. "Skip" Hall, American Intercontinental University
Devinder Sud, DeVry Institute, North Brunswick, NJ
Muhammad Obeidat, Southern Polytechnic State University
E. Edward Blevins, DeVry Institute of Technology, Dallas
Dan Wright, DeVry Institute of Technology, Phoenix
Ron Grob
Bonnie S. Rucks, DeVry Institute of Technology, DuPage, IL
Tim Hilboldt, DeVry Institute of Technology, Kansas City
Paul Stephanchick, DeVry Institute of Technology, Kansas City
Anilkumar Bhate, DeVry Institute of Technology, North Brunswick, NJ
Donald Stelzer, DeVry Institute of Technology, Phoenix
John Blankenship, DeVry Institute of Technology, Atlanta
Glenn G. Boylan, Project Management Services, Inc.
J. Tim Coppinger, Texas A&M University—Corpus Christi
Joseph Orczyk, Purdue University
David E. Wagner, Tri-State University
John K. Best, Oklahoma State University

Many of our colleagues also made inestimable contributions, in particular Bob Lewis and Susan Chin, as well as the many people we interviewed while researching this material. Thanks also to Emily Heminger and Dana Smith, who were involved with compiling the original notes. Finally, we are grateful to Paul Mallon for developing the testbank in the Instructor's Manual as well as questions for the Companion Website and the online courses.

R.G. and S.M.

I want to thank my wife Mona and my sons Joseph and Jimmy for their support and giving up a lot of our times together to make this happen. Many thanks to Dr. Dennis Young and Dr. Tom Clark of Young, Clark, and Associates for introducing me to project management training. Also, I wish to acknowledge the person who made this project come into reality through perseverance, hard work, prodding, coordinating, and much more: my co-author and colleague, Sandra McKee.

R.G. Ghattas

I want to express my appreciation to everyone at Prentice Hall who nurtured this project along: Carole Horton for instigating the team approach for the book; Steve Helba for supporting our concept; and Katie Bradford, Tricia Huhn, and the copyeditors and art and graphics people who pulled out all the stops to bring this effort to press. I also want to thank Raouf Ghattas for giving me the opportunity to partner on such an important book.

Sandra L. McKee

About the Authors

Raouf (RG) Ghattas, PEng, CPIM, CIRM

A professional engineer, Raouf Ghattas has nearly twenty years of experience in project management in electronics manufacturing, including plant start-up, turn-around, product introduction, and quality improvement. His industrial experience is in senior management and consulting with Fortune 500 companies as well as several projects for the government at the federal and state levels, and includes consulting and training in Project Management, Total Quality Management, and Operations Management. He has also conducted project management training for the American Management Association (AMA).

Ghattas received his B.S. in Mechanical Engineering from the University of Riyad and his M.S. in Industrial Engineering from the University of Windsor, Canada. He is certified by the American Production and Inventory Control Society (APICS) and is currently a professor in Operations Management and Business Information Systems in the Business Department at DeVry Institute of Technology, Atlanta, Georgia. Mr. Ghattas' professional affiliations include American Production and Inventory Control Society (APICS), Council of Logistics Management (CLM), Canadian Society for Professional Engineers (CSPE), American Institute for Industrial Engineers (AIIE), and American Management Association (AMA).

Sandra L. McKee

Sandra McKee's career has had many corporate interactions, and by maintaining an active consulting, training, and speaking business, she keeps her hands in the world she writes about. McKee's industry experience includes developing a training manual for telecommunications technicians, handling corporate communications and organizational development at a technology research and development company, and conducting marketing research for the U.S. government. As a seminar leader, she has taught project management for first-time project managers, presentation skills, technical communication, and leadership in organizations. In addition, McKee has coached CEOs, managers, salespeople, and entrepreneurs.

Sandra McKee received her B.A. from the University of North Carolina at Greensboro and her Master's from Winthrop College, and she did post-graduate work at Louisiana State University. She is a senior professor at DeVry Institute of Technology in Atlanta. Prior to *Practical Project Management,* Sandra co-authored *Life Management: Skills for Busy People,* also published by Prentice Hall. Currently, she is on sabbatical directing a web development project for Enrev, a high-tech company in Atlanta, and she is marketing a novel she wrote with her teenage son.

To The Student

In your work, you may find yourself serving on a project team or leading a team as the project manager. In the latter case, you may be suddenly pushed into the role of managing projects with complex task relationships, often across disciplines. This, along with complicated resource constraints and people interaction elements, is totally new and often frightening territory for the first-time project manager.

Practical Project Management introduces you to the particular discipline imposed by project management practices, providing relief to the new project manager who is overwhelmed by the new level of responsibility. The text's practical, day-to-day approach explains in simple, achievable methods, the challenges real project managers face daily.

You will notice that the book is divided into people issues and process issues. Chapter 1 introduces you to the field of project management. Chapters 2–6 explore the complex interpersonal relationships in heterogeneous workplaces. The remainder of the book, Chapters 7–12, covers the challenges the project manager must face while working with processes.

This book follows a training seminar given to six management professionals. The seminar is led by a two-person team, the facilitator and the content area specialist. Throughout this training we will concentrate on two theme problems:

(1) Kitchen remodeling—This common situation will help present concepts that will transfer easily to your project management experiences.
(2) Millennium Enterprises—This more ambitious business-oriented project will let you polish your skills.

The theme problems above are presented across multiple chapters and will grow in complexity as you learn more about managing projects. Each highlights and refines a different issue that will help you control a complex process in your role as a project manager. Written in an easy-to-read narrative style, the text lets you concentrate on the ideas and strategies being presented.

Imagine managing a project in which you enjoy the support of end users, upper-level management, clients, and peers. Imagine having committed participants who apply their skills and expertise with enthusiasm, cooperate across teams, and overcome obstacles with creativity. Imagine bringing every project in on time, within budget, and with impeccable quality. This is successful project management. Successful projects are led by project managers who understand that projects are a unique combination of people, processes, and tasks.

Project managers who are able to provide a stress-free environment and cultivate highly involved and motivated team members can consistently achieve these results, and so can you.

Finally, all the principles and techniques presented in this book fit together in a cumulative mosaic of a highly effective model for project success. We strongly recommend assimilating them in their entirety.

Here's to your highly successful project!

Contents

1
Introduction to Project Management 2

2
Change 24

4
COMMUNICATION 66

10
Resource Management 200

11
Project Control 226

12

PROJECT CONTROL TECHNIQUES 244

PRACTICAL PROJECT MANAGEMENT

CHAPTER 1

Introduction to Project Management

Chapter Preview

The Project Management Seminar: Session 1

Hilda Jensen looked around as she sat in the lobby of the posh hotel. This was so much more relaxed than the way she usually started her day, which typically involved a 7a.m. project status or customer meeting, a review of the e-mails that had come in overnight, and signing several memos for her secretary before a quick dash down to the plant to see what was going on. Hilda was a senior control specialist with a prosthetics manufacturing firm. She enjoyed her job immensely, finding great satisfaction in helping others. But she was still glad to get away for a few days to attend this project management seminar, which had been suggested by her boss.

Arriving in the training room for the seminar, Tom Bryant discovered that he was the first to arrive. It was nice to be early, but then he usually was. He helped himself to some coffee and one of those institutional Danish pastries that hotels always provided. The early arrival allowed him to settle down and look over some paperwork, but soon he was interrupted by Yury Tomicovic, an older, heavyset Russian man who went straight to the coffee without acknowledging Tom. When Tom spoke, Yury was startled, and only grunted in response to Tom's introduction.

Tom's sales background made him the natural choice for greeter as the others arrived. A third man rushed in and looked around guiltily as he deposited a travel mug on the table, liquid sloshing over the edges. As a production engineer, Ragdeesh always had a crisis problem to solve and this morning had been no exception.

"Oh, I'm not late?" the man asked Tom, who smiled in welcome.

Hilda, walking into the training room, assured him,"No, you're not late."

"Thank you, good morning. I am Ragdeesh Patel, and I am pleased to make your acquaintance." Formal and proper, Ragdeesh's greeting, complete with British accent, made a positive impression on Hilda. It was still 20 minutes till 9 o'clock.

"This training has come at a very bad time for me, " Ragdeesh said. "I still am not quite sure why we are here."

"That is what I was thinking," Yury said, scowling.

"Well, I'm looking forward to learning this stuff," Tom volunteered with enthusiasm. Yury cut a disapproving look towards him and again grunted, while Ragdeesh sighed.

Ralph George, the training facilitator for the day, and Tracey McElroy, the content area specialist, had just stepped into the room. Overhearing the tail-end of the discussion between Ragdeesh and Yury, Tracey thought, "This is going to be a tough group."

One look at Ralph told her that he had come to a similar conclusion about the trainees.

Tracey and Ralph introduced themselves and quickly checked that the hotel had provided them with all of the necessities for the day. Soon, Jaime Martinez, another member of the training class arrived and, after more hurried introductions, they got started. Noting one was still missing, Tracey asked the participants to break into two groups to discuss any concerns they wanted to cover during the first day of training. After writing their responses on a flip chart, she tore off the sheets and taped them to the wall.

- Why are we here?
- How can project management help me?
- I can't spare the time for this training, things will go crazy while I'm gone

Group A

- Why don't my projects run smoothly?
- Why does everyone else seem so much more in control?

Group B

Tracey and Ralph pondered the group's concerns and adjusted their opening outline appropriately:

- **The need for project management**
- **Terminology—the language of project management**
- **The key objectives of project management**
- **Project constraints**
- **People focus in project management**
- **Stress**

Tracey and Ralph encountered a curious mix of skepticism and curiosity from each new group to come through their seminar, but this bunch seemed to come with the most diversity of experience. Ralph looked forward to the different contributions the participants could make from their own fields, while Tracey couldn't wait to see the group dynamics at work.

1.0 The Need for Project Management

Today, project management is used for projects big and small—from building a huge skyscraper over a period of 3 years, to remodeling a kitchen, which can be done in a few weeks. Almost everyone who works in the public or private sector today has been a member of a project team. Smaller projects often don't require the highly formal control needed for larger projects. Formal project management goes back at least to the days of World War I, when Henry Gantt developed a simple but effective control tool known as a Gantt chart, which is still widely used today. Formal project management became popular during World War II, with the development of warplanes and weapons. Other enormous projects, such as Operation Overlord—the invasion of Normandy—required thousands of hours of coordinated planning.

As discussed in a later chapter, the Critical Path Method (CPM) and the Program Evaluation and Review Technique (PERT) were developed at approximately the same time in the 1950s. Engineers at Remington-Rand and DuPont developed CPM. The U.S. Navy developed PERT during the design and deployment of the Polaris missile. Today, CPM and PERT charts adorn the walls of managers' offices worldwide. These charts are often vital ingredients of frequent project status meetings.

The world today is quite different from the world of 50, 20, or even 10 years ago. New products appear on the market every day and are replaced by even newer models faster than we can purchase the older ones. For consumers, this means lower prices over time, but also increased frustration. Shiny new possessions become obsolete almost before the packaging reaches the garbage.

The life span of any new version of a product gets shorter and shorter over time. Remember the abacus? This early version of the calculator was used for thousands of years before being replaced by the slightly less cumbersome, but more mentally taxing, slide rule. Slide rules stuck around for a few hundred years before being forced off the market in the 1960s and 1970s by hand-held calculators. Early calculator models were bulky, expensive, and limited in their performance, allowing the user to perform only a few basic operations. Today, you can purchase a sleek scientific calculator for about $15 or $20 in the checkout line at your local drugstore. It will more than meet the needs of even the most advanced student of mathematics. Spend a little more, and you can choose one with all kinds of different features—graphing capabilities, and full keyboards that will even remind you that your mother's birthday is coming soon.

What does this have to do with project management? When a new calculator appears on the market, it means that a team of individuals worked together to develop it. They were led by a fearless and skilled project manager. Life cycle, which is the span of time a product is issued to the time it is replaced by a flashier version, has been reduced to only months for many industries. This includes computers, automobiles, or any product we used to think of as being a relatively long-term investment. The career of the average project manager now involves managing a multitude of small projects, rather than overseeing the life cycle of one long-lived product.

■ ■ ■

At this point Hilda, the prosthetics manufacturer, jumped in. "I see exactly what you mean," she said. "In my industry, new developments are being made every day. People are surprised to learn that whole teams of scientists and doctors dedicate their research time to improving our products, but it's true. And every time a better prosthesis is designed, we don't just begin production. We have to redesign our manufacturing equipment, retrain employees, and reconfigure the setup of our plant. This happens more than just every couple of years–it's more like every couple of months or even weeks."

"And what happens, Hilda," asked Ralph, "if you don't get the equipment redesigned or the employees retrained quickly enough?"

"Believe it or not," answered Hilda, "we do have competition in the prosthetics industry. If we can't get a product out quickly enough, there is another company out there that will get it out sooner. It makes our company look bad in the long run."

■ ■ ■

In today's market, companies have more projects going on than they can possibly provide all of the necessary resources for. The same corporation that is developing the new robotic system that will feed your cat and wash your car is also developing the latest hand-held television and working on a technology that will make your telephone reception clearer than you thought possible. As project manager, it's your responsibility to make the most of limited resources so that the company can carry out its full load of projects.

Without good project managers, products may die in the planning or early production phases. Another company with a faster team, or better technology, will beat you to the finish line. Effective project management skills allow you to shorten the time line from product inception to market, thereby maximizing your chances of meeting or beating the competition. And in today's world of shortened life cycles, project management skills are more important than ever. (See Figure 1–1.)

Figure 1–1
The amount of time from introduction to obsolescence has decreased dramatically in the last 5 years, especially for high-tech products.

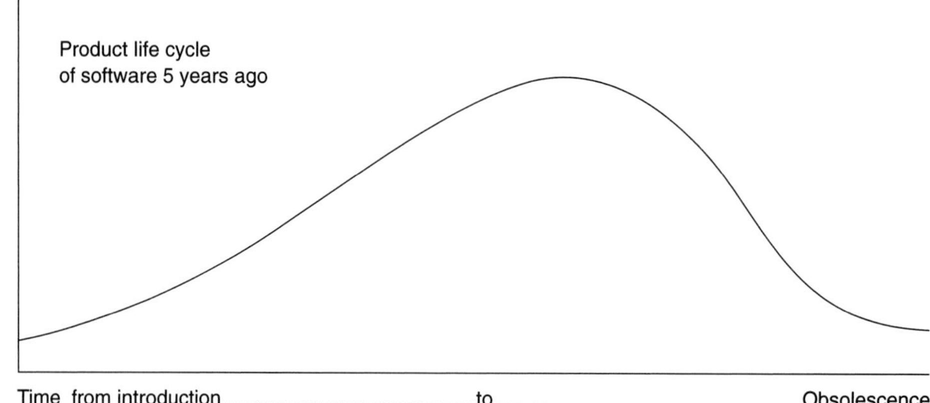

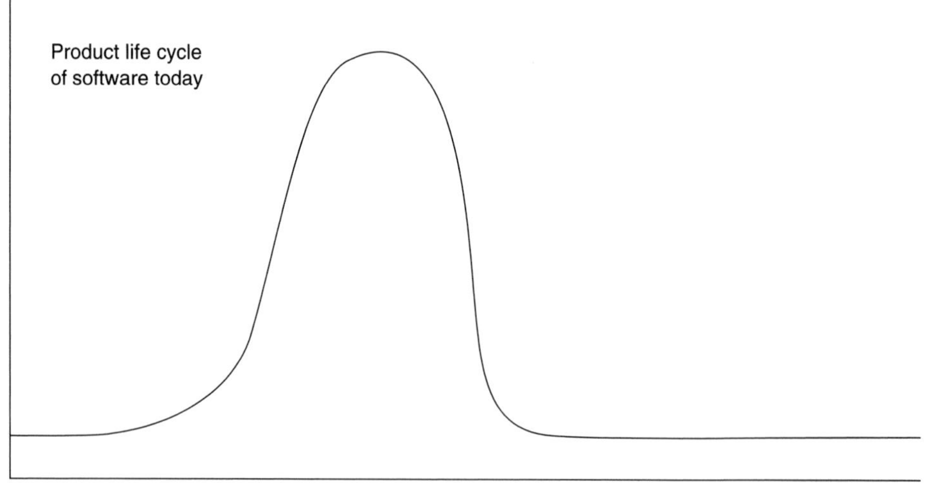

The organization of today's industry management also makes project management skills essential. Downsizing is now a way of life. For the past 5 or 6 years, middle management has been thinning its ranks, resulting in a flattening of company organization. Consider the organizational charts in Figure 1–2 and Figure 1–3.

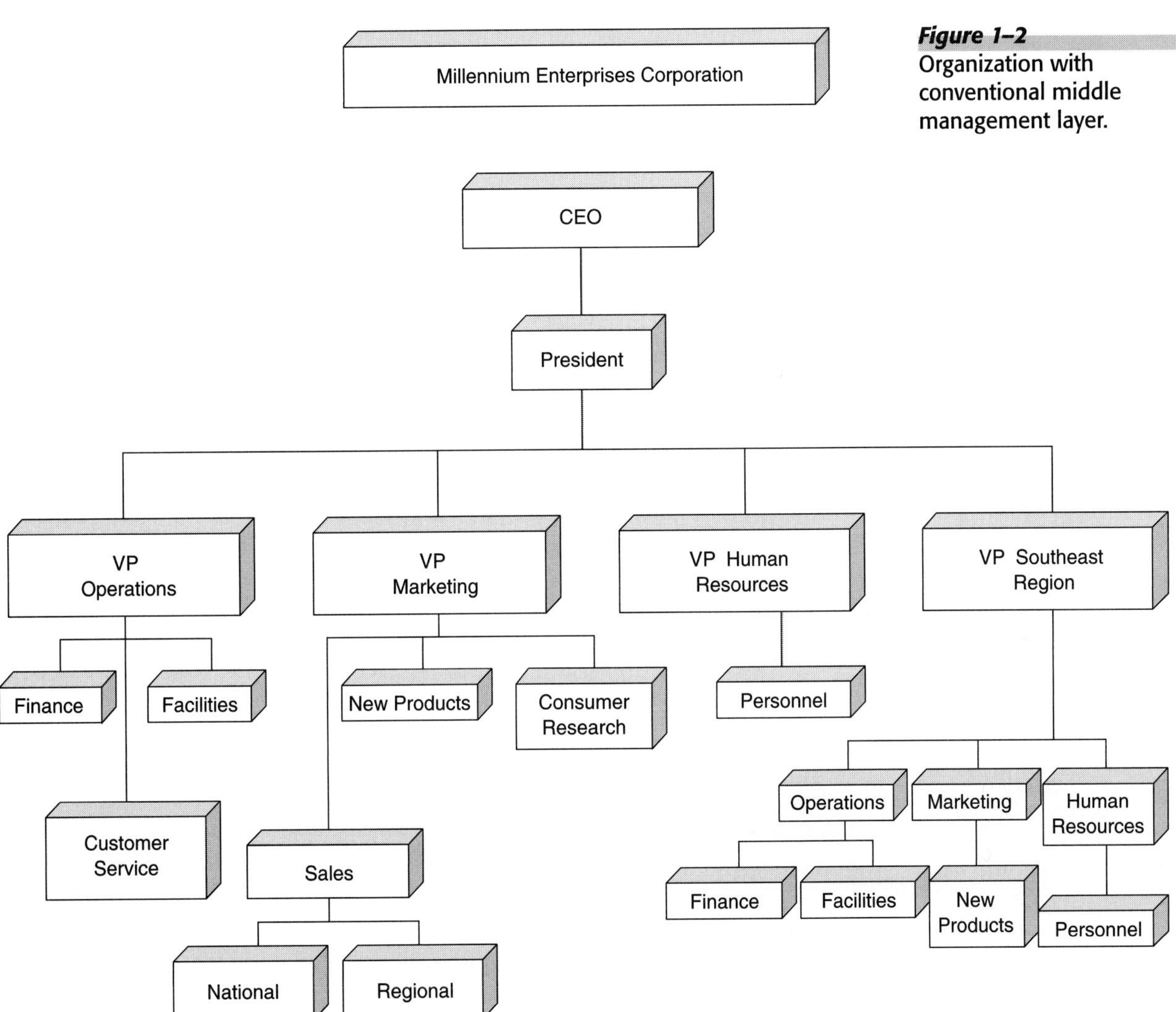

Figure 1–2
Organization with conventional middle management layer.

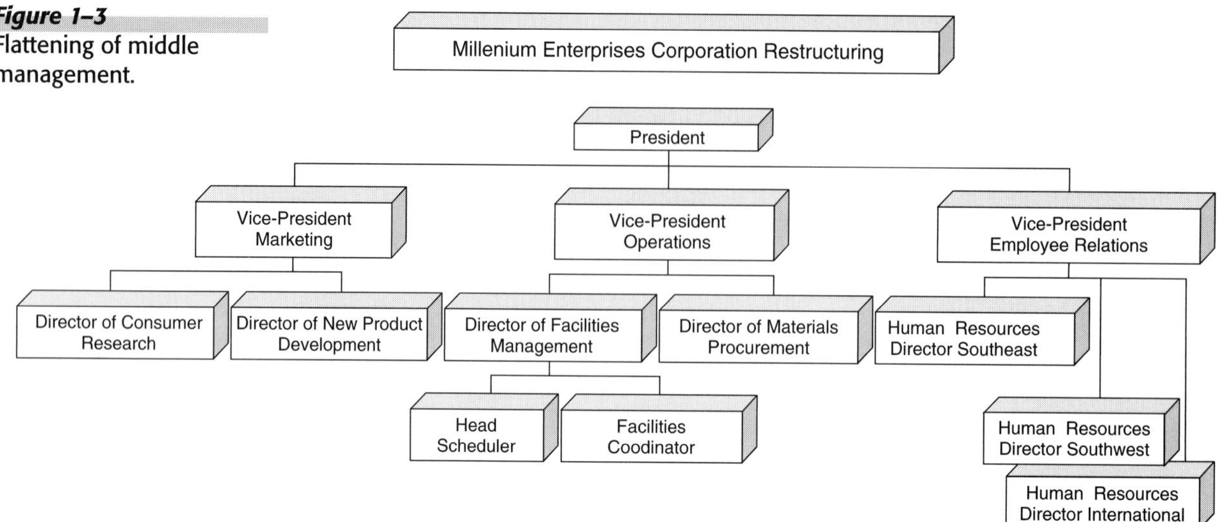

Figure 1–3 Flattening of middle management.

As middle management is pared down, more people in the workplace are responsible for a larger number of projects than ever before, with less time at their disposal. True, flattened management has a lower overhead cost, but the project manager's attentions are spread too thin. Project management skills give you the edge that allows you to concentrate on each project under your command, in its turn, without compromising the integrity of any one.

Never forget that your projects involve all kinds of people, both within your company (in-house) and outside (out-of-house).

In-house team members are from (among others):

- Research and Development department
- Marketing department
- Cross Functional Teams
- Accounting/Control

Out-of-house team members may include:

- Architects
- Vendors
- Sub-contractors
- Customers

Project team members may represent many different occupations. Many project teams also contain representatives of the customer, to ensure that the planning matches the desired end product. The project manager is responsible for putting all of these different individuals together to form a cohesive team—individuals who come to the project with different loyalties, agendas, and priorities. Accounting will always be concerned with money, and will generally disappear from your project at the end of each month to handle the obligations of the accounting department. Marketing members will be especially concerned with the timing of a product release or the competitive implication of a project. Production engineering will want a final result that is easy to reproduce and manufacture, while research and development wants the product to have as many cutting-edge features as possible.

In addition to managing the diverse (and sometimes opposing) needs of the project team members and customers, the project manager will at times receive a project from some other area that is in deadline, budget, or resources trouble. Inevitably, a company usually decides to take action on an idea only when it becomes abundantly clear that there is no escaping it. So by the time a project is handed off to you, the deadline that comes along with it is probably tight. Project management skills allow you not only to effectively handle a tight schedule, but also prevent many hardships from happening in the first place.

For example, suppose you're a college student. You've just returned to campus feeling that this is going to be a great semester. You don't have class on Monday or Friday, or before noon on any day in between. You signed up for a class in communications. Communications, you think, my forte! I talk on the phone all the time. I'm a great communicator. The first day, your professor assigns a project that's due the last week of class, 15 weeks from now. She gives you a vague definition of what the project is to comprise, and leaves it at that. For about the first 3 to 4 weeks of the semester, as you get into the groove of your new classes, you don't worry about the project. This is called the period of **Uninformed Optimism** (see Figure 1–4).

uniformed optimism period of time at the beginning of a project when worry and stress are low

Soon, you begin to receive projects and assignments from other professors in other courses. You begin to worry a little bit about how you're going to get all of this work done. This is called the **Vague Concern Phase.** But you still have roughly 10 weeks left in the semester, so you quickly put the concern out of your mind and move on to more pressing matters, like how awful the cafeteria food is.

vague concern phase phase of a project when concern begins to mount

Before you know it, you're about 11 or 12 weeks into the semester, and that final deadline looms near. Suddenly, probably at about 2 or 3 o'clock in the morning, you wake up covered in a cold sweat, and it dawns on you that you've waited too long. There's no way you're going to get your communications project done, finish your thesis paper, and prepare for all of your finals. **Panic** has set in. Now you're very worried.

panic phase worry phase of the project, when the project manager realizes that it take an enormous effort to accomplish the task at hand

For the next 3 weeks you shut yourself off from the world in the library. You live on canned soup, pizza and coffee as you try desperately to finish the project. You call the professor, who you thought was nice and laid-back, and ask, actually beg, very politely for an extension. Maybe I could turn it in on Sunday night or Monday, you ask, instead of Friday? Just one more weekend would really help me out.

The answer is no. So you miss the deadline, finally turning the project in on Tuesday, knowing that the work is unacceptable, but at least it's done. Your level of worry drops sharply as you look forward to the semester break. This is the **Wince and Take It stage.** You resign yourself to whatever fate is yours for being a poor manager of your time. If you are clever, you will learn from your mistakes and do better next time, with a positive result more likely. But somewhere in the back of your mind you know that you'll return only to start the whole cycle over again.

wince and take it stage stage of a project when the project manager must accept the outcome, though it may be unpleasant

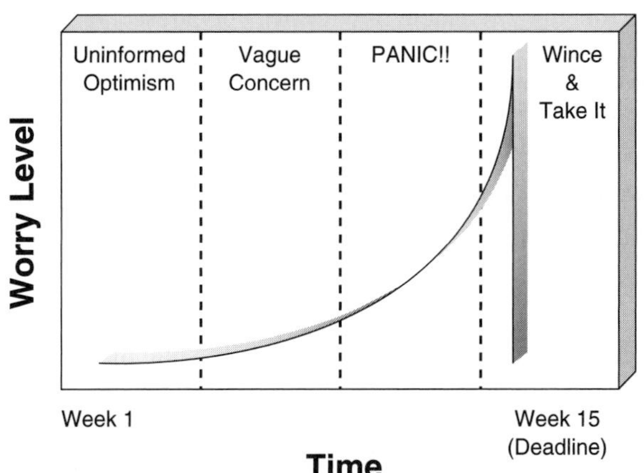

Figure 1–4
As the deadline gets closer on a poorly managed project, the level of worry increases.

Suppose this scenario is changed slightly. You are still the college student with the great schedule. You're still taking the communications class and your professor still assigns a project. But instead of leaving you to fend for yourself for 15 weeks, she tells you that by the end of week 1, she wants you to pick a topic. You're not too worried because this is a reasonable request and one that, most importantly, won't take up too much of your time. You choose your topic, write it on a piece of paper, and turn it in. Any worry you might have felt is now gone.

During week 3, your professor asks you to design the title page for your project and develop a table of contents. You worry a little bit, because you hadn't really thought about the project enough to be able to make a table of contents. But you spend a little time thinking and get it done on time, and you feel good. During week 5, your professor wants an abstract in which you define what you will be doing in the project. Every other week after that, the professor assigns another small portion of the project, called a deliverable, until finally you have the entire thing done, before you even know it. Best of all, your worry level has never risen above mild concern (see Figure 1–5).

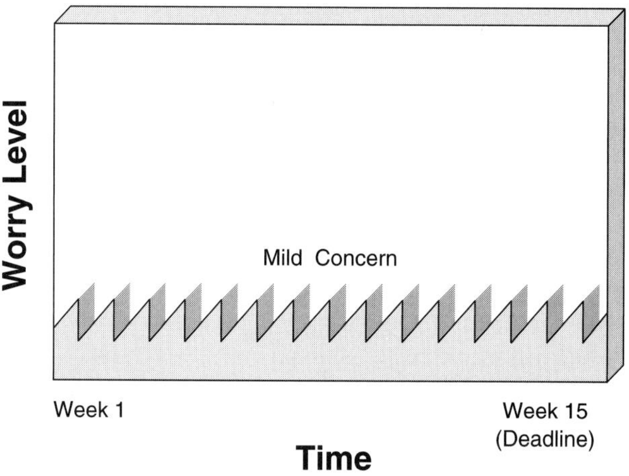

Figure 1–5
In a well-managed project, the level of worry stays within more reasonable levels throughout the project life.

Week 1:—pick topic and turn in

Week 3:—create title page and table of contents; begin research

Week 5:—write abstract; interview expert

Week 7:—write introduction; finish research

Week 9:—finish draft one; put in sources

Week 11:—revise draft—edit for flow and errors

Week 13:—add illustrations to final version

Week 15:—turn in finished project

Providing a project team with enough guidance to restrain their worry to a reasonable level, one in which team members never reach the panic stage, is one of the most important contributions any project manager can make. Knowing how to set up a schedule of small, manageable deliverables (completed tasks) reduces the stress level of your team

members, improving the overall quality of the work they produce. In this textbook you will begin to understand the techniques of managing the tasks of projects.
But the job of project manager is much larger than that; it requires a way of looking at a project as an intricate set of interdependent relationships, with priorities and potential problems that you will handle using your talented people and the resources assigned to you. Inputting data into software and generating graphs and charts help you track and report the tasks. Project management in practice consists of managing people, anticipating problems, utilizing resources, and pulling all the parts together. It is a way of organizing your thinking.

2.0 Project Management Terminology

Having a big vocabulary is not a requirement for being a successful project manager, but being able to speak the language of the profession is. There is certain terminology common to any project, and these terms should be a part of your vocabulary whether you're building a new space shuttle for NASA, or opening a new franchise for a fast food chain.

What exactly is a project? Like the above examples, the actual goal of a **project** can vary widely from company to company, but each one has a few things in common. In general, a project can be defined as a group of multiple *interdependent* activities that require people and resources. It has a definite start and end date and a specific set of criteria that define successful completion. When these activities are combined, they achieve the desired results. Operation Desert Storm was a medium-sized project taking only a few months, while the goal of landing humans on the moon was a very large project that took more than 10 years. A smaller project might consist of the development and marketing of one product—such as a new perfume or snack food—or writing a research paper.

project a group of multiple interdependent activities that require people and resources

The student of project management today must realize that the discipline and rigor that have been so effective in managing product development, manufacturing, and even construction, are now being applied in a larger sense. Whereas at one time we used to refer to a project as a process that results in a tangible outcome—a product prototype or a new manufacturing plant—now we see the term applied to many more types of operations. AT&T might call a customer-service process changeover a "project," just as Advanced Charger Technology would call the development of a 15-minute battery charger prototype a "project." It might therefore be helpful to provide you with other definitions of a *project,* as well of *project management.* Note the diversity of interpretation of each term:

- "A project is a one-time job that has defined starting and ending dates, a clearly specified objective, or scope of work to be performed, a pre-defined budget, and usually a temporary organization that is dismantled once the project is complete." (*The Project Manager's Desk Reference,* James Lewis)
- "A project is a unique undertaking, is composed of activities, involves multiple resources, is not synonymous with the 'product of the project,' and has a managerial emphasis on timely accomplishment of the project." (*The AMA Handbook of Project Management,* Paul C. Dinsmore)
- For an "official" definition we look to the organization, the Project Management Institute, which publishes the *Project Management Body of Knowledge* (known as PMBOK): "A project is any undertaking with a defined starting point and defined objectives by which completion is identified. In practice, most projects depend on finite or limited resources by which the project is to be completed."

- And further in the GOAL/QPC Project Management Memory Jogger™, the project manager's job is defined as supplying "project teams with a process that helps them coordinate their efforts so they may create the right product (or service, process or plan), at the right time, for the right customer, within the resource limits established by the organization." (GOAL/QPC, 1997)

goal what exactly needs to be accomplished

project scope documented set of standards and criteria that the customer defines as successful completion

objective a combination of tasks that concern specific functional groups or structural areas

tasks a combination of activities that lead to the achievement of a definable result

activity a time-consuming piece of work with a definite beginning and end

duration the elapsed time from the beginning to the end of an activity, task, or objective

So, a human resource "project" to develop a re-organization plan for a 3000-employee company fits the definition the same as an engineering company's "project" to build a highway extension. The **goal** (what exactly needs to be accomplished) and the **project scope** (the documented set of standards and criteria that the customer defines as successful completion) then, will define the project.

Once you know what your project is, the next step is to break it down into objectives. An **objective** is a combination of tasks that concern specific functional groups or structural areas. Imagine you work for a major-label clothing manufacturer and it's your job to open a new factory in Brazil. One of your objectives might be to come up with the operations plan. As part of this objective, you would determine how you're going to provide the facilities, people, and materials for the plant. Another objective would be to develop a marketing plan.

Each of your objectives is further broken down into **tasks.** A task is a combination of activities that lead to the achievement of a definable result, or deliverable. A task you might assign to your marketing team might be to develop a promotional plan or pricing strategy. Each task must in some way contribute to the completion of one of your objectives.

Meeting objectives in the larger sense can seem daunting. For example, if you tell a particular group to restructure the manufacturing facility, you might come back two weeks later to find they have become mired down trying to figure out their approach. For this reason, each task must be broken down into a series of activities. An **activity** is a time-consuming piece of work with a definite beginning and a definite end. If you had told your research group, "One of you must evaluate the existing structure, another will secure input from manufacturing personnel, and the third person is responsible for comparing current value of the property with costs of a relocation," they'd probably have gotten the task completed much more quickly. Each activity needn't be assigned to a different individual. One person can be responsible for an entire task, or tasks, but by being broken down into activities, the task becomes much more manageable.

To plan your project, each portion must have a specific **duration.** Duration is the elapsed time from the beginning to the end of an activity, task, or objective. This is not to be confused with effort. Your team may spend only two hours developing its consumer research survey, but, because of their other responsibilities, the duration of the activity may be two days. From the time an activity is supposed to start, to the time it is delivered, the elapsed time is known as duration.

Why is it important for you to know this vocabulary? These terms are the outline of your project. Remember the college student approaching the research paper? When left on his own, he procrastinated, but when someone defined small, manageable steps for him to take, the entire process was almost enjoyable. When you are planning and scheduling, you need to know that you are going to break your project down into objectives, tasks, and activities. If you accurately predict the duration of each of these components, you will be that much closer to bringing the project in according to your schedule.

3.0 Project Constraints

If planning a project is as easy as knowing a few simple terms, why isn't everyone a good project manager? There are several reasons, but one of the most important is that every project is subjected to certain constraints: simply put, cost, schedule and quality/scope (see Figure 1–6). Not every project manager is able to appreciate these constraints, but those who do are well on their way to success.

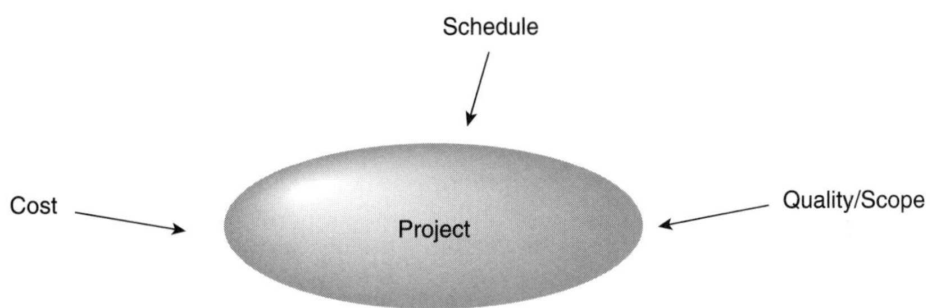

Figure 1–6
The three main elements of quality, cost, and schedule drive the project.

Constraints are those things that control your ability to bring a project to completion. Time (schedule) is one very pressing constraint. Being told, "We're shooting for completion sometime around the end of the year, but the product won't go on the market until the following June," is a different story from the admonition, "The competition is breathing down our neck, and we have the trade show coming up at the end of the month." You will likely approach each project differently depending on its time constraints.

What if you're short on cash, or people? These are constraints in the form of resources, and can be very damaging to your plan if not recognized and taken into account. When you hear the phrases, "We can't spare him until . . .," "The cash won't be available until . . .," "The facility is booked until next week," "The other project is higher priority," or "We're having closing this week so I can't work on your project until next month," you know you're dealing with a scarcity of resources.

The project's scope might be the document that reins in the creative design people in your team and keeps them on track to the customer's needs and specifications. This important link between the customer (could be internal or external) and the project team helps ensure that no one is going outside the parameters at the company's or the customer's expense.

A good project manager will know how to recognize the constraints acting on any given project. But the successful manager will use the strategies in this book to work around or within those constraints and, sometimes, even turn them into assets.

4.0 Key Objectives of Project Management

Project management skills are important. Rarely would any project reach fruition without a manager who is qualified and capable. But how does one become a good project manager, and what separates the good from the bad?

Any project must meet several objectives in order to be considered successful. Each objective is made up of many concerns, or constraints that must be addressed. Your thought process and your teams will benefit from a document that has all of the details of each concern spelled out:

OBJECTIVE	DOCUMENT	CONCERNS/CONSTRAINTS
Quality requirements	*Specifications/ Scope*	• Definition of the end product • Form, fit, and function • Description of the end state
Deadlines	*Project Schedule*	• Must complete by . . . • Must start by . . . • Can't start before . . . • Can't have until . . .
Cost limits	*Project Budget*	• We can only spend . . . • Bring it in under . . . • If you can beat their price . . . • Our minimum profit margin is . . . • The market will bear . . .
High levels of team commitment	*Project charter* *Team constitution*	• We understand the purpose/vision. • Each person's role is clear. • Team members have mutual respect and trust. • Team members are motivated. (They don't have to be told what to do.)

4.1 Quality Specifications

With each project assignment, you will always receive some kind of quality specifications. These may come in the form of a verbal description of what the product must be capable of achieving, or as in a long printed document of detailed requirements. The exactness of the specifications you receive will have a lot to do with the industry in which you work. Government-based projects are likely to come with a great deal of paperwork detailing the product, while private industry projects may leave you much to your own accord. The quality specification gives the end definition—the form fit and function of the project—which defines the final state of your project. It is important that you ensure that your project meets or exceeds these specifications.

4.2 Deadlines

Every project on which you work will come with a deadline. The deadline may be fuzzy or not stated at all, in which case it's your job to establish an appropriate deadline. Your project may be handed to you with specific start and completion dates. Deadlines can be determined by trade show dates, production start-up dates, or even an anxious client who wants a product in hand as soon as possible. Once the deadline is established, spell it out to your team members in the form of a schedule. It is important that you as project manager have a firm idea of the project deadline in mind when you're planning your schedule. Your team will be much more motivated and helpful if they know what the real time line of the project requires. Team members will be able to better pace themselves and make better contributions when they know what the schedule really is.

4.3 Cost Limitations (Constraints)

Lastly, you will be asked to stay within certain cost constraints in carrying out your project. As with deadlines, cost constraints may not be presented clearly. Sometimes you are given an exact budget that is presented up front, down to the last cent, but this is more the exception than the rule. Even when you are presented with a very general budget, it's your job as the project manager to come up with a detailed one. Once you've had some time to plan the project, you should be able to tell your company or client exactly how much the job will cost. Because they are the people that make your project happen your team needs cost information as much as the client does.

Project teams can be highly self-directed and committed to the vision set up by the project's champion or sponsor. These projects seem to almost run themselves, and members show initiative in completing the tasks to carry out the objectives. A written document outlining project tasks and objectives that everyone understands and agrees to will support the project manager's efforts.

Even if all of these criteria, quality specification, time line, and cost constraints are inexact, you have to keep in mind that they are *real* constraints. These are the "box" in which you must place the project.

■ ■ ■

At this point Ralph stopped. "So your project must meet scope specifications, stay within budget, and be completed on time," he said. "Which of these three things do you think is most important?"

Ragdeesh jumped in right away. "Of course quality is the most important," he said, and a few of the others nodded in agreement.

"Why do you think this is?" Ralph asked.

"Because a project isn't worth doing if you're not going to produce quality work that meets the client's specifications," Ragdeesh replied haughtily.

"Do we have any other opinions?" Ralph queried.

"Wouldn't cost be fairly important?" asked Tom, a young account executive, uncertainly.

"Let's think about it this way," said Ralph, smiling, "What happens to quality when you're out of time? When you feel a time crunch on a project, you're likely to cut corners. Our college friend, the one working on the communications assignment, produced work that he knew was inadequate. He was pressed for time, focusing solely on getting the project done, so the quality of his work suffered."

Ralph looked around and saw agreement on most of the faces. He continued, "What happens to your budget when you're short on time? When you fall behind schedule, you usually have to pay someone overtime, you begin shipping materials overnight, you fly in experts from across the country. All of these are expenses that could have been avoided if you'd just stayed on schedule."

"So while all three objectives are important, if you can just stay on schedule, you stand a much greater chance of meeting your quality and budget specifications," Ralph concluded.

At that moment Jerry Benjamin burst into the training room, still carrying his bags. Everyone watched while he tossed his bags down in the corner and took off his coat. He looked up, noticing everyone was staring at him. "I missed my plane, all right? Had to take a later flight."

"And how much more was your ticket?" Ralph asked, smiling.

"$300, so what's your point?" Jerry snapped back.

The group laughed out loud, and Jerry muttered as he took his seat.

■ ■ ■

All of the information in this book is designed to allow you to master and meet schedule and cost objectives. Quality specifications will vary widely from project to project. You must be prepared to motivate your project team to meet or exceed these specifications.

5.0 People Issues in Project Management

When glitches occur, materials are late in arriving, or machines break down, deep investigation will probably lead you to a people problem as the source. The difficulty might be a communication problem, a motivation problem, a territory or infighting problem, or even a personal problem that interferes with the carrying out of your project. Because people drive processes, it makes sense to build competence in people management skills as well as in quantitative and analytical process management.

Today's managers are often responsible for 20 or more employees. Project managers may even have to pull together teams of people who do not all work for their company. Contractors view themselves as colleagues or peers and must be managed differently from your own employees. Firing difficult employees is not a simple solution anymore. Many federal laws protect employees who fall into specific categories, and the potential for lawsuits requires endless documentation to justify dismissal of just about anyone. The demand for skilled and competent people far exceeds the supply in the human resource market, so replacing an employee fired in a fit of temper may ultimately cost the company a lot of money. In addition, your job may be in jeopardy if you are unable to keep and lead good employees.

Furthermore, the working culture has changed. In years past American companies were by and large run by white, upper middle class males with military service as part of their profile. Thus, the military model was the norm. In addition, the workforce as a whole was racially and ethnically homogenous. Obedience was absolute; the company owned its people, but it also offered lifetime employment to anyone who showed loyalty.

Today, companies cannot offer lifetime employment, nor can they guarantee raises, benefits, job definition, or management stability. They cannot repay loyalty with loyalty, or hard work with compensation. Thus, the challenge of motivating employees goes far beyond "donkey management"—the use of either threats (kicks) or rewards (carrots). Today's project manager must lead and inspire commitment in very different ways than in the past.

With changes in hiring laws and the addition of anti-discrimination guidelines, a new mix of managers and employees has emerged. The workforce is increasingly diverse, not only culturally and ethnically, but in other ways as well. It includes, women, older workers, handicapped workers, homosexuals, and any other group protected by law from discrimination in hiring. Also, with the demands for skilled, high-tech workers at all levels, employee searches span the globe and cross cultural barriers. One California-based semiconductor manufacturer had to recruit and hire people with Ph. D.s in semiconductor design. Can you imagine how many people there are in the world with a specialty like that? Or, more realistically, how few? This same company reported 29 different culture groups among 1,000 employees.

Managing such a diverse group of highly skilled employees is a fact of life for today's project manager. In addition to processing the magnitude of the skills and knowledge required, project managers work in environments that commonly require 50-hour plus weeks from their employees. Stress is a way of life! Amazingly, however, increased knowledge and skill in all the areas of people management can remove the biggest stressor in human relations—the lack of understanding of why your employees do what they do. Helplessness in the face of such a challenge naturally elicits fear, in any of us. Processing knowledge and tools for dealing with employees makes us feel prepared, and we become better able to solve problems with energy and creativity.

Horseback riding is a good example. Many people are naturally afraid of riding a horse. A 1,200-pound animal completely out of your control is a frightening thing. However, some rudimentary instruction in understanding, handling, and riding horses can lead to a pleasant experience. However, you can choose *not* to ride the horse; you cannot choose *not* to manage your people.

Thus, in chapters 2–6, this book goes beyond instruction in process management to include an education in interpersonal and leadership skills required of project managers in today's professional environment. The effects of **change**, as well as the methods for managing change, are discussed. **Leadership** discussions will take you through concepts of motivation that will help you encourage commitment in your project team members. An examination of **communication** will help you to increase your knowledge and skills in getting your message across to others. Because every project is a team effort, the dynamics of **teams** and the skillful crafting and maintenance of teams will be presented. Finally, the **cultural and ethnic diversity** within the workforce demands that project managers become at least somewhat familiar with the implications of cultural background for performance and communication.

Orchestrating the outcome of a successful project and meeting the challenge of bringing a product or process to completion create a sense of satisfaction that makes the headaches you experienced along the way worth it. However, by learning the processes, practices, skills, and even a few tricks presented in this text, you will dramatically increase your chances to bring about that outcome and significantly reduce the stress related to project management.

change transformation

leadership providing guidance or direction

communication exchange of message or ideas

team a group of people dedicated to the achievement of a common goal

cultural and ethnic diversity peoples of various cultures and ethnicities come together in the "melting pot" of the US workforce, making it necessary to understand the practices and traditions of their various backgrounds

6.0 Achieving Low-Stress Project Management

Stress has become second nature to many of us, almost a way of life. Think about your workplace. How many times a day do you think or hear the word "stress" compared to the number of times you hear the words "happy," "satisfaction," or "fulfillment"? A day at work is not meant to be like a relaxing spa treatment or a journey of self-discovery, but neither should your team members be commuting to work with a knot in their stomachs each morning.

It is possible for you as a project manager to cultivate a low-stress or stress-free environment for your team members. Have you ever stopped to think about what exactly creates stress in the workplace?

Major Sources of Stress

Lack of planning
Ambiguity of project goals or project organization
Lack of support from upper-level or peer management
Imposed plans or details; technical second-guessing
Imposed activity duration
Crashed activity plans
Lack of communication
Lack of feedback or visibility of progress
Conflicting objectives or priorities

Hurry up and wait: overtime followed by layoffs followed by more overtime
Micromanagement
Lack of recognition of changed circumstances
Inability to deal with change or diversity
Badly run meetings
Lack of response to major problems
Lack of recognition of accomplishments; stealing the credit

This list isn't meant to scare you. The idea is, if you know where problems may originate, you are able to anticipate and avoid them.

Besides making people miserable, stress is a major killer of individual performance. Stressed people are more likely to make mistakes and generally perform at less than their optimal level. The more mistakes an individual makes, the worse he feels about his job and himself, and the more likely he is to experience burnout. A high burnout rate means a high turnover rate, and more time for you spent on re-hiring and retraining.

A stressful work environment leads to stressed employees, who in turn contribute to a more stressful environment. It's a vicious cycle, but there are several preemptive strategies a project manager can take to break it.

Have you ever been assigned a project with very few guidelines and an undefined goal? For some, this situation can be incredibly liberating, for others it's unbelievably stressful. Employees who don't know exactly what their job is become easily stressed. They're not quite sure why they're here, which means that there's no security that they'll be around tomorrow. When you provide your team members with adequately defined goals and show them the pathway toward achieving them, not only are your employees less stressed, they truly feel themselves a part of the project and can be proud of the results they achieve.

Not only should you provide your team members with goals, it is imperative that you get them involved in setting those goals and planning the project in general. When you let team members help with the planning, you will be much more likely to spot any developing problem areas early on. Members will also feel much more committed to a project in which they had a stake in setting into motion.

If you learn and apply the time-proven strategies in this chapter and succeeding chapters, not only will you develop and bring to completion more successful projects, you'll also find that the individuals you work with are much happier, less stressed, and actually come to enjoy their work more than ever before!

One of the best tools you have at your disposal to help prevent stress, as well as to keep tabs on all aspects of the project, is the project meeting. The following Skill Extra provides guidelines for holding successful meetings. Skill Extras are included throughout the book as tools for project managers and team members.

Skill Extra—Guidelines For Meetings That Work

The most despised element in many businesses is the meeting. The common feeling about a meeting is that it is a boring event that can last forever and take away from valuable work time. This feeling shows that the meeting is being poorly used. Following these guidelines, you will be able to construct the basic, successful meeting. Guidelines for specific kinds of meetings follow in other chapters where appropriate, but this will get you started.

Clear Goals

There are two keys to a useful and productive project meeting. The first is to have a clear-cut goal for the session. What *exactly* do you expect to accomplish? Having a general idea is not acceptable, because a lack of a clear goal often leads to a rambling meeting that wastes everyone's time. Most people dislike meetings for this very reason—there is no sure point. If you know precisely what the goal of the meeting is, productive work can follow. The true goal of any meeting is problem solving. Everyone should leave in agreement and with a new version of the schedule, if appropriate, which brings the project back on track.

Length

Especially if there is a clearly defined goal, most meetings should last a maximum of 45 minutes. Still, there is much to be said for a meeting that starts, gets the job done, and is finished inside of 20 minutes. The easiest way to keep the meeting length short is to develop an agenda and then stick with it. Don't allow significant deviations or tangents. You might find it useful to take off your watch at the start of a meeting and place it in a visible place. This focuses the participants' attention on time at the outset. As the end of the meeting approaches, place the watch back on your hand. This signals that the end is near and you are ready to wrap up.

Frequency

How frequently you have meetings depends on the type and length of the project. A complicated project, like building a ship or relocating an entire division of a company, may require meetings twice a week. Some things that are more simple may only need a "touch base" meeting every two weeks. Certainly, it is wise to schedule meetings at major checkpoints and events in the process. For example, in the case of the relocation example, a meeting should be held prior to the delivery of the equipment to the new facility to ensure timely and proper unloading and installation of equipment.

Schedule meetings at a regular time. This allows the people involved to make attendance a predictable part of their schedule. However, never hesitate to call a meeting to resolve a problem. If a problem arises the day after a regularly scheduled meeting that could impact the schedule, you as the project manager should hold a meeting immediately to resolve it, if that's what is required. Remember, people may actually appreciate short, effective frequent meetings.

Location

Often, little thought is given to where to hold a meeting. "Let's meet in Joe's office." Or "I think the conference room is free, let's try that." Busy, noisy offices; unreserved conference rooms where people have to stand outside and wait while you find another place; and meeting areas that are convenient to you but require excessive transit time by others—all are contributors to poor meetings. In addition, these problems make you appear disorganized or not truly serious about the importance of the meeting yourself—creating the same attitude in your people. Choose a sensible location and try to meet there every time, unless rotating places on some type of regular basis is necessary for fair distribution of convenience. At any rate, a clean room, equipped with dry erase board or easel and flip chart, even overhead projectors or computer projection devices, will contribute greatly to a successful meeting.

Attendance

Appropriate attendance is vital to making a meeting productive. Little will stop a meeting dead in its tracks as the absence of the main participants in a discussion. Participants should therefore clearly understand that there are serious consequences for missing a project meeting. A meeting with too many people will also be unproductive. Who, then, should attend the meeting? Only the people who are essential to the day's agenda should attend. Others will merely be bored and resent the time away from other responsibilities.

The basic rule of selecting participants is to invite (a) decision makers, and (b) technical experts. Do *not* invite (c) bystanders.

a. *Decision makers* include those who can assign and commit resources and those who approve technical decisions. Functional managers, supervisors, vendors, subcontractors, and team leaders are typical decision makers.
b. *Technical experts* include those who advise on the advantages, disadvantages, and suitability of technical approaches; and make recommendations. Engineers, accountants, technicians, tradesmen, researchers, designers, and attorneys, are typical technical experts.
c. *Bystanders* are any of the above who do not have a direct responsibility for the tasks or activities being discussed within the scope of the meeting's agenda.

Size

The effective size of a meeting depends entirely on the purpose of the meeting. But because many project management meetings are intended to resolve problems, the most effective size is two to five participants, depending on the complexity of the problem. A meeting to make a choice between two technical approaches to fabricate a part may require no more than two experts. On the other hand, a meeting to select a management information software package will likely involve a lot more.

Large meetings are more suitable for information dissemination or gathering. When it comes time to solve problems, split up into smaller meetings. In the case of the software package selection, use the larger meeting to clarify the objectives and answer questions. Then go to predetermined breakout groups of five or less, each with specific objectives to accomplish.

Preparation

You cannot achieve the perfect meeting if you are not prepared. As the project manager, you will set the standard for the preparedness expected of all. Define the goal of the meeting, create an agenda, and distribute the agenda to each participant at least one day before the meeting. This will allow them to target their own preparations. Update the schedule so that the participants are working from the best available information. Have in mind contingencies for delegated responsibilities.

The participants in the meeting must know the status of their activities. They should:

- Update you about where they are in the current tasks and how this affects their completion times.
- Be ready with their current cost information, including the amount of money and resources they will require to finish.
- Be prepared to present their major needs and recommendations.

Note that much of the benefit of the meeting is derived from the preparation for the meeting. Many a useful nugget of information has been mined preparing for a meeting. The meeting proper is for the many and varied participants to arrive at consensus for an action—not debate why something hasn't been ideal in the past.

Accountability

Everyone should leave the meeting with a clear picture of two things:

- What the meeting has accomplished.
- What action each person is accountable for

Closing a meeting with anything less clear affects your credibility the next time you call an "important" meeting that will be "really short." Always summarize at the end what was accomplished and repeat assigned action items and names of those responsible. This way, everyone feels that the meeting was worthwhile, and you secure the commitment and action you need for future meetings.

Chapter Summary

As operations within organizations grow in complexity and size, project management concepts and procedures could be applied to any area of activity in a company. Considerations of project scope, duration, quality, resources, and commitment all enter into successful attainment of goals in an organization and reduce project managers' worry. Staying within time and cost limits goes a long way toward stress-free project management within the process and people issues that come with the job. Many problems can occur to throw project processes off schedule, but managing people issues well can do a great deal towards keeping things running smoothly. An important skill in handling projects is the meeting. Done well, project meetings can effectively uncover problems and solve them in a timely manner.

Chapter Questions

1. In what types of professional environments would you expect to find project management techniques being used?
2. What are the constraints within which projects must be managed?
3. Some practitioners have called project management a carefully created illusion; they argue that organization can only barely exist in complex projects. Agree or disagree and explain.

4. Give three characteristics of the current environment in which project management professionals must operate.
5. Explain the relationship between people and process in the successfully managed project.
6. Who sets the budget and time deadlines for projects? (Be sure to include every interest that must be included in the decisions.)
7. Outline at least three guidelines for effective meetings.

Project Challenge: Applying What You Know

A. Alton is planning to move his entire household across the country (from North Carolina to New Mexico). He has a family: his wife works and will need to find a job right away in the new location, and his children are in elementary school. He has two cars, several expensive antiques and art pieces among his furniture, a dog that gets car sick, and a constraint of 2 weeks to accomplish the move. Although he has already purchased a new home, he doesn't know if it will be vacant so that they may move in immediately. He has been given two first-class plane tickets and an $8,000 moving budget.

1. Determine all the separate activities that will need to be done for a successful move.
2. Estimate durations on each of the activities and fit them into the 2-week time allowance.
3. Anticipate any problems that might occur that would prevent an on-time completion.
4. Develop a set of contingency plans and cost for these. (For example—if the house is not ready on time, what would they do and how much might temporary quarters cost?)
5. Write out a "to-do" list for the day the family and furniture are to leave.
6. What might happen if Alton arrives late?

B. In the situation above, Alton decides to rent a truck and ask his brother and two friends to help him move.

1. What are some of the issues Alton should consider when he manages the people involved in this project?
2. Would his relationship to the helpers make a difference?
3. Is there a possibility for conflict?
4. How much would he have to budget to pay them?
5. What difference might it make in determining the scope of the project if Alton chooses the driving option?
6. If Alton chooses the driving option, what might he do with the remainder of the money he has been given for the move?

Interview with an Expert

***C. Robert Suggs,** Associate Manager of Product Development, Florida Power and Light*

On the question of "why project management?" there is no question. There is very little done in an organization that doesn't require a critical look at planning time, cost, and resources. So project management principles, in some form or other, are practical nearly everywhere in a company. Take the planning process, for example. The focus of planning is to have:

- Explicit, detailed description of the final goal or finished product
- No overlap of effort or people
- No omissions of tasks or resources needed to complete the job
- Agreement on roles and responsibilities of people and/or departments

What a lot of people don't understand is that project planning can be as simple as a "to-do" list or assigning tasks to individuals and holding them accountable for their output. Developing, publishing, and distributing a detailed project plan that includes timetables, precedence relationships, and resource allocations keeps everyone "honest." No one can point fingers and say, "They're holding up the project," when, in fact, a quick look at the plan and completed tasks will show immediately who's holding up whom.

The worst case scenario I remember working with was the development of component parts by an outside contractor. He was to conduct research and development and build a prototype. This individual was selected for this because of his creative brilliance in his field, but he had no organizational skills or understanding of operational cause and effect. After the project became so far behind as to be in jeopardy, we sent in someone to handle project management, but the contractor just couldn't grasp the concept. By constantly re-tooling and failing to delegate, he fell further and further behind, losing so much money his company eventually went under. He never connected the time /money drain—the more time something takes, the more it costs.

Here are the steps I use to set up a project:

1. Define EXACTLY what the result will be––prototype, production, service re-vamp, etc.
2. Anticipate EVERY step required to get to the result.
3. Starting with due date, establish durations––how long each can take to reach deadline.
4. Evoke the plan and do whatever it takes to catch up if you fall behind.

What so many people don't understand is that project problems impact everything in your personal life as well: the amount of time you spend at work, the time you're away from your family, the amount of sleep you get (and the impaired decision making that comes with not enough sleep), and sometimes your pay, if there is a late penalty. Each employee, regardless of his or her official designation as a project manager, should understand, and act on the understanding, of the time and resource relationship—this is the project management mentality.

CHAPTER

2 CHANGE

CHAPTER PREVIEW

THE PROJECT MANAGEMENT SEMINAR: SESSION 2

"Today, we'll be moving rooms," Ralph announced at the begining of the session. "And I'll be away at a conference, so Alan Twan here will be running the workshop. Oh, and the schedule has been altered; lunch won't be until 1 p.m. because of a conflict with a banquet in the dining hall." When he finished, the group as a unit stared at him for a second.

"What? We're just getting started with this training," Yury protested. "Now, you're heading out. We have to move all our stuff to another room, and lunch is late. What's going on around here anyway?"

"Yeah," Jerry agreed, "you'd think there would be more organization than this."

Jaime, with his usual optimism, offered, "Hey guys, the other room might be better, and what if this Mr. Twan is a real expert?"

Ragdeesh obediently packed up his briefcase and started for the door. Tom walked over to Alan Twan and introduced himself. "Hello, I'm Tom, I'm looking forward to today. Don't worry about the others—change is harder for some people to deal with than others. . . ." Tom caught himself, his eyes lighting up as he glanced quickly over at Hilda, who was beginning to smile. Then he looked at Ralph and Tracey, who were laughing out loud. A sulking Yury jerked his head up from his preparations for the move. "What?"

"Gotcha!" Ralph smiled. "You guys have just illustrated the concepts for today. You were great! You couldn't have done better with a script."

Yury scratched his head and Jaime chuckled. Ragdeesh sheepishly turned to walk back to his seat.

As everyone settled in, Ralph and Tracey opened the discussion, which yielded the following ideas.

- People hate change.
- Why do we have to do new stuff all the time?
- Worry

- Why is everything moving so fast?
- Mergers and buyouts
- What's a change agent?

Because change affects everyone, the conversation was lively, and it took Ralph and Tracey a while to focus the group on the objectives for the day.

- **Understanding external forces that drive change and the effects of change on the project manager**
- **Identifying and handling individual responses to change**
- **Surviving professionally in the face of change**
- **Managing organizational change**

Ten years ago, and probably all the years since the beginning of the 20th century, parents advised their children, "Get a good job with a stable company and stay there. If you're loyal and dedicated, you can retire with a good pension in 30 years. Stability, that's the thing." Mom and Dad notwithstanding, it's just not that way anymore. Change is the only predictable element in today's professional life.

1.0 External Forces That Drive Change

Figure 2–1
Forces in the environment act on companies.

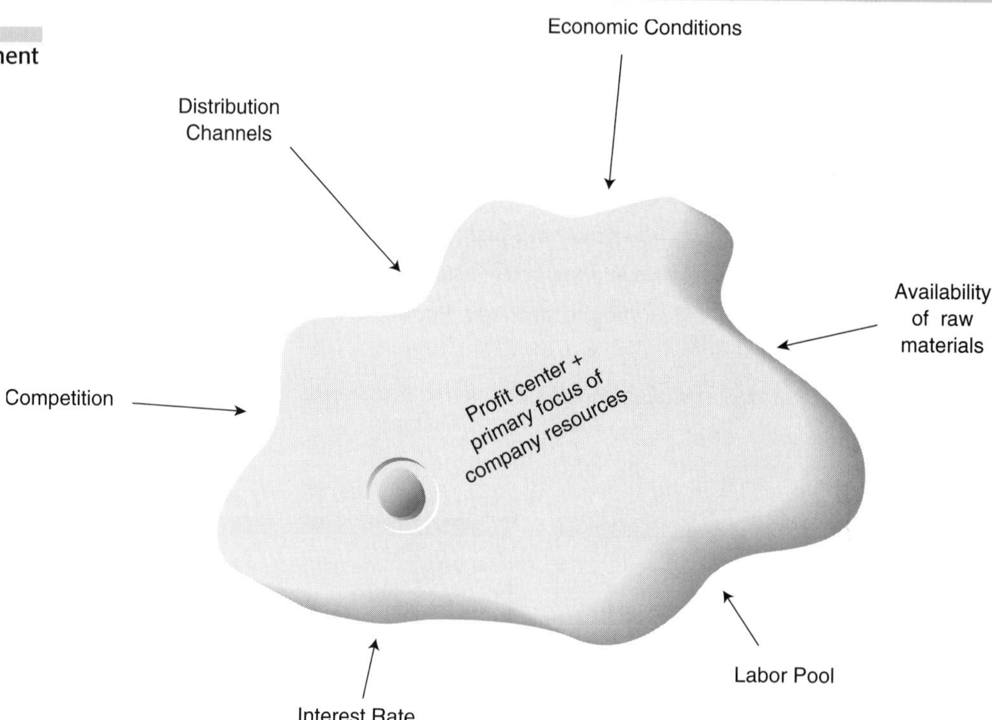

Environment affects the way in which businesses operate, much in the way an amoeba is affected by its environment (Figure 2–1). Success and failure in terms of profit and loss are directly related to a business's ability to respond to conditions in that environment. A business survives as it is able to react to trends and opportunities in its operating environment. Systems within the organization respond and evolve to meet these environmental shifts, which take place internally—within the business—and externally—outside of the business. These conditions change constantly. Some changes that take place in the world economy directly affect your company, and ultimately your projects. Some do not.

Changing conditions may be seen as a strategic opportunty if the company's reaction to these new conditions would likely be profitable. For instance, a company that builds houses and apartments might easily move into a profitable situation of building office complexes if the company has plenty of trained people, and if the equipment and sources of materials required are compatible with the current needs of the company. If instead, the company would have to buy millions of dollars of new equipment, or work with materials suppliers they had never done business with before, then the venture could be a failure.

Companies must adapt to change constantly or be consumed by it. Conditions that are changing rapidly now include:

- Expansion of economies to include global markets—we sell jeans and motorcycles to Japan, and cars to Mexico. We contract construction of everything from clothes to pagers to other countries.
- Abundance of easily accessible information and markets—for the first time in history information is available to individual homes on any topic imaginable. Also, any person or company can put a page on the Internet and market goods or services.
- Rapid technological growth and obsolescence—the sales life of software is 90 days now before obsolescence. More computing power is in children's games than existed in the first supercomputers.
- Gap between skill requirements of today's companies and skill levels of employee pools—companies that used to require degrees or certifications along with work experience for hiring now accept "working knowledge" of new technologies.
- Constant mergers, downsizing, and buyouts—it is possible for a worker now to change "jobs" as often as every two years due to buyouts, layoffs, and restructuring. In some cases he or she won't even have to leave the office, just do different things for different owners and/or managers. Personal career management becomes the responsibility of the employee because companies can't promise longevity or promotions.
- Fluctuating availability and prices of resources—in highly competitive markets, many companies vie for scarce resources (raw materials, components, labor). Prices vary with availability and can affect the price of the final product, so bidding on contracts can become a potentially costly "guess."
- Increasing interdependence of systems as opposed to isolated technologies—since the Telecommunications Act of 1996 the lines drawn between separate parts of communication, such as television, cable, phone and data communications, are disappearing. We compute on our TV and watch videos on our computer monitor.

And this is just the short list.

It is difficult, or maybe even impossible, to discuss the external forces that drive change in a company without discussing marketing. The name of the profit game in business is competitive advantage. Every successful company offers the buying public a reason to purchase products or services from it, rather than from its competitors. Since the competitive field changes all the time with new technologies and even new companies, maintaining a competitive edge requires constant monitoring of what's going on outside the company. In addition, as quality improves in the areas of product refinements and service offerings, monitoring of what's going on inside the company is necessary also.

What's going on inside the company is called the **company culture.** Peter Bijur, Chairman and CEO of Texaco, Inc. defines ***culture*** as "what people do when no one is telling them what to do" (1999). The way an employee internalizes the vision and operating policies of the company—the rights and wrongs—determines the way that employee acts. Cultures are sometimes fast-paced, sometimes light-hearted. Some are fierce and fraught with conflict. Some cultures are very positive and energetic; some reflect worry and tentativeness. (Bijur, 1999)

company culture the informal rules that govern peoples' behavior

culture "what people do when no one is telling them what to do"

Whatever the culture, good or bad, successful or unsuccessful, Bijur suggests, "For sustainable competitive advantage, you have to change the culture" (1999). No company can continue growth in a dynamic and evolving marketplace without constantly re-inventing itself. Whatever you did well last week is old news. To stay competitive, companies, and the individuals that make up those companies, must constantly look at what has been accomplished today, and at what will be the victories of tomorrow.

That string of victories makes up the life force that must be fed to keep the organization alive. Each department and each employee responds to trends in the market or new technologies that can help a company to stay competitive and profitable. To stay alive, the organization must adapt. Thus, we return to our amoeba example. If an opportunity opens up, the company must move in that direction and move quickly. The move may require the reduction in, or elimination of, a unit or department in the company in order to supply the new area. Thus, energy centers can shift inside a company, but the overall vitality of the organization will be maintained; the net result is healthy profitability. (See Figure 2–2.)

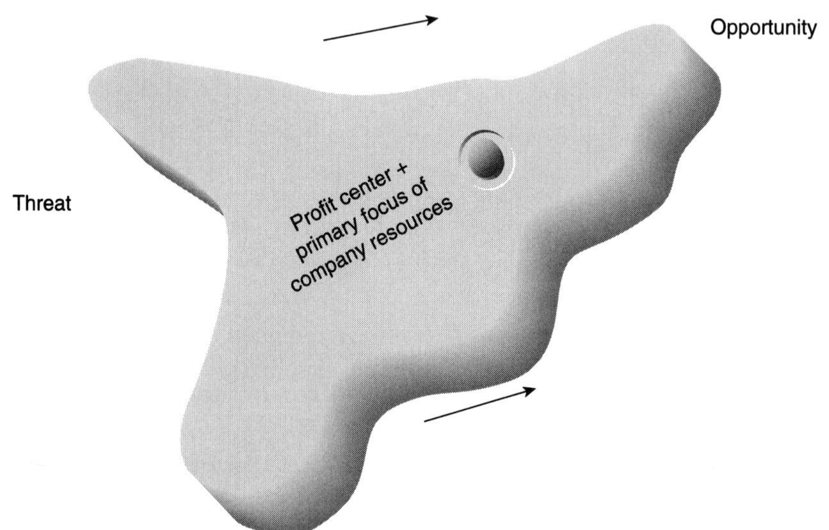

Figure 2–2
Energy in a company moves away from threats and toward opportunity. This is how a company survives by adapting and responding to changes in its environment.

To allow the organization to adapt, resources—capital, process, and human—must be brought to bear. This not only requires the ability to react to rapidly changing external conditions; but it also demands that the culture of the company be oriented towards change as a positive. For this to happen, employees have to be aware of conditions that affect their business. In the best of all possible worlds, a line worker would see a new technology profiled on an educational television channel and, realizing the possible impact on her company's products, would share the news with a manager. Moreover, the employee should already be thinking of ways her department could rise to the potential challenge or even the threat the new technology might pose to her company. Many times the employee who must manage the adaptation is the project manager.

2.0 Effects of Change on the Project Manager

Many changes land on the desk of the project manager on a daily basis. Sometimes the changes are little ones: new reporting forms, a change in specification for a product, new phone equipment, different purchasing procedures. Sometimes, however, they are major ones: new materials suppliers, complete re-design of a product at near ready stage, change in management, acquisition or loss of a highly skilled project team member.

Whatever the change, or magnitude of that change, project managers are in a uniquely qualified position to deal with it; project managers adapt constantly to variations in schedule, supplies, specifications, and so on, on a daily basis as part of their job.

Project managers by definition are called upon to manage all sorts of projects: long-and short-term, small and large. Specific changes in processes, facilities, products and resources often become defined as projects, with a project manager given responsibility for creating the change. Interestingly enough, it is not always the career project manager that runs these change projects. Often an employee with high levels of expertise within the area to be changed is "drafted" and told to "make it happen." There are many perils in this type of situation, as you might well guess. Project management is a skill and discipline that must be developed, not designated. It is easy to see, then, why so many of these appointed "project managers" eventually throw their hands in dismay and cry for help.

When this happens, if the company is smart, it will bring in professional project managers from within the company or secure the services of outside consultants with expertise in the area of the desired change. Problems with either of these scenarios may arise if employees are insecure and try to protect their "turf." The outsider, even if it's someone from within the same company, may be viewed as an intruder or even as an ugly reminder of the department's failure to effect the change by itself. Without a proper company posture towards the change, the project manager may find himself knocking on locked doors or making phone calls that will never be returned. For this reason the person designated to create a managed change must balance many roles, including technical expert in the area of the required change, visionary who can connect the change to individual employee success, expert communicator, conflict manager, influence master, team builder, process analyst, designer, and so on and so on (Figure 2–3). (Most of these skills are covered later in this text.)

Figure 2–3
The project manager must balance many roles.

Here is a timely example.

TechArt (fictional company name) is doing well, with many internal projects under way. A facilities project is planning to convert a warehouse into an expanded printing area. Included in this is a reorganization of the current printing area into a larger software design unit and private conference rooms for meetings with clients. The systems area has a cross-departmental project to design an internal communications network to connect all areas, both on-site and off-site. This project affects all functions: marketing, design, production, printing, shipping, accounting, and supplies.

Several other internal projects are either ongoing or in the making, including a customer service training program for all employees and a hardware upgrade. These are in addition to external projects with customers. Because the company is doing well with almost no debt, but market share growth is fairly static, the owners have decided to offer the business for sale, to "cash out" and retire. Investors are in almost daily, and there is some talk about the company going public due to its unique design technology patents.

Now comes the impact to project managers. Here is what is already happening:

- Rumors about the sale have caused some of the talented employees to "jump ship," or leave for jobs with other companies, before the official announcements are made.
- Recruiters and headhunters—private human resource locators—are calling daily to try to hire away the skilled design engineers as well as the project managers.
- Many projects, including the customer service training and some parts of the software upgrade, have been put on hold.
- Any projects affecting the "bottom line" or short-term profitability of the company have become priority number 1, such as the expansion to the unused facility, which will increase production capacity 80% and allow for a larger, more varied customer base.
- The project managers who don't leave in the first wave have to recruit team members from departments already stretched to the limit or from departments that fear layoffs and are fiercely trying to protect their jobs.
- Fear, infighting, and negativity abound while the company pretends to conduct business as usual in order to look good to investors.
- All expenditures of money are scrutinized carefully, and many sign-offs are required to prevent too much spending in the short run.

Left in the wake of this situation, the project managers have:

- inordinately high accountabilities (not only to their usual work but to bottom line appearances as well),
- limited resources that are closely held and that require excessive effort to secure, and
- teams made of skeleton crews and already overworked draftees from other departments (with maybe an occasional contractor thrown in for a few weeks).

So why do the project managers stay if things are that bad? One reason might be that they like the company and the work and hope they will be allowed to continue doing something they love. Or they believe they will be rewarded financially if they stay with the company and support it—maybe in the form of shares of stock. Maybe, they welcome change and truly enjoy new challenges. Their reasons for staying, as well as others' reasons for leaving, are based on how individual people react to change in their lives.

3.0 Individual Responses to Change

With the constancy of change a way of life in today's industries, you might imagine that a lot of research effort has been put into trying to understand people's reaction to change and into facilitating the rapid assimilation of employees into new conditions. If employees don't "get up to speed" quickly on the new product or process, then the company's future could be in jeopardy. Whether perceived as a threat or promise, a change scares many people and is greeted positively by very few.

Unfortunately for the project manager, the way an individual responds to change at work has as much to do with his personal experience as with his professional situation. So, if changes have brought positive experiences for a person, then there is a good chance that person will respond well to an anticipated change; change is seen by him as opportunity and potential. But, if the person has a history of experiencing change that is negative (family breakups, job loss, etc.), then that employee may be expected to overreact in some way; change is viewed as threat and loss. (See Walters & McKee, 1997, for a more detailed discussion of this reaction.)

Actually, it is possible to find out a person's approach to change with psychological testing. The term for describing reactions to change or uncertainty is **tolerance of ambiguity**, which means the degree to which a person gets upset or stressed when faced with change. Ambiguity may be broken down into three categories: novelty, complexity, and insolubility. (Whetton & Cameron, 1998). **Novelty** describes the new or unexpected and includes not only new things we choose to experience (generally less stressful), but also new things that come at us without warning (more stressful). An example would be taking a different route home (less stressful) versus taking a detour that unexpectedly occurred due to a gas line break (more stressful, especially if the alternate route is completely unfamiliar and not well marked.)

tolerance of ambiguity the degree to which a person gets upset or stressed when faced with change

novelty new or unexpected situation

Complexity has to do with an environment, or problem, that seems to have a lot of unrelated or disconnected elements to it. A new job in a small company, where the pace is frenzied and employees seem to do everything without a job description, is an example. Another example is a project team comprised of many different functional areas, working together to create a new system. Individuals carry out highly complex and varied tasks that must converge in a meaningful way.

complexity environment or problem with unrelated or disconnected elements

Finally, **insolubility** is another form of ambiguity resulting from problems that seem to be unsolvable with the current knowledge, tools, or systems. Some view this type of problem solving as a challenge, a puzzle that is fun to engage. Others see it as a problem for which they cannot possibly get the right answer, and so feel doomed.

insolubility form of ambiguity associated with seemingly unsolvable problems

As you might guess by now, project managers and their employees are faced with high degrees of novelty, complexity, and insolubility as they carry out their projects. Managing change and employees' reactions to it might present seemingly unsolvable problems. Project managers must develop a positive approach to handling situations of this nature.

■ ■ ■

"Okay, let's look at what happened this morning and figure out the reaction each of you had to the change situation we created." Tracey suggested. "Tom, what was going on in your mind?"

"That's easy. As a salesperson I have to be ready to roll with the punches and capitalize on any opportunity. I actually enjoy seeing how I can turn a surprise into a sale."

"Okay, then, would we say Tom is comfortable with novelty?"

"Yeah, but that's his job," Jaime responded. "I'm supposed to keep new stuff from popping up. If something unexpected comes into the picture, I haven't stayed on top of things and it makes me look bad."

"Then it's probably safe to say," Tracey said, "that in a highly changeable and complex environment, you would feel stressed because it might look like you weren't doing your job. Right?"

"Something like that."

"What about Ragdeesh? Did anyone notice what he was doing?"

"He picked up his briefcase and headed for the door, so what?" Jerry observed.

"Ragdeesh probably looks at change as just another element of the job. If the company says 'It's time to change,' then he accepts it and goes about his work." Tracey stopped and looked at Ragdeesh for approval. "Is that about right?"

"Yes. I don't understand all the talk. We work for the company. It's not our place as project managers to second-guess management. It just wastes a lot of time," he explained.

Yury, who had been silent up to this point, spoke up. "But my managers come from marketing. They are always jumping on the newest thing. They make me crazy. Expect me to change the machining of a part just to make it look prettier. Who cares if it's pretty? It is good as is. I don't agree with much they do," he grumbled.

"Anyone have a comment on Yury's input?" Tracey surveyed the group.

"In our business, if we don't react quickly enough to a new technology or a new need in the market, our competitor will," Hilda responded matter-of-factly. "We don't have time for the engineers to tell me they can't make the change when we need it."

"So, we've heard a lot of reactions to change and the reasons for them. Let's classify some and put names on them, so we can know how, as project managers, we can deal with them. Your project team members are having the same feelings in the face of change that you have voiced here."

■ ■ ■

Some generally observable and predictable reactions to change are listed below. Keep in mind, however, that the project manager should know the employees themselves in order to best guide a team through a change process. You will observe each of the following reactions in response to change. By understanding the sources of concern and having some alternatives for managing these concerns and the problems they create, you as a project manager or team leader will be better equipped to keep productivity high.

3.1 Reaction #1—Negative

Source of concern Employee assumes new must be bad due to past experiences with negative change events or due to toxic effect of negative employees who influence others. These employees see change as a loss, whatever the outcome. The employee may also have reason to believe his or her job is in jeopardy because of the nature of the change. Homeostasis, the human's desire for things to stay the same whether they are good or bad, adds to this. (See Paul Alcorn's discussion of this situation in *Social Issues in Technology*, Prentice Hall, 2000)

Recognizable characteristics Employees may exhibit to varying degrees similar responses as would occur with other losses, such as denial, anger, and sadness. Arguing and complaining over little things will become more and more prevalent. Previously cooperative and open employees may become reluctant to discuss plans or projects with other departments in an effort to protect territory. Arguments between employees and managers may occur, but covert activity is more likely: whispered conversations that stop when managers walk up, long lunches either in defiance or for job-hunting, hoarding and misrepresenting resources, missed deadlines and decline in new project ideas. Morale and creativity generally decline drastically.

3.2 Reaction #2—Accepting

Source of concern Some employees in this group feel they have nowhere else to go or no recourse within their company and realize that they must adapt to survive professionally. Others by experience have learned that many changes come and go and believe that "riding out" the change will eventually allow things to return to normal. And finally, there is the "good soldier" group who generally does what management says and trusts (or hopes), realistically or unrealistically, that the outcome will be for the general benefit.

Recognizable characteristics Employees may say, "Well let's try the new way; what's wrong with something new?" or "I'll do whatever you want me to, just tell me." Some will be enthusiastic and helpful in implementing new systems or procedures; others will just comply with management directives without any real zeal or commitment. This group will stay with the company because that's what they do; they may not, however, be the ones you would necessarily choose to keep.

3.3 Reaction #3—Inciting

Employee concerns If things aren't changing, they are stale for this group. These employees are passionate about ideas, especially theirs, and are constantly driving managers and the company with news about the latest strategic directions "we should be going in." They crave the excitement of change and cause as much of it as they can. Often opportunists, this group can detect a change coming and find a way to capitalize on it for themselves or their group before it is even implemented. As drivers and creators of change, some in this group, interestingly enough, still do not respond wholeheartedly to changes forced on them from the outside or from above. As a group, however, these employees are information gatherers and innovators and are rarely caught by surprise. They derive power and satisfaction from being "on top of things."

Recognizable characteristics Questions such as "Why don't we do this?" or "Don't you think we should be implementing that?" are often heard from this group. Unsolicited articles and proposals for new equipment, markets, or processes flow from these employees to management at all levels. They volunteer for feasibility studies and beta tests of new software or equipment. Frequently, these are the ones that request professional development and skills training to support their need for growth. They will attend seminars and volunteer to lead in-house sessions on the changes. Because they devote time and attention to researching change indicators, they expect to be listened to and taken seriously when they suggest new actions.

It is not always possible for project managers to know their people well enough to anticipate their reactions to changes, so understanding that each of the above reactions will likely occur will help you to prepare. Another important consideration is that you, as the project manager or project team member, examine your own feelings about change and understand the need for change in thriving organizations.

4.0 Professional Survival in the Face of Change

As has already been discussed, rapid and dramatic changes are becoming characteristic of the workplace in many, if not all, industries. To survive, companies must rise to the challenge of these changes, and so must every employee in them. For the project manager (or even members of project teams) to survive professionally, he or she must adopt several behaviors:

- Develop awareness for external conditions that drive company success.
- Recognize cause-and-effect relationships in the workplace.
- Take creative action.
- View change as positive.

4.1 Develop Awareness of External Factors

Because project managers often have to carry out the activities that allow the company to adapt to changes in the external environment, it makes sense to know what those conditions are. Too often employees are oblivious to factors that directly affect their industry and their jobs. In the past these concerns were, admittedly, relegated to upper management, to the strategic planning function. Today, however, it may not only be foolish, it may be professionally suicidal, to ignore or not seek out this information. The more employees understand about the competitive world in which their company operates and the economic challenges in that world, the better able they are to prepare for and adapt to changes.

4.2 Recognize Cause-and-Effect Relationships

Another element in this individual survival plan is the awareness of cause-and-effect relationships within the company itself. Too often employees think of themselves as independent contractors: "I do my job; they can do theirs." Life outside their own department is a fuzzy world of "not me." Clearly in the best-run and most successful companies, the interdependence of departments and functions, as well as the recognition of each one's role and relationship to the others, is common knowledge among all employees. Understanding and fostering these relationships help the employee or manager ensure his or her central role in whatever happens in the change process.

4.3 Take Creative Action

"Taking creative action" does not mean constantly reacting after the fact to changing conditions—a kind of problem-solving-on-the-fly approach. It means, instead, taking the knowledge gained from the previous two steps—developing awareness of external conditions and understanding cause and effect—and building structures and processes that will allow the company (or even just your department) to capitalize on the change. Doing so results in the creation of a productive opportunity out of a new set of conditions. What do you do, according to the proverb, when given lemons? Make lemonade! In taking creative action, you should have the foresight to see the role of lemons in your company's future success, and therefore plant lemon trees.

Taking creative action also requires practice. Creativity in meeting life's challenges can be a learned skill, but when we become complacent in a familiar job, we tend to lose our edge. Practice can help.

4.4 View Change as Positive

Finally, the attitude element enters into the survival equation: embrace change as necessary and valuable. Viewing change as positive is difficult for most people because they become good, even expert, at their jobs. Change means that they may have to start over in a new area, to become a beginner again, which most people associate with feelings of awkwardness and discomfort. So, many are reluctant to give up their feeling of personal competence and control, especially if they are among the older group of employees.

In *The Artist's Way,* an engaging and especially helpful book for retooling and re-creating your life, Julia Cameron (1992) offers this example from a conversation, "I can't start the piano at my age. Do you know how old I'll be by the time I learn to play the piano?" The response was, "Yes, exactly the same age as if you didn't" (p. 138). The observation, though cryptic in this example, is true: change is difficult to accept, but can change your life for the better.

■ ■ ■

"May I interrupt here?" Ragdeesh politely raised his hand.

"Yes, please do." Jerry interjected, a sarcastic edge to his voice. "What is this 'embrace change' stuff, anyway? Like it's supposed to be a good thing. Look, in my business, we get a competitive edge, as you call it, by being able to produce our products more cheaply than the other companies. We can do this by economies of scale: long production runs and increased efficiencies over time. You can't tell me that constantly making changes and fouling up my processes are something I should get excited about."

"Excuse me, Jerry, but I had a question," Ragdeesh persisted.

"Sure, go ahead, Ragdeesh," Ralph answered.

"What if the change that management wants to make is not a good one for the company in my opinion?"

"That's a great question, Ragdeesh. Who wants to field that one?" Ralph turned the question back to the group.

The silence in the room suggested that the group may have had that same question, so Ralph answered. "First you have to figure out the reason you are resisting the change. Have you done the research we talked about to know why management is asking for the change? Second, are you like Jerry here and feel that any changes mess up the process and create inefficiencies? And, if so, could you think of any possible ways the change could be a positive one? Remember, few of us like change, even good change, and sometimes we resist just because change rocks our carefully constructed boat. Eh, Jerry?"

"Aye, aye captain." Jerry returned, still not completely convinced.

Noting Jerry's folded arms and challenging expression, Ralph knew there was more work to be done.

"Well, Jerry, I have two answers for you," Ralph continued. "One is that the change is probably coming anyway, and fighting is just a waste of time, so why bother? The other is that managers today are beginning to look at employees as those that are 'with the program' or in the way of it. It's survival, Jerry. Plain and simple. You can see the change coming and figure out how to make it work for you, or you can dig in your heels and be dragged out the door."

Jerry nodded thoughtfully.

■ ■ ■

5.0 Organizational Approaches to Change

How organizations handle change strategically is a book in itself. However, the way the leadership of organizations views the management of change internally has a direct effect on the project manager. Following are comments by change consultants that reflect three common views of approaches to creating change within companies.

- **Slash and Burn**

"You can't make a culture change. You have to come in, fire enough managers to make an impression, then hire in people who think like you want. From the ones that are left, those that can come along with us with the new plan can stay; the others get left behind. It takes too long to try to change people's operating style and attitudes. By the time they bring me in, change has to happen . . . and fast."

- **Support and Nurture**

"Change is the death of the old, and even if it is a merciful death, or a death that brings new life to a failing company, people experience loss. We look at the steps of grief (denial, anger/sadness, dealmaking, acceptance) and try to hasten the movement through that process. If you don't address the fear and loss in people, it's going to take a long time to get commitment to the new way, maybe never."

- **Inspire and Motivate**

"I've seen a lot of success with what we call 'firestarters.' These are compelling visionaries with a lot of credibility due to past successes and a lot of charisma to really inspire people. Lee Iacocca was like that as a manager. He just has that spark that makes people believe things can be better and that the individual employees can make them better. Anyway, the firestarter comes in, gets things going in the right direction, then moves on, usually leaving behind a hand-picked management team to carry out the plan and keep the momentum going. These guys rarely stay around for the long term."

These are three very different approaches to how management can handle and facilitate major company change. Although the project manager, as has been stated before, seldom makes the large change decisions, the project manager is responsible for implementation of those decisions.

5.1 Urgent Change Management

Urgent change management relates to upheavals that dramatically affect operations, including buyouts, mergers, downsizing, bankruptcy, market (competitive) threats, and changes in senior management. Companies in crises have made the news in recent years—the poisoning of a major pain reliever, stock market dips, and airline crashes resulting from unknown causes. Many of the situations that affect the project manager are less newsworthy and more subtle. However, because they ultimately impact the people and deliverables within the project manager's accountability, they can certainly be called "urgent."

The situation with TechArt, described earlier, is an example of an "urgent" situation. A company offered for sale presents one set of challenges; a company after a sale presents another.

5.1.1 Challenge #1—Bailout

Uncertainty about the future can cause many talented employees to "bail out" of your project and pull back to protect their own turf.

Prevention Provide information (as you are allowed to release it) so that employees feel that they are not going to be dropped on short notice. People become more fearful if information is withheld and they know it. The assumption is that things must really be bad, causing them to panic. Realistically, you aren't going to be able to prevent all employees from being fearful and panicking, but you can show your team members how finishing major projects can enhance their value to the company and possibly help them be the ones who are kept.

Damage control Meet with upper management and secure a projects priorities guideline. You need to know where to concentrate your time and limited resources. If you have to drop something, make sure it's not one of the projects upper management feels is critical. In addition, you will need to survey the organization for support to replace those who have left. This is the time where carefully developed internal relationships across areas of the company could pay off. You also may have to gain a commitment from management for resources to complete the high-priority projects. Unexpected expenses, such as contract help or overtime pay, need to be covered. Be very clear to management what is required to bring the project in on schedule. This is not the time to whine about the difficulties you are having; they already know that. They are interested in results regardless of the reason for the crisis.

5.1.2 Challenge #2—Poor Morale

Morale is poor, and management needs everyone to "behave" when potential investors or new management come through.

Prevention Remain realistically positive. You can't say for sure what is going to happen, but if you are overly positive, your employees will see through the deception and you will lose credibility with them. However, negativity is in itself an unpleasant and self-defeating attitude. You may have to be a bit creative with finding positives in an uncertain situation, but keeping people focused on their tasks and continuing to reward those who demonstrate commitment and achievement will go a long way towards maintaining a good working environment.

Damage control If the end is indeed near, you should try to pin management down as to what is going to happen when. If the end is a buyout, you should find out when new management will take over. If the end is a merger, you are entitled to ask which divisions will be retained and which will be divested or taken over by another company's similar department. Keep in mind that new management is not necessarily the end of people's jobs; if a company is doing well, a new owner would be foolish to come in and ruin a good thing. However, companies are bought with a vision in mind of how to make them successful. Thus, business as usual will not likely take place.

This doesn't mean things will be awful, necessarily, but it does mean that working conditions and goals may be very different. You will need to convey this to your employees if you intend to stay yourself. You also should ask for planning meetings with the new management as soon as possible, if for no other reason than your own peace of mind about what is happening. The key survival question to new management, both for you and for your employees is, "What do you want me to do?"

If the end is bankruptcy or the closing of a plant or department resulting in layoffs, you should attempt to negotiate an outplacement arrangement for employees to help them transition out of the organization from which they are being asked to leave. In the case of a layoff, it is not always the fault of the employees that the division is being closed or that the company is going under. There could have been a market shift that management did not see or could not rise to meet. Actually, today, because this kind of layoff is commonplace, a resume showing a nonvoluntary departure from a job is not necessarily viewed as a red flag signaling a problem employee.

Ways to Speed Change Acceptance

Explain reasons for change
Project positive outcome
Hold a "wake" for old ways
Create group "memories"
Get change implementation ideas from departments affected
Ask employees to drive change process

5.2 Ongoing Change Management

Change affects everyone, on a personal and a professional level. Project managers deal with changes every day, and most have learned to approach new challenges with a circumspect and analytical manner. However, there are still many people who view change as unsettling or threatening. In the world in which today's project manager operates, a high tolerance for flux and a real skill at adaptation are not just helpful; they are necessities.

The job of managing change as an ongoing condition is more realistic and more easily accomplished, however, if the company posture is one of commitment to the change and if the employees buy into and welcome the project manager's presence as a facilitator. The concept of facilitator is very important, as project managers themselves can only go so far in creating change. Because they cannot do all tasks of the project themselves, they must foster support for, and create a commitment to, a change that is going to benefit the company. At some point, though, managers and employees themselves will have to take action that will create changes in their own departments. Project managers, then, must deftly unravel old goal commitments and attachments and weave in new ones that support the new processes.

Yes, "attachments" is the right word here. Attachment to workgroups, familiar equipment and procedures, workspaces, and even job titles is strong. But nothing new will come of "same old, same old." And until those old frameworks for doing business are altered, forward movement is not possible. The complexities of restructuring these old relationships are intensified by individuals' own perceptions of change and its meaning for them.

As project manager you are the proverbial "captain of the ship." And, as captain, you are looked to as an example of how to respond to situations. Often, employees will follow the manager's lead in circumstances of uncertainty. Project managers must model the appropriate behavior for employees. If the project manager panics, so will the employees. If the manager is negative, many of the employees will be negative as well. However, even if the manager is positive, some employees will greet change with fear and dread.

There are many specific actions you, as project manager (or as a project team member) can take to foster a constructive work environment in the face of constant change, as outlined below:

1. Set an example. Though your day-to-day actions and attitude, show employees how they should behave in the face of ongoing change. Remain positive and resilient. Approach tentative and ambiguous situations calmly.
2. Behave consistently. You send an alarm to employees when you are cheerful and open one day and ill-tempered and secretive the next.
3. Recognize employees for demonstrating creative adaptations or showing ingenuity. Make it clear change for constant improvement is expected and rewarded.
4. Nurture growth in employees. Constant change requires constant skill upgrades. Challenge employees with new and varied duties and situations. Cross-train team members where feasible, so someone can pick up the duties if a team member leaves.
5. Involve employees in setting goals for future competitiveness. Hold improvement meetings and information sessions about where the company is going and what its strengths and potential threats are. Then tie this information directly to the daily activities of the department, team, and individual employee. "What are *you* going to do differently to further growth in the organization?"

Managing change has become a way of life for employees of any company that wants to stay competitive. Projects you will manage are often tied directly to that competitive drive: new product development, retooling a manufacturing facility, setting up a new computer network or data management system, changing a process. Because of this you are the change agent, whether you conceived or ordered the change or not. And you are responsible for seamlessly managing daily changes in team make-up, resources, specs on deliverables, deadlines. The better you teach your people to be adaptive and positive, the easier your job will be.

■ ■ ■

"Jaime, how long have you been with your company?" Ralph asked.

"About 16 years, 5 as a project manager."

"What changes have you gone through in that time?"

Jaime laughed. "I feel like you're setting me up here. We've had the founder die and be replaced, the company merge with a larger competitor, and my job title and division change."

"How many times?"

Jaime shook his head and chuckled again, "I've had 12 managers, two of them twice, 5 department changes and 6 job titles." He paused, "And before you ask, I've directed 28 projects."

Ralph looked around the room at the heads nodding. "Is that about typical for all of you?"

Yury spoke up. "I think Ragdeesh and I have even more. We've both moved from other countries in addition to all that Jaime said."

Hilda interrupted with a question. "How do we as project managers deal with our people's reactions as well as the changes themselves? How do we ever keep it all together?"

"That's a real concern", Ralph agreed. "Why do you think stress levels are so high in project managers? Changes occur all the time. But if you remain clear, about the objectives and the need for creative adaptation, you will help yourself and your employees. Commitment to the goal, and an organizational posture toward change as a good thing, will help you respond both to the people and to the challenges."

With an impish grin, Jerry chimed in, "Great, I hear you. But now can you guys tell me what I'm supposed to say to a 10-year employee who recently had a sex change operation and now wants us to call him Shirley?"

Ralph, throwing his hands up in mock exasperation, commented, "I'm not even going to attempt that one."

■ ■ ■

Chapter Summary

Change is a way of life for companies that need to adapt to changing conditions in their competitive environments. These include global markets, abundant information, technological growth, acute scarcity of skilled employees, mergers, fluctuating prices and resource availabilities, as well as system complexities. Designing and implementing those adaptations within the company or for customers is often the job of the project manager.

Individuals for whom the project manager has responsibility may react in a variety of ways to changes in their situation. They react to novelty, complexity, and insolubility in different ways. Thus, the project manager must recognize the many reactions—negative, accepting, or inciting—by their characteristics. To drive change, the project manager must look at his or her own survival in terms of awareness of conditions that affect the organization and what the organizational need for change is. A positive attitude toward change can help ensure this survival. Project managers are responsible for ongoing change management, which includes being an example of a positive attitude for other employees and encouraging future orientation and creative adaptations. Urgent change may occur in the occasion of a major event—buyout, merger, and bankruptcy. In these cases an early and straightforward meeting with management can help the project manager assess the situation and convey important information to employees.

Chapter Questions

1. What are some examples you have seen in your own experiences of the changes outlined in the first section of this chapter?
2. Name three different effects of change on project managers.
3. Why is a positive reaction to complexity such an important trait in a project manager?
4. What problems can you see resulting from the constant driving force of "incitors"?
5. In your own field, give an example of the movement away from isolated functions or operations and towards interdependent systems.
6. What can you, as a project manager, do to foster a change-oriented environment?
7. How could you as a member of a project team work to facilitate change?
8. Name at least three conditions in the business or technical environment that could directly affect companies in your field. What effects would changes in those areas have?

Project Challenge: Applying What You Know

Read the following situations and make recommendations for the best methods to facilitate the needed change.

A. TechArt, the example in this chapter, was finally sold. The new "owner" was a large, multinational company. Because it was fairly profitable, TechArt was chosen to take over the graphics function for the parent company, which had contracted that function out to various vendors prior to the purchase. In addition to providing graphics design and printing to large accounts, the parent company has decided to create a division that develops and produces operating and instruction manuals for all the technical products it produces. TechArt will be expected to take on this function.

1. Suggest an organization for TechArt, which covers all of the services it will offer now, including the new division responsible for generating instruction manuals, as well as the original services—graphics design, large-scale commercial printing, and development of graphics design software. Make a chart that includes your recommendations for the names of the different divisions, as well as the reporting lines to TechArt management, the parent company, or a division within the company.
2. List reactions you might expect from employees after they are told that they have a new owner, and tell what strategy you would use to ensure a positive change.
3. Write a brief speech you would give to the employees explaining the change and how it will affect their positions.
4. Define at least three projects that will grow out of this change. Include the name of the project, anticipated time frame, and division in which it will occur.

B. You have been managing a project, the addition of a 15,000-square-foot freezer compartment in the warehouse of a wholesale foods distributor. You are responsible for managing the construction of the storage area itself, as well as coordinating the installation of the refrigeration system and setup of the monitoring/alarm system as well. Your contractor is nearing completion of the construction, and some of the refrigeration equipment has been delivered. The monitoring/alarm people are waiting for your call to schedule that installation. So far you are on schedule. However, you receive the following memo from an upper-level manager of the new parent company:

> "We want to change to a variable temperature system and some sort of division in the freezer space. I know this is a major change, but we've studied some others and think this is the best setup. I know you'll carry this off."

1. What could management have done to prevent your having to make this change after the project is already under way?
2. What, if anything, could you have done to prepare for this possibility?
3. How will you determine the effect this change will have on your completion date?
4. As project manager, how would you feel about what has happened?
5. What's the most constructive thing you can do in response to this change?

Interview with an Expert

***Chris Cole,** Human Resources Business Partner, AT&T.*

turnaround the term used to describe a change forced by management to correct problems with productivity or profitability in a unit or whole company

Turnarounds

The first element to keep in mind in a turnaround is that the **employees know there's a problem, and they tend to hear management's messages defensively,** as if we've said, "You're the problem." In addition, there is some confusion, "Why didn't I see this earlier?" So, no matter how positive the message is going in, the employees are going to hear blame. **Establishing trust, then, becomes a priority.** Responses around lack of trust include, "Why should I believe you have the right answer? I know and trust what I have today, good or bad. How do I know the change will be good for me?"

This view is interesting in the way it looks at change. Positive change is generally referred to as "transition" or "improvement," not necessarily as change. Alternatively, a view of a turnaround might be, "I know this change can't be good for me." When we talk about continuous improvement, we are talking about change too, but it is couched differently. The spirit of continuous improvement is "Let's do more of what we're doing that's right." It gives credit for people doing a good job.

Management's posture must be a careful one; and **it is a mistake to come in suggesting you have the right answer. Address change by identifying which parts need change, and which don't.** Ask, "What do we have that is good?" This allows building on a base of success and moving change out from that point.

Also, it is a necessity **to involve the entire team, at least at some level.** My favorite method for this is the **"town meeting."** Management makes a statement or two about the status of things, then the floor is opened for questions. This eliciting of input scares some managers because they're afraid all that will come out is anger. However, hearing the issue at the source of the anger is the first step toward solving the issue. You can actually ask for volunteers to investigate the issue and report back to the next meeting. If a request is made for some new concession from management, for example a 4-day workweek, then management has the right to respond, "There is still pressure on us to improve cost versus revenue and productivity. If you can show us how that can happen, we can consider it. Does anyone want to investigate this?" In this case they did and offered full commitment to the outcome. The town meeting and follow-ups like this demonstrate clearly that not all intelligence in the company lies with the managerial few.

In a turnaround situation, **one of the hurdles to get past is the fear held by the managers themselves.** They resist opening up the information coffers because of the power in, "I know something you don't know." They also worry that their jobs will be eliminated in the change. Actually, they are, but that is so the managers can move to something else that the organization needs them to do. Still, they resist leaving the old position.

The important next step is to **take action.** If the team makes a recommendation, begin action on it that day. Try the plan, check it, and then revise if necessary. Perfection isn't necessary, but learning to learn from mistakes is. You can build off any degree of success. As soon as you begin implementing action, you need a way to reward and celebrate success. If your group is committed to this, you will find you can be creative with ways to do it. In our case the budget was cut, as is typical in a turnaround, so we had to come up with a way to reward with no money. We allowed winning employees to have their cars washed by members of the management team. They held us to time and quality parameters and sent back any cars that didn't meet the standards. It was a great experience all around, and it didn't cost anything!

Finally, it became apparent to management and employees that **to improve productivity and quality, training was the next step.** Because information comes best from one of your own, we sent employee representatives to training and had them come back and train the others. On a shoestring budget we raised the skill level of all our employees and involved in the process the people who had asked for the training.

To summarize, in a turnaround you have to be clear on the important issues. Think about these questions:

- What do we need to achieve?
- How do we measure success?

The guidelines for making a turnaround a success are:

- Communication
- Recognition
- Process (time, cost, and quality)
- Training

CHAPTER 3

LEADERSHIP AND MOTIVATION

CHAPTER PREVIEW

THE PROJECT MANAGEMENT SEMINAR: SESSION 3

Jerry Benjamin slammed down the receiver of the pay phone outside the training area. His face was red and he flexed his jaw several times.

"If we just had some leadership, maybe something would turn out right for a change," he shouted, then swore under his breath.

Checking in to listen to his voice mail, he had learned that things weren't going well in his absence. "I don't have time for this ridiculous class. No one can make any decisions or seem to get anything done if I'm not there. What am I doing wasting my time here?" he muttered as he walked back to the training room. Hilda Jensen followed him in.

"Sounds like you have some of the same problems we've run up against," she said to Jerry. "When the cat's away, the mice become mice."

Jerry chuckled at the twist on the old cliché and relaxed a little. "The thing that gets me is that no one in my group shows any leadership, and really, a lot of the time I don't feel like the people I report to have a lot of skill in that area either."

"Yeah, they got rid of a lot of deadwood with the downsizing stuff," Hilda agreed, "but moving responsibility for big projects to people who have never run even a small job is just not the answer. They don't know what to do. My own designers and engineers won't even deal with purchasing on their materials issues or take any initiative at all with customer inputs. It's frustrating."

"Not everyone wants to be a manager." Yury Tomicovic joined in. "My job is quality control on three projects all running at the same time. I just want to do my job, not have to figure out how to get other people to do theirs."

Ralph and Tracey walked into the room. "Whoa, sounds like you guys are into this stuff already," Ralph said. "How about taking a seat and we'll start? "

"I've got just one question, can you teach people to be leaders?" Ragdeesh Patel challenged.

Tracey noticed the edge in his voice right away and realized that he might be speaking for the group's concerns. "We're going to deal with that today, but to give you an answer right off, I will tell you that every individual has a different need to run things. Training won't change that need. But when people understand what makes their co-workers tick and why they do what they do, it sort of demystifies the whole leadership thing."

"Demystifies?" mumbled Jerry. "This I gotta hear."

After the initial discussion the group came up with these topics to be covered:

- Leadership in projects
- What managers and leaders do
- How do you get people to do things?

- Motivating peers
- Inspiring commitment
- What do you do when no one will take responsibility?

Ralph and Tracey looked over the ideas from the group and generated an outline for the day's training:

- **Project managers as leaders**
- **Motivation methods—for self, for others**
- **Artful influence**
- **Effective delegation**
- **Accountability, Authority, and Autonomy**

The concerns that Jerry, Hilda, and Ragdeesh had are common ones for project managers who have had no prior management or supervision training. As technical professionals in their fields, most project managers have worked up to positions of responsibility because they were good at understanding cause-and-effect relationships within their projects. What they probably missed along the way, however, is a close look at the cause-and-effect relationships in the other factor of project management—the individual motivation and commitment of the people involved.

■ ■ ■

1.0 PROJECT MANAGERS AS LEADERS

A popular belief among employees in company after company is that a move into management is the kiss of death. Repeatedly, companies reward good engineers, line workers, systems developers, quality control specialists, and others like them with a "promotion" to management. With a crash-and-burn rate of just under half, it would appear that such a promotion is not always a favor to the honored employee.

Academic and business researchers have tried to figure out what happens to good people when they hit that management wall. Some say the problem is one of not understanding the different duties of managing projects other than just their own (Flammholtz & Randle, 1987). Some suggest that not everyone can "cut it" as a manager, while still others say that people just reach their level of incompetence. But keep in mind an important focus: no one takes a job of responsibility with the intent to fail. What happens along the way that causes new managers to fail is a set of things, not just a lack in any one area.

Project managers come into that position as successful professionals. They know how to manage time, materials, and even unexpected foul-ups. They are excellent "doers," but they often have not learned to lead people. Leading requires some skills that aren't necessary in carrying out those prior jobs. Some of the things project managers do as leaders that they probably didn't do before as technical or skilled professionals are:

- Coordinate different functional groups and diverse personalities.
- Evoke commitment from people who don't report to the manager.
- Gain a sense of accomplishment from others' achievements rather than their own.
- Take initiative in looking ahead of deadlines toward larger company goals.
- Become accountable for others' performance or lack of performance.
- Develop the skills of employees.

(See Figure 3–1 for comparison of skills of manager and technical specialists.)

Technical Specialist	Project Managers
Technical expertise	Understand relationships among tasks
Hands-on problem solving	Lead and delegate to others
"Doer"	Develop goals
Creativity	Develop budgets
Meet goals	Gather and communicate information
Meet budgets	Relate to customer and team
Follow guidelines	Accountable for work of others
Work with/for others	Develop skills of others
Work with end product	
Accountable for own work	
Develop own skills	

Figure 3–1
Differences in activities and skills needed—technical specialists and managers.

Simply put, the project manager must lead others to the successful completion of the goals of the project. Perhaps for the first time, that person is responsible for a project that is larger than he or she can do alone, regardless of time or dedication put in. Successful project managers have learned to adhere to a variation of an old saying: lead when necessary, follow when someone else knows better, and get out of the way of good people who know their jobs. What derails so many project managers (who were probably excellent technical professionals) is the inability to transfer satisfaction derived from their own work to satisfaction derived from the work of others. Thus, when the pressure is on, the project manager may try to jump in and "save the ship" by doing many of the tasks by himself, letting the management of the project slide in the process.

As project manager, you experience an undeniable feeling of helplessness when a part of a project is slipping, and you have no direct control over the person who is causing the problem. You can hold a contractor accountable because of the nature of the contractual relationship—money for specified work. "Borrowed" employees, who make up most of your team, are accountable to other projects besides your own, and to a functional area "boss" who determines the employee's professional fate.

People will often ignore the requests of someone they do not feel any obligation to on an official level. They will, however, respond favorably to good leadership, and they will give first priority to well-run projects. The project manager must pull a final deliverable out of diverse, often transient and, generally, shared resources—and accomplish this frequently without direct authority over team members' time and effort. People recognize good leadership and will follow it; conversely, they also recognize poor management and will avoid it whenever given a choice.

To return to Ragdeesh's question earlier, "Can people be taught to lead?" The answer is, "Yes." Of course we all know examples of people who were born leaders. An 11-year-old boy convinced neighborhood children to help him move firewood—a task he was assigned—and people like Ted Turner could probably be dropped into the Amazon rain forest and create a successful business. But most people can be *taught* to lead. You, the student of project management, can learn to do what leaders do and can become much more effective in the process. In the sections following you will learn some characteristics successful leaders share—a lot of what works and what doesn't, what tricks you can use, and how you can become a leader by first "pretending" to be one.

You may not have any desire to be a leader, or may not have ever thought of yourself as a leader, but successful completion of any project requires effective leadership. The first step in the process is to look at your own motivation level and how to manage that, then to concentrate on how to motivate others. Remember, a leader is not someone who tells people what to do; a leader instills commitment in others to work toward the goals of the company. Thus, the project manager as an individual must be highly motivated toward that end.

2.0 Motivation Methods for Self

It would be great to say that as a project manager you could count on your own manager to provide regular motivation for you as you pursue the deadlines for your projects. Wrong. Your manager (or the person to whom your project is accountable) if you're lucky enough to have only one, now probably has 20–25 people reporting to him or her instead of the 8–10 of several years ago. So don't assume that your manager will pop into your office on a regular basis to give you a pep talk when things are going badly. In fact you may have been made a manager of a project against your will. This is the, "Well, no one else can do it" situation. Figuring out what to do as a leader is tough, especially if you have had no training in the role and if you have just been asked to manage people you worked with as equals or peers in the past.

Leaders often emerge out of situations in which no one else is able or willing to take the responsibility. The military, for example, puts untried young recruits into situations in which they are forced to lead, maybe for the first time in their lives. To earn one of their badges, Eagle Scouts must demonstrate leadership on projects that often involve service or volunteer work. Scouts must take responsibility for their project's successful outcome in order to receive their badge. Women leaders often come from small women's colleges where there were no men to fill leadership positions, so those responsibilities fell to them.

In short, as a project manager, you may for the first time have an opportunity to discover the leader in you that you never expected was there. Whether you were motivated to lead in the past or not is irrelevant. This is your chance to realize potential that you have never tapped before. A project completed on time and in budget is quite an accomplishment, and there is a heady feeling of success that goes along with the knowledge that you were a big part of making that happen.

You are not going to wake up every day ready to seize the project and inspire the troops, however. Some days the dragon wins, and you, the stalwart knight, will feel more like retiring to your home to lick your wounds than leading or inspiring anyone. You may, temporarily, lose focus and enthusiasm. This is to be expected in the ups and downs of project management. Two things you must keep in mind in those difficult times:

1. The leader has intensity of vision and a high expectation of success.
2. When your own motivation wanes, you can borrow some from someone else.

2.1 Vision

Leaders understand the importance of each task related to the outcome of the project. Sometimes, the leader is the only one in a highly complex and long-term project who truly does know all the tasks and their contribution to the whole. The project manager, as leader, keeps the vision of the completed project foremost, both in his or her own mind and in the minds of others who are charged with making the project happen.

In addition, leaders are people who know that success does indeed breed success. Expecting positive outcomes colors your approach to everything you do. If you expect most things to turn out well, you are enthusiastic, energetic, and committed. Negative expectation makes you hesitant, lethargic, and indecisive. Sure, not everything will work exactly as you would like. It's always possible that the diodes your engineers need will not be available in the numbers you need them, or the materials that were supposed to be delivered last week are still not in and what has arrived is damaged. But **negativity** affects our ability to think clearly and solve complex problems. Good decisions require energy, and your employees will draw energy from you; they will follow your example. By modeling motivated behavior, you will create an environment of positive approaches to problems and of positive expectations in the face of roadblocks. When you do have those "I just can't do this anymore" days, it is often helpful to borrow motivation.

negativity affects our ability to think clearly and solve complex problems.

2.2 Borrowed Motivation

You can borrow motivation from at least two sources:

1. Motivational tapes
2. Professional support networks

Motivational tapes are an invaluable source of energy in the face of tough situations. Many professionals use them daily in their car instead of listening to the radio. Tapes work by suggesting an alternative, upbeat way of looking at the world, and when things are going wrong, right and left, brilliant alternatives are sometimes hard to come by. Regularly exposing your brain to the positive messages in motivational tapes balances the negative ones that occur in all our lives. This also provides a balance the project manager desperately needs sometimes. Relaxation and creative visualization tapes, played before bedtime, help you disconnect from the demands of the day and sleep better on those tough nights. A lack of a good night's sleep makes a positive outlook difficult to achieve.

Another way to borrow motivation is to create a professional support network. Seek out other people who have jobs similar to yours. It is helpful to have one confidante in your own company, because not only will that person readily understand what you are dealing with, but he or she will also be nearby during trying times. You may also gain valuable insights from people on the outside, because there are many commonalties to project management across industries.

Finally, it is nice just to have people who speak the same language you do who share "war stories" about projects headed for disaster that ultimately turned out okay. Keep in mind that you shouldn't call these people only when the walls are crashing in; you have to be willing to support them in their time of need as well. Call sometimes just to exchange ideas; don't call only to whine or moan.

3.0 Motivation Methods for Others

"If I just had a handful of motivated employees, I could get something done around here." Managers often use this complaint when they are concerned about the lack of output in their areas. Funny, though, many of those same employees that the manager complains about were highly motivated when they took the job. Wonder what happened along the way?

People can be productive only if they are working under conditions that foster productivity. In the eyes of the manager, productivity is often the measure of motivation. If an employee is performing well, then he or she is perceived to be motivated; if not, then the employee is assumed to be unmotivated. In most cases, however these "unmotivated" performers believe that they are trying hard to do well, but that external circumstances keep them from performing at the highest level. But because managers see poor performers as incompetent, it is no wonder employees become unmotivated after a time; they feel like they are in a no-win situation—powerless to do their job well and criticized unfairly by managers (Yukl, 1998).

Figure 3–2 is an especially helpful model to guide you when you are dealing with what seems to be an unmotivated employee. (Note: this is a variation of the Mager and Pipe Human Performance Model, 1970)

Figure 3–2
Why employees may be unmotivated.

What leads to the inability to produce is a complex set of factors. The problem could be that the employee is asked to do something he or she has never been trained to do. It could be that the employee doesn't have the ability to do the job, or that factors outside the workplace are spilling over into the job in a negative way.

■ ■ ■

At this point Jaime Martinez interrupted, "I know what you're talking about. I had to do a budget for my department last quarter and present it to the brass when they came down from the home office. I'd never done a budget or ever had a class in how to do one. The meeting was horrible! Two of the other managers were in MBA classes at night and one had a professional coach. Their presentations were great, and the manager fell all over himself telling them so. When it was my turn, I did the best I could, but he ripped me to shreds, right there in front of everyone. I felt like dirt. He never even asked if I knew how to do a budget." Jaime's face was downcast as he told his story. Everyone in the group, having been there, empathized.

Tracey responded, "That's exactly what we're talking about here. Managers are in some ways responsible for the motivation level of their employees. To lead people into commitment and high levels of performance, we have to understand what motivates our people and what they need to get their jobs done right."

"Just a minute," Jerry said, "are you saying WE have to go around and hand-hold every person in our projects? You gotta be kidding!" he barked, incredulous. "I can't be fussing over every supervisor or worker that has an attitude problem. Why can't they just do their jobs? Isn't that what they're paid for?"

"Yes, that's true," Ralph said calmly. "But think about it Jerry. You, as project manager, are the only one who understands completely how all the pieces are supposed to come together. If everyone involved doesn't see, and see clearly, what his or her part is and why that part is important to the ultimate success of the project, there isn't going to be a very high level of motivation. Your people may be working very hard, but on the wrong things. Then, when you beat up on them for screwing up, they get mad because you've attacked them for no reason. So, they begin to slack off, and you get madder, and the problem gets worse."

He studied Jerry for his reaction before he finished. "You have to communicate what is needed, why it is important, where each group fits into the total picture. And you have to make sure all have what they need to do their jobs. You're the only one with the knowledge and authority to do all that."

"Just hang in there Jerry," Tracey said, "we're going to give you some ways, right now, to help you do just what we've suggested."

■ ■ ■

Ways to motivate project team members

- Judiciously discern project team members' task preferences and skills.
- Clearly communicate the picture of the goal to be accomplished.
- Jointly define the team member's role in the success of the project.
- Regularly recognize contributions to the final outcome.
- Openly invite solutions.

3.1 Determine Task Preferences

Project managers have to do more than merely assign tasks related to project goals. They have to assess the competencies of all those on the project management team. By knowing what your people are good at and not-so-good at, you can free up talent and support weakness. A quick formula for failure as a leader is to put the right person in the wrong job. Don't take a "big picture," creative, problem solver and assign him to reporting minutiae. By the same token you shouldn't look to the highly-regimented, detail-oriented operations person and expect her to orchestrate the relationships among the cross-functional teams.

A note of caution is necessary here. Humans are infinitely adaptable; that is, they can learn or manage to do most anything, eventually. But, that doesn't mean they would necessarily choose to spend most of their time doing all the things they are able to do. And when they don't particularly like the activities they are assigned day after day, they may do them, but lack commitment and enthusiasm. Find out what tasks or roles your team members gravitate to naturally. Let your people help you define their roles in your projects.

In her book, *The Conative Connection* (1990), Kathy Kolbe contends that people will spend more time doing things they like to do. So, if you as the manager, can discover what your employees like, and place them in jobs where those activities are required, you are more likely to have motivated employees. In this way, you may discover that instead of an engineer for a job, you need someone to do engineering drawings, or you may need a technical writer, to fill in a gap in performance. Being able to do this quickly is critical because often team members are assigned or "lent" to you from another department. Without the luxury of choosing all your team members, finding how best to utilize each is the project manager's challenge.

Kolbe classifies people based on the types of activities they like to do, as shown in Figure 3–3. Whereas everyone may have a little bit of each type of person in them, most people will fit squarely in one single category.

Figure 3–3
Task preference categories.

Fact Finder	Follow-Through	Quick Starter	Implementor
Looks up information	Operationalizes	Takes risks	Likes hands-on
Substantiates strategies	Plans activities to carry out strategy	Thrives on pressure	Builds
Accumulates data	Defines and oversees process	Gets things "off the ground"	Troubleshoots

Discover the real talents and desires of your people, then turn them loose and let them do what they love. You will be amazed how the apparent "motivation" level of these properly placed and directed people will increase. Lead by nudges that channel talents and preferences into productivity.

3.2 Communicate Goals

Your project team will not be motivated when they do not know what to be motivated towards. Just as you can't tell a child to "be good" when you haven't specified the exact behavior you want him to exhibit, you also can't tell an employee to "get with the program" when the actions these words translate into aren't clear.

Communicate goals by doing the following:

- Paint a picture of successful completion of the project and all this entails.
- Spend as much time as you need filling in the details.
- Make sure all those contributing to the project understand exactly what to do, and exactly what "doing it right" looks like.

Although all of this is time-consuming in the beginning, it will prevent a myriad of foul-ups later.

3.3 Define Role in Success

In addition to clarifying successful completion, you will have to work with the employee to mutually develop a set of goals or action plans that will define that employee's contribution. If you set the goals, the employee may resist openly, because adults hate to be told what to do, especially if they think they are already competent. The problem can be, though, that they are extremely competent and are working hard, but not prioritizing properly. Having joint goal-planning sessions accomplishes two things:

1. It lets you know the employee understands what needs to be done.
2. It affirms the employee by making him or her feel a part of decisions being made about the project.

3.4 Recognize Contributions

If you don't recognize, or at least notice, the hard work and the contributions being made by your team members, they will begin to feel unappreciated. Although feeling unappreciated may not seem like a big deal, think about this: Employees are more likely to leave your organization because they feel unappreciated than because of too little money or other adverse working conditions. Also, keep in mind that those on your team who don't report directly to you may feel like they are doing you a favor. It never hurts to reward people in some way, even if it is just recognition.

Take, for example, the case of Ron, a technical support person for the sales and marketing group of a telecommunications company. Because of his outstanding work, his manager, wanting to give him recognition, nominated him for the President's award to be presented at the annual banquet. When it was time for Ron to receive his award (in front of 300 of his peers), the district manager stepped to the microphone, chuckled a bit and said, "This award is for Ron, uh, I can't pronounce his last name. We don't know exactly what he does, but we believe he's good at it." The man was noticeably embarrassed and became, understandably, no longer motivated at his job. He actually engineered a transfer out of that group within a few months after that, and his manager never understood why. Members of your project team are not just a set of resource competencies; they are humans who need to be affirmed from time to time. This doesn't mean you have to coddle or fuss over them; it means treating people with the respect they deserve.

Ways to Affirm and Reward

Say, "Thank you."
Give company sports event tickets.
Take employees to lunch.
Shake employee's hand.
Say, "Congratulations."
Broadcast appreciation via e-mail or voice mail.
Recognize outstanding employees at employee meeting.
Implement cash awards program.
Give employee afternoon off.
Give first choice for vacation dates.
Give "goodies" such as t-shirts, cups, and so on.
Frame certificates of appreciation.
Invite employee input to plans.
Ask employee's opinion.

Assign an interesting project.
Send employee to training.
Send employee to conference.

3.5 Invite Solutions

solution should be presented along with the problem

Another observation you will have to make as a project manager is to note progress in ways other than studying your employees' weekly reporting into the Gantt chart. Invite them to alert you to difficulties they see coming *before* they hit. Be certain they know that when they do see a problem, they should match it with a proposed **solution.** Motivated people think in terms of solutions and requirements for success, not explanations and reasons for failure. Train your people that when they discover any problem that impacts progress, they should address it and work to solve it. Encouraging them to report progress honestly and to address impediments proactively will help everyone to be more motivated. Additionally, when people exhibit a positive attitude, managers should pay attention and encourage this attitude. Conversely, whiners and complainers should not receive inordinate amounts of your time or attention. Naturally, you as leader and project manger will have to discipline yourself to communicate this way as well, avoiding negativity and excessive criticism.

■ ■ ■

"I think you want us to look at things with rose-colored glasses," Yury remarked. "That is foolish."

"Yeah, Yury, I agree with you," Jerry put in. "Don't make it pretty; tell it to me like it is."

"Okay, pretty we don't need," Ralph conceded. "But, wouldn't you rather have an employee expect to come to you with a plan to fix whatever's wrong instead of sounding an alarm? I mean, you'd have to send him back to look into it, look into it yourself, then figure out what to do. Motivated employees become even more so when encouraged to take charge in their own areas."

■ ■ ■

But if you are looking for commitment in your employees, you should make sure you are clear on not only the definition of commitment, but but also on the behaviors you expect. Some managers who are preoccupied with control want obedient followers who check every operation and every decision with the manager. They want yes-people. In this situation, employees will likely show commitment only to the manager.

Commitment to the goal of the project means that team members understand what their contribution is and that they direct energy towards that goal—without having to be told. Actually, highly committed employees require little from project managers. Any time a project manager can reward someone for working ahead or for being prepared for a meeting or for any behavior that reflects a positive, committed attitude, then the manager is a step closer to having that "group of motivated people" that managers dream about.

4.0 Artful Influence

Ideally, all those connected with a project are committed, motivated and proactive in their work activities. However, leaders understand that **influencing** people is a necessary part of getting the job done. The power a manager is granted by virtue of the position is just not enough to create a real dedication to projects by all involved. Everyone has known managers, or for that matter other authority figures, that just did not command anyone's respect, and, consequently, no one seemed really inclined to do what the manager asked, let alone demonstrate any real dedication. No, the **power** a leader has is only what others are willing to defer to that leader. That is such an important concept that it bears repeating: a leader has only as much power as others are willing to give, or defer, to that person.

influence to have an effect on the condition or development of a project

power possession of control, authority

4.1 Deferred Power

deferred power power you allow others to have from you or which you grant to others

You might defer power to your mechanic regarding the things you do to maintain your vehicle. You respect his knowledge and understand that his requests or suggestions are based on expertise and experience. For that reason, if he says to change the oil at 3,000-mile intervals, you will. On the other hand, if he makes suggestions about your finances, you probably won't give much heed to what he says and will not likely act on the information.

Generally, if people recognize someone as deserving of their cooperation and commitment, they will give it to him or her. But there are several criteria on which people make decisions about allowing others to have power over their time and energy. One is certainly, "Does this person in this position have the right to ask this of me?" This question can extend from requests such as, "Would you get me some coffee?" or "Can you work the next two weekends? or . . . stay late?" If your team members agree that the requests are legitimately part of the job, then they will do what you've asked. They may not be happy about it, or particularly committed to the tasks, but they will likely do it. Many times all you will need is cooperation, not necessarily enthusiasm.

One problem comes in, however, with the technically expert employee. In today's project management environment, as in many other situations in business, there will be those on your team who are going to be more technically adept and expert than you are. So, the old notion of the most proficient at the task being the leader is not altogether fitting anymore. Often employees feel that managers, project managers included, are out of touch with the nitty-gritty of getting the individual parts of the job done. This is true to some extent. But the expertise of managing diverse people is the sum of accumulated experiences that the hard-core "techy" does not generally have. Gaining the dedication of employees who are more skilled in their areas than you is a complex influence challenge and cannot be accomplished by just trying to know more or by invoking threats.

Still, inexperienced managers do commonly threaten employees to get them to comply with their wishes. College students, when presented with a scenario involving a resistant employee, will invariably vote to fire that person. It's not that easy. Highly specialized technical expertise is getting harder and harder to find. Larger companies actually recruit from all over the world now to fill positions in **hard-to-staff jobs.** In short, firing or replacing a team member who has a specific, crucial skill set may very well not be an option.

hard-to-staff jobs jobs that are difficult to fill because of a number of reasons, such as there being too few people with a particular specialty in the workforce

In addition, threats—of firing or of any kind, for that matter—could make the threatened employee, even a fairly loyal one, seriously entertain an unsolicited offer to go elsewhere. Highly skilled employees often are solicited by headhunters—people hired by companies to locate good employee prospects for them. Project managers who cannot hold onto good people are ultimately deemed a liability to the company and are eventually invited to move on themselves.

So, today's employee will probably not respond well to strong-arm techniques. A new approach to influence is emerging that involves allowing employees to participate in decisions that affect them and inviting their input regarding project planning. Inclusion in decision making sends a positive message to the employee.

■ ■ ■

"You mean manipulate them by telling them what they want to hear and saying 'good boy'?" Jerry scoffed. "My Labrador retriever responds real well to that. He'll do anything for a toss of a ball or a pat on the head," Jerry challenged snidely.

Tom hurried to respond, his neck reddening. "No, Jerry. What's wrong with making people feel good about what they do?"

"Well, using psychology stuff to make people jump through hoops isn't honest," Jerry argued.

manipulation disrespectful, overbearing influence

"Jerry," Ralph countered, "I think it's just a definition thing. ***Manipulation*** *—or pushing people around just to prove you can—is wrong. It's disrespectful and pointless. Influence has more to do with guiding employees to be successful at their jobs and to support the goals of the company—without that the company wouldn't go very far, and they wouldn't need managers like you." Directing his attention back to the group, he asked, " How do you get your projects in on time? Each of you?"*

Jaime volunteered. "My team is proud of our success rate so far. We have never come in over time or budget. Pride in that makes us all work hard."

"So, Jerry, how is it you handle your project teams?"

Jerry didn't say anything for a few seconds, but Ralph seemed content to wait him out. Finally, he responded. "It's simple. We get a new project. We meet. Everyone knows what to do and does it. That's all."

"Why do you think that is?"

"It's their job. That's all. And I'll tell you. I don't worry about their 'needs'. "Jerry crossed his arms in front of him.

"Ever had any quit, Jerry?" Ralph asked softly.

"Yeah, so?"

"How many?"

"Maybe one or two each project," he said. "But that's to be expected. Happens everywhere."

Hilda spoke up. "My design team has been stable for 6 years. Rick has an ailing aunt who lives with him, so we let him work at night when he needs to. He doesn't punch a clock, but I bet he puts in more hours than a lot of others. Anya's worked with handicapped people for years, gets involved with them personally. Franz patented most of the basic controller algorithms used in myoelectrics. He's known around the world for what he has done with us. Misha likes to holiday in France, so we let him bank days for vacation by working double shifts. It works because everyone gets what they need, and so do we. High loyalty, high productivity, high commitment." As she ended, she looked right at Jerry, who looked straight ahead and said nothing else.

■ ■ ■

4.2 Met Needs

Artful influence, then, is the ability to create in members of a project team a desire to meet the goals in a timely and cost-effective manner. Remember, also, that some members of the team do not report directly to you all of the time, yet you need what they do in order to make the project turn out right.

artful influence the ability to create in members of a project team a desire to meet the goals in a timely and cost-effective manner

Today's professionals just don't respond to the old "donkey management": the carrot in front or the boot behind. When asked why they stayed at their obviously demanding jobs, when there were so many enticements to move on, many highly expert members of a project team had the following responses:

"I like the ownership of my projects. I feel real pride in handing off what I've done to the next group in the chain."

"For me it's the freedom. As long as I'm producing, no one really cares when I work or how I get things done. Few other places offer that; they're on a rigid clock schedule."

"Yeah, I could go other places, but where could I find such interesting projects to work on? They move me around to different groups. It's never the same old thing."

Hmmm. Sense of accomplishment, freedom, variety? This sounds like the project manager really has nothing to do with the employees' commitment. Absolutely not true. Instead, the clever manager helps to connect the employees with what they need to feel good about their work. As you have probably figured out by now, your people don't have to work for you. Your influence, by showing them what is valuable and internally rewarding about their work, helps to connect them to the job satisfaction they need to be committed. (See Figure 3–4.)

Figure 3–4
Why people stay.

You can't offer them loyalty. Your company could be bought; you could be transferred; management could downsize them out of a job. But your influence in the form of:

- clear definitions of what the path to success looks like,
- a working relationship built on mutual respect, and
- a willingness to accept employees' input into the decisions that affect them,

will encourage them to defer power to you and to follow your lead. This, as you might guess, requires some creative thought on your part and some time investigating your employees' needs.

4.3 Internal Motivation

intrinsic motivation employees derive satifaction from their work

Committed employees are **intrinsically motivated**—they feel that they get something out of their work. It may be pride in their expertise; it may be that they do something that helps people or that brings them recognition. A person who is internally motivated will not require you to constantly provide external incentives or rewards.

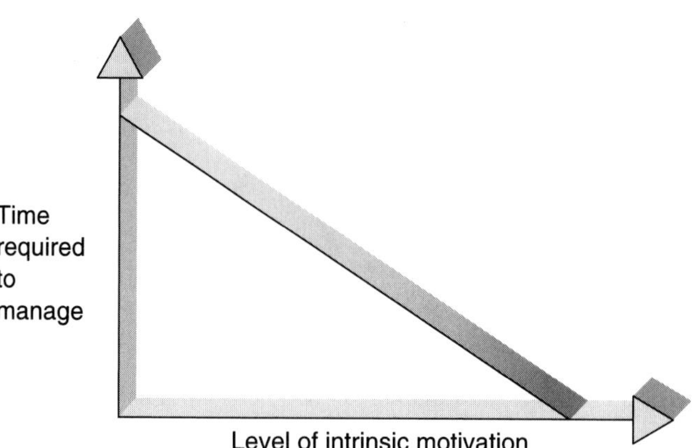

Figure 3–5
Employees with low intrinsic motivation require more time to manage.

In Figure 3–5, intrinsic motivation is measured, not happiness. A happy team member is not necessarily a productive one; she may be happy because she is doing nothing. An unhappy person, who derives little satisfaction from work on your project, though, is often unproductive.

In fact, highly committed employees require mostly an occasional pat on the back or a timely check-in to catch any problems before they become unmanageable. They defer to your influence and direct energy into the job because the relationship works for them, as well as for your project. Thus, it's to your advantage to show each of them how to derive satisfaction from the job you need them to do.

5.0 Effective Delegation

Now that you have positive, motivated, proactive, and committed employees and team members all around you, what do you do? Unfortunately, like too many project managers, you will occasionally become too involved in what they are doing. Inability to delegate is a major deterrent to success and is most common in project managers who have expertise in several areas that are critical to project completion. These managers need to "get their hands into" crucial activities because they worry that no one can do these activities as well as they can.

Occasionally dipping into others' jobs will do little harm; however, when the project manager is so involved in doing everyone else's tasks and not doing his or her own, then there is a problem. Mature and effective project managers have learned to balance delegation with the need to hold on. There are two reasons why holding on is bad:

1. It shows disrespect to the team member or contractor and a lack of confidence in that person's ability to perform the assigned job.
2. A gap eventually shows up in the overall coordination effort of the project. Pieces will eventually begin to slip through the holes left by the project manager's lack of attention.

Inability to delegate effectively is not necessarily an issue of a project manager's confidence in his or her employees; rather, it points to a difficulty in the project manager's ability to let go of old tasks in which he or she had been successful in the past. Managing an entire project creates a gulf between the manager and the ability to see a direct outcome of his or her work. For this reason some are tempted to get back into the old, hands-on activities that were so fulfilling. **Delegation** does in some ways remove the project manager from directly observable outcomes. It throws him or her into a sort of no-man's-land where everything is in limbo until a milestone is reached or the project is completed—sometimes 2 months later, sometimes 2 years later.

delegation handing parts of a project off to a competent team member

Effective delegation does not mean that you should hand over everything to anyone who happens to be willing. As already discussed in the section on motivating others, you have an idea of who has what skills, and this should make you confident of what others can do. You can't do everything yourself, so, you must hand some things off.

■ ■ ■

"I must speak here," Ragdeesh broke in. "I am responsible for the project. If I give it away to my workers, they will think I am not the manager."

"Do you think you will lose power or respect?" Tracey asked. As Ragdeesh thought about it, she continued. "Each of you has a fulltime job just keeping track of the projects you are responsible for. If you don't hand off certain duties to your people, who rightfully should have them, you are hoarding something that is detrimental to you. If you get sidetracked on some adminis-trivia, you run the risk of missing something important as the project reports come in. You are paid to be captain of the ship, not to cook or to row."

Jerry looked over towards Ragdeesh and saluted. Ragdeesh gave no response.

■ ■ ■

The best way to wean yourself from the habit of doing everything yourself is to make delegation something of value to you, instead of viewing it as a loss. Each responsibility you can hand off, appropriately and sensibly, of course, *enhances* your performance as a project manager; it does not detract from it. Don't worry, no matter how much you hand off, there will still be plenty for you to do. There are a few rules to effective delegation, though:

- Don't overload the best employees by always delegating to them.
- Prepare people for the task you are handing off to them.
- Be sure that the employee you hand off to has the competence, skill, and ability to complete the task. If not, find a way to get this person trained.
- Remind yourself that too much to do makes you do everything badly.

- Check to see if the delegation is working; if not, shift the task to someone else who is more qualified or willing.
- Remember that your employees work very hard. Respect and show gratitude for their acceptance of the tasks you delegate to them.

Delegating well is an act of confidence and trust. Many never learn to delegate well because they don't believe in the value of it. You allow your team members to grow professionally by giving them some of your management-level tasks. In addition, you free up some of your time, so you can pay attention to the needs of your people and of the project itself.

6.0 ACCOUNTABILITY, AUTHORITY, AND AUTONOMY

■ ■ ■

"Have we answered all your concerns yet?" Ralph George asked the group.

Jerry responded, "I still don't see how I can get my people to take responsibility for projects when I'm away. Things are going down the tubes while I'm here this week, and it's the same way every time I'm not right on top of 'em."

"I agree with Jerry," Hilda chimed in. "My workers look to me for guidance, and when I'm not there, no one can seem to make a decision."

The others turned to Ralph, curious to see his response to this latest issue. "Thanks for giving me the intro for the final topic. We can have an effect on our employees' motivation and commitment, but getting them to buy in to taking a leadership role when we aren't there to approve every step is a very real challenge." he answered.

■ ■ ■

This issue can be addressed by discussing three terms: accountability, authority, and autonomy. All have to be present for projects to go smoothly, and all are leadership issues.

6.1 Accountability

People are hesitant to take on responsibility when the price could be too high. Managers have been heard to laughingly say, "The price of a mistake here? Oh, we cut them off at the knees." Anthropologists tell us that in many cultures people laugh and make jokes about things that make them uncomfortable. If that's the case, then these managers understand how untenable such an environment is for employees, so much so that they laugh about it. Unfortunately, when employees are held accountable for all their actions in unreasonable ways, then the desire to innovate, take risks, or champion an "iffy" decision goes away quickly. When the cost of failure is death, then no one fails—or at least no one appears to fail.

accountability responsibility for a project

Thus, employees who make decisions in the manager's absence may find themselves in a potentially very risky situation, one to which few are willing to subject themselves. **Accountability** is the issue. Managers want their people to be accountable for the deliverables within their departments. Employees will be more willing to do so if the project manager creates an environment where mistakes can be openly admitted and addressed in a constructive, problem-solving way. No one takes risks or admits to problems without this kind of atmosphere. Forward movement and candid, honest status reports will not occur either.

Allowing, or even encouraging, team members to take on certain tasks that may be perceived as marginally threatening, and then walking them through the decisions related to those tasks, will build their confidence in their ability to handle tough situations. When employees are clear on policies and guidelines for decision making, such as, "How much is too much?" and "When does the problem need to be escalated up the management ladder?" they are more comfortable with accepting responsibility. The choices aren't so nebulous, and they can see themselves making the right ones.

6.2 Authority

authority taking the lead and moving ahead with projects

But you can't expect employees, even good ones with high skill levels and confidence, to willingly be accountable in areas where they have no authority. For example, picture a secretary trying to plan a company-wide meeting at an off-site location. Her manager tells her that this is *her* project, and to show some initiative and handle it. However, when it is time to put down deposits to reserve meeting places and order the t-shirts, she has no authority to sign checks. With her manager out of town a lot, she is unable to take care of the reservations and ends up not having the arrangements made when the manager returns. The manager thinks she is incompetent and holds her "accountable" for things not being ready. Actually, the problem is a lack of authority to comply with the manager's instructions.

Another reason employees don't act with authority is that they don't know how. Not everyone is comfortable with taking the lead and moving ahead with projects on their own. A good manager takes the time to initiate team members gradually into authority behaviors. By giving a subordinate a small task that requires some leadership, then conferring with, and guiding, him or her through the task, project leaders can raise the confidence level of the subordinate. When this happens, that subordinate is more likely to show initiative in other tasks. And you as project manager are more comfortable telling employees that they can sign off on project reports or purchase orders.

6.3 Autonomy

autonomy the desire, ability, and authority to make decisions and act in the interests of the project without direct supervision

This nurturing of employee growth leads ultimately to a knowledgeable, committed, and autonomous employee. We can define autonomy in this sense as the desire, ability, and authority to make decisions and act in the interests of the project without direct supervision. Doesn't that sound like the kind of team you would like to be on? Chapter 5, Teams, goes into more detail on the need for teams that can make their own decisions and act on them. But here it can be concluded that every autonomous employee who is committed to the goals of the project makes your job easier.

■ ■ ■

"Jerry," said Tracey, "do you think you've heard enough to have an idea of what to do with your engineers when you need to be away?"

"Yeah, I have to understand their needs, evaluate their skills, train them if needed, inspire them, delegate, support, affirm, and give them authority so they can be autonomous," he responded sarcastically.

"Yes, it's an involved process, I know," Tracey agreed. "But remember that having motivated employees is not a matter of chance or hiring; it is a process, an investment. You get what you put in."

■ ■ ■

Here are some brief guidelines to serve as a quick reminder for leading your project. You must provide:

- Direction
- Guidance
- Support
- Encouragement

Direction: Keep the project team focused. There is a real tendency in some employees to be sidetracked by attractive but tangential issues. These absorb the time, money, and energy of your employees. Recognize these for what they are and steer your people away from them.

Guidance: Coach your people along. Help individuals address their weaknesses and recognize their strengths. Have frequent one-on-one sessions with individual members of your project teams.

Support: Back your employees. Use your resources to help them along and smooth their way. Encourage creative thinking. Your people will respond much better if they are certain that your clout is supporting them and not a threat to them.

Encouragement: Some call this cheerleading. There is nothing wrong with a good, effective cheer. Show them the light at the end of the tunnel (make sure they know it's not a train) especially if things are not going well. The proper words of encouragement can go a long way towards developing a positive attitude and the commitment that goes with that.

Chapter Summary

The tasks of projects must be managed. People, however, should not only be led, but also taught to lead in their own areas. Keeping self-motivated is a challenge for all employees, but for project managers especially. Being once-removed from the individual tasks denies them the sense of accomplishment that they had as hands-on professionals, before being moved to management. Motivating others often consists of helping team members discover personal satisfaction in the job well done—however the employee perceives that satisfaction. Making employees accountable for all their actions stifles creativity and innovation by setting the price of error too high. Team members and employees should be held accountable for their areas of responsibility as long as they have the authority to make decisions and get things done. Autonomous employees require less guidance and result from effective delegation.

Chapter Questions

1. Why does the project manager have to think of himself/herself as a leader?
2. Give two methods a leader can use to motivate himself or herself.
3. What does the term "affirmation" mean as it is used in this chapter?
4. If delegating or deferring power to others is a good thing, why do you think so many managers resist doing it?

5. Discuss the difference in possible employee reactions between excessive displays of power and the more subtle use of influence.
6. The ability to read people and adapt your behavior to fit what will work most effectively with them is a good skill or talent for a leader to have. Why is this? Why is this ability especially important for a project manager?
7. Discuss the ethical implications of making people accountable for tasks over which you give them no authority.
8. The term, "intrapreneur" has been used in business to describe autonomous employees who conduct their activities as if they actually were running their own business within the company.
   a. Suggest possible positive and negative effects of this approach on the welfare of the company.
   b. Suggest ways to create this kind of attitude in employees.

Project Challenge: Applying What You Know

A. Jeron has been assigned a project group. It is his first leadership position. Here is his situation.

■ ■ ■

My three senior people are system design engineers; they make the intricate electronics of modems work smoothly. They are always pushed for more and more refinement because someone always wants better, smaller, faster. The major computer companies are our largest clients.

Others on the team are technicians, a plastics molding specialist for the housing, and various chip and fabricating groups. I think that Fred, the one who has been with us the longest, should lead on most of the projects because he has some history with what we do. But time after time, when I've tried to pull him into that role, he either begs off or just doesn't do anything to drive the process.

Beth, our new plastics molding expert, is just out of college and tries to tell everyone what to do. She has a lot of energy and interest, but she doesn't have the electronics background to run the projects. The technicians will actually sit around until they are told to do something. Honestly, it makes me crazy, and no one will take responsibility for the final product. I have to tell them when to order materials, how to schedule the projects, what problems to bring to me, and what to solve themselves.

■ ■ ■

Suggest a plan for Jeron to develop a high level of motivation and commitment in this group and to encourage autonomy in the actions of the individual team members toward the goal of a smooth-running project. Recommend possible motivators for the team members and for Jeron. The project is expected to take 8 months. Define the goals and the vision of a successful project. As specifically as possible suggest tasks Jeron should delegate and to whom. Also, investigate what books on leadership are available.

B. Angela is a communications network designer who is leading a project that is converting her company's system from a DOS-base to a UNIX base. A large part of her job is extensive information gathering from the end-users of the system, such as salespeople, customer service people, and accountants, as well as the engineers who design the telecommunications equipment her company manufactures. She is an excellent systems engineer, but not very good with people. All team members are in-house employees, and comprise two programmers, a certified network administrator, and a customer service trainer. In addition, Angela will be using several technical consultants and contract employees.

She is nervous about her role as leader because it is her first leadership position since she was president of her engineering organization in college. The former leader of the project was an older manager, who had been with the company a long time, but was removed from the project because of lack of knowledge. Although the others were fond of him, they did not respect his ability, and therefore, the project floundered.

1. What is Angela going to have to do to prepare herself to handle the challenges of the first few weeks with this new group?
2. What possible leadership problems might spring up right away?
3. Because she has a weakness, should she be the leader of this group?
4. What kind of support system will Angela need to set up?
5. Give one suggestion for motivating the contractors to be committed to the project.
6. What might she do with the two programmers who have become problems due to their unwillingness to work days (they were originally hired for the night shift) and to turn in reports on time? They are both excellent at their jobs, otherwise, and they are the only ones in the project that know both the old system and the new one.

Interview with an Expert

***Richard Cope,** USMC Retired, former director of Advanced Research Projects Agency for the federal government, now COO of Advanced Charger Technology*

Leaders have to take responsibility for putting together the elements that make motivated employees.

- Do your "homework." Really listen to your employees or team members to find out what they enjoy about their work and what underlying need they want their work to meet: money, satisfaction, recognition, etc.

  They can't verbalize this need, you have to investigate by seeing what makes them "light up." This is done in many conversations, such as, "If you do this, your name will go into the technical journals." Or "Success on this project will get management's attention." Or "Bonuses go to the projects that come in on time." What appeals to one may not appeal to another. This takes time; you may have to listen to some boring (to you) conversations in order to understand just what motivates each employee. Listening on your part fosters a willingness to communicate on the part of the employee.
- Create the vision that employees can take part in. A two-sentence description of the "endgame" done in concrete terms, that are clear to everyone, will link the goal with the individual's own success. You have to create a desire for achievement by making the end result seem real—by putting them in the scene. On the other hand,

you must check to see if they understand the goals by asking questions; get them to explain what they're going to do to meet the goal.

- Ask your employees what they are doing, and get their perspective on how the project is going.

  Many managers are afraid to ask employees to explain things for fear of looking less than expert. Asking does two things: it affirms the employee by showing that you respect, and want to understand, what he or she does. Also, the more you understand what your employees are doing, the better able you are to lead them intelligently and the more willing they are to follow your lead.

CHAPTER

4 COMMUNICATION

CHAPTER PREVIEW

The Project Management Seminar: Session 4

The group milled around the coffee pot. Hilda seemed particularly intent on downing as much as she could. In addition, her hair, which was usually perfectly styled, was in disarray. Jerry walked over to her. "Rough night?" he asked with a smile.

"Yeah. With the difference in time zones I have to stay up all night solving problems with my people. You're lucky, you don't find out about yours until the next morning. This one was a real bear."

"Don't tell me. Let me guess. An engineer forgot to tell the project manager a really important piece of information, and now the whole project has jumped the track because of it. Communication debris is lying around, and the scene appears to be a total loss." "Am I close?" queried Jerry.

Hilda cocked an eye at him, startled, at first by his apparent insight into her problem.

Jerry hurried to explain. "No, Hilda, I haven't suddenly developed psychic powers. You and I and everyone else in business have the same problem: people don't communicate enough and when they do, it's usually pretty badly. Actually, in all the things we do as professionals, communication is the thing we probably do worst. I wanted to be early for this session today. Looks like you could use some help too," he added sympathetically.

"I think you're right, but I'm so exhausted, I'm not sure I can make it through the whole day," Hilda agreed.

"Don't worry, if you begin to snore loudly, I'll toss something at you." Jerry laughed.

"Thanks a lot. You're a real friend," she responded sarcastically, but managed a smile.

The opening discussion was particularly lively, with the exception of Hilda, who mostly studied her coffee cup, and quite a few issues came up for the day's training session.

- Why don't they listen?
- She won't report on paper.
- Nobody understands.
- Sales won't talk to engineering.

- I can't ever get him on the phone.
- Do I have to ask for everything?
- What about e-mail?
- He talks all around the issue.
- She always says the wrong thing.

With their work cut out for them, Ralph and Tracey posted the objectives for the day.

- **Meeting project communication needs**
- **Uncovering the reasons for ineffectiveness**
- **Matching communication styles and media**
- **Gaining access for communication**
- **Ensuring efficiency and confirming "appreciation"**

Managers everywhere have the same lament: "We have terrible problems with communication." For some managers, poor communication means "Nobody listens around here." For others it might be, "We're duplicating effort because the right hand doesn't know what the left hand is doing." Some problems are corporate problems, while others are individual skill or process problems. With differences in communication style, preference for certain types of communication media, and variations in personalities, backgrounds and experiences, it is actually a wonder that we communicate at all. Maybe that's a bit of an overstatement, but untrained communicators, although they can survive in general, cause many difficulties in business: from messing up a sales deal to incurring liability for the company on a project that has crashed.

1.0 Meeting Project Communication Needs

The project management environment has a set of challenges that are different from those faced in the standard business situation. Because of the nature of the activities and accountabilities involved in projects, they require some specific types of communication. Following are some of the formal and informal types of communication you might expect to generate, receive, or take part in over the course of a project.

Formal Project Communication

- Meetings
- Status reports
- Change orders
- Conference calls
- Project scope (or project map)
- Control reports
- Test results
- Problem detection and notification
- Problem solving

The list goes on and on. Some of these forms of communication will be very structured, such as control reports, which allow many people to understand what is within plan parameters and what is not. Control reports might be forms to fill out or software-generated reports from data. Test results might also be reported in specific forms, such as a lab report. Chapter 12 provides a detailed discussion of reporting forms and methods.

Informal communication may take the form of a casual conversation in the break room about a problem, or a problem solution meeting over a few beers in the pizza place next door.

Managers complain consistently about communication problems. Project managers have an even greater challenge because of the nature of the project team:

- Project team members often come from diverse departments and are unfamiliar with each other.
- Projects are made up of highly specialized people who may prefer to interact only with those of their specialty.
- Project team members understand less about the intricate interdependencies of the tasks required than the project manager.
- Project managers are responsible for soliciting input from team members who are reluctant to communicate, and therefore project managers must be superior communicators themselves.

The project manager must ensure not only commitment to the project, but commitment to communication regarding the project. The project manager's job is to (a) motivate project team members to communicate regularly with each other and with the project manager (and in some situations, with the customer); and (b) encourage or train team members to communicate well.

2.0 MATCHING COMMUNICATION STYLES

Members of your team who seem unwilling to communicate, may not necessarily be uncooperative. Instead, they may merely be unwilling to communicate in a way that is not comfortable to them. If you prefer to talk with people to exchange ideas, you probably feel that filling out forms or writing reports is arduous and irritating. On the other hand, if writing or generating a report from software is easy for you, you might see the verbal interplay of a meeting as a waste of time. So one approach to motivating team members to communicate is to ask for **communication** from people in the style that suits them best.

communication information is exchanged between individuals through a common system

- People tend to send out messages in the manner they take in information best.
- Some avoid certain media altogether even when doing so may create a problem for them.

Thus, to encourage communication (and to ensure that we are getting through as well), we have to know which gate to choose, or in this case which media channel or set of conditions to select, to get the response we want. The descriptions in Figure 4–1 can help you to discover which channel works best for which of your team members. Take special note of your own preference and understand that you will generally fall back to this method unless you are diligent about choosing the most efficient form of communication. (These categories are roughly based on the work of James and Galbraith, 1987.)

readers in communication, those who prefer printed correspondence to other forms

2.1 Readers

For those who prefer print, send messages and ask for responses in writing, including letters, reports, memos, or bullet points on a presentation. Print-oriented communicators like to read and study ideas rather than depend on briefer, less precise methods.

Advantages	Disadvantages
• Ability to explain complex ideas or numerical data and keep it available for referral. • Documents provide a record of communication. • Things in print seem to have enhanced credibility.	• Without nonverbal cues, possibility exists for misunderstanding. Requires greater attention to word choice, grammar, and punctuation. • An error in print could be taken as fact and be legally binding. • For people who don't prefer print, follow-up may be required to ensure communication.

listeners in communication, those people who prefer phone and face-to-face correspondence to other forms

2.2 Listeners

This category includes telephone and face-to-face communication. Busy managers or team members who are "listeners" often prefer you to "tell them the short version." These people will remember what they hear, rather than what they read. Because they absorb information better this way, they are likely to send out information verbally as well.

Advantages	Disadvantages
• Quick feedback and response during real-time communication. • Sender can adapt message if he/she perceives it is not being received correctly.	• Risk of error, of "not hearing you right" or forgetting important facts. • Most people are not efficient listeners and are influenced by biases in some way or another.

exchangers in communication, require a true dialogue

2.3 Exchangers

Exchangers require an exchange, a true dialogue, and do a lot of their deep thinking while talking. This type must constantly process (usually verbally) to clearly understand message. Often, exchangers will want to "talk through" problems or "run an idea by you" before making a decision. Internet "chats" may help with exchangers as well as conference calls and meetings.

Advantages	Disadvantages
• Both parties to the communication are actively involved. • Feedback is automatic. • Often many relevant issues emerge during exchange.	• Conversation may drift off-target unless sender is skillful in keeping on track. • Process constantly, may step on ends of sentences of others. • Must have some kind of exchange. • Conversations often aren't documented.

2.4 Movers

movers in communication, those who need to move around to think or process clearly

These people need to move around to think or process clearly. Quite a few of these types may have been hyperactive as children. It was thought in years past that children outgrew this, but professionals now pretty much accept that is not always true. It is highly unlikely that a mover will sit still long enough to fill out endless forms or write up reports, no matter how important they are to their jobs.

Advantages	Disadvantages
• Think well "on their feet" or on the run, and process quickly and generate ideas rapidly. • Get through to movers by joining them for a walk around the plant or communicating during some sort of physical activity.	• May not sit still at meetings, might rock or get out of seat frequently, which distracts others. • Will not process as efficiently if required to sit still while information is being distributed; may pace or fidget when doing presentations, which will distract listeners.

2.5 Manipulators

manipulators in communication, require a hands-on approach to take in messages

Manipulators require a hands-on approach to take in messages. Highly mechanical people who are natural "tinkerers" fit this category. We often use the word "concrete" to describe this type, as opposed to "abstract" processors who prefer to deal in ideas instead of things. Manipulators might want to show you the actual physical problem rather than tell or report about it.

Advantages	Disadvantages
• Generally easily comprehend an idea if allowed to manipulate equipment or to work through an operation rather than just watch. • When an abstract concept is involved, an activity or object to reinforce concept will ensure successful communication.	• If they cannot physically be involved in the procedure in some way, they will not retain the ideas as well.

2.6 Viewers

viewers in communication, require drawings or videos, diagrams, flow charts, or models

Viewers love drawings, videos, diagrams, flowcharts and models. Things represented graphically make sense to this person. Printed words projected on a screen, whether as overheads or software graphics display, are *not* going to get through to this person as well; they are merely projected print. Viewers will be Gantt and Pert chart fans and will probably feel they have communicated all they need to when they generate their charts or diagrams.

Advantages	Disadvantages
• Pictures can substitute for words or can enhance meaning for viewers. • Might feel like your ideas "make more sense" if you have represented them graphically and another presenter has not.	• Difficult to accomplish goals with words with viewers. Viewers will likely assign more importance to drawings and charts than to words.

Figure 4–1
Communication Styles

■ ■ ■

"So now, what do each of you think of this?" Tracey asked. "Can you find yourself in these descriptions?"

Yury volunteered, "I like books, so I guess I'm a reader."

"Tell me, Yury," Tracey asked, "do you send out a lot of memos or E-mail and ask that your project team give you written reports?"

"Of course I do. Everyone does," he retorted, folding his arms defensively.

Tracey continued to question him. "Do you have any in your group who don't turn in reports on time? And yet, do these same people stop you in the hall to tell you what's going on with their projects?"

"Yeah. I have one manufacturing supervisor who always wants to talk, but he won't even return my E-mail. He's a real problem," Yury returned, leaning back in his chair.

Jerry had been listening closely to the responses, but was beginning to frown a bit. "Okay, Jerry," Ralph said, "I see it coming. I know you've got some sort of problem with what we're doing. Let's have it."

"I'm a manager. Do you mean that I have to figure out the communication style of all my project team members and adjust my delivery and communication requirements to them? What happened to meeting the boss on his own terms?" he said gruffly, thumping his pencil on the table. Yury and Ragdeesh nodded in agreement.

"I think I'll let the group field that one. Everyone, what's the answer to Jerry's question?" Ralph asked.

Hilda, who was beginning to wake up, answered, "Jerry, if you don't use their style, you won't get through. The people who communicate like you do will understand and respond. The others just won't get it, or won't get back to you, and then you've got a mess on your hands." She paused as she stood up. "Now, if you'll excuse me, I've got an E-mail and a fax to send, a phone call to make and a chart to overnight."

"I think Hilda pretty much said it all," finished Ralph.

■ ■ ■

Meeting Channel Preferences

Readers

- Memos
- Letters
- Articles
- Proposals
- E-mail

Listeners

- Phone
- Conversation

Music added to presentation
Meetings
Videoconferencing

Viewers

Movies
Multimedia presentations
Charts
Graphs
Line drawings
Photographs
Words inside shapes

In the ideal world, team members would ardently seek to adapt their style to the project managers and communicate in the most constructive ways. But because this rarely happens by itself, the responsibility for fostering open, regular, and positive communication falls to the project manager. Project communication has, by nature, and necessity, its own separate style because the accountabilities are different from those in personal or other workplace communication situations. If you forget to tell your spouse to get the bread on a grocery store trip or he picks up the wrong brand because he couldn't read your handwriting, no great loss occurs; inconvenience, maybe, great loss, no. If in your job, you reverse the order of two pages in a report, or if you are too casual in an E-mail, you can cost the company money or can offend important people. Because accountability is so high and communication is so crucial in carrying out a successful project, messages of all sorts must be handled with attention and care.

By examining all that is involved in communication, you will quickly see why communication is a complex process and why it is so difficult to do well.

3.0 UNDERSTANDING THE COMMUNICATION PROCESS

There are so many models and theories of communication that a serious study of the subject might take more time than it takes you to complete your most complex project. In addition, there is no "short version" that will give you a few quick steps or truths with which to guide all your communication. However, being aware of some of the communication factors in the project management process, plus the addition of a few tools and skills, will help you approach a more strategic, more efficient, level.

The diagram in Figure 4–2 is a picture of what goes on when we communicate. The area of overlap is between the idea originally offered by the sender and the idea assimilated by the receiver. Whether the occasion is a conversation or an E-mail or a proposal or a report, that small amount is about all that actually gets through to the receiver in any meaningful way.

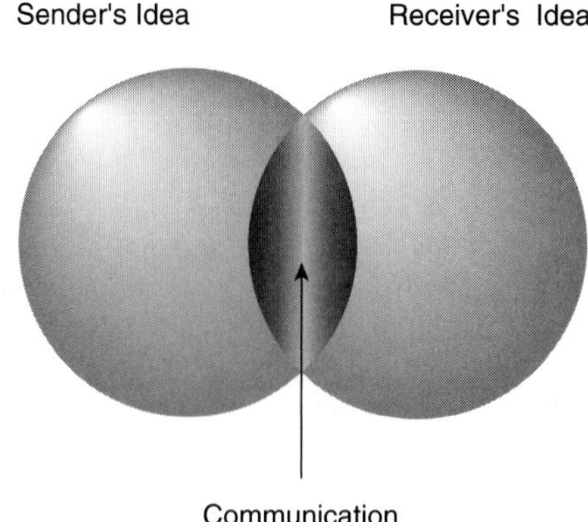

Figure 4–2
Only a small part of a sender's ideas are transferred intact to the receiver.

In the project management environment, many factors affect how closely the idea that originated in the sender's head matches the idea that is ultimately formulated by the receiver. The good news is that there are many ways that you and your team members can improve communication skill and thus widen the area of mutual understanding.

First, a look at the elements that make up the process will help establish a working vocabulary about communication. Amazingly, when you and your employees begin to talk about communication and communication improvement, it actually does improve. But you have to have a common language to do that. The terms used here will allow you to pinpoint communication problems and to head off possible developing ones. It is first assumed that the sender accepts responsibility for the communication. Then, the important considerations in understanding the receiver's perspective are explored.

3.1 Elements of the Message Sent

3.1.1 Purpose

purpose motivation for the communication

Purpose is the motivation for the communication. Rarely, though, does the receiver intuitively know what the sender's purpose or idea is. For example, when the phone rings with an urgent call, it may take you several seconds, or even a minute before you understand what is so important. You might, however, understand the urgency more quickly if the caller clearly states the purpose in the first sentence or two. Pinning down your purpose before you communicate, then organizing what you will say or write so that it clearly conveys that purpose, will foster successful idea transfer.

3.1.2 Body Language

body language nonverbal communication

When we have a message or idea, we communicate it often without using words at all. Some experts tell us that nonverbal communication, or *paralanguage* as it is sometimes called, is anywhere from 75% to 90% of what we send and receive. Although often we don't consciously think about it, we can choose to send certain messages with our body language. Wearing certain clothes sends a message, just as how fast we walk or how we posture ourselves sends a message. Some gestures are perceived as being submissive in some cultures, and signs of respect in other cultures. (See Chapter 6, Diversity.) Eye contact is another important form of nonverbal communication, as is a smile or a handshake.

3.1.3 Proxemics

proxemics the physical distance between people during an exchange

Although *proxemics* generally refers to the physical distance between people during an exchange, here it will be used also to refer to how we treat people's time and personal space. Crowding someone who has a large personal space need (larger than the average American space of 3–4 feet) will make that person feel threatened or challenged.

Similarly, if you don't respect people's time and the value they place on it, then they will see your communication as an encroachment, and they won't be receptive. An example is, "Call me" versus "I'll call you by 3 o'clock tomorrow." "Call me" conveys no commitment, whereas "I'll call by 3 o'clock" sets a priority on the call by both parties. The first message respects the sender's time; the second message respects the receiver's time.

3.1.4 Inflection

inflection any change in loudness or pitch in a person's voice

Another choice the sender makes is how lively the message should sound. Variety of pitch and rhythm is a necessity in a speech; it is also helpful to add a little bit of energy and animation to conversations over the phone because the phone makes the voice sound flat and uninterested. Inflection relates to the idea that "It's not what you say, but how you say it." It tells the listener whether to perceive a comment as a joke instead of an insult, or as a sincere compliment instead of teasing. Unfortunately, inflection is lost in written communication, and because of this we have to be more careful how we say things in writing.

■ ■ ■

"No, no, no. You have to be joking," Yury cut in. "I don't make all those decisions every time I want to tell somebody something. You're making a big fuss over this. If I've got something to say, I just say it."

Ralph smiled. "Thank you, Yury, for opening that discussion for us. That is exactly what we're cautioning against here. If you don't plan what you want to communicate and consciously select the best strategy for doing it, you run the risk of not achieving your goal. Now, I know your people are supposed to follow direction, but do they ever seem to just not get what you mean?" Ralph pressed.

Yury thought about it, relaxing a little. "Sometimes they forget what I have told them. They don't understand how important what I tell them is."

"That's right," Ralph affirmed. "Your message isn't getting through because there is a lot of rough ground between your idea and your employees' understanding. Let's look at the receivers now and see what has to happen there for your ideas to actually show up in their heads."

■ ■ ■

3.2 Elements Affecting the Message Received

On this side of the communication process, the person you wish to talk to has a myriad of thoughts floating around in his or her head at any time you choose to communicate. These ideas compete in importance with the one you are sending. In addition, the receiver may think that he or she has clearly heard your idea and understands perfectly, even though this may or may not be so.

Senders are responsible for the effectiveness of the communication, and in a fast-paced and complex project management environment, you as project managers have to use specific follow-up techniques to help you. These are discussed later in this chapter.

3.2.1 Listening

listening hearing something with thoughtful attention

During any exchange your receiver may drift onto other ideas that have nothing to do with yours. The brain operates at much higher speeds than most people speak or read, giving it time to play and to possibly get distracted with other things. Have you ever asked someone a question on the phone and gotten no response? The receiver most likely went elsewhere mentally. Active, intent listening is rare because few receivers understand the importance of your message enough to care about it. You must assume that there will be many times the receiver is not listening actively.

bias inclination to think good or bad thoughts based on prior attitudes or experiences

3.2.2 Bias

Bias is the inclination on the receiver's part to think good or bad thoughts about your message depending on prior attitudes or experience. If you look professional and speak with clarity and assertiveness, people will be biased in your favor and tend to receive what you say more readily. However, if you appear too young and inexperienced, or have an abrasive manner, people may discount what you say or ignore your comments completely. Be careful of discounting the good idea just because it came from someone you do not much like.

connotation value placed on certain words; implication

3.2.3 Connotations

Similar to bias, connotation refers to the value the receiver places on certain words. Words and phrases such as, "boss," "new kid," and "girls in the office" often have more than one connotation depending on the relationship and situation of the people communicating. Less loaded words, such as "manager," "recent hire," and "office staff" have a better chance of not offending the receiver and closing the communication channel.

■ ■ ■

"I have to jump into this one," interrupted Tom. "We have been beaten over the head about sexual harassment so much, I don't know what to say anymore to a woman at work that won't cause trouble. What's this stuff all about? Everything we guys say seems to have the wrong connotation."

Tracey spoke up. "I'll take this one, Ralph." She turned to the group, "Tom is right. Connotations can cause trouble, and sexual harassment is a serious thing. Actually, it's as much the body language and attitude as it is the words that cause the trouble."

"You mean I have to mind my P's and Q's every time I talk to a woman at work? Sheesh! It's not worth it," Tom added, shaking his head in exasperation.

"Look, it's really simple," Tracey said. "Avoid words or forms of address that are obviously objectionable: honey, toots, baby, like that. Mostly, though, if you treat everyone with respect, and occasionally ask if something might be offensive before you say it, you'll probably have good working relationships. Otherwise, you're going to get nailed and dragged into court or fired."

Tom was quiet, digesting Tracey's last statement. "Aren't you glad you came?" Jerry said, jabbing Tom playfully in the arm.

At this point Ralph suggested, "Hey guys, let's break for lunch."

"Guys? Did I miss something here?" Hilda interjected with just the hint of a smile.

"Oh no!" Tom groaned with a pained look on his face and put his hands on his head. Everyone laughed as they headed out the door.

■ ■ ■

appreciation understanding message sent and believing it has value and merit

3.2.4 Appreciation

Appreciation has multiple meanings. Here it means not only hearing and comprehending the words being sent, but also agreeing that the idea has value and merit, *and* being willing to act on it. In business there will be many occasions where you just can't "agree to disagree"; you have to make decisions, and your employees or co-workers have to "appreciate" and support those decisions.

As is probably becoming clear by now, there is a huge margin for error in communication between senders and receivers. Many reasons exist that create these errors.

4.0 Reasons for Ineffectiveness

Many elements can ultimately drive a wedge between the sender and receiver. These wedges create understanding gaps between your purpose and the other person's response (see Figure 4–3). Classified as chasms, barriers, and noise, wedges must be anticipated, recognized, and addressed.

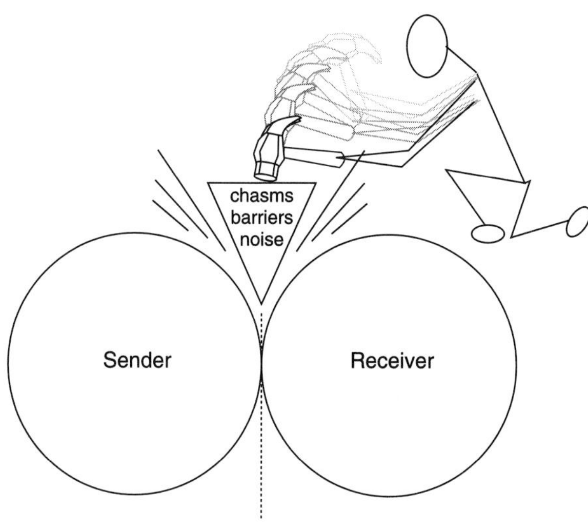

Figure 4–3 Some factors drive a wedge between communicators.

4.1 Chasms

chasm the physical distance between you and the person with whom you are communicating

A chasm is the physical distance—whether physical or in terms of purpose or intent—between you and the person with whom you are communicating. The further physically removed you are from each other, the further you are separated, the more likely you are to have a miscommunication. You have a greater chance to communicate well when you communicate in person. You also have a lot more power to encourage someone to engage in communication with you when you are face-to-face. Furthermore, it is harder for people to lie face-to-face.

Going to someone's office, crossing the chasm of physical distance, is a show of respect, sending the message that you are willing to come to him or her. However, if you make an unannounced visit, or startle the person you are meeting, that person may perceive your visit as an invasion. In a study done by Kinney and Panko (1996), only 44% of project teams had all members on-site. Further, 25% had half or more of project participants located at other sites. It is safe to assume that the problem of chasms, or physical distance, is to be expected.

Phones give access to people who are too far away to be reached, but they lack the personal connectedness of the face-to-face meeting. Conference calls work best when participants have met face-to-face previously. When the phone is the only medium of communication used, people are more hesitant to cement an agreement. The phone connects voices, but the impersonality of it can create resistance, especially if the person receiving the call feels a face-to-face meeting is preferred and takes the phone call as an insult.

Some people actually use phones to create distance. Shy people, or those who are otherwise uncomfortable talking face-to-face, are actually more open when talking on the phone because of the anonymity it creates. Remember, though, that the more distance, the less efficient the communication, and the more likely you are to be misunderstood.

Figure 4–4
Many barriers can get in the way of a person's understanding of an idea.

4.2 Barriers

barriers anything that gets in the way of communication

Another wedge that can drive apart communicators is **barriers**—anything that gets in the way of communication. Barriers come in many forms, but physical and perceptual barriers are examined here. (See Figure 4–4.)

Working environments themselves often are made up of many physical barriers to communication: closed doors that people sit behind, meeting rooms too small for all to fit into, cubicles that prevent private exchanges, walls that people have to talk over, team members located physically too far from each other. One reason off-site retreats and workshops are helpful in improving communication is that the physical barriers between people and departments disappear around the dinner table or in the bar after the meetings are over. Managers who close their doors or refer employees to their official appointment calendars put up physical barriers between themselves and the employees, often resulting in lessened communication. Managers who complain that they have too little communication from team members might look at how they may be discouraging contact through the creation of artificial barriers.

Perceptual barriers—or barriers that aren't physical—can be as forbidding as physical ones. Sometimes a manager's or employee's appearance erects barriers. A scowl may put people off, as may an insincere smile. Some people put up barriers around employees with disabilities, because they feel uncomfortable around them and don't know what to say. Usually it is the able-bodied employee who puts up the barrier. Barriers are also apparent between people of different racial or cultural backgrounds, and also hamper communication. (Chapter 6, Diversity, discusses this issue in more depth.)

perceptual barriers barriers that aren't physical

Another barrier is the brain's own filtering system, called the **perceptual screen,** which is a kind of sifting device that keeps the brain from going into overload from too much "stuff" or data. Data can be anything from ads to newscasts to talk from friends to information you have read. In fact, in today's information age, working people currently experience data overload. People are forced to filter out all of the information coming at them, or their brains would explode. The brain chooses its own pattern for retaining and screening out information.

perceptual screen kind of sifting device that keeps the brain from going into overload from too much data

The project manager must be the one to bridge or plow through the barriers, when they exist. Barriers of inaccessibility and perception deter the message in its attempt to get through. It is in the project manager's best interest always to have good and open communication by removing barriers.

4.3 Noise

A final wedge in communication is noise. **Noise** muddles the message so that what comes through to the receiver is fragmented and incomplete. Noise may be actual physical noise, from a bad signal on a cellular phone to construction work in the background of a conversation. It might take the form of interruptions during a conversation in person or on the phone. Or, it can be mental noise: outside concerns occupying the mind of the person you are talking with, questions not answered right away, concerns that are not voiced.

noise anything that muddles the message being communicated

5.0 Gaining Access for Communication

Now that you are beginning to understand some of the difficulties you have to overcome to communicate well, what follows are some guidelines for doing just that. First, in order to convey your message, you must know the level of accessibility team members are comfortable with. This is an area that has not been discussed at length in textbooks because it falls into the category of "trade secrets" instead of academic research. Successful business professionals have learned techniques for motivating people to return their phone calls or to see them for a meeting. They have also learned how and when to locate people when they are most amenable to talking business. Information in this section will be presented as hints or strategic alternatives to help you engage people in communication, and it comes from long experience dealing with busy business people.

Everyone is different in his or her need to communicate. Feelings about the need for privacy versus the need for accessibility affect an individual's responsiveness. You will always have to observe carefully or ask the person's preference. Although you rarely can make assumptions in these areas, there are some clues to the different strategies required.

5.1 Clues to Accessibility

If someone hands you his/her card and says, "Here's my fax number, and it's on all the time," it's safe to assume that person reads faxes and maybe picks them up at odd hours. Some people like to control time on their end of the communication, although they have a high need to communicate. Someone who has a high need to communicate but needs little control of time would most likely have a cellular phone on at all times and gives out that number to a lot of people. The high-need, high-control person will have a pager and give you that pager number or have an automatic paging setup on the voice mail system. That way he or she knows who calls, but can control when he or she calls back. (See Figure 4–5.)

Some of the people on your projects prefer face-to-face communication, but don't like surprises that can result from unlimited access. These people might say, "My assistant has my calendar," or "I'm in my office and see people from 4 to 6." For this type you might do best to make an appointment to ensure that the receiver is as receptive as possible to your communication, since the receiver will be able to prepare for your visit.

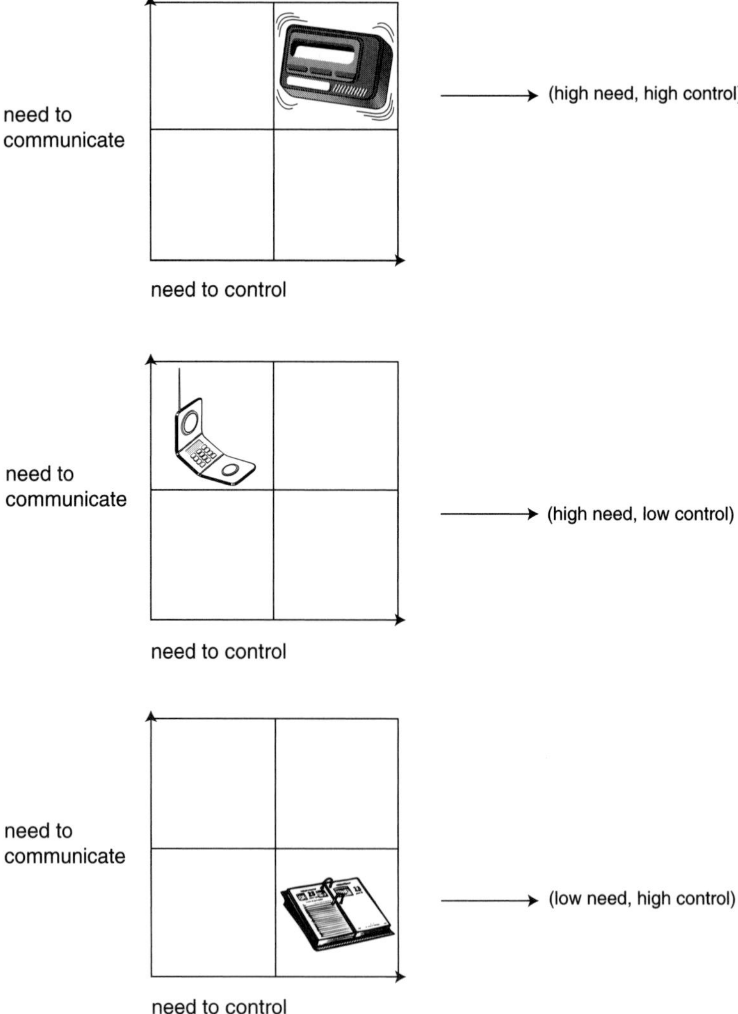

Figure 4–5
Need for control vs. need to communicate.

5.2 Electronic Access Alternatives

E-mail and voice mail, among others, are methods of access brought to us by the information age. E-mail and voice mail protocols are still young enough not to be set in the corporate etiquette books. Remember, though, that both are recorded messages and can be held as evidence of what we have said. The same amount of care therefore must be given to wording in E-mails and voice mails as to letters.

Voice mail or E-mail gives us 24-hour-a-day access,which is especially helpful when doing business across time zones. Don't assume, though, that just because someone has voice mail, E-mail, or both, that it is used. Some people screen the subject line on their E-mail and trash messages that don't catch their attention as immediately relevant. The same is true of voice mail. And there are still those who refuse to use either. Learn to send good, succinct messages via both these media, and you will be light years ahead of others in the communication competition. In addition, construct your subject notations carefully to capture the attention of the receiver.

5.3 Personal Time Accessibility

Personal time accessibility is another issue. Is it okay to call people at home? Some parents prefer to be physically around their families, but can be contacted under certain conditions. Remember, though, that many of your co-workers and project team members are on a clock that is different from yours. At 6 A.M., when you might think your departmental supervisor would be home, he might actually be at the office and doesn't mind talking to you during that early, quiet time. In fact, you probably won't catch him any other time.

Pagers, cellular phones, E-mail, voice mail, conference calls, meetings—all are variations of your employees' needs for communication balanced with their need to control accessibility. A quick inventory of your team members might facilitate the level of communication required to execute the kinds of complex projects you will have to run. A questionnaire that each member of a project team fills out at the start of the project can tell how team members can be reached and when access is preferred. (See Figure 4–6.)

Communication Access Form

Project: Name:

Department: Extension:

E-mail: Pager:

Cell phone:

Can call at home? Yes No Home phone:

Between ____________ and ____________

Figure 4–6
Communication access form.

Much of a noncommunication problem can be attributed to the project manager's not knowing accessibility information about his people or his not making communication easy. Project managers must make themselves accessible in many different ways at many different times and still do the work required to direct operations. Each of you will have to strike that balance between need to communicate and need to control accessibility.

6.0 Ensuring "Appreciation"

The goal in project communication is not only to get through to your people but also to make certain they appreciate the value of your message enough to take the appropriate action. Otherwise, they will respond by nodding in a vague manner, then promptly go about their business in their own way. Your message will go right past them.

People will not commit to or act on messages they don't either believe or see the value of. Thus, your challenge becomes how to make them see the value. There are several things you can do to cultivate that "appreciation" and evoke action. Several elements in the environment of communication can help (Figure 4–7).

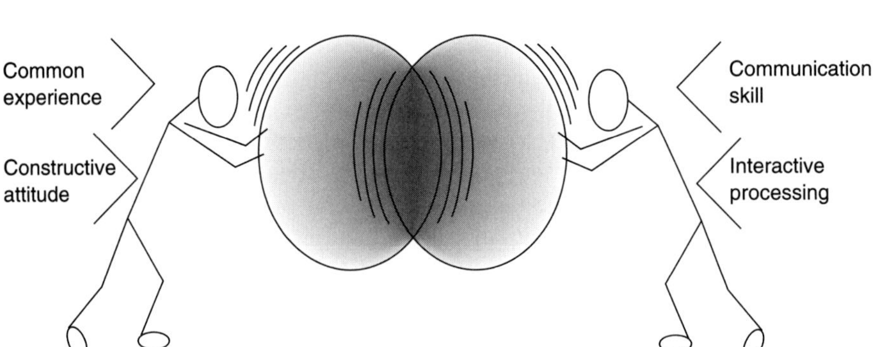

Figure 4–7
Certain elements improve understanding.

6.1 Common Experience

We tend to communicate better with people we know better. Communication between people of the same culture is often better than between people who have serious cultural differences in the way to express ideas.

In addition, engineering and other technical fields use a lot of specialized words that have meaning only to specialists in that field. A "warm boot," for instance, means something quite different to a computer user than it does to a deer hunter. Specialized language is useful among groups with a common professional background, and using it can establish one's credibility and increase understanding between communicators. In short, the more we have in common with our audience, the more we are likely to be able to achieve understanding.

In a project management environment the same holds true, and has its advantages and disadvantages. People tend to communicate more readily and more often with those they are comfortable with. But, for those on the team they do not have a lot in common with, they should improve communication by discovering or creating some common experience both between themselves and their project employees and among the team members.

Sending people to training classes together, and having social or sports events involving the employees all can help. The best method, though, is to get to know your people and find out what experiences you and they may share in spite of other differences. Then, you can build on these bases for communication and expand communication to more complex and unrelated areas.

6.2 Communication Skill

Everyone can improve communication skills with skillbuilding activity. Good communicators are able to convey their ideas in spite of all the screens and barriers they encounter. Project managers who constantly pursue excellence in their own performance and model good communication skills generally experience fewer misunderstandings and elicit better responses.

There are many skill training programs, courses, and consultants out there to help with this process, as well as books and articles on the subject. But the most important element for skilled communication is recognizing the importance of conveying messages well. When you think about what your communication goals are at any given time or for a specific situation, you select a strategy for achieving that goal. Thus, you send your message in the manner it is most likely to be received well, and you greatly enhance your chance for success. Training to improve your communication skills can be a real boost to communication on any project.

6.3 Constructive Attitude

The general attitude of employees toward each other and toward management influences the quality of communication. For you, the project manager, the situation is even more tricky because the members of the project team do not technically work for you. The term "supportive communication" (Whetton et al. 1998) is used to describe the most effective form workplace interaction can take. Working on a project, you don't have the luxury of telling people off in a very nasty and aggressive way because you will probably have to go back to that person for a favor or service later. The person may even be the customer. So, preserving relationships—the ability to continue to work together in a positive way—is the goal.

Because of this goal, good, supportive communicators demonstrate several characteristics in the way they interact with people:

- Reasonable, problem-solving approaches
- Concern for mutual agreement, not one-sided dominant solutions
- Respectful posture, affirmation of the other's needs and viewpoints
- Constant pursuit of understanding—on both sides
- Acceptance of responsibility for success of communication

There is no room for verbal muscle-flexing or sneaky agendas in the demanding world of project management. So the motivation to handle all communications positively and effectively should be a priority for everyone.

6.4 Interactive Processing

The difficulties of communication are compounded when there are no checks to determine whether an idea got through or not. Also, when you "talk at" people instead of "talking with" people, you hurl ideas at possibly unreceptive audiences. Sometimes you think you have made a point or have gotten the idea or direction across, when, in fact, you have only sent words flying towards a target.

Figure 4–8
Poorly planned one-way communication can miss the target completely.

Interactive processing requires the expenditure of energy on the part of both (or all) communicators. The project manager formulates a clear message in a manner he or she thinks will be understood by the employee or team member. The team member actively processes the message and seeks to clarify and appreciate the meaning and the motivation behind the message. If any part of the exchange breaks down, either communicator should notice it and immediately ask for feedback or use some other method to determine what part of the message didn't get through.

Skillful communicators experience less frustration and higher efficiency in their work exchanges, but the intensity of attention and thought required for this skillful communication can be exhausting. This is probably why most people just settle for "okay" conversations and message exchanges. But when a client or a company's multimillion-dollar project is on the line, the project manager and every member of the project team have an obligation to operate at the highest levels attainable.

To ensure high-efficiency, interactive communication, project managers should:

- Model excellent communication patterns themselves.
- Affirm superior communication skill in employees.
- Value clear, open communication (good news or bad news).
- Persist in encouraging skill improvement through training or coaching.
- Remove as many communication barriers as possible.
- Provide person-to-person, electronic, and other formalized platforms to encourage frequent and candid communication.
- Provide ample opportunities for informal idea exchange to foster cooperation.

Interactive processing involves sending clear messages and giving clear feedback to confirm the message. Trained conflict managers or negotiators will often use the phrase, "What I hear is . . . Is that what you meant?" If everyone in your project group is trained to clarify messages to ensure efficient communication, then fewer costly mistakes will occur.

Chapter Summary

Good communication is both necessary and difficult. Project managers are called upon to recognize communication problems and to ensure the most effective communication possible given the responsibility they have to their companies and the projects they manage.

Reasons for ineffective communication include factors that drive a wedge between communicators' ideas. These wedges include chasms, barriers, and noise. Being able to match the communication style of the receiver improves the chances of the idea getting through. The styles include: readers, listeners, exchangers, manipulators, movers, and viewers. To gain access for communication, senders read clues receivers send, utilize access alternatives, and determine personal time availability.

Some elements improve understanding and ensure appreciation. These are: communication skill, interactive processing, common experience, and constructive attitude on the part of communicators. In addition, project managers can help the process by setting a good example themselves, offering training to employees, and rewarding employees who display proactive communication and skill.

Chapter Questions

1. Why is it, do you think, that so many managers say that poor communication is the biggest problem they have to deal with?
2. Since the word "communication" is such a broad term, give three possible specific communication problems that can plague the project manager.
3. How does the meaning of the word "appreciation," as defined in this chapter, differ from the meaning of "understanding"?
4. How can the telephone both cross, and create, chasms?
5. Define:
   - **a.** *interactive listening*
   - **b.** *supportive communication*
6. Name three conditions that can facilitate better communication.
7. Why is an overhead presentation of text or a computer-projected slide show of bulleted text not truly appealing to a graphics-oriented person?
8. Discuss why a sexual harassment lawsuit might be considered a serious example of a failure to communicate.

Project Challenge: Applying What You Know

A. Communication in projects is often formalized, so the success of the project does not depend on any individual's willingness to communicate on any given issue or situation. Communication protocols and or expectations can come from the project manager as forms (or E-mail reporting formats) and/or reporting procedures.

Suggest a communication process or procedure to ensure that project team members and cross-functional teams within the project keep in touch with each other. (You may include informal methods as well as formalized procedural or posting, such as on a listserv or electronic bulletin board.)

a. Design a "quick communication" form or E-mail format that encourages easy and frequent interaction that will foster a more open communication environment.

b. Write a short memo to team members explaining this communication procedure and offering reasons why good communication is important to the project's success.

B. Develop a brief presentation storyboard for a topic in your field of study or your work. Make sure you will meet the communication style or channel needs of at least three different types of people who could be in your audience: readers, viewers, listeners, manipulators, exchangers, or movers. A storyboard is a series of frames or panels that show how you will carry out the presentation (Figure 4–9).

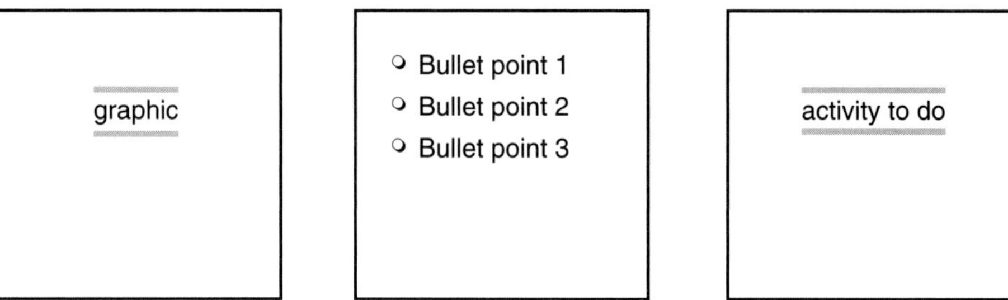

Figure 4–9
Sample storyboard.

Try to be as specific as possible on your selection and don't be afraid to be a little creative. Write out or draw the graphics you will put into your presentation as well as the bullet points. For extra practice, you might put the presentation into some of the graphics presentation software out today. Just remember, print is still print, even on a colorful background with special effects. (For a detailed guide to doing oral presentations, see the reporting meeting section in Chapter 12.)

Interview with an Expert

Gary Floyd, *Project Manager, Electric Vehicle Commute Program, Georgia Power*

Question: You have an unusual communication challenge in your project. Can you describe it?

Floyd: What makes this project unique is that I must communicate different information to many different people with different interests. For example, the participants in the project may need technical information or general information about dates and provisions of the project that affect them. Other employees want to know what's going on because this is a highly visible program within the company. Senior management is looking at the project to determine furture directions for the electric vehicle in communities and fleets. Certain information must go to the legal folks. Finally, the public is another audience that I'm accountable to for updates and information about electric vehicles in general and about our program here.

Question: How do you manage all that information flow and still run the project itself?
Floyd: Communication, accurate and frequent, is absolutely necessary for the success of any project, and this one in particular because of its public visibility and strategic implications. Several communication channels have evolved in this one that would be of help to all project managers.

1. Company intranet—this is a web page devoted to information updates and general resource information on the program. Anyone within the company can access this, and it cuts down on the number of specific answers to the same E-mail questions over and over.
2. Departmental newsgroups—these allow those with a particular information need to communicate with each other more easily and don't require their wading through other reports that they don't need.
3. Meetings—staff directly related to my department meet once a week, other staff meet every 2 weeks, more general feedback sessions once a month, and in our case, a special Electric Vehicle club was formed to connect our project participants and other EV owners or drivers. The club has its own internal network.
4. Brochures, press releases—these public communications comprise a deliverable the same as the nuts and bolts operations. Public visibility is one of the elements of our accountability on this particular project, where it might not be on other projects. We coordinate with corporate communications on this, but we are responsible for generating the information on a regular basis.

Question: What have you learned about communication strategies in projects that would be helpful for a new project manager to know?
Floyd: There are several things. In the first place, not everyone wants to know everything. Some people just want communications that are immediately relevant to them, where others may want to know it all. Another thing is that management needs to know about any problems immediately. Managers should never have to hear of a problem from someone outside the department or from the public.
Question: How does the communications situation differ for a project manager from that of a department or other company manager?
Floyd: Project managers have a wide diversity of levels and departments with which they have to communicate on a regular basis. Other managers, though they do have to communicate with other departments, aren't necessarily as involved with the coordination of effort or information across so many functional areas. Project managers, because their information and communication efforts relate to specific projects, may not have as many routine or established communication channels or occasions as other functional managers would. Where a functional manager may have a weekly meeting or progress report requirement, a project manager may meet with a different group each week, based on the demands of a particular project at the time.
Question: Any general comment you would make about communication in project management?
Floyd: Yes! One is that you can't communicate enough. The other is that you have to be creative with ways to get information out, especially with the diversity of groups that need your communication.

CHAPTER

5 *Teams*

Chapter Preview

The Project Management Seminar: Session 5

Ragdeesh and Yury stared in disbelief at the obstacles ahead, then looked at each other. Tom and Hilda walked up, dressed in their jeans and hiking shoes. Tom voiced their thoughts: "We're not really going to swing across this gully, climb that rockface, and then rappel off it, are we? Who are they trying to kid here?"

Jerry, decked out in camouflage pants, shirt, and hat complete with heavy lug hunting boots and utility vest, jogged past them. "C'mon you guys. We're a team, remember?" he laughed. They frowned in return.

"Great," Tom said, throwing his hands up. "A team is supposed to have expertise in the task. We're the blind leading the blind." He went on, "I mean, do any of you know anything about swinging across a gorge? And that rock. It's too big to climb."

Ralph arrived. Obviously fit and seemingly self-assured in the face of the task ahead, he addressed the group. "This program is designed to teach you to work together. You can accomplish all the goals if you use your talents and help each other. There are no superstars here; we all win or no one does." He paused a moment to assess the group. "Yury, you're large and strong. You'll make a good anchor man. Jerry, you say you've done some rockclimbing. That will help out later. Tom, you're tall and not too heavy, and younger than the rest of us. You'll heal quicker," Ralph said, laughing. Tom didn't laugh. "Hilda," Ralph went on, "you're small and will be able to get through some of the close places we have to manage. And Ragdeesh, you've shown yourself to be a good problem solver so far. There will be situations where you'll have to figure out how to get out of difficult spots. So, you see, each of you contributes to the team."

"Look, I want nothing to do with this," Yury said. "What's this got to do with project management training?"

"Yury, some of your project team members feel just like you do now," Ralph answered. "They don't know what they're supposed to do or how to be successful. They didn't choose to be on the project, and they don't know who they can trust or depend on when things get tough . . . Yeah, I think we've got a good start on understanding this whole team thing."

At that point the training director called the group together to orient them on the survival skills exercise they would be doing that day. She outlined the challenges they would face as a team and described what successful completion of the tasks would be like. Then she opened the discussion for questions and comments. The group offered the following:

- How do we know what to do?
- Goals that challenge.
- What do we do if we disagree?
- How do we decide stuff?
- Why do we have teams anyway?

- Whose responsibility is it?
  - Motivating team members
  - Where is the leader?
  - We want to win.
  - Handling lazy team members

Now resigned to the activities of the day, the group listened carefully to the objectives:

- **Recognizing the need for team structures**
- **Identifying elements of successful teams**
- **Constructing the team**

1.0 Recognizing the Need for Teams

Project teams, quality teams, customer teams, design teams, operations teams, assembly teams, and on and on and on. American business today appears to have embraced the concept of teams in a very big way. Anyone moving into the workforce for the first time, or even those who have been with a company for many years, will likely find themselves in some sort of team arrangement. There are several reasons for this, and an entire organizational history of the evolution of team management is not necessary here. Two factors are important, however, and will be explored in depth:

1. Downsizing with the elimination of layers of organizations increases the number of people reporting to each manager.
2. Increased per-employee productivity rates occur when effective teams are utilized.

cross-trained trained in a variety of areas

After several mini-recessions and a general belt-tightening by businesses, a pattern of economy emerged: flatter organizations. These organizations have many teams whose members are **cross-trained** and assigned to more than one project or set of tasks. This set-up allows for more flexibility and best utilization of human resources to meet the varied challenges the organization must face to remain competitive. The illustration below shows what has happened and why it leads to a preference or need for team-style management (Figure 5–1).

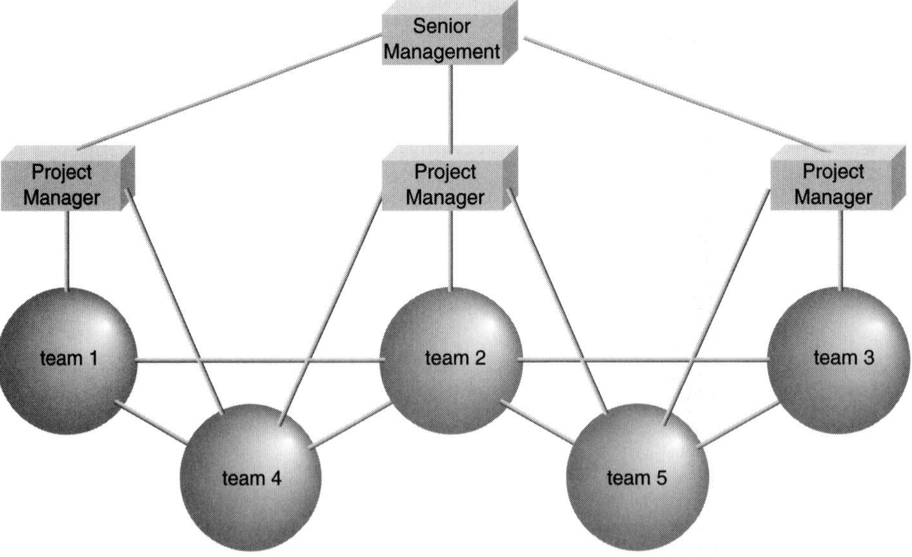

Figure 5–1
Project management teams eliminate the need for a direct reporting structure.

Today's highly competitive marketplace demands quick turnarounds on new products, superior quality, and constant improvement of service and delivery systems. This demand requires the combined creativity and energy of all employees in companies with tighter budgets. Small companies, utilizing teams of skilled, knowledgeable, and energetic people, are accomplishing feats of manufacturing, construction, system development, and start-ups that would have been considered undoable years ago. Thus, teams have become the organizational method for meeting diverse and immediate needs to ensure the company's survival. For this reason many types of teams have evolved:

- Management teams—heads of different departments to do strategic planning
- Cross-functional teams—representatives of design or development for individual components to produce complex systems
- Self-directed work teams—employees grouped by complementary skills set their own goals, carry out own processes, and distribute own rewards
- Project teams—often temporary (though could be in place for years) groups of all necessary skill sets and functional areas brought together for a specific task or operation

A variation of these teams in times past, especially the cross-functional and project teams, was the matrix organization. Businesses would pull out representatives of relevant functional areas within the company to form a group that was responsible for carrying out a specific project or task. For example, to revamp the customer service delivery system, representatives of marketing, logistics, accounting, systems, telecommunications, and even customers themselves might be included on the team. When the goal was reached successfully, the team would be disbanded.

Similarly, today's project teams often have responsibility for several projects at once with undefined connections to any individual manager. Some teams have the luxury of being on only one project at a time, but these projects have such vast reach and complexity, that many departments and functions in the company may be involved. Project managers, then, become conductors of highly-orchestrated operations carried out by educated, skilled, and expert professionals in intense and sometimes difficult environments.

The ever fast-paced, challenging world of industry demands more and more of the project manager. The skill set required to select, develop, and facilitate these teams is scarce because both high-level technical and interpersonal skills are required. Managing teams requires a focus that is slightly different from managing individuals. Understanding the factors that make effective teams is a helpful first step.

2.0 Identifying Elements of Successful Teams

Managers entering a team environment will have one or more of the following scenarios:

- A task for which the project manager is allowed to select team members
- A group of already assembled employees who may or may not work well together
- Multiple teams on multiple projects, sometimes with borrowed or "rented" contract and/or temporary workers

In an examination of the way we build teams, different scenarios are described and recommendations for their successful implementation and management are offered.

Putting a group of people together and calling them a team does not automatically make them act like a team. In fact when questioned, many job applicants really don't know what being on a team means. Following is a typical scenario:

Interviewer: Would you describe yourself as a team player?

Applicant: Oh, yes. Absolutely.

Interviewer: And what does that mean to you exactly?

Applicant: That I can take orders well and work really hard.

In today's business environment, few employees have the luxury of just doing what they're told. For a company to be successful, each and every member of the team must be a leader and a follower at the same precise moment. If a team member hears something on the radio about a shortage of some materials that he knows are needed by the project, then he must take leadership initiative to involve the team in solving this potential problem. He must demonstrate leadership-level strategic thinking, and he must defer power to the team to come up with a solution.

At any given time, any member of the team may be called upon to exercise leadership, to "step up to the plate" and demonstrate initiative that positively impacts the goals of the team. That is a very different way of thinking and behaving than being able to "follow orders well." The most successful teams have the following characteristics:

- Each member shares and supports the vision and goals of the team.
- Each member takes responsibility for both the task needs and the workplace relationship needs of the team.
- Each member understands and is able to respond to the factors, internal and external, that impact the team's potential for success.
- Each member possesses the skill to manage his/her own parts of the project and to support others' contributions.
- Each member demonstrates superior skill in workplace interpersonal communication.

So what does it take to have a good team?

Knowledge	Skill
Attitude	Intimacy
Supportive organizational culture	

These elements are all necessary and can be thought of as a mobile in delicate balance (Figure 5–2).

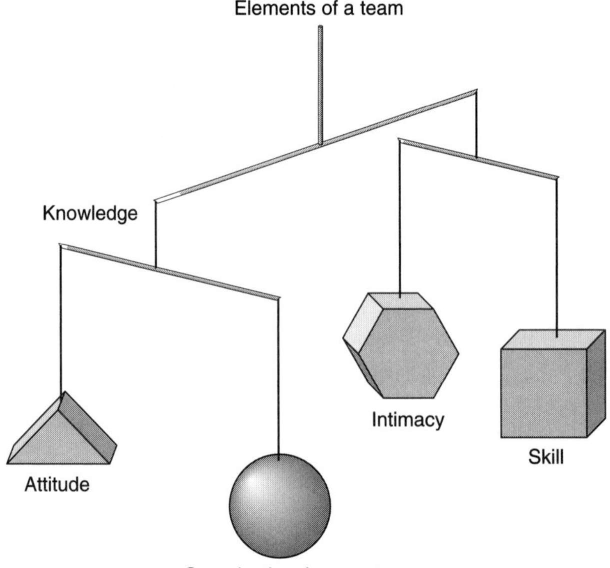

Figure 5–2
When all elements of a team are present, the team is in balance.

If one element is too light or is removed, the whole team dynamic gets out of balance and doesn't function properly (Figure 5–3).

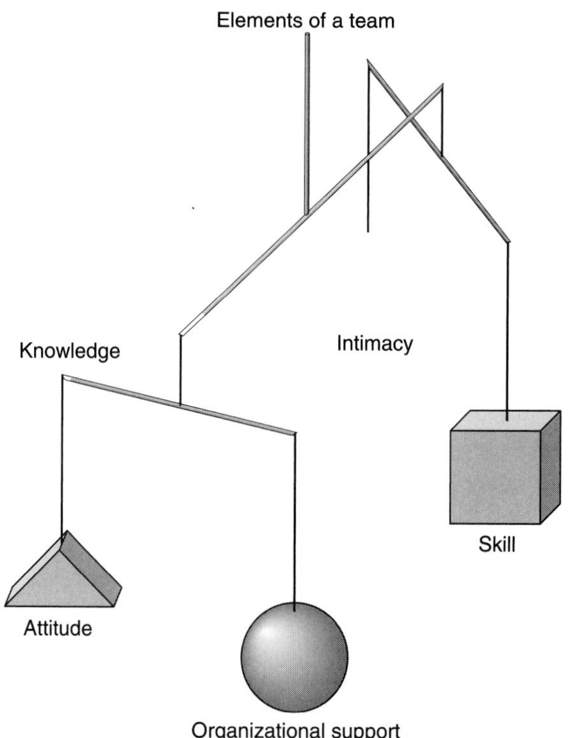

Figure 5–3
If one element is missing, the team is out of balance.

Thus, all the elements must be observed and valued for the highest levels of productivity.

2.1 Knowledge

Knowledge is often missing in low-performing teams. Grouping a set of skilled people without letting them know why they are working together, what affects their task, who brings what expertise to the project, what the possible pitfalls might be, or what the successfully completed project will look like, will result in failure very quickly.

Each team member must know:

- What the goal is
- What his or her role in the completion of that goal is
- How internal or external constraints affect the process

This is why a manager or an informed facilitator (sometimes an outsider, consultant, or even a ranking officer in the organization) must lay out the vision and objective of the group early on. In addition, this facilitator or "germinator" should be responsible for ensuring that each team member understands the capability and expected contribution of every other team member. Highly productive teams have "buy in" or commitment to the value of the goal of the team and to the value of the contribution of team members.

Team members should also have knowledge of:

- Possible obstacles to the success of the project and resources available to overcome these obstacles
- External factors affecting the business they are in, such as materials availability, or competitors' innovations
- Internal constraints imposed by budgets, personnel, processes, and policies

With these conditions and their effects on the outcome clearly understood, teams are equipped to be proactive in heading off problems. Depriving project team members of valuable knowledge is counterproductive. Ensuring that everyone is well-informed contributes dramatically to success.

2.2 Skills

project-task-related skill skills related to the tasks needing to be accomplished

interpersonal relationship skill skills related to dealing with the people necessary to accomplish the task

Skills can be divided into two major categories: technical **(project-task-related skill)** and group harmonizing **(interpersonal relationship skill).** Ideally, a project manager is able to select a group of people for their specific and complementary skills related to the needs of the project. Not all project managers do this well. Like other managers, sometimes project managers will choose members based only on technical qualifications, disregarding people skills. Others include only those with whom they enjoy working. Whereas there is something to be said for being with people you like, a demanding situation ultimately requires a pooling of skills for success.

Just because a group gets along well does not necessarily mean they will be productive. Although chemistry (see section below on intimacy) plays a part in the level of a team's success, chemistry alone is not enough when a skill gap occurs. The needs of the task—not personal preferences—should dictate the technical skill makeup of the team.

group harmonizing skill the ability to help maintain the relationship aspect of the team

The second skill category, **group harmonizing skill,** is the ability to help maintain the relationship aspect of the team. Interpersonal skill at the level required for effective teams must be learned, as workplace relationships have to be handled differently from personal relationships outside work. Technical expertise and interpersonal skill rarely occur at the same levels in the same person.

However, as we are moving to teams and group decision-making structures in companies, high-level skills in communication, conflict management, group problem solving and peer relationships are becoming priorities. Very little in the technical expert's education prepares him or her for this. Many colleges and universities have minimal or no communication skill mandates for their technical graduates, and thus, these specialists are often less expert in the relational aspects. The answer to this problem should be obvious: training. Engineers (even Ph.D. level) and many other types of technical experts can be very receptive to training in this area and actually quick to learn the skills. However, it is unrealistic to expect your project team to come to you well-equipped to handle difficult interpersonal situations effectively, especially when the pressure is on.

As project manager, determine what your team members might need in the way of orientation or coaching to ensure the best possible team interactions. The following Tool Box Tips list many of the team skills needed for constructive group interactions.

Team Skills Requiring Training

Goal setting
Planning
Conflict resolution
Facilitation
Problem solving
Peer review
Offering feedback
Leadership in teams
Supportive communication

As a concluding note on this topic of skills, it is helpful if the team is made up of members with skills that are complementary with little or no duplication, but with some overlap. Having too many people with the same skill can invite comparisons and competition. On the other hand, if members don't understand any elements of the other member's jobs, serious problems can result. Your people have to need each other's expertise, but they also have to be able to support each others' efforts as well. The project manager must maneuver these diverse skill sets into a profitable and successful result.

■ ■ ■

"Now before we cross this rope bridge, we have to teach you a few things and explain how each of you is involved in this," the instructor began. "I will show you how to grab the guide ropes and to place your feet on the bridge itself. Do all of you have rubber-soled shoes: tennis or running shoes or hiking boots?"

"I have shoes and gloves and all that," Yury scowled, "but I have no desire to cross that ravine on a rope and like a fool."

"Look Yury," Jaime began, "this is new for me too, but we all need to make a stretch every now and then; do something risky."

The instructor continued, "Jerry and Tom, I'd like you two to anchor the lines at this end for each person to start off." She showed them how to hold the lines and steady a team member at the same time.

"Look, I know how to cross one of these things. Can't I go first?" Jerry questioned, a little miffed that he didn't get to show off what he could do.

"Jerry , that's precisely why you're needed at the beginning. What you know is more helpful to your teammates in getting each one started off right," the instructor responded. Jerry grumbled a little, but moved into position opposite Tom. "I'll go to the other side to help you at that end. Who'll go first?"

"I guess since I've opened my big mouth, I'll have to," Jaime volunteered, approaching the start. He had a rough time finding his balance on the rope, and Jerry and Tom had to work quickly to keep Jaime upright. Finally, he started across.

■ ■ ■

2.3 Attitude

How many times have you heard the phrase, "Attitude is everything"? Knowledge and skill are just not sufficient by themselves to produce a successful team.

To be motivated to work together, team members must have the attitude that:

- The goal of the team is in the best interest of the company (and ultimately their own professional well-being as a result)
- The project is indeed doable with the skills and materials available
- Each team member needs and respects every other team member's ability to contribute

facilitator team leader, responsible for nurturing team's positive attitude

The team leader or **facilitator** is responsible for nurturing this attitude set. If employees believe they are working on a project that is foolish, or they will not be able to complete the project with the resources allotted, then they will not commit. Or, if the team members feel that others of the team lack skill or integrity in meeting deadlines and production exigencies, then they will not commit. The team leader or facilitator (and this person can be appointed or can emerge naturally within the group) must accept responsibility for setting the stage appropriately for a positive attitude toward the team's project.

Attitude also plays an important role in maintaining team closeness and cooperativeness in the planning or problem-solving meetings. If every team member has a constructive, solutions-oriented attitude, then planning sessions will be creative and productive. Those on the team with bad attitudes (we'll refer to them as "toxic") can truly poison the atmosphere or spirit with which the group operates. Subsequently, the productivity of even the best teams will be affected.

Finally, the attitude that team members have towards the whole idea of groups will have an effect on the team's productivity. In American culture we honor the individual: in sports, music, even politics and the arts. When was the last time you heard, "Oh, wasn't he great in his contribution to the team? You could hardly tell where his efforts ended and the others' began?" Not in this society. Other cultures have varying approaches to cooperation in their traditions and value system. Many Asians, for example, will relate harmony, respect, and mutual achievement as being more important than singular, outstanding achievement. (See Chapter 6, Diversity)

Also, some group members may prefer to work alone and think teams are a waste of time. These people must be made to understand the importance of the roles of the other team members in their success. Otherwise, their "loner" attitude will keep them from sharing or seeking important information.

2.4 Intimacy

"Oh, no! We're not going to hug now are we?" Jerry moaned as the subject of intimacy in teams came up. The group was taking a lunch break after training in the woods all morning.

"No, Jerry, but you've been in this business a long time, haven't you?" Ralph asked. "And you've been on some successful and some unsuccessful teams, I'll bet."

Jerry answered cautiously, "Yes, I have."

Ralph pushed further, "What was it like working on those successful teams?"

"Well, we got the job done on schedule and in budget," he answered somewhat warily.

Ralph continued, "No, not how did it turn out? What was it like?"

"We worked hard, and played hard. We hung out together, sometimes we went out for a beer after work."

"And did you like the folks you worked with on the project? Did you trust them and value their ideas?"

"Yeah, yeah, what're you getting at?" Jerry began to fidget a bit.

"Jerry, and the rest of you, I hope you see that a kind of bonding occurs with people who respect each other and enjoy working together. They share confidences, happiness, sadness, and know they will be accepted. They support each other, press conflicts until they are resolved, and choose to spend time together even when work doesn't demand it." Ralph said, surveying the group.

"You know, it's funny," Tom spoke up, looking a little sheepish. "I'm beginning to understand this woods training thing. By forcing us into situations where we have to depend on each other, we're getting to know each other more. I remember Hilda saying her mother fell while hiking and broke a leg, and that made her nervous about the climb. Jaime is afraid of small places, but he's a good man on an anchor rope. Jerry's gruff, but I'd sure want him in my corner in a pinch. Ragdeesh can figure out how to engineer a piece of equipment out of a pocket knife and twine if needed. Yury complains about being old, but he outpulled me on the hoist." He stopped and looked at the group, then at the instructor. "Am I close here?"

She smiled at him and shook his hand, "Congratulations. Now you're getting it."

Tom looked a little surprised, but recovered quickly. "Thanks."

The others nodded and smiled warmly, despite their fatigue.

■ ■ ■

High-stress situations, such as wars and natural disasters, create close relationships that can bond people for life. So, why would it be such a stretch to assume that the day-in and day-out pressure of working in today's fast-paced companies, along with the long hours and the mutual understanding that grows out of solid working relationships, might lead to deeper bonds than those of just casual acquaintances? However, when groups do not develop personal connections in addition to the professional relationship, they rarely reach the highest levels of achievement .

Two interesting benefits of teams relate to this* intimacy *idea:

- Increased employee loyalty
- Higher satisfaction with work

intimacy
personal connections

Workers in this rapidly changing time are feeling the loss of workplace relationships. With the instability of their situations, they find no reason to be loyal to a company that can't possibly (realistically) be loyal to the employee. In addition, the place where a person spends most of the waking hours of the day can be desolate if the employee feels disconnected from what is going on. Thus, teams provide a natural and, actually, a positive substitute for the "caring" company. Team members become the reason people enjoy their work.

The following anecdote points to the value of intimacy. For 18 years, a family friend worked as a quality control specialist for a cigarette company. Translated, that means she picked flawed or bad cigarettes off a conveyor belt, all day, every day. After 18 years, she became the supervisor of the people who picked cigarettes off the conveyor belt, all day, every day. When asked how she liked her work, she replied, "Oh, I love my job . . . look forward to it every day. My group is the best in the plant; there isn't anything we wouldn't do for each other. They're like my family." It's easy to see how team relationships can fill a very important need people have for meaningful affiliations in their place of work.

There can be dangers, though, in this closeness that develops. This intimacy can begin to take the place of other relationships outside work that each of us needs to balance our lives. When the time at work becomes more satisfying than the time at home, serious complications can develop. I have seen companies where the **burnout rate** was 50% or better (people quitting and experiencing illness due to stress and overwork), and the divorce rate was higher than the national average. But in these companies the workers expressed high satisfaction with the workplace relationships and often chose to stay at work long hours rather than to go home—including weekends and holidays.

burnout rate the rate of people who quit or experience illness as a result of stress or overwork

Finally, the obvious problem can occur. When people work closely together, like and respect each other, and have everything in common, chemistry can take over and personal relationships evolve and move outside work. As long as these relationships are going well, everything may progress still. But when things go sour, the fallout with the team is potentially disastrous.

2.5 Supportive Organizational Climate

For teams to perform successfully, management must remove all organizational barriers and demonstrate through actions continued support for the team structure and autonomy. To call a group a team, and then not fund training or provide meeting rooms or authorize communication systems, sends the negative message that teams don't really count there.

Barriers come in all shapes and disguises, and the clever project manager learns to ferret them out and eliminate them before they sabotage a good team.

These barriers are:

- Inadequate release time
- Territorial behavior
- Lack of funding for training and support systems
- Lack of guidance or upper management direction

One barrier is time commitments to multiple projects or functional areas. If an employee from the materials area is assigned to a project, yet she is still held accountable for all her regular departmental responsibilities, she will not be a committed team member, regardless of her attitude or intent. She simply will not have the time. In addition, her yearly salary review will probably be done by the manager in her functional area, so that's where her employment accountabilities will necessarily lie—if, of course, she wants to keep her job.

Territoriality is another barrier that is evident, especially in organizations that are transitioning from hierarchical structures to team structures. To keep from being another casualty in the downsizing tidal wave, the few managers left may try to micromanage or poke their noses in every team member's job. They are trying to appear important or necessary, to justify their place on the payroll list. The very nature of teams demands that the group be allowed to direct itself, at least in most of the areas for which it is accountable. And a controlling manager will eventually destroy the building success within the team by interfering.

territoriality protecting one's own territory, often to the point of being too controlling and detrimental to team success

Other barriers include lack of money for training and communications systems support. In addition, lack of guidance in the early stages of team formation or the absences of a "champion" for the team's task itself will translate into lack of organizational support and ultimately failure for the team. Ways organizations can support teams include:

- Designate a ranking person to "kick off" and mentor the team in the early stages.
- Provide funding for and set a value on training.
- Facilitate group gatherings with availability of meeting rooms and a budget for food functions for the team.
- Funnel critical strategic information to the team to assist them in their planning.
- Release and/or assign authority for decision making as much as possible to the team.
- Be aware of the achievements of the team and celebrate them.

3.0 Constructing the Team

Given all the requirements for a solid team, it should become painfully obvious why so many teams ultimately fail: too little preparation, training, information, commitment, support, or all the above. Thus, the term "construction" when applied to teams makes sense. Without the necessary materials, tools, labor, and plans, a contracted building becomes an unidentifiable heap. An investment in company time, money, and energy as well as a willingness to guide teams through the learning process, is the only way companies can expect a solid productivity (translated: profit) return on its teams. In short, you as a project manager cannot assemble a group of people, call them a team, then tell them to go forward and from that day forth act like a team, and realistically expect an autonomous, fully integrated, smooth-running team to emerge magically. But, sadly, too many companies do just this.

Thus, project managers will not always find support within their companies for the time and training it takes to develop teams properly. Team construction responsibility falls to the project manager, who must either secure training and support systems or provide them personally.

The steps in construction follow:

1. Carefully analyze the task and determine both the skill set and work styles required for a complementary and synergistic mix.
2. Indoctrinate each team member in the vision and goals of the team as well as the expected contribution of each.
3. Provide the necessary skill training and process tools (software, information systems, communication protocols, etc.).
4. Guide the team through initial formation stages including rules and operating guidelines development as well as role and task definition for each member.
5. Monitor progress to ensure continued team cohesiveness and movement toward goals. (This is not as important in more mature teams as in newer teams.)
6. Note and celebrate with the team successes along the way.
7. At the time of dissolution (project end), help team members transition out of old team relationships and into new ones.

The flow diagram shown in Figure 5–4 will guide this discussion.

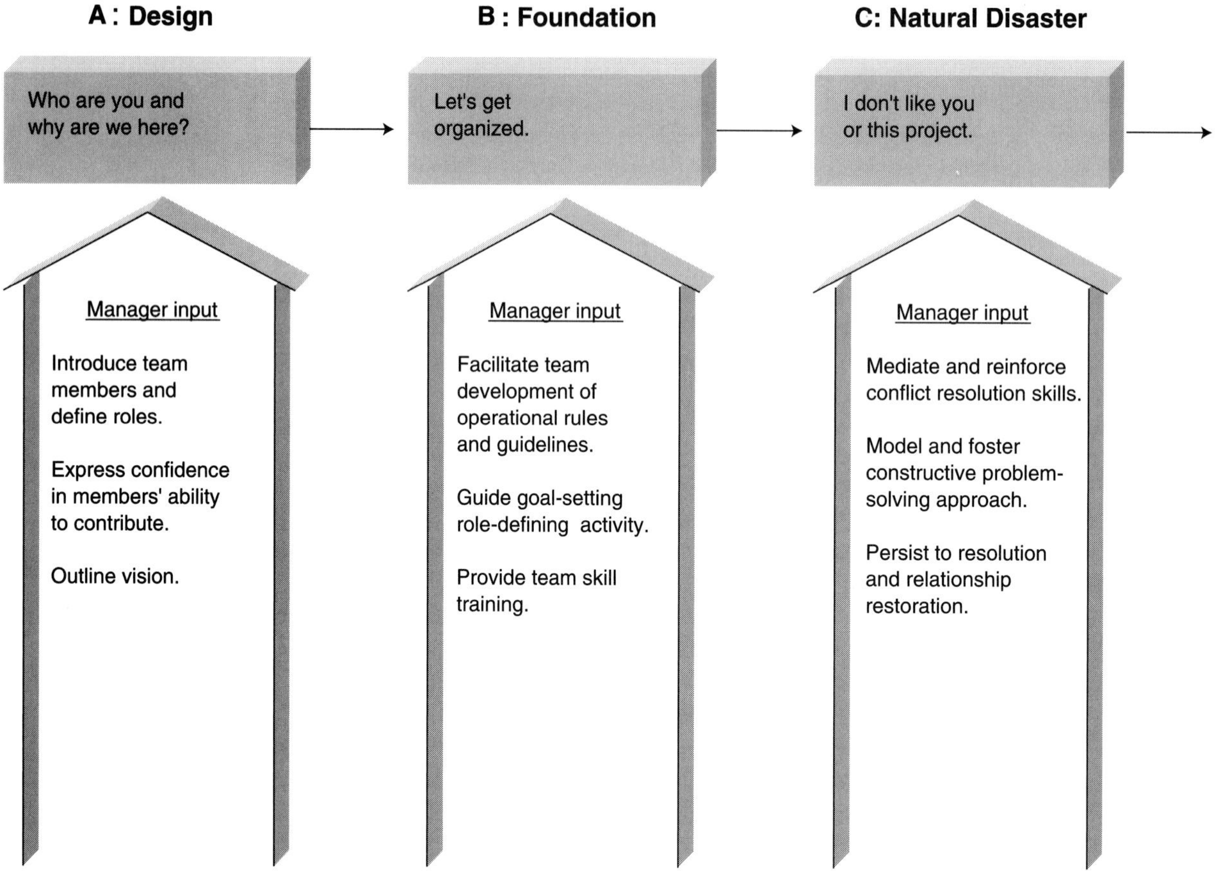

A: Design

Who are you and why are we here?

Manager input

Introduce team members and define roles.

Express confidence in members' ability to contribute.

Outline vision.

B: Foundation

Let's get organized.

Manager input

Facilitate team development of operational rules and guidelines.

Guide goal-setting role-defining activity.

Provide team skill training.

C: Natural Disaster

I don't like you or this project.

Manager input

Mediate and reinforce conflict resolution skills.

Model and foster constructive problem-solving approach.

Persist to resolution and relationship restoration.

Figure 5–4
The stages of team construction (continued on next page)

3.1 Level A—The Design

Project managers who can select and construct teams that are effective and that run smoothly are highly valued in industry. The following guidelines for Level A and team member selection will help to improve your chances for a successful project team.

1. Clearly analyze the task and develop accurate job descriptions and human resource needs.
2. Choose project team members on the basis of skills, professional team attributes, and problem-solving ability. If everyone on your team approaches tasks and problems the same way, though, then you need to make some changes to form a more diverse group.
3. Introduce team members to the vision of the project and to each other; express confidence in each member's expected contribution. Acquaint members with each others' knowledge and operating style preferences.

In the case of an existing group that you have been assigned to convert into a team, the process at this stage is a little different, but not much. In an existing group relationships have already been established, good and bad. If there are dysfunctional relationships, negative experiences, and bad history, starting as if this were a new group can sometimes disconnect from past problems. But you as the project manager must take a strong role in this, and finding an emergent leader (one from within the group) that can support you can be a lifesaver. You may be the "new kid" coming into their "neighborhood."

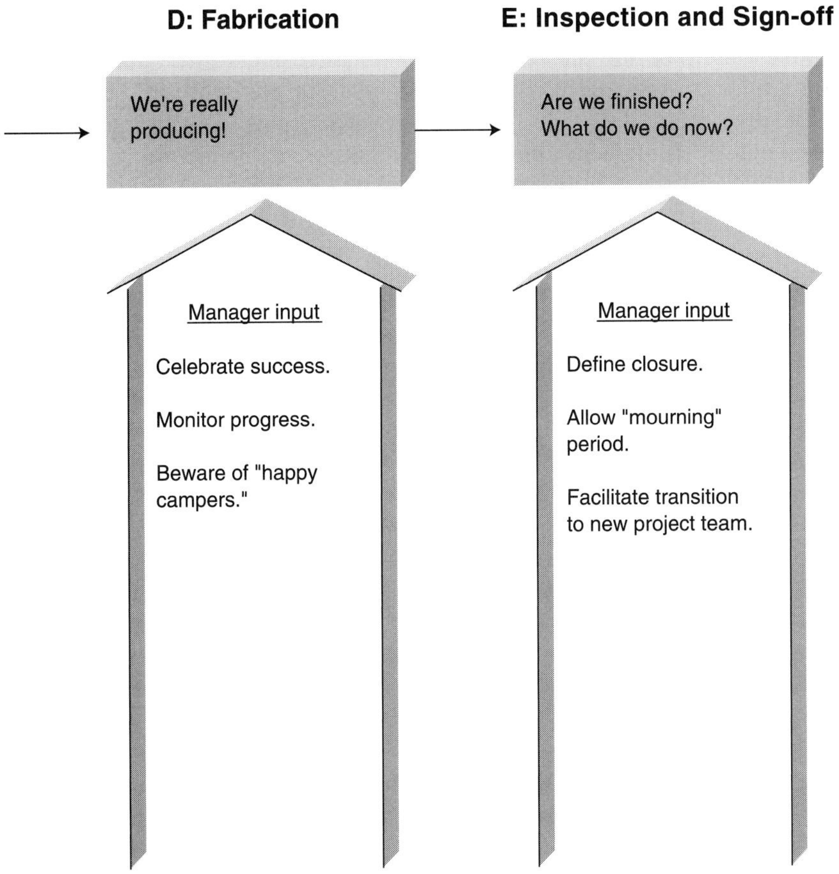

At this stage, or actually at any stage along the project's path, outside people may also be assigned, not necessarily selected by you, creating similar problems. For example, a project manager might say, "I need a software engineer who can program in C++." This request may be answered by someone in-house, unknown to the project manager, or by a contractor brought in just for the project. In either case there was little or no choice or selection involved. A situation like this is quite common, and requires even more careful handling to ensure commitment and team orientation.

3.2 Level B—The Foundation

Successful teams take the time in the early stages of their endeavors to lay groundwork important to the team's ability to operate smoothly under many different conditions.

It's amazing how important a discussion of "what do we do if a member stops coming to meetings?" is to ironing out a lot of attitude and commitment issues. And similarly, the group's consensus placed on a team goal statement creates a firmer commitment to that goal. Other issues, such as how conflict will be handled, what approaches to communication will be used (e.g. check E-mail daily or use voice mail meetings, or even, do not swear at meetings) and what constitutes the need for an emergency meeting, are worked through prior to their occurrence. The more the project manager can refrain from meddling too much in this process, other than to ensure it actually occurs, the higher the level of ownership each team member will have. Some sources recommend the generation of a team "constitution," a sort of "rules to live by" document that can be evoked when problems occur—and they will.

At this stage the team really doesn't have any authority within the company structure—this should, and hopefully will, come later. Therefore, the manager will have to authorize money for training. As much as possible, though, the team should be encouraged to determine and voice its own needs. Several years ago Hewlett-Packard wanted to make some changes in its customer service structure and processes. Instead of bringing in an outsider to assess the needs and make recommendations, H-P selected an internal team to do just that. Although the analysis and subsequent report took some time, the teams that grew out of that internally driven process became some of the better-performing in the company.

Reverse engineering is the process of looking at an end result and backtracking through the steps necessary to achieve that result. In this manner many companies have found a better way to develop products, build structures, and design service processes. For existing groups that you want to reshape into working teams, you will find this process of working backwards profitable, especially where there is a stubborn adherence to doing it the way its always been done.

3.3 Level C—The Natural Disaster

Not unlike any relationship, eventually a team hits a "wall" that signals the end of "let's all be nice." In other words, real loyalty has not developed yet, nor have mutual respect and trust among team members. This level may be characterized by any of the following symptoms exhibited by team members:

- Information withholding, territoriality, unwillingness to share ideas
- Sniping or even open clashes during meetings
- Silence, sullenness, grumbling and negativity
- Inability to reach agreement on important issues
- Lack of enthusiasm in problem-solving sessions
- Marked decrease in productivity

Just as a relationship may reach a point where the old "contract" won't work anymore, so does a team. For the members of a group to move from "making nice" to the gut-level bonds seen in the best teams, they have to somehow work through this stage. It is called the "natural disaster" because it *naturally* happens in close groups. Project managers who expect it as a normal stage in the construction process can guide the group through it to the next level.

Project managers who enter into an existing group may find that this is the stage they have fallen into. Sometimes it is futile to try to repair all the old damage and cover the festering wounds of the past. However, the manager should make attempts at fair resolution of old ills, emphasizing that they can be used as springboards to the new relationships. Some companies have even brought in psychologists to conduct a sort of group therapy forgiveness session to allow group members to lay down old resentments and move on.

Conflict management, problem solving, and constructive communication skills, if well-established, can help to resolve the skirmishes that can result in this level. The project manager must, however, reaffirm the group goals, assist in conflict resolution, and model solutions-oriented behavior. Groups who do work their way through this problematic level realize a higher level of understanding, communication, and commitment. Until groups learn that they can have conflict and, importantly, see those conflicts through to a positive resolution for each member, they do not experience the highest level of trust and mutual support. This is not to say that every group must have conflict, but when it does occur, constructive outcomes are possible.

3.4 Level D—The Fabrication

Fully integrated, autonomous teams are the project manager's dream, so all the hard work of construction does have this as its rewards. Team members at this stage are working together towards the goals originally set, and maybe a few more that the group has developed along the way. The project manager should continue to monitor progress, but on a more occasional basis, as the group becomes mature in regulating itself. Regular celebrations of success in both visibly dramatic ways and in subtle "thank you's" should be part of the project manager's operating style for this level.

It is possible, however, for highly bonded teams who have now had some success to reach a stage of mutual admiration at the expense of critical thinking and continuous improvement. Although intimacy is a desirable element to contribute to team productivity, there are dangers. When everyone begins to like and respect each other, "the happy–camper syndrome" sets in. No one challenges ideas or decisions; there is so much support, that constructive criticism or healthy conflict never occurs. In these cases critical thinking and creativity give way to, "I like your idea," a pattern of thought known as **groupthink** (Janis, 1972).

groupthink a pattern of thought among group members characterized by mutual admiration at the expense of critical thinking and continuous improvement

A happy group is not necessarily a productive group; the relationships may become so satisfying that the tasks take a backseat. When this happens, productivity actually drops. Therefore, someone must have responsibility for monitoring the results of the group's efforts and must step in when things become a little "too happy." To do so, the project manager may have to change the "hands-off" approach used prior to this point. Appointing a devil's advocate or bringing in an outside creativity consultant can stir things up a bit.

Reminding the group about the need for continuous improvement can be healthy. One company reported that their quality groups had reduced error in their production area to less than .01%. That having been accomplished, the group didn't know why they needed to meet anymore. Here is where the vision failed; it was too short-sighted. There were cost issues with waste that could be addressed, personnel skill shortages that could be solved, and communication foul-ups with other departments that could be remedied; all were being overlooked since the "goal" had been met.

Project managers must be alert to productivity variations in even the best teams. As many of us experience in our own lives, we become complacent and cease to seek out growth opportunities when we have become good at something. Teams are no different.

3.5 Level E—The Inspection and Sign-Off

This stage is called "inspection" rather than "completion" because construction of any type (including the process of developing this book, by the way) is not truly complete until the one who is paying for the project approves it. When this happens, the highly committed, motivated, and bonded group of people who brought the project to fruition are suddenly out of a job. That is not to say they are unemployed, although in the case of temporary employees, this might be true. The project manager should understand, however, that they are going to experience some kind of loss reaction, at least in the short term.

This is why "inspection" is such a good name for this stage. By allowing the team to inspect its work in finished form—the installation at the customer's site, the finished system with all parts in place, the building, or the highway—and affirming the successful completion of the task, the project manager can hasten all the team to more readily "let go" and move to the next task.

prototype the original model or first working form of a new construction design or type

buy-in commitment to a project

One operations manager who worked for a car manufacturer said they had such a problem with the design team not wanting to release their "baby" to the production people that they finally initiated a "divorce ceremony" of sorts. The **prototype** was brought out and officially handed over to the production group who promptly moved it to another site for disassembly and retooling for production. Design said their "goodbyes" and turned their attention to the next project.

Teams sometimes have so much **buy-in** or commitment to their projects that they have a hard time closing the book. Thus, a passage ceremony, to mark the end of one journey and the beginning of the next, will help team members mourn, if needed, and certainly separate, from what they have done for so long. In addition, it will release them to move on and be committed to their new team project and new team members.

This step is often overlooked by project managers, especially in fast-paced environments that demand instant shifting of gears and require commitment to multiple projects at once. Helping employees stay focused is critical to maintaining productivity. It is easy for project team members to become lost in the melee of the many different pulls on their time and commitment. Project managers must be proactive in guiding them back onto their priorities track.

Chapter Summary

Downsizing and the need for tighter, more efficiently run organizations has spawned the highly adaptive organizational structures that now include teams. Successful teams have members who support the vision, share responsibility, respond to the environment and demonstrate skills in task and group maintenance. The basic elements of successful teams are: knowledge, skill, attitude, intimacy, and a supportive organizational culture.

Teams do not occur naturally (outside sports) for the most part, except in times of extreme duress or danger, so a construction process is necessary to build a solid and fully integrated team under less threatening conditions. The levels of construction must be guided, or at least facilitated by a leader—from management in the initial stages, from within the team itself in later stages. The levels are: design (selection and introduction of vision), foundation (rules and goals), natural disaster (conflict and productivity crashes), fabrication (integration and performance), inspection, and sign-off (affirmation and closure).

Chapter Questions

1. Why have so many American companies begun the move to team structures?
2. List four characteristics of a productive team.
3. Why is the word "construct" used to describe how effective teams are made?
4. What happens at Level C—Natural Disaster? List two possible outcomes of that level.
5. The term "dysfunctional family" has been used to define teams whose relationships have failed. Relate this term to the role of intimacy in team interaction.

6. Why do threats from competitors, natural disasters, and wars make for cohesive teams in the short term? What happens, do you think, to this cohesiveness when the threat is over? Why is that?
7. What are some ways a manager might turn a group that has already been working together with moderate success into a highly productive team? Be as creative as possible with your suggested actions.
8. Why is it helpful to understand the style and personality implications of other team members?

Project Challenge: Applying What You Know

A. Complete the following exercise in groups of four to five. As you complete the exercise, your group should:

1. Consider the problem and its implications from several different perspectives.
2. Come up with many possible solutions, especially creative or out-of-the-ordinary solutions.
3. Select the most workable solutions and make a plan for their implementation, including details.

Instructions: Analyze the following situations and suggest *three* courses of action the senior manager might take to increase productivity. Be aware that firing people is difficult to do these days, and technically knowledgeable people are hard to replace. However, toxic team members can hamper productivity. Weigh your alternatives carefully. Try to come up with some creative approaches to this complex problem.

Ben Vanosch is a consultant who has been called in to work with a group of customer service specialists in a computer re-manufacturing company. The success of the company depends on both meeting the design needs of the customer and also doing so in a timely way. An important customer has become concerned about the process involved in getting out its highly complex and large-dollar order and has asked to see a written version of the plan for developing the custom hardware it needs.

On the company side, the project is dangerously behind, it appears, but no one seems to know for sure because none of the heads of each of the different system divisions has told the other when his part of the system will be ready. Ben discovers that this process is primarily a hand-off situation: one group finishes its part, then hands it off to the other group. He determines that creating a team of all parties in the process will speed up the production and also allow them to write up the process for the customer. At this point, no one is working together.

The first meeting is a disaster. Each manager blames the other manager for the delays. The situation quickly erupts into a yelling and swearing match. No work is accomplished, and two people walk out of the meeting. Ben's report to the senior manager profiles of the individuals involved:

Arnold, a 55-year-old retired military, is of the old school: process, rules, and "do it by the book." He is white, conservative, and uncomfortable working with people of other cultures and with women in management.

Hajid is 30, from India, highly intelligent, trained in British schools, has a good technical understanding of the process, and offends people every time he talks to them in his disdainful manner.

Linda is a 25-year-old-design engineer, recently graduated with a technical masters and very knowledgeable in her area. In the meeting she vacillates between pushy and sullen. She swears when angry.

Aaron is the sales rep who works with the account. He has some basic understanding of the production and design process, but doesn't have technical training. His rapport with the customer won the account, and he is very concerned about the unresponsiveness of these people in his company to the customer. All the others think Aaron is an idiot because he's not technical. He thinks they are not interested in the welfare of the company and are trying to sabotage the account.

These people are going to have to work together to become a team if for no other reason than to provide documentation of the process that the customer is demanding. Since a $1.5 million account is involved, Ben has been called in to assist.

He reports, "These people have extremely poor communication skills. They seem unaware of professional decorum and unmotivated to resolve anything—they just seem to point fingers at the others. All seem to know plenty about their own areas but almost nothing about the other areas."

Your task as analyst is to look at what can happen if this group doesn't get together, as well as to define a vision and action plan for a successful team. Write down word-for-word what you would say at the first meeting you would hold with these people. List any actions you would take and provide details on what would be required to accomplish this action. For example, if you decided to fire Arnold, find out what the implications of firing someone over 50 would be, or if you want to replace Linda, what would it cost to locate a masters-level computer design engineer?

Check with the Yellow Pages of the phone book for consultants who work with team training and get prices of different team-building programs. Find out also what professional coaching for any of the individuals would cost. You might look for a local chapter of the American Society for Training and Development, which should have a listing of professional trainers and coaches as well as consultants in your town.

B. Many types of people make up a team. Some like plans, logical steps, and definition while others like to be more free to manage things in their own way. Some are open and talkative while others are quiet. In each group are also strategic types who see the larger goals or purpose, and then there are operations types who take care of the details. Some adhere to a regular schedule, whereas others work in fits and spurts. A good tool for determining what you bring to a team style-wise is the Meyers-Briggs Type Indicator (copyrighted material published by Consulting Psychologists Press), which is available at most colleges, in either the counseling department or career placement. In companies, the human resources department can usually offer this assessment to you. An interesting web site that gives some additional guidelines on assessing your types is *www.teamtechnology.co.uk/tt/h-article/mb-simpl.* After you have determined some things about your own type, explain here why having one of each type in a team might make it more productive than some other random grouping of people.

Interview with an Expert

Renee Walkup, *consultant, seminar leader with SalesPeak, co-author of* No One Succeeds Alone: Success is a Team Effort *(James and Brookfield, publishers) www. salespeak.com*

Question: How is project management connected to sales, which is your business?
Walkup: That's easy. Take a company that sells office furniture-maybe chairs, a desk or table or four or five in each sale. Then, someone closes a contract for an entire building or even a multi-location set-up by a client, and all of a sudden, you have a project, sometimes a big, very complicated one. They might have to coordinate delivery and installations of everything from technology to wall panels, furniture and telecommunications systems.
Expertise is required in interior office design, traffic flow, many different areas.
Question: Where does the team come in?
Walkup: Generally one or two salespeople secure the contract; then sometimes they will hand over the filling of the order to an internal team. Of course, they tell the team what the customer wants.
Question: How well does this work?
Walkup: It's just like any other team situation; depends on whether all the important parties are in on the team planning. If the salesperson, who was the contact with the customer, doesn't write the specs in enough detail, and the operations team isn't in direct communication with the customer, then disaster can happen easily. The best teams involve the customer who contracts for a product or service, to ensure what was promised was indeed delivered. That ultimately is reflected as customer service.
Question: How do you put together a good team?
Walkup: I've had good success with some personality inventories where people leam more about their own operating style, and about what they can expect from other and how to work better with other types of people who are motivated differently. Obviously, you wouldn't pick a team just on personalities, but when I'm called in to work with a team gone bad, differences in approach do seem to be big contributors to the problem.
Question: Like what?
Walkup: The really risk-averse people might want to be more careful and gather as much information or testing as they possibly can. Where others take the attitude of "do it and ask forgiveness later." Those attitudes clash with each other, and until both sides learn the value of the others' views, conflict will probably continue. Some people like to lead and might resent another leader—competition, I guess. But at different times different people in the team need to lead, depending on what the situation is.
Question: What problems do you see in teams that the project manager can prevent?
Walkup: A lot has to do with communication—does everyone communicate enough? Does the project manager? Do people communicate the right things? For example, in reporting the person responsible for the end result would rather hear the answer to "how much is needed to complete" than "how much completed so far." Different personalities communicate different ways—some in writing. some need to be on-site "see it to believe it": some need information confirmed, from more than one source before they buy-in. The project manager has to step away from their own ego or role and involve other team members, to focus on the individual strengths within the team. Better communicators should communicate, some more detail oriented people should handle details. The strong project manager will recognize talents and styles in people and direct them to tasks more consistent with their style.

CHAPTER 6

DIVERSITY

CHAPTER PREVIEW

THE PROJECT MANAGEMENT SEMINAR: SESSION 6

Ralph George opened the session by introducing a guest instructor. "Folks, if there's anything I've learned as a corporate trainer, it's when to defer to an expert. I'd like you to meet Susan Chou, a diversity consultant and retired professor."

The group surveyed the facilitator for the day, a diminutive woman with graying black hair and Asian features. The brief smile she gave them on greeting disappeared almost as she began to speak. "In case any one is wondering what my qualifications are for leading this session today," she said curtly, "I'm a vertically challenged, middle-aged Chinese-American woman. Any questions?" Her face remained expressionless, bordering on rigid. Jerry rolled his eyes and muttered under his breath. Yury frowned. Hilda, however, regarded the woman and sat patiently, as if waiting to hear more. Suddenly, the instructor smiled. "Was that stereotype good enough for you? The inscrutable Chinese person? Obviously over 50, female, and short! Isn't that what you expected?"

Realizing they had been caught in their own biases, most of the group laughed. Chou started out with a card game. She divided the group into two tables, and gave each table a deck of cards and a set of rules. Cautioning them not to speak, she gave the trainees several minutes to become familiar with the rules of play, running them through 3 or 4 practice hands. "Okay, now rotate—one from this table exchange with one from table B. Begin play." Very soon into each game disgruntled looks and sighs of frustration could be heard. After a few minutes she stopped play.

"Did you get it? Each table had different rules. When we switched, one person at each table was playing with a different set of expectations of what it took to win." She paused to let the explanation soak in. "That's what your employees from outside cultures feel like in your company and on your teams."

Everyone nodded.

- What's this diversity stuff?
- Why should I care?
- Why are those people so weird?

- They need to learn to adapt to us.
- We're hiring from everywhere; how can I know about all of them?

In the last 10 years, just as the cultural makeup of American society has changed, the workforce has also changed. Project managers are facing, and will continue to face, more and more diversity in the work population. This chapter is a guide for managers who need greater understanding and skill to meet the challenges of an increasingly diverse and complex workforce today.

Areas of concentration for this discussion include:

- **Multicultural teams**
- **The danger of assumptions**
- **Potential issues in diverse work teams**
- **Strengths of alternative views**
- **Guidelines for a constructive diversity climate**

1.0 Multicultural Teams

heterogeneous culture a culture in which people from many different nations and backgrounds have come together

culture a set of consistent beliefs, attitudes, and behaviors within a group

homogeneous culture a culture in which most of the population is made up of people from the same ethnic group

Waves of immigrants over this country's history and the contributions made by groups, such as African Americans in the farm economies and Chinese in the building of railroads, have made the United States a **heterogeneous culture.** The term **culture** means a set of consistent beliefs, attitudes, and behaviors within a group. Many different and diverse groups have created a complicated set of written and unwritten rules for interacting with others. The population of the United States continues to change, and this change is reflected in the workforce. Over the next 10 years it is estimated that the bulk of new entrants into the American workforce will be *not* American-born white males; more than half will be minorities and women (Bloch, 1994).

A **homogeneous culture,** on the other hand, is one in which the population is made up largely of people from the same ethnic and racial group with customs and values that are part of long-held and accepted traditions. The Japanese culture, for example, is seen as highly homogeneous. Curiously enough, however, there are many ethnic groups within the population of Japan, but the cultural orientation towards conformity makes them appear nearly the same in their outwardly observable social behaviors.

Since the American culture is already heterogeneous, why is diversity a topic of concern and discussion? The first reason is power. Power in the United States has traditionally been held by white, upper middle-class males of western European descent, and of primarily Protestant faith. Thus, language, religion, holidays, value systems, and customs have been imposed or legislated based on this background. However, there has been a variety of changes, ranging from the social revolutions of the sixties and the ensuing affirmative action mandates, to the high demand for sophisticated technical expertise found to be in short supply within American shores, that make work today a very different place.

In our attitudes about the infusion of diverse cultures into the American workplace, however, we have been through many stages historically (Carr-Ruffino, 1996):

- The "melting pot" mindset, in which everyone is supposed to become like everyone else
- The legal approach of affirmative action amidst the prejudice that existed during that time (and the ensuing tokenism that emerged)
- The acceptance of diversity and honoring of differences

All the above attitudes remain in our culture, and each can be found among our employees—of all races and ethnic groups. Now, however, we have come to the era in which managing diversity of all types has become a necessity. The next step in the evolution then becomes:

- The utilization of diversity to create the next level of competitive advantage.

ethnocentricity the belief that one's own culture is the "correct" culture

Although this sounds like a concept that holds great promise—the old "two heads are better than one, especially if they have different viewpoints"—many barriers stand in the way of making this happen. One is **ethnocentricity,** the belief that one's own culture is the "correct" culture, and all others are inferior in some way. "Cultural pride" is in its own way ethnocentrism, and carried to extreme, can become a negative force in human relations. There are groups around the world who do despise each other and refuse to have any interaction at all.

Some people have a negative attitude towards others just because they look different. Though dissimilar looks are disconcerting to some people, for example in the case of a handicapped or racially different person, differences in the way diverse cultures interact in day-to-day activities of work create even more of the problems. Human relations with people of similar background is difficult enough to manage well; adding additional elements of foreign workstyles and communication conventions muddies the situation even further.

You as a project manager are being asked to play a complex game for which there may seem to be too many rules, most of which are unwritten. If you feel overwhelmed at the idea of learning to deal with differences, you might want to ponder the following idea. In a homogeneous culture people of like beliefs and backgrounds are grouped together, so they generally agree on larger issues of values and social rules. Reaching goals and conveying employee responsibilities are more easily done when people agree. And if your cultural value system says that you do not question the authority of the group, then agreement is even more easily reached.

However, what if too much agreement becomes a limiting factor? What if tomorrow's world market leaders grow out of those companies that have successfully harnessed the energy of radically different ideas and the varying talents and approaches that other cultures bring? If this is the case, the synergy created by the multicultural team is the next stage in the evolution of international competitiveness. (See Figure 6–1.)

Figure 6–1
More globally competitive ideas come from culturally diverse teams.

Before this goes too far into a discussion of international diversity, though, many other diverse elements already exist in the workplace including: gender, communication style, sexual preference, size, handicap, motivation, needs, and so on. The list of differences among us is huge without the factors of culture, race, or religion even entering the picture. This chapter focuses on areas where clashes of interpersonal style and work values can create misunderstanding and mistrust. This chapter will in no way delineate in detail the social and communication conventions and needs of every culture group the project manager may meet. It will, instead, show areas where the alert project manager can address differences and foster understanding and cooperation by being aware of potential sources of friction.

attribution the projecting of assumptions about people's needs and/or behavior based on generalizations or conclusions drawn about them

Some friction between people or groups is caused by what psychologists call **attribution**—the projecting of assumptions about people's needs and/or behavior based on generalizations or conclusions drawn about them. Assumptions caused by attribution create a dangerous trap for project managers.

2.0 The Danger of Assumptions

2.1 Communication Problems

Paul Blodgett, a workplace relationship consultant, offers some very good advice to anyone working in a culturally diverse environment. "When there appears to be a communication problem, be sure not to write it off as a diversity issue alone; it may or may not be." He goes on to remind us that communication is a complex process and all sorts of interpersonal elements may enter into the problem (Blodgett, 1998).

Some people are talkative; others are quiet. Some speak clearly; others do not. A few look at the larger issues, while many focus on details. You may recall in the chapter on communication that there is a great deal of variety in the way people process information and the media they prefer. None of these differences go away when diversity also enters the picture. It is important that your work groups agree on certain rules of communication, such as: everyone is expected to give input in meetings; conflict is to be brought out and resolved; problems are to be solved, not hidden; and so on.

The "rules" that "go without saying" for one group can create misunderstanding, because everyone assumes everyone else is operating by the same rules. Thus, a miscommunication is often construed as a deliberate attack, or an assumption is believed to be the truth. Teaching employees to verify meanings in communication is a good plan, regardless of whether the workplace is culturally homogeneous or heterogeneous.

Assumption #1 to avoid If there is a conflict or communication breakdown among employees of different culture groups, don't automatically assume it's a cultural issue.

2.2 Country of Origin

People from different racial or ethnic groups often complain that Americans make assumptions, often incorrectly, about their country of origin. A favorite example about that comes from a student. He was telling the class about his home country of Jamaica and his immigration to the United States. He expressed surprise at the way he was treated in the Florida high school. "When I moved here, I thought I was Jamaican. When I got to school, I found out I was black." Dark-skinned peoples hail from many countries, and each is dismayed when addressed as someone from a different country. And, to add to the confusion, some areas within one country are quite different from others. Swiss people may speak French, Swiss, German, or Italian among others. Irish people may be Protestant or Catholic. A black person from Haiti will speak a different dialect, and maybe a different language, from a black person from St. Thomas.

Another group that experiences similar frustration in interactions with Americans is from the Pacific Rim countries. Martial arts movies have been popular in this country for a long time and have contributed to the assumption that all Asian-looking people are Japanese or Chinese. (See Figure 6–2.) Vietnamese, Laotians, Koreans, and Thais do not feel that they look at all like Japanese or Chinese and are quite disconcerted when lumped together by Westerners who don't notice the differences. Southeast Asia (Indochina) alone is made up of several countries. In fact, among some of the countries in that part of the world, there is still conflict stemming from the past, and those hostilities can be carried over to American soil, or your project, as well.

Figure 6–2
Sometimes it is difficult to determine people's country of origin by their appearance.

In addition, Americans often fail to differentiate among Spanish-speaking people, calling them Mexican or Puerto Rican, depending on what part of the country they are in. Latin countries include not only Mexico and Puerto Rico, but also the countries in Central America, South America, and the West Indies as well as several other colonies—nearly three dozen individual nations in all. Most do speak Spanish—generally a local variation of the more formal language—but all consider themselves distinct and do not like to be referred to incorrectly. Cubans resent being called Puerto Ricans and people from Colombia look very different from people in Mexico, but again, Americans will group them all as "Hispanic," which often appears as a category under "race" in census and other forms. Thus, we come to the second area of assumption that can lead to trouble.

Assumption #2 to avoid Don't automatically attribute characteristics or ethnic labels to someone who looks different from you. In addition, don't assume that just because two people speak a similar language or look similar, that they are culturally the same or even that they share a cultural affinity.

2.3 Language

Language differences are probably obvious when an employee speaks in broken English. What may not be obvious, however, is the depth of misunderstanding that can take place when neither you nor the employee knows the other's language intimately. American English is full of idioms and expressions which, if taken literally, make little sense and can therefore be confusing to those not completely fluent in English. "Cut it out!" and "You're putting me on" are two such expressions.

Communication goes far beyond merely deciphering words in a sequence. Although a Chinese employee or co-worker may learn the words of English, the indirect nature of Chinese discourse does not translate into English on a word-for-word basis. Thus, pauses will occur while the employee is trying to translate before speaking. Americans dislike pauses, so much so that we often step on the ends of each other's sentences. In contrast, the Japanese view a pause in conversation as a time to reflect on what has been said; it is both a show of respect and a signal that ideas are being thought carefully through. The same occurs with American Indians, who tolerate broken English patiently and value silence amid speech.

If English is not a person's first language, misunderstanding may occur, no matter how good the person's command of English seems to be. And, depending on whether the person learned British or American English, pronunciation, some vocabulary and many spellings may be very different. Conversely, second- and third-generation Asian Americans, who speak none of their "native" language, are often spoken to as if they don't understand English.

Assumption #3 to avoid You can't assume that an employee has heard and comprehends all you have said, even if he seems to speak English fluently. Actually, in quite a few cases, you can't be sure that what you heard from the employee is what he or she actually meant. (This seems to be true even for speakers of the same language sometimes.)

2.4 Attitudes Towards Americans

For this next assumption we must revisit the notion of ethnocentrism, which is apparent in citizens of many countries, including the United States. But not everyone in the world aspires to be American or even to be like Americans. Historically, the notion that the American way is somehow desirable, comes, no doubt, from this country's being a society founded and built by immigrants, many of whom came to escape persecution or to build a fortune. Today, however, those who come here might not be representative of their culture group. Individuals who immigrate to the United States may, indeed, aspire to an American lifestyle, but that does not mean others in the native country have the same ambition. There are many Africans, Indians, and Asians, living in the United States, who have sent "home" to find spouses familiar with their own culture of origin. (There is an excellent discussion of the views other cultures hold of Americans in Sherron Kenton and Deborah Valentine's book, *Crosstalk,* Prentice-Hall, 1997.)

Some specific culture clashes will be discussed in the next section, but suffice it to say here that Americans are often seen as brash, arrogant, and disrespectful with people of other cultures. What problem this can present to the project manager is this: fast-paced, high pressure projects require teams whose members are intimate and trusting of each other.

The African or Korean worker who might not want to socialize or be "chummy" with other team members might appear to be disloyal or arrogant to Americans who don't understand the behavior. Actually, you might expect a great deal of loyalty to the project because honor is important to both these groups; you just may not see camaraderie with the other team members. There may be a respectful but clear line of demarcation between work commitment and interpersonal closeness. Or, an employee may be reluctant to communicate because he or she lacks language skill.

Some employees who come from other countries might build a community within the workplace of people of like culture. Although such a group may serve to give them a sense of connectedness and cultural continuity, it can be damaging to relations with the project team. Immigrants who have difficulty with English may begin to immerse themselves more and more into groups of other employees who speak their same language. This fosters mistrust in your team and should be addressed; it also impedes progress with language acclimation.

Assumption #4 to avoid Be careful not to jump to conclusions when the new employee from another country doesn't seem to be interested in becoming one of the group. His or her dedication to the task and commitment to the project may be thorough, but strong cultural differences may make socializing awkward or may seem inappropriate to the newly indoctrinated employee.

Each culture group from each different country will present many potentially problematic issues within your team. However, the project manager can start asking questions that will help improve communication within the team. By building a working knowledge of areas of possible culture clash, the project manager can help ease relations.

Figure 6–3 provides an illustration of how different cultures handle the same process—a salary or performance review, which is a common and necessary practice in business, especially so for a new employee. Different cultures handle this process differently, so your assumptions about its purpose may be different from those of employees from different cultures. The example uses the cultures that seem to have the most divergence from typical American expectations and assumptions: Asian and Middle Eastern (specifically Arab).

PERCEPTION DIFFERENCE #1–PURPOSE OF A REVIEW

U.S.	Arab	Japanese
Develop employee and fairly distribute rewards (money).	Determine placement within a set of possible jobs; provide an opportunity for employee to express loyalty to manager.	Talk about company goals and how employee must fit, to allow employee to develop internal excellence.

PERCEPTION DIFFERENCE #2–PERSON CONDUCTING REVIEW

U.S.	Arab	Japanese
Immediate supervisor	Manager	Mentor

PERCEPTION DIFFERENCE #3–METHOD OF CONDUCTING REVIEW

U.S.	Arab	Japanese
Direct criticisms and affirmations are provided in writing.	Criticism is always subtle, always oral, never written.	Respect is important; criticism is subtle, verbal.

PERCEPTION DIFFERENCE #4–ROLE OF PRAISE

U.S.	Arab	Japanese
Individual praise to show appreciation and to motivate.	Individual praise to show appreciation and to motivate.	Praise for the whole group; it is embrassing to be singled out.

Figure 6–3
Perception Differences among Different Cultures

As is becoming apparent to you by now, language, though generally one of the most obvious differences among groups, is probably only the proverbial tip of the iceberg in workplace relations.

3.0 Potential Issues in Diverse Work Teams

First impressions, as we all know, are a major contributor to our view of a person. How many times have we heard, "Oh yeah, I knew he was right the minute I saw him." We'd like to think that we are not so quick to jump to conclusions about people, but we are. Consequently, a person's manner, carriage, eye contact, and body language in general often determine what we perceive. These perceptions are guided by culture.

We are taught throughout our lives what is okay and not okay in behavior with others. "It's not polite to stare." Or "Don't raise your voice to me." Or "Keep your hand in your lap when eating." All these rules, or "mores," as anthropologists call them, we learn, and begin to expect that others have learned the same rules. Consequently, when we meet someone who violates these rules, we too often assume some sort of aggressive intent or a generalized ignorance.

What follows are several areas that seem to crop up over and over as differences that create uncomfortable relations. The finer points of social behavior regarding meals are purposely omitted here, as there is a great deal of ritual and variety in meal rituals, especially formal, celebratory, or business functions. If you have one of these occasions to attend, in your own country or in a foreign country with those of a different culture, you should research in depth the proper conduct expected. There are many sources on the Internet for information on this topic as well as in books and from private consultants. Some are listed in the sources section at the end of this text.

Some likely areas of misinterpretation are in :

- The way respect is shown
- The way conflict is handled
- The requirements one has for personal space
- The work ethic one holds
- The speed at which business or conversation is conducted

3.1 Respect

Managers often say "I don't trust him; he won't look me in the eye." In some cultures, direct eye contact is considered a challenge to authority and is always avoided with managers and those one respects. In American culture we say, "I can always tell if someone is lying when I look him in the eye." Interestingly enough, women in this country have a difficulty with perceptions about eye contact. Taught to make strong eye contact when dealing with males, as in introductions and meetings, women report that when they do, they are perceived as "coming on" to the men as a flirtation. (See Figure 6–4.)

Figure 6–4
Eye contact or lack thereof has different meanings for different cultures.

Another area where respect becomes an issue is the manner with which one affirms the person in an interaction. Many cultures are very careful not to cause someone to "lose face" or be embarrassed. As one Chinese interviewee explained, "Even if you feel that you could not agree with someone, you would never say that. You would, instead, part company with the phrase, 'that merits thought,'" in order not to openly challenge a belief or idea and possibly embarrass the person. Another way this is demonstrated is in the structure of conversation for business. Some cultures (Latin particularly) expect a certain amount of chat about families, not just the business at hand, as a way of demonstrating respect for the person.

Often, women, regardless of culture or country, perceive that at work they are not treated with respect and have to consistently assert their right to contribute and make decisions. The issue of women in the workplace is a book in itself. Deborah Tannen's book, *Talking 9 to 5,* directly addresses the differences in perception of women in American industry. One study she refers to examined the way in which female medical students were perceived in the classroom. Questions posed to instructors by male students were seen as inquiring; questions posed by females were seen as indicating lack of knowledge (Tannen, 1998). So, culture or value issues around respect extend to gender issues as well.

In general, however, there are culture groups that see Americans as disrespectful in the way they conduct business. If you are a project manager working with a diverse employee team, a short seminar or discussion on what makes employees feel respected is helpful. We even see this in college classes with diverse populations. A discussion the first day on how the students feel they should be treated to show respect for their time and goals, as well as what the professor needs to feel respected, goes a long way towards preventing problems later on.

3.2 Conflict

Conflict is another area where differences in approach add to the problem. First, it should be emphasized that few people handle conflict as well as it needs to be managed in professional environments, mostly because they bring their personal methods into the situation. Conflict in the workplace is a different element entirely from conflict in one's personal life, and must be handled very differently. Adding cultural differences in what is socially accepted conflict behavior complicates the situation further.

Some ways in which people differ in their approaches to conflict include:

- Their assumptions about the nature of conflict and conflict behavior
- The degree to which harmonizing is a priority over winning or over surfacing a problem or conflict

We have all seen movies in which family members belonging to a certain ethnic group are screaming at each other one minute, then hugging and kissing the next. Quite a few cultures place value on "a good argument to clear the air" or "I argue with her to show respect for her ideas. If I didn't argue, it would show I didn't care." Sometimes this can be merely a personal thing; some people, regardless of culture, just enjoy getting a rise out of someone to liven things up. Thus, an employee or manager who yells or gesticulates vigorously in conflict may have been taught that is the way one behaves in those situations. Broaching this topic, about the way conflict will be handled, can be helpful while the diverse team is still developing its rules about how communication will take place.

The next consideration is **harmonizing**—the idea of encouraging the group to get along and pull together and subjugating individual goals to those of the group. Harmonizing is foreign to some and a way of life to others. Many American Indian and Asian groups view the group needs as a priority over individual needs. Where some cultures place high value on interdependence (perhaps stemming from a historical survival necessity), the typical American view is the individual "success story" or the superstar. Thus, when Americans, with a view towards winning, controlling, and leading the pack, encounter harmonizing behavior, they often interpret it as lack of assertiveness or "giving in."

harmonizing the idea of encouraging the group to get along and pull together and subjugating individual goals to those of the group

In some cases this lack of assertion damages an employee's chance of a raise or advancement because it is perceived as lack of commitment or as weakness. Harmonizing translates into non-assertiveness because importance is placed not on calling attention to the self or individual achievement, but rather on contribution to the group goals.

A harmonizer:

- Allows others to go first
- Apologizes for misunderstanding whether at fault or not
- Redirects conversation rather than disagree or offer a negative response
- May not offer facts and statistics that might disprove someone's statement
- May smile when the discussion becomes uncomfortable or offensive

You can readily see how those from harmonizing cultures would be perceived poorly not only at work but particularly in job interviews. Failure to promote or "sell" the potential employer on achievements or superior skills is a sure ticket to failure in a job interview. Yet in harmonizing cultures, this self-promotion would be seen as inappropriate and boastful. Thus, it is essential for project managers to interview carefully with an eye out for this behavior.

Problem-solving sessions present another potential difficulty with a harmonizer. The project manager must be alert to situations in which everyone seems to agree. Agreement may just mean a reluctance to "make waves," not a belief that the strategy or solution agreed upon is acceptable. The harmonizer, especially if he or she is the technical expert on the project, will have to be sought out in private and asked tactfully for more information.

3.3 Personal Space

As discussed in the chapter on communication (Chapter 4), individual needs for physical distance from another speaker vary. Americans typically require approximately 3 feet of space between themselves and the speaker to feel comfortable in a conversation. Closer contact suggests intimacy as with significant others, family members, or close friends, or it can also mean a challenge in the form of invasion of space. A complaint Americans have is that people from some cultures "stand too close, like they're crowding me." This can be disconcerting and make team members possibly avoid having consultations or discussions with the non-native employee. (See Figure 6–5.)

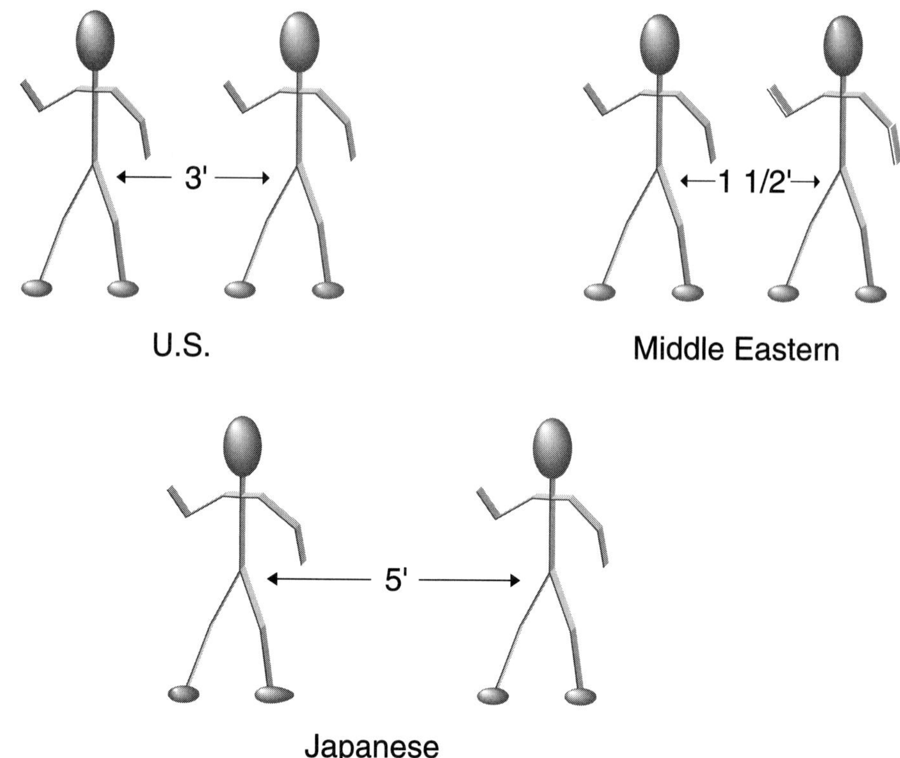

Figure 6–5
Personal space requirements vary from culture to culture.

On the other hand, Americans, especially white males, will touch each other in greeting or playfulness: a slap on the back, a punch to the arm. Touching of any sort suggests a degree of informality or intimacy that some cultures feel is inappropriate in public. Commonly, respective cultures have specific views on this issue as it relates to interactions.

There have been clashes between Korean business people and African American customers, the complaint being the Koreans put change on the counter instead of placing it in the hands of African American customers. Actually, they put change on the counter for all customers, as it is considered impolite to touch someone in a public transaction.

Appreciating differences and becoming tolerant of people who look or speak differently is one thing, but Americans' discomfort with violations of personal space is one of those subtle intolerances. For this it might be better to indoctrinate the new employee from another culture to the concept of personal space and to find out what his or her expectations about it are as well.

3.4 Work Ethic

The value placed on work varies from person to person. Length of work day, desire for promotion or transfer, need for recognition—all are subject to interpretation based on culture. In some countries the workday is sunup to sundown. In others a 2-hour lunch spent in leisurely conversation is an expected revitalization in a long work day. Australians have more holidays than Americans, and the Japanese may continue their business at a restaurant or club after regular hours. These differences go from being the subject of interesting conversation to the inciting of clashes and resentment.

During an interview, a Korean businessman commented, "Koreans believe in working hard, and this makes them successful." He didn't take vacations or long holidays, although he did close his business on typical American holidays. This isn't a big deal for someone who owns his own business, but in the workplace some employees may feel that this approach to work might make them look bad by comparison. Another employee of a different culture may leave every day right at 5 p.m. Before you interpret that behavior as a lack of commitment to work, you might understand, instead, that family and community are first priority for some groups (or individuals for that matter). This same employee might turn down a promotion or transfer if it would separate him or her from the extended family and the associated obligations and support.

Holidays of a religious or historical significance in the country of origin of your employee might interfere with work. Absences at critical times because of these observances can be a problem, but just as any other anticipated difficulty, you can prepare in advance if you know what the employee's needs are. An upside is that you may have someone willing to work during typical American religious or historical holidays.

Differences in work style exist within any group of employees because of individual preferences, so working with each to ensure commitment is not so different in a culturally diverse workforce. Understanding your employees and their approach to work is necessary. In a workshop with a culturally diverse group that could not seem to get into the "team mode" and bond with each other, everyone had to come to the next session dressed to show "the real you." What we saw was both amazing and profoundly helpful. One older man showed up in a suit and tie to explain to us that he was raised to think that was the way successful people dressed. Another came in a Hawaiian shirt and a chef's hat to illustrate the other-than-work aspects of how he defined himself.

But the most telling one was the manager who was from India. Raised in British boarding schools from a very young age, he explained that he really was uncomfortable in any form of casual dress. Detailing the rigor of his upbringing, he took out his handkerchief to show us that, even today, he is careful to fold and crease it just so. This man came from a country whose culture is sometimes viewed by outsiders as haphazard and unstructured in its approach to conducting business, yet somehow jobs end up complete by the end of the day. However, the overlay of the strict British boarding school created a firmly entrenched methodical and highly structured style of conducting daily affairs, especially work. Hearing this explanation, the others began to understand this manager's seemingly overly ordered and unforgiving methods of doing his job and of directing his employees.

Gaining insight into work styles will not solve all your diversity management problems, but it will help you to begin to trust what your people can and will do. "Different" can work, also, but not if "different" creates suspicion in others who don't understand style variations. Making assumptions about the degree of commitment or the competence of an employee based on your perceptions is an error.

3.5 Speed of Business

The first point to understand about this issue is that Americans are viewed by many cultures as being in a hurry and thus unmindful of the needs of others engaged in business interactions. In Latin countries and in some Pacific Rim countries, a suitable amount of time is expected to be devoted to developing the relationship among the principals in the deal. Jumping right in to business is considered discourteous. When a Japanese businessperson hands you his business card, you are expected to read the whole thing and show proper respect to the station or rank the person holds in his or her company. This takes time. Americans typically shake hands, take a business card and put it in their pocket. You can see the impression this creates.

■ ■ ■

"Guys, I have to share a story on this one," Hilda interrupted. "When I first started with my company, I was assigned a project with a Japanese company. So, when the four representatives of the company came, I was the one who greeted them. I was a little flustered, so I became overly enthusiastic. I didn't wait for introductions; I extended my hand first and vigorously shook hands. The first two, who were more westernized, smiled and returned my handshake. The other two looked surprised and uncomfortable, but politely allowed a handshake as well. After I had escorted them to the conference room, my manager explained to me how I had inadvertently been rude." She smiled, remembering. "Fortunately, my manager explained I was young, and the visitors graciously forgave my social error."

■ ■ ■

brainstorming problem-solving and idea-generating technique in which group members spontaneously contribute ideas

On the other hand, however, the time-consuming practice, that Americans call **brainstorming,** is viewed as a pointless waste by some Oriental cultures. Being pragmatic and geared towards practical solutions, they are impatient with the apparently unstructured and pointless, free-flowing idea sessions Americans find so helpful in solving complex problems. The perception of time required for business, then, and the value placed on how it is spent, does vary with culture. Like so many other differences, this doesn't have to be a problem. An understanding of an individual's perception of the appropriate rate at which to conduct business will help ensure success.

4.0 Guidelines for a Constructive Diversity Climate

Many companies are becoming aware of the need for managing diversity into a competitive advantage. They are also becoming aware of managing diversity as a human resources, team, and communication issue. However, too few companies are doing the job well. Michael H. Smith, a diversity training consultant, offers these guidelines.

- Know how to attract, hire, and retain talented people.
- Learn how to treat employees in a way that is consistent with their needs and values.
- Educate all your employees about the issues of racial and sexual harassment.
- Discover how to use each employee's strengths in the most effective manner (Smith, 1992).

Additional suggestions include:

- Perform a needs assessment to determine what the real issues are in your work teams.
- Secure or develop training and awareness programs to improve understanding.

4.1 Hiring and Employee Retention

In United States history there have been many models of society and models of workplace behavior. Whereas the profile of the "average American worker" is changing radically with the addition of more women and minorities, the rules of the corporate culture are changing very slowly.

Thus, talented minority or foreign individuals who are hired into companies with poor diversity climates will likely not stay. In one company, 29 culture groups were represented by 1,000 employees. They had few women in positions other than clerical or administrative. Because of the highly specialized expertise required in their rapidly growing division, recruiting was worldwide, and little attention was paid to whether employee "A" liked employee "B." The primary question was "Do you have this knowledge?"

The company was high-tech, and most of the employees were engineers. Curiously, it seemed that they had fewer communication problems than some other culturally diverse companies, because engineering design is a common language and because they were used to differences. According to the women (and confirmed by some of the men as well), the culture had a "macho" character which all the males seemed to understand and accept to one degree or another. This masculine-dominated style was somewhat familiar to all, regardless of culture.

Anyone, however, who did not embrace this approach might not be inclined to stay, presenting several problems. Not only might the organization lose highly specialized talent, it will have to incur the excessive costs of a worldwide search for expertise it so badly needs. No company can afford to do this very often. So, taking steps to create an accepting and supportive environment can, in fact, be very beneficial, and profitable to a company.

■ ■ ■

This time it was Yury who spoke up. "But what about the cost? Doesn't it cost my company more to find these people, just so we can all be different? I don't understand."

Chou responded quickly, "Yury, I know you are from a country that historically was made up of many different cultures blended into one. This made it seem homogeneous. But did you ever reach the point where you needed a fresh approach?"

"I guess so, we are capitalist now." Yury looked briefly around the room and laughed out loud.

Chou chuckled with the rest, but only briefly. "What's happening today in our high-tech everything world, is the playing out of the old proverb,

> *For want of a nail the shoe was lost; for want of the shoe, the horse was lost; for want of the horse the soldier was lost; for want of the soldier, the battle was lost.*

"Each skill needed to bring our project to completion is a nail. If I need an engineer with a background in high-voltage power supplies, I need that, period. If he or she happens to be from India or Korea or Australia, I will pay whatever it takes, because if I don't, my competition will. If I don't make that person feel welcome and utilize talents constructively, I'll be responsible for a problem far beyond the cost of hiring."

Jaime, who had been quiet up to this point, interjected, "I was hired in 1983 to fill a quota. I was the first Hispanic the company had, but I had experience in product design. I knew why I was hired over the other guys who applied, but I didn't care. The company moved me and my family from Guatemala. Since my hire I've won bonuses for early completions, been recognized by the president of the company for my contribution, and most important, I've become the one they call when a project needs a boost. I think my company has gotten its money's worth."

Yury nodded respectfully to Jaime.

■ ■ ■

4.2 Needs and Goals

The issue of meeting employees' needs and goals in the workplace is not just one of diversity. Although the challenges of doing so with people of a different culture may require a little more investigation and discussion, the practice is sound for all employees. Retaining an open mind about what an employee needs is important. Second-guessing what someone needs based on some generalized perception can lead to trouble.

Not all people have the same professional aspirations, including the needs for travel, promotion, exposure, power, and so on. And, it is unfair to assume or project goals for someone else. Individuals differ in their approaches to life and in the degree to which they may want to embrace the values of a new culture—including the corporate culture of your company. Broaching the subject of goals with each employee is just good management. Remember, however, that ambition, as Americans know it, is not seen in the same light in all cultures. Knowing what is important to all your employees is the key to keeping all of them motivated and committed.

4.3 Racial and Sexual Harassment

No company in today's environment can afford to allow or ignore any situation that could be construed as harassment. Thus, creating a positive set of working conditions is a necessity for legal if not for motivational reasons. It is one thing to explain to employees the legal implications of prejudicial or dominance behavior; it is quite another to move people to change old biases and quick judgments and to acceptance and trust.

Where there is a past history of hostility, prejudice or oppression, an essential element is forgiveness. Everyone has to start with a clean slate. So leading employees through a process of laying old stereotypes and resentments aside becomes a first order of business (Smith, 1992).

■ ■ ■

"I know about this you speak of," Yury said, so softly and out of character for him that the group as a unit showed surprise.

"Yes, Yury, can you tell us what you mean?" Chou gently encouraged him to explain.

"I am a Russian Jew. In my country this was not allowed. When I was able to leave during Glasnost, I was excited. But my friends warned me that we were not always accepted here. I worried about bringing my family here and finding a job."

"Go on. How did you get started in your work?" Chou asked.

"My first interview was set up for me by the group that sponsored my coming to the United States. On the phone the man had a British accent. When I arrived, I was surprised to see a black man. Instead of being helpful, he was very short with me and didn't seem interested in what I knew at all. He said, 'You Russians, so backward.' Later I interviewed with a new company, just starting up. It was a gamble, but the president was a woman, and she treated me with respect. She even hired several of my friends and brought in a language trainer to help us to communicate better."

"So you've done okay over the years?"

"Yes, now I drive a Lincoln." Yury smiled, and the others laughed.

■ ■ ■

In this country individuals receive protection by law from discrimination and harassment, so the personal prejudices or hostilities that may be harbored by any of your employees have no place in your projects. There will always be people who choose to avoid or despise someone because of size, race, religion, or nationality. They do not, in any case, have the right to infringe on anyone else's right to work in a non-hostile environment. Project managers would do well to attend a seminar on the legal implications of workplace behavior in order to protect themselves and to ensure professionalism among and towards all workers. Also, project managers should tolerate no inappropriate behavior towards any employee.

To Improve Understanding

Ask about family.

Find out religious observances.

Offer voluntary language classes.

Invite suggestions and input.

Discuss in private notable social interaction problems.

Encourage others to interact with foreign employee.

Affirm different perspective when voiced.

Respect social distance.

Inquire about food preferences/avoidances.

Openly treat non-native employees with respect and require others do the same.

4.4 Needs Assessment

In sales, experts teach that when it is determined the prospect has heard enough about a product to agree to buy, the salesperson should shut up. To continue to talk further might raise objections or questions in the prospect's mind that didn't exist before. The same is true with this diversity issue. Take a look around at your own situation. Are your people working well together? Are differences understood and respected? Is cooperation shown among all members? An old saying covers this well: "If it ain't broke, don't fix it."

Sometimes, however, face-to-face courtesy may be a cover for deeply-seated prejudice or rankling mistrust that can undo the best efforts at creating a high-functioning team. A needs assessment can be conducted by someone in your group, by the human resources department where you work, or by outside consultants. Generally, needs assessment information is gathered using several methods: interviews, questionnaires, focus groups (a small segment representing the larger group that talks openly about conditions in the company), and observations. All employees who are involved in the activities of the group are asked for input—some in formal ways, some in chats in the break room. The custodian may hear or see something the secretary misses; the programmer may have an idea about the situation that the manager doesn't. All comments, compiled and classified, will appear in the report submitted to you or to management. Conclusions about the situation and recommendations for corrections or improvements are also included.

Although a needs assessment will not solve diversity problems, it will tell you what is working in your group and what needs to be addressed. It will give you a road map for corrective or supportive action and might outline training content suggested. At any level, a needs assessment is a better place to start than a full-scale diversity training marathon.

4.5 Awareness Training

If you've ever seen a handicapped person around his or her friends, family, or work group, then seen the reactions to that person outside the familiar circle, you will understand a lot about problems created by diversity. A man at a recent party was talking with a group of co-workers. Periodically, in the middle of a sentence, he would emit a tirade of obscene and crude words or phrases, then immediately return to the sentence and finish it. The group around him was unfazed by the outburst and waited patiently for him to finish his story. They were familiar with the behavior his Tourette's syndrome condition caused, understood it, and generally overlooked it. A woman on the other side of the room, however, heard what he said and was shocked.

We can learn tolerance, acceptance, and finally, trust if we have information. The unfamiliar is always threatening; the familiar is more comfortable. Training programs that help employees see similarities instead of differences, and that set behavior in a cultural context, go a long way towards creating a higher level of comfort.

Managing a diverse employee population productively requires a commitment by upper management to create an environment that fosters understanding and respect for all. The issues of affirmative action, sexual harassment policies, quotas, false perceptions and assumptions, prejudice, and ethnocentricity can all be worked through constructively if management is committed to fully utilizing and affirming all employees. Without management "thinking right" about diversity (this includes you, the project manager), training becomes a waste of time and dollars. Change and differences foster creativity if viewed positively. The global economy could use a little of both.

4.6 Advantage of Alternate Views

People on a project team are rarely equal in all areas of need a project may have. The clever manager recognizes the unique abilities each team member may have to contribute. To do so, however, the project manager must be aware of employees' work styles, performance record, skills, and commitment. Only the most open-minded of us see differences as potential strengths; most of us, regardless of our cultural background, see differences as potential weaknesses. This bias may make us overlook, or fail to utilize, the potential power in a synthesis of differences.

In furniture manufacturing there is a method of joining corners of drawers that is considered to be strong and long-lasting. This is called dovetailing, and is illustrated in Figure 6–6.

Figure 6–6
Dovetailing

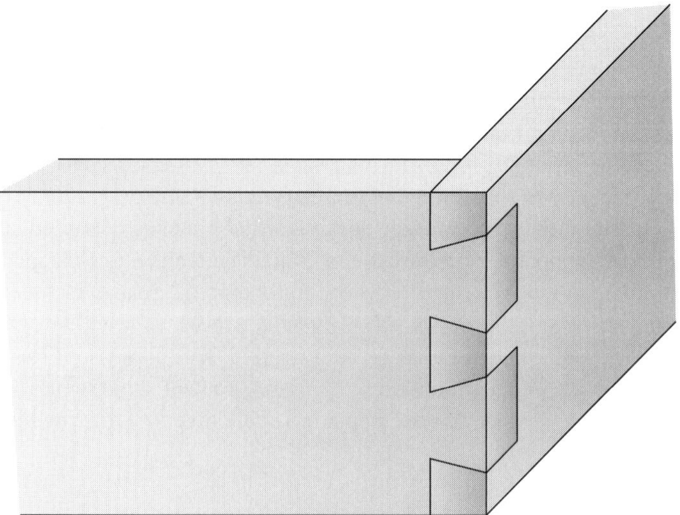

The strength comes from the interlocking pattern. In the same way the many disparate viewpoints that occur in a diverse workforce can interlock to make a stronger team.

In working on a project, some people look at the big picture or vision, seeing the operational details as less important, while others consider the steps and "small stuff" as essential to completing a project. These two types of people make each other "crazy" because they have incompatible styles. The vision person finds the operational, detail-oriented person to be preoccupied with minutiae and seemingly set on slowing down the project. The operational person sees the vision person as being lost in far-out ideas. Fundamentally, they are both correct and incorrect at the same time in viewing projects and decisions in their singular way. Projects require *both* vision and operational detail. Thus, to design sound and successful projects, the project management team must utilize and welcome these seemingly opposing views in the interest of a sound project.

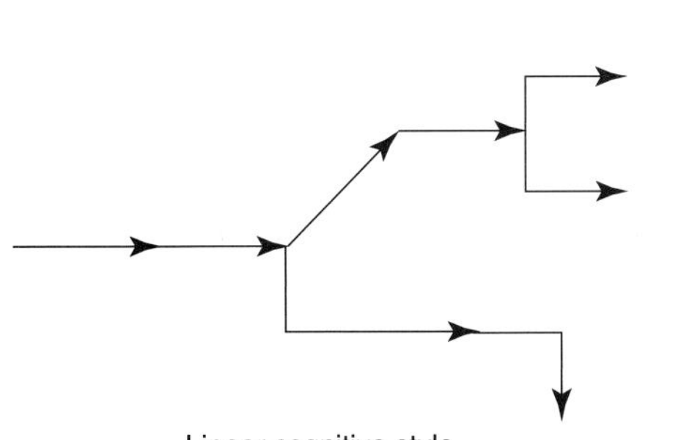

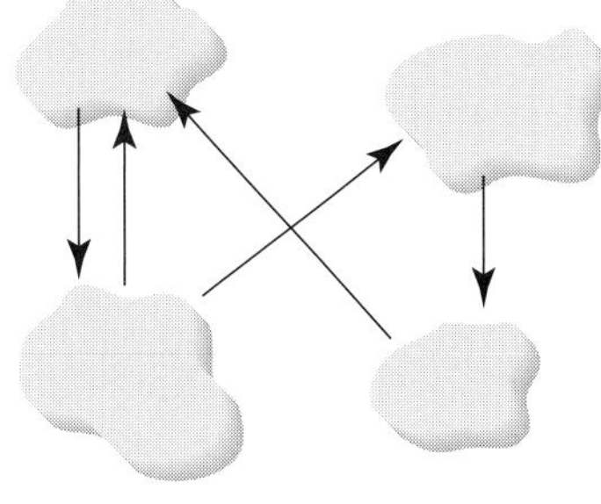

Figure 6–7
Recognizing diversity can mean acknowledging different cognitive styles.

Granted, a plethora of differing viewpoints does slow the decision-making process down, especially where consensus is required, but heterogeneous groups in general seem to generate more new ideas and reach higher quality solutions than homogeneous groups (Block, 1994, referring to Robert Lattimer's research). There is a lot of evidence building for the argument that different is better, as Rich Templeton of Texas Instruments points out: "Development of the future workforce is a critical issue for high technology companies. We must find ways to remain creative and innovative, and diversity of thought is fundamental to creativity" (Baum, 1999). Other anecdotal evidence includes Solectron, a Silicon Valley company with 30 nationalities speaking 40 languages and dialects. Cultural awareness training in this situation yielded triple the revenues and an award. A textile company that had lost money for many years attributed a profit turnaround to "a diverse management group" (Block, 1994). (See Figure 6–7.)

■ ■ ■

"Now, do any of you have stories of situations where opposite, or at least different, views led you to a better decision?" Chou asked.

No one spoke for a while. Finally the silence got to Jerry, who blurted, "Okay, yeah. We have this really 'out there' kind of idea guy in our group. He makes us all crazy because it's something new every week we should be looking into. Then there's this Egyptian guy who's always looking for an angle no matter how ridiculous a task may seem to be to accomplish. He takes impossible situations and somehow engineers them into projects. Vish, our Indian guy, makes math out of everything and crunches the numbers on our probabilities, risk, that type of thing."

"So what are your meetings like?" Chou asked, only partly restraining a smile.

"They're outa control sometimes. Vish stubbornly sticks to his numbers; Jim, the visionary, is trying to explain the big picture, and the Egyptian guy is already delegating work to everyone."

"Okay, that's the bad part," Chou replied, with a smug smile. "Now tell us what the good part is."

Jerry looked around the group. "It works. Our group generally gets the toughest projects because we have a track record of on-time and in-budget completions."

"Jerry's situation is not uncommon," Chou remarked. "Diversity brings change and requires new learning. People tend to prefer same old, same old. But once they look past the initial, 'oh no,' they find that they can become a more sophisticated thinking machine."

■ ■ ■

In business decision making we teach that conflict presents a mutual problem that requires creativity to solve. If it were not a complex problem, it would have been solved already. Creativity and the ability to solve complex problems are enhanced when large numbers of ideas come from many different and distinctly disparate viewpoints. The careful management of such diversity may be the next level of strategic advantage in this dynamic global marketplace.

Chapter Summary

With the increasing demand for highly skilled people, recruiting has now gone worldwide. This has contributed to the increasing cultural variety in companies and to the challenge of managing and motivating people of different values and needs. Unfortunately, ethnocentricity and concerns with power have led some groups or individuals to be intolerant and/or resent others. Attributions and assumptions make managers draw conclusions about employees and may sometimes be incorrect, causing misunderstanding. The biggest error is to think understanding is taking place when it is not—on either side of a bicultural conversation. Assumptions about where someone is from or about the extent to which a foreign employee might want to be like Americans can also be false.

Issues that occur within multicultural teams often result from areas of friction between operating styles of one culture or another. Points of friction where differences likely will occur are: the way respect is shown, the way conflict is handled, the way personal space is treated, the work ethic one holds, and the speed at which it is acceptable to do business. However, in spite of these areas of potential problems, there is an important result that can come out of working with such differences. The result is greater creativity and higher quality solutions to complex problems. Each approach to a problem, culturally guided or not, has a strength in forcing decision makers to look at different aspects of a problem.

To synthesize success out of diversity, project mangers should create a work climate that fosters understanding and respect for everyone's ideas and contributions. This includes hiring good people and meeting their needs for respect and affirmation.

It also means educating employees on the legal ramifications of racial and/or sexual harassment. A needs assessment that uncovers the strengths and weaknesses of the working relationships will help the manager decide what training, policies, awareness, or accommodations need to be made. The net result will be a workforce that is uniquely equipped to meet the challenges of a complex and highly competitive industry environment.

Chapter Questions

1. Explain what *ethnocentricity* means and how it can be a problem in a culturally diverse workforce.
2. Give examples of assumptions and attributions you have heard about various groups. Do you hold any of these biases yourself?
3. Discuss at least two areas where other cultures' approaches may clash with the American "rules" of interpersonal communication.
4. Why should project managers concern themselves with the diversity issue?
5. What are the projections for workplace population mix in terms of homogeneity or heterogeneity through the new millenium?
6. Recommend three specific actions a project manager should take to ensure the highest level of productivity in a culturally diverse project team.
7. Is the following statement true or false?
   It is easy to figure out where someone is from and to know things about him or her by the language the person speaks or by his or her physical appearance.
   Explain your answer.
8. How should a project manager handle cases in which racial or sexual harassment has occurred? Justify the actions that you recommend.

Project Challenge: Applying What You Know

A. An Indian (from India, not an American Indian) woman you recently recruited heavily and won to your company has come to you with a problem. Brought in as an engineering design manager in new products development, she has education and experience you have been unable to find other places, and you very much need to keep her in your group. She states her problem as follows: "I cannot work with your people. The men will not follow my directions, and they openly refuse to turn in the status reports I have asked for. This is a "cowboy culture" here; they all work until 7 p.m. and on weekends and criticize anyone who does not. They hold meetings that I did not call and don't attend the ones I do call." She further stated that she felt uncomfortable with everyone, that they were too familiar and didn't show her proper respect in her position. Threatening to quit, she has come to you for a solution.

1. What are the issues in this problem? Which ones are culturally related?
2. What do you think the other employees (mostly male, all American-born) would say about her?
3. Cite any legal or ethical problems that may exist in this situation.
4. What is the best solution in this case?

B. Design a questionnaire that will be used to conduct a needs assessment of the diversity climate in a company. Determine what questions should be asked to discover what the real problems as well as the real strengths are. Once you gather the information, what would you do with it?

Interview with an Expert

Sunil Robert, *Corporate Communications Manager, ACER* Bangalore, India

A project management situation with international implications.

This project involved a CD-ROM presentation that was to be done in English, French, and German for a European Union exhibition my company was participating in. The vice president and I planned well in advance with clear project management charts and checklists each week to monitor progress. Expectations were high for this highly visible project.

The translator, the only one available, would not keep his deadlines. Pushing him would not solve the problem as his involvement was critical. The chap who was to do the English voiceover fell ill. Delays were mounting. The following day he called off the appointment because he felt his voice would be better at dawn than at noon; this required re-slating the time for the studio. The translator pitched a tantrum and said that translated work had to be done in the outdated WORDSTAR format, and of course no modern multimedia software is compatible with it.

Another problem came up. Some of the visuals we had used for the English version presentation were JPEGs and when the rest of the material was translated, the visuals would still be in English. The vendor whose studio we were using was getting sick of the chaos, and the guillotine of a deadline was dropping closer. Between carrying on conversations about cricket matches to one of the designers and offering career guidance to another, I managed to use sympathy to keep them moving the project along.

Then another hurricane hit. The entire French translation of 40 slides had arrived, but in an English word file, so the marks peculiar to the French language were not in it. It fell to me to manually convert this "frenglish" document to acceptable French. Finally, voiceovers and translations were complete. But, the next day, while copying the material for the final publishing, the design chaps managed to delete the voice files. Though I wished the earth would open and swallow me, we instead retrieved the raw voice recording and re-synchronized everything. Since this was not the time for "blamestorming," I waited for the two CDs. The time of my wait was extended because an idea for the visual cover for one CD came at the last minute. The finished product was a multimedia show for our booth at the exhibition, which would play in French, German, or English as the listener desired. On the way to the airport, my boss said, "Hey, good show. It was a great effort!" That last sentence was worth all the agony.

CHAPTER 7

Setting Goals and Securing Commitment

Chapter Preview

The Project Management Seminar: Session 7

The day's session hadn't yet begun. Hilda was chatting quietly with Ragdeesh and Yury when Jerry walked in, talking on his cell phone. He was shaking an angry fist in the air and his face was a deep shade of red. Hilda watched Jerry stab the "off" button on the phone so hard that he flinched in pain, and put his finger in his mouth. She approached him with a smile. "Looks like you're having a great time."

Jerry removed the finger from his mouth. "It's maddening! I don't know what top management is looking for. And I'm beginning to think they don't know either. We spend hours in concept meetings and when the meeting is finished—if there were 10 people at it, there would be 11 different versions of what we need to be doing."

"I know what you mean," Hilda said, nodding sympathetically. "We think we know what the goal of a project is before we start, but it seems to morph somehow during the process. Most of the time the target appears to be moving."

"You got that right! I get the team up and running and then find out that my boss wants them going to point B, not point A. If we just had a clue what it was that we were running towards, we'd stay away from the do-anything-even-if-its-wrong syndrome."

By this time Ralph and Tracey were calling the group together, and the day's topics were on the easel.

- Why do we need goals?
- How do you get them to agree?

- Getting buy-in
- Maintaining commitment
- Conflicts—how to handle them

This discussion will center on the following objectives:

- **Defining the project goal**
- **Developing goal statements**
- **Managing goal conflicts**
- **Maintaining commitment**

1.0 THE PROJECT GOAL

The very first thing that any project leader needs is a clearly defined and understood goal. Why is this so important? If you have ever tried to assemble a jigsaw puzzle, you know that the easy way—even on a hard puzzle—is to look at the picture on the box. The picture is the end result—the goal of the project. Suppose someone took the lid outside and left it in the rain. The picture, if it even survived, is now very difficult to see clearly. Now you have a job on your hands that is much harder than before. If you had wagered that you could do the puzzle in a set amount of time, you might find that without the picture, the puzzle is much more time-consuming. That is why the goal is necessary. The goal, just like the picture, is the **final result.**

final result the goal of a project

A word that strategic planners often use in a similar way is the "vision." This is the picture that is in the minds of everyone who has an interest in the project. Unfortunately, everyone will likely have a different "view" of the outcome. The vision is the situation that would occur if everything were to fall into place exactly as everyone wishes. The goal, like the vision, is often different in different people's minds. Some may value some aspect of the specification of the outcome more than the rest.

For example, marketing may value the product's competitive value, while engineering may stress functionality of the product, yet field service may be concerned primarily with the product's maintainability. Financial stakeholders will be most concerned with the cost of the project as it relates to revenue. Top management's usual focus is on the timeliness of the outcome. Design engineers are passionate about the latest and greatest technologies to employ. Buyers are looking forward to a better, cheaper, or faster product. Sales reps may be craving to finally land that big elusive account that will make them rich.

You, as the project manager, are responsible for achieving the goals set by all the stakeholders, as well as maintaining the parameters set by the end user, whether an internal customer, such as management, or an external customer, such as an original equipment manufacturer.

More often than not, even the end user has not fully defined the project's goal, but has a high-level, fuzzy definition of what is envisioned. This is a dangerous situation for the project team, because it will bring about an endless series of midstream changes, delaying completion and escalating costs. Even then, the end user's real needs are often not completely met by the projects results, causing contention, dissatisfaction, lawsuits, withheld payments, not to mention ruined reputations.

1.1 Defining the Project Goal

project goal A statement of the end result of the project, which will satisfy the major reasons why the stakeholders are undertaking the project, defined in terms of three critical dimensions: specification objectives, time objectives, and cost objectives

What is the actual definition of a **project goal?** There are many aspects to a project and many reasons a project is undertaken. Including all of them in a single definition is not reasonably achievable.

First, let's break up the two words in an attempt to arrive at a working definition.

1.1.1 Project

A specific, unique plan or design. An *idea.* A planned undertaking. One that involves many people, resources, activities, entities, cultures, skills, and so on.

1.1.2 Goal

The end result toward which the effort is directed. Measured in as many ways, perhaps, as there are people involved.

So with the two words joined together, the project goal should be defined as:

A statement of the end result of the project, which will satisfy the major reasons why the stakeholders are undertaking the project, defined in terms of three critical dimensions: specification objectives, time objectives, and cost objectives.

1.2 Goal Myopia—The Activity Trap

Knowing what the real goal of a project is can help you avoid a rather nasty trap: focusing on a small part of the goal picture at the expense of the larger goals of the company. Henry Ford initially fell into just that trap. He revolutionized the automobile manufacturing industry by inventing the concept of standardized production on assembly lines—repetitive production for increased production efficiency. On the day that Ford's plant achieved one of the highest efficiency ratings ever, the plant was shut down. Although the operation was efficient and tight, it lost sight of the real goal, which was to sell lots of automobiles. The customers asked for automobiles in different styles and colors, but for the sake of standardization and efficiency Henry Ford said, "You can have any color you want, so long as it's black."

General Motors had opened, offering cars in several colors; so did Studebaker and Chrysler. They "cleaned up" at the expense of Henry Ford. He had, with the best intentions in the world, made automobiles affordable to the masses by focusing on the goal of making the most efficient automobile plant in history. The real goal, however, was to *sell* cars, to satisfy the customer's needs.

Consider the difference between *doing things right* and *doing the right thing. Doing the right thing* has to do with acting based upon what is important. *Doing things right* is doing whatever task you are involved in very well. Many technical people pride themselves on doing specific tasks right—but this can lead to doing the wrong thing.

Say you were in charge of the construction of a chain of restaurants. There are going to be thousands of them all across the country in 2 years. Things are going great for a while until suddenly, several of the construction sites report they are falling behind. The project managers at the local level can't seem to find a solution that meets the deadline for the grand opening of the chain. When you inspect one of the sites, you find that the specifications required the bar be made of mahogany, and that there is none to be had for 3 months.

Nothing can happen with the rest of the construction until the wood is installed. The interior designer on the project is insisting on mahogany. All over the country, teams of workers are looking at each other and waiting for mahogany. The interior designer is *doing things right*—the mahogany would look great, and is called for in the specs. He is *not doing the right thing*—finding a nice substitute, say red oak, and finishing the project on time. The goal is to build a chain of restaurants, not win awards for splendid mahogany interiors.

The railroads of yesteryear should have been the airlines and trucking lines of today. Their goals should have focused on the *transportation of people and goods.* Instead, they focused on running efficient railroads, which now are mostly aging, dying enterprises in need of major government subsidies.

Deliberate and careful consideration is to be given to the formulation of goal statements. These statements are to capture the true underlying needs, which motivate the undertaking.

2.0 DEVELOPING GOAL STATEMENTS

Goals are the driving force behind shaping the focus of your project. Goals define *the right thing!*

The specific description of the goal should be simple—a single-sentence description of the end result. To come up with such a description, ask a lot of questions.

Think of remodeling a kitchen. The vision is for new cabinets, flooring, and appliances. What the cabinets, flooring, and appliances should be like are very clear in the mind of the person who initiates the job. However, specific questions must follow: What kind of cabinets—oak, laminated, or birch? What kind of flooring—vinyl, tile, or wood?

In designing electric vehicles for sale to the public, engineers had to go beyond issues of drag, battery life, and user-friendliness, and include the ability of the car to pass federal government standards for crash testing. The most efficient car might not have met this important criterion. If the goal from the investor (or customer) was a commercially marketable vehicle, the design with the highest mileage between recharges might turn out to be a failed project—if the car does not meet crash-test standards.

Once you have formulated a goal statement, testing it on other people is a good idea. They may not have been at the original concept meetings and have a less clear notion of the goal. To help sharpen the goal, encourage the people you are talking with to ask questions if they are unclear about the goal. And remember, some people are better than others at articulating what they expect. Quick turnaround time to one person may be 3 days and to another might be 3 weeks. The unasked question is most often the one that creates the problem.

Different interest groups (stakeholders) within the organization will have a say about the goal. Asking several different people helps in examining different understandings of the goal. Examples of various people one should ask are:

- **Upper management,** for questions that pertain to the company's mission, goals and objectives
- **Accounting,** for questions that relate to cost objectives and the expected financial performance of a project
- **Engineering,** for questions that deal with the design and development of a product or a process
- **End users,** for questions about the utility of the project's results

All of these preceding individuals will have different concerns and understanding of various questions. People are motivated differently. The result of all this feedback will help formulate your goal statement for the better.

Table 7–1 shows the evolution of a goal statement from the synthesis of ideas of the various stakeholders involved in an automotive project.

Table 7–1
Evolution of goal statement

First-pass formulation:

Customer	Marketing	Engineering	Production
Clean emissions for use within resort communities. Contemporary looks, affordable for fixed-income retirees.	New market with built-in resale, for short trips and low-budget users to beat upcoming Japanese intro in 2001.	High-efficiency vehicle, low-drag, with latest motive technology.	Fewer parts, off-the-shelf components. Standard design, suitable for high volume production.

Second-pass formulation with more specific refinements to goal expectations:

Customer	Marketing	Engineering	Production
Price between $9,000–$10,000.	Small two-seater. 25-mile range, high economy; 75 mpg, for 2001 model year. Gross profit margin to be 50%.	Electric vehicle design. Off-board charger. Less than 1,100 lbs. gross weight.	Golf cart drive-train parts. Dune-buggy composite body.

Third-pass formulation:

Specifications: Two-seater, E.V., 25-mile range, 75 mpg, off-board charger, gross weight under 1,100 pounds, sealed batteries, standard configuration only.

Cost Objective: To sell for under $10,000. Allowing for 50% gross margin, direct cost not to exceed $5,000 each.

Time Objective: Complete the design phase, prototyping and testing phase, production tooling, start-up, and initial shipment by September 30, 2000.

Final Formulation:

Goal Statement: "A simple two-seat, electric vehicle of streamlined appearance, with 25-mile range and the equivalent of 75 mpg, to sell for under $9,995, on the show floor by October 2000."

Project Name: "Resort Electric Vehicle (**REV** for short)"

2.1 Define Goal Standards

It has been said that if you can't measure it, you shouldn't be doing it. If performance is not weighed against a standard, there will be no objective way to determine your **success** or **failure.** Without clearly stating that the goal is to build a 40-foot racing sailboat, with its attendant specs, you may find some of your project teams hard at work on developing a sailing yacht, and others a pleasure craft—each group feeling that its understanding of the goal is correct.

success completion of a project with all goals accomplished in the amount of time specified

failure non-completion of or wrongly-completed project

"Improve quality" is not a clear goal. Reduce scrap by 20% is! Simple measurements are the best. Simple measurements are easy, inexpensive, and readily understood by everyone.

Some useful examples of measurements (other than technical criteria) include:

- Margin—usually a percent of sales or a percent of cost
- Readiness for production in "x" weeks
- Percent of error or waste reduction
- Production cost to sale price ratio
- Capacity in pieces per year

Sometimes, however, the real trick is to find a technique for measurement. Customer satisfaction, for example, can be difficult to measure. Recently a major banking company was trying to improve customer relations. They had hired some rather expensive consultants to help find the answer to improving customer relations. The consultants did a series of tests with the tellers and the customers. They decided that friendliness is a key factor, and that it starts with the tellers. But the problem was what do you measure, and what kind of tests can you perform?

Do you track the amount of time a teller spends in small talk, or the number of smiles per transaction? After surveying the customers, they concluded that calling the customer by the correct name was the most important factor, and that names were confused or not used some 70% of the time! The teller-training project that followed had a goal of 95% accuracy name recall and use.

Use a standards tool that fits the type of project you are doing. Practicality should rule all measuring activity. So many companies are responding to the push for total quality management, that they are measuring, calibrating, calculating, and storing huge amounts of data for no practical purpose. But a simple standard can become very helpful when all understand it:

An economist may understand stochastic process analysis, but marketing may not have a clue. There is going to be difficulty getting both to agree that a goal has been met using this technique.

■ ■ ■

"Oh yeah," Tom interjected. "I worked in a plant one summer that gave us the error rate we were allowed and the production numbers expected. They told us that when we reached production numbers within error standards, we could go home—whether it was 2 p.m. or 5 p.m. You can believe everyone in that plant made a point of knowing what it took to leave early," Tom finished, chuckling.

"Yes. That's what I'm talking about here," Ralph said, nodding his head. "Without a standard to put performance up against, you have a hard time telling when you're done."

■ ■ ■

2.2 Gain Consensus for Buy-In

It is common for various parties of a project to have different impressions of the project goal. It is vital that this be rectified so that everyone connected with the project agrees on a unified definition of the goal. Consensus, though sometimes hard to reach, is absolutely necessary for a unified pursuit of the goal.

buy-in all members of the cross-functional team agree and understand the underlying vision for the project's development and marketing plan and that this is the best possible plan for the project

It is extremely important for all members of the project's team to "buy in" on a product's specifications. **Buy-in** means that all members of the cross-functional team agree and understand the underlying vision for the project's development and marketing plan and that this is the best possible plan for the project. When someone opposes a project's plan, or doesn't buy in, the plan should continue to be reviewed until consensus is achieved. Remember, objections raised at this stage are gold nuggets. They allow you to discover and resolve problems now, which otherwise would surprise you during the implementation phase, when problem resolution will come at a higher cost and risk to the project.

Consensus from all parties is absolutely necessary for the project's (and your own) best interest. The most important people who must agree to your goal are the end users, who most often are your customers. Although it might be easier in some ways to keep the customer out of the picture, you run the risk of not meeting the customer's expectations at the end of the project. If the end user doesn't agree with your goals, then the product, service, or process will not be fit for their use.

There are two ways to get the end users to agree to your project's goals:

1. Show them how the goal fulfills their desires and needs.
2. Modify the goal until it does fulfill their desires and needs.

When it comes to goal agreement, the customer is indeed always right. A typical process of customer involvement in product development goal setting is shown in Figure 7–1.

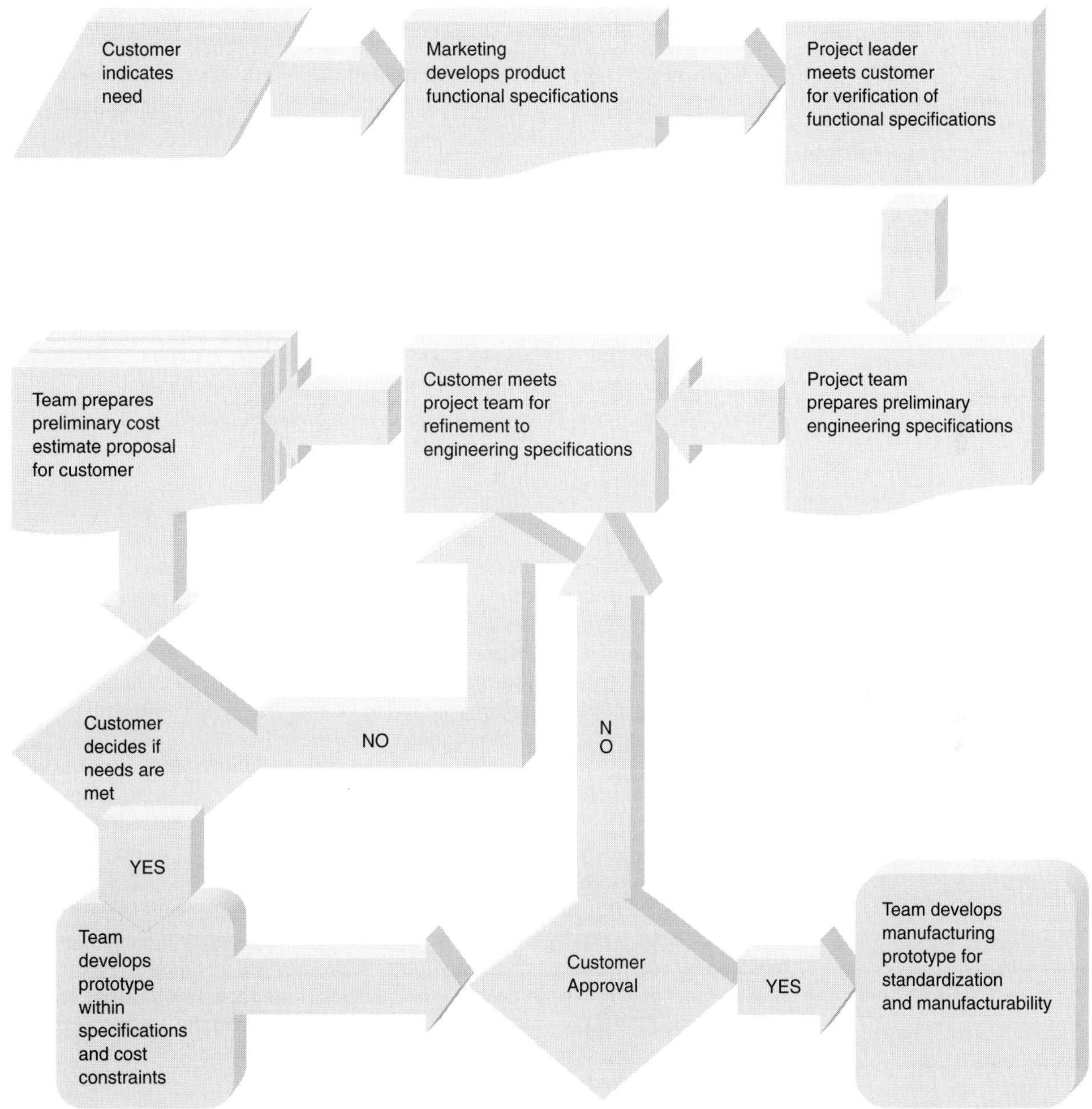

Figure 7–1
Customer Involvement in Product Development.

Project subteams and functional groups must also concur about the final goal and their part in achieving it; there should be no individual agendas.

Who must ultimately agree to the goals of a project? A partial list might include:

- **The project's end user.** This will make or break your project's chances of success.
- **Upper management.** They set the strategic plan and sign off on the specifics that are created by the rest of the teams.
- **Your immediate superiors.** You need to make them look good and should know what their expectations are. They need to know what you are doing and want you to succeed. They can help with access to resources beyond your reach and to buy you critically needed time when you most need it.
- **The check-signers.** They can express their disapproval by being late in payment to you and your subcontractors. They may even withhold payment completely if they suspect the project to be "off-track," and bring a quick halt to your progress.
- **Your peers.** These are the people you rely on for support and assistance. They need to agree with the goals of a project in order to lend their efforts to yours, and to help out when you are in a tight spot. Their most important contribution is in resolving priority issues in your favor when assignment conflicts arise.
- **Subcontractors.** If they agree with the goals, and the specifics can be worked out to comply with both of your needs and their capabilities, then supplies will flow more smoothly, have fewer quality problems, and possibly cost less.
- **Your subordinates.** They will work much more intelligently if they know and agree on what the result is supposed to be.

■ ■ ■

"Everything thus far has made reasonable sense," Jerry commented. "But what about cases where you have relayed the goal perfectly to everyone, but management wants insane deadlines? I 've been through this many times in my career. And I noticed that a lot of corners were starting to get cut for the sake of the project's progress. This type of workmanship caused quality to go out the window, and my staff and company started to look bad. So how do we deal with upper management creating unreasonable deadlines?"

"Excellent point, Jerry," Ralph said, and turned to the others. "Well, group, how do we deal with this situation?"

Ragdeesh spoke up. "I think we should advise upper management of the deadlines arrived at by our team of experts and tell them we can't be done with the project any sooner."

Tom turned to Ragdeesh and asked, "But what if the product your team is manufacturing is a new swimming pool pump that is to be out for this summer season? And your team of experts says that the product will be ready a month after the pool buying season ends? Do you tell upper management that you are unable to build the pump because it would be a month late to the market, or do you go back and see if you are able to modify the schedule to allow for the product to be finished sooner?"

"Great point Tom," Ralph said. "Thanks for the lead-in "

■ ■ ■

2.3 Set Doable Expectations

There is no honor in accepting goals that cannot be met. The expression, "It was a tall order, but we gave it our best shot," is not something that the manager of a project wants to say or hear. A successful manager must avoid the traps that created the unrealistic goal in the first place.

There is a guaranteed no-miss formula for creating the magic of goals set well. It contains the three elements that are the minimum for a realistic goal. If any of these elements is missing, then maybe you should reevaluate your involvement in the project. A realistic project must have:

- **People.** There must be enough people to do the work. Further, they must possess the right types of skills. A new piece of software is difficult to create with a team of beginners instead of seasoned programmers. It is almost as difficult to create it without enough programmers.
- **Money.** A shoestring budget will generally buy only shoestrings. There has to be enough money to get the goods and services that will make the project go. Enough money to pay your people is a necessity. Unanswered questions about money should set off alarm bells.
- **Time.** The single most overlooked aspect of many projects is the time line. Even a well-staffed crew of highly skilled and lavishly funded experts will not be able to produce the new standard in desktop operating systems in a couple of weeks.

3.0 Setting Budget Goals: Time and Money

Everyone seems to agree that time is money, but in reality, time and money are two separate elements here. You, as project manager, are responsible for both. The administration of these elements is, of course, your responsibility. However, you should also make sure that you have both elements provided to you to administer. Let's break them down.

3.1 Time Line

You must see to it that the project has reasonable, known deadlines. This means that the overall project *can* be done in the allotted time. It does no one any good at all to try for the impossible. All you will have done is create the environment for failure. If by some miracle you could meet the unrealistic deadlines, you will most definitely violate the project's other constraints by pushing your resources to overload and putting your people into crisis mode. Subsequently, the project will cost significantly more than it should have and the quality achieved will be questionable, which spells failure.

Beware of lead-in phrases such as "How quickly can it be done if everything went well?" or "if you had all the resources you can use?" Neither of these conditions has much of a chance of actually happening nor will anyone remember them when the deadline you committed yourself and your teams to rolls around.

A customer's multimillion-dollar market launch may be held up waiting for your project's product, since they scheduled around your unrealistic promise date. The losses resulting from such a situation far exceed any possible gains from the project.

Make sure your teams agree to the deadline as well as to those for major project milestones. The chances of project success are slim if you are the only one committed to the deadlines. These milestones may include major design components, major testing dates, launching marketing campaigns at trade shows, and/or grant renewal deadlines. A key factor to keep in mind is elements that may be out of your direct control, like delivery of needed parts or obtaining a critical approval. If you are using someone else's resources, that person is in control of the process, not you. First, get their agreement. Then, leave yourself and your teams some flexibility for contingencies. A schedule that is excessively tight will crash around your ears if there is any problem. Conversely, you want to be able to beat the time line should the opportunity arise. Everyone is grateful for exceeded expectations. You need not only the ability to alter the schedule, but also the authority.

3.2 Cost Factors

capital budget involves the purchase of the physical plant and the machinery required to make the product

expense budget includes everything accept capital—payroll, electricity, water, etc.

A reasonable budget goal is one that will meet the project's spending profile. This will allow the project to proceed without the necessity of requesting additional funding midstream, or doing without something needed (like your check). There are mainly two types of budgets—capital and expense. A **capital budget** involves the purchase of the physical plant and the machinery required to make whatever the product is. A furniture manufacturing plant will have a capital budget to purchase lathes, saws, and sanders. An **expense budget** covers everything else: payroll, blades for the saws, electricity, and so on. The government will tax you differently on each type of expenditure, and the company probably has different policies regarding the two types of cost. You will need to budget both kinds. Make sure that you have adequate funds and authority to cover both, as well as the freedom between line items. You should have control over your budget; after all, you are responsible for working within it.

Here again, though, it is important to remember what a budget goal means to a business. A company spends money throughout its operations based on budget expectations. If you tell them the project will cost $110,000, and the company is charging the customer $200,000 for the work, then that difference is anticipated and assigned to other areas. If the real cost exceeds your budget goal, then the company's other operations and projects may be in jeopardy. So another vital issue in a reasonable budget is one that the company can live with financially and that will help the company meet its financial goals.

Both your budget and the ability to meet it have a direct impact on the chances of the project being approved. One project manager interviewed said that the comptroller (person who controls the money) of his company assured approval of any project that could break even within 2 years—a 50% return on investment.

Credibility in estimating the project budget is a key factor in having the project approved, in addition to the ultimate success of the project. Your track record for accurate budgeting will help get the okay for your projects when others might be turned down.

■ ■ ■

Ralph George called on Tom. "Forecasting revenue from a project often falls into the marketing realm, but it is good for a project manager to understand where budget constraints come from. Tom, can you give us an example of a forecasting situation?"

"Oh yeah," Tom said, "and this one was classic. Our plant manager, at the monthly production planning meeting, asked for product demand forecasts for 18 months into the future. When he asked for the forecast in dollars of sales of their 355 Connector to the Empire Company in the month of November, almost in the same voice, two account managers spoke up. Vince replied $30,000, and Brenda replied $60,000. They argued right there in the meeting about who had the right forecast. The manager asked, 'Why are they so far apart?'

"Vince, our hotshot MBA, replied that he had used all these sophisticated forecasting models. Brenda, an older woman, who had been with us forever, said that she did her forecasting by sitting in her customers' offices. She explained that

she kept in daily contact with her customers, and added that she had gotten the $60,000 figure from Empire's buyer the day before!"

"So what happened?" Jaime asked. "What did they use? Because we get this stuff all the time, and I never knew where the numbers came from."

"Well, the plant manager finally made Brenda call the buyer right there from the meeting and confirm the numbers. And you know? The final actual purchase was $59,600. She was right on the money."

"Maybe so, but I still think they make some of that stuff up," Jerry said, frowning.

■ ■ ■

No matter how good you are at estimating budget needs, make sure you have a contingency budget—a "fudge factor" if you will! There will always be emergencies and unforeseen expenses. Setting up a contingency fund of 5 to 15% of the total budget can save major headaches and embarrassment. Make sure you have already identified all possible budget items first, so that only truly unknown and unanticipated items are covered by the contingency fund. The contingency fund, and the authority to use it, can save you and your projects.

4.0 Managing Goal Conflicts

Inevitably, in robust businesses that have multiple projects and limited resources, even after the goal statement is agreed upon, conflicts will arise. Choices are made and priorities are set based on several factors:

- Market conditions: Time windows of opportunities and unanticipated changes
- Compatibility with other projects: What other activities conflict with this undertaking?
- Ownership of individual projects: Which V.P. "likes" this project?
- Resources available: What do we have and which project should it be spent on?

If the market shifts, and the number one priority project is moved to the back burner, the champion of the project will likely have a problem with that. Sometimes a goal becomes unrealistic due to lack of resources: they just couldn't find enough engineers, full-time or contractors. Other times, different managers may compete for leadership in a project that has high visibility to upper management and that could advance their careers. Any time there are different goals within an organization, there is the potential for goal conflict. With goal conflict, the project manager can take three basic paths:

- Influence: Sell the idea or his or her version of the goal and why it's important.
- Early detection: Invite constructive criticism and adjust accordingly.
- Conflict resolution (sometimes negotiation).

Each has its merits and place and is an important tool in achieving goals. Goals without support won't get very far. The project manager who repeatedly has goal conflicts because he or she didn't secure "buy-in" from all necessary parties or doesn't anticipate conflicts of interest will have a short life with the company.

4.1 Influence

Influence involves many elements: salesmanship, barter, peer influence. To sell an idea or a goal, or even the method for measuring the goal, the project manager must be able to figure out who cares about the outcome. To sell a V.P. on making your project the highest priority, and thus an objective of the company in assigning resources, you have to understand who is in a position to profit from the successful completion of the project. Maybe your V.P. needs visibility with product development and likes working with big-name, flashy customers. If your project fits this description, then your project may need to be presented to this particular manager.

To sell your idea, you will have to find out who has something to gain from your project's successful completion and who has the authority to free up resources to help you meet your goals. The old adage, "It's all in the way you explain it," is very true. You will have to describe goals in terms of the benefits of reaching those goals—not only to your managers and higher-ups, but also to your project team. If you can't think of a good reason for someone to support the goal, then that person will not likely think of it on his own.

Among peers, managers, or resource holders of other departments who do not report to you, you may have to use other techniques. Barter, or trading favors, is a common method of influencing others to make your goals become theirs. Any time you have an opportunity to do a favor for someone else within the organization, you should welcome it; it's a chance to get into the plus column if you need a favor down the road.

Peer influence is accomplished in a way similar to that of barter. Over your professional life you will, hopefully, cultivate a group of professional "friends," people who know and respect you. These people will respond favorably to your ideas if you present them well and with a tactful approach. Not, "Hey, we're friends, aren't we? How about signing off on that transfer for your development engineer?" but "Ben, this project has a lot of merit for the company, and that new materials person you have could get some valuable experience helping out with it. Would you consider it?" Understand that this technique will work only if you have made the initial investment in networking within your organization to get to know people and if you have proven to be committed and trustworthy yourself. Project managers who only take without giving something back soon find their requests falling on deaf ears.

4.2 Early Detection

A little conflict is a good thing (a little healthy argument stimulates ideas), but time spent in conflict is time taken away from goal activity. Also, if team members have some disagreement about what the goal is or should be, then support for that goal will be diminished. So, it truly is in the project manager's best interest to surface conflicts and resolve them as early as possible. Many who have experienced ugly and painful conflicts wish to avoid conflict at all costs. However, conflicts in a professional setting that are not uncovered and successfully put to rest will, inevitably, become crises at the worst possible time.

In customer service environments, successful companies have learned to ask the customer often, "How are things? Was this situation resolved to your satisfaction?" They don't wait until there is a problem; they look for smoke and deal with it before a blaze is burning their toes in the form of lost customers. Clever project managers invite critical thinking and positive conflict resolution techniques. They further make sure conflicts with the goals are confronted and settled satisfactorily.

4.3 Conflict Resolution

Project managers who are faced with conflict from time to time must guide the situation to a constructive conclusion. It is highly recommended, however, that all project managers train their people in conflict resolution skills by utilizing either outside trainers or internal support personnel for that purpose. By training and supporting team members in solving their own conflicts, the project manager will have fewer "fires" to put out and may even eliminate the parade of small squabbles that file into his or her office. Following are guidelines for constructive conflict resolution.

4.3.1 Guidelines for Resolving Conflict

The goal of conflict management is to maintain a balance between constructively keeping things stirred up (which stimulates critical thinking and creativity) and destructively allowing differences of opinion, conflicts of needs, and clashes of personality or communication style to interfere with the completion of projects. Following is a technique for handling conflicts. By stepping through each guideline as you assess a conflict situation, you will develop a more methodical and strategic approach to managing conflict when it occurs.

Guideline 1. Consider: Is this a conflict or a problem? A conflict often grows out of a difference in need or in understanding. A problem can be generally recognized by the group as a situation that should be solved. (Views on religion can create a conflict; starving children present a problem that most agree should be solved.) If it is a problem, use problem-solving techniques. If it is a conflict, proceed to the next guideline.

Guideline 2. Do I (as the project manager) need to be involved in this? Sometimes the issue is not one you should be spending your time on, especially if the situation is not directly related to the project. Often, though, seemingly unrelated issues have a way of spilling over into the project's productivity profile. If the project or the team's harmony is in jeopardy, then intervention is required. Proceed to guideline 3.

Guideline 3. What are the issues and the emotions connected with the conflict? So many people who try to resolve conflicts with others become more and more emotional out of frustration at not being "heard." If the issue is emotionally volatile to one or more parties, then the source of the emotion must be addressed along with the issue itself.

Guideline 4. Are the parties involved committed to resolution? This is where the manager must lean a little on the participants. All involved must agree to persist in the discussion and process until the conflict is resolved for all concerned. (Some managers have been known to lock their doors until the situation is solved.) Further, each must agree to say if the issue is still not resolved. Squelched conflicts seem to stop for the time being, but will erupt again over and over until they are addressed and worked through. One Japanese company locks the conference room doors from the outside until all parties sign off on the annual budget.

Guideline 5. Are all discussions characterized by a genuinely constructive attitude and by positive, nonloaded (not sarcastic or accusing) statements? The project manager must curb any abusive or unprofessional words, gestures, or attitudes including non-participation on the one extreme and swearing or violence on the other.

Guideline 6. What is it going to take to make this okay with all parties? Use problem-solving techniques to resolve issues and affirming, interactive listening (see Chapter 4, Communication) to address emotions. Encourage creative solutions and affirm any who suggest options that benefit all and not just their own interests.

Guideline 7. After resolution seems to have occurred with the problem-solving session, ask each affected party again, "Does this resolve the situation for you and can you support the solution?" This second check can sometimes uncover unvoiced objections suppressed by fatigue or stubborn nonparticipation.

Guideline 8. Celebrate the resolution with all concerned and congratulate all on their commitment to the project by their resolving the issue.

Methods to Defuse Goal Conflicts

Have each side state the other's position.
Brainstorm creative and unconventional solutions.
Use humor to ease tension.
Negotiate over a meal.
Use a professional arbitrator.
Use a surprise experience or outing to build common ground.
Physically move discussion away from the workplace.
Have people dress casually.

■ ■ ■

"When a team is divided, and unsure of proper method or direction, I can see this method will help it to find the path through forest." Yury seemed to be almost talking to himself.

"That's right Yury," Tracey said, "managing conflict is another way to gain agreement, and to get your people to buy into the project in the same way that you already have." She was pleased that Yury had grasped this important concept so quickly.

Jerry wasn't quite convinced. "This all sounds great, but who has time to sit around and do all this conflict management stuff?"

"Among others—you do," Ralph replied. "Because if you don't, you won't get commitment, and you will end up spending the time many times over later in the project when you can least afford it. Unresolved conflicts divide people's attention and draw the focus away from the goal of the project that you are accountable for. Is it getting clearer now?"

Tom jumped in. "OK, that makes good sense. But the biggest problem that we have in the sales force is that we know what the goal is, but it's hard to keep people psyched up about it."

"No," said Yury. "Once they know what to do, there is no reason to worry about psyche. The team will produce once they know what is expected." Yury still believed that a strong hand covered a multitude of sins.

"Have you experienced what Tom is talking about? Have you ever had a group who knew what they were supposed to be doing but just couldn't seem to stay motivated?"

■ ■ ■

5.0 Creating Goal Commitment

There are two parts that make up commitment. They are *securing* the commitment and *maintaining* that commitment. It does you no good to motivate your workers at the start, and then halfway through the development process, allow them to lose interest. Once you gain the enthusiasm from everyone, keep it!

5.1 Securing the Commitment

When attempting to capture the commitment of your employees, return to the vision. The originally conceived vision may need to be rephrased or reworded to make it easily adopted by all on the team. The wording will help to create a distinct view of the project's goal. Be sure to remind team members throughout the process of the end result that you are working towards because often it is this idea of the end result that you are working towards because often it is this idea of the end result that gives people the motivation to work.

A critical element in securing commitment among team members is the project name. A project's name can determine the level of focus and commitment from its workers. The focus of your project and the means of committing your workers should be clearly evident in your project's name. For example, a worker who defines her project as "ensuring uninterrupted operation of a medical database" is likely considered to be more focused and committed than one who says she "does programming." Perhaps you are the project manager for a new supersonic airliner for the President of the United States and his staff. A name to reflect the focus might be the "Air Office One."

Finding a name to gain the commitment of workers is harder than finding the name for the focus. The name for the focus is usually a dressed-up term for the product's advantage. In fostering commitment, you must analyze what gain there is for your workers and connect the goal to the gain. Bonuses for reaching goals are one of the more popular incentives, but these are not always the most effective.

■ ■ ■

Jaime's growing smile and eager expression finally caused Ralph to call on him. "I know you have something here, Jaime."

"Yeah," Jaime said, nodding. "A few years ago we had this design contract for an ultralow-power chip to be used for a battery-powered cell phone. They called it the 'Chatter Box' since it allows extended talk time. Then, when we found out that finishing early would earn the team a vacation on the French Riviera (where testing was to be done), it became the 'Chatter Box in the Sun.' It's amazing how motivated everyone was on just an ordinary chip design project," he finished, laughing. The others laughed along with him.

■ ■ ■

The key point in naming a project is to tie its success in some way to the project team's needs for recognition, money, time off, whatever. Sometimes it is necessary to relate the vision to a basic aspiration, or to build on a common discontent. People will work with much more enthusiasm if they feel purpose in their job.

It is also very necessary to ensure that all participants understand their role in the project vision. They should be able, at some point, to lay claim personally to their part. For example, "I designed the housing for that radio." It is important for you to start to relay these roles in the final product as early as possible. This will get everyone involved and ready to go from the start.

5.2 Maintaining the Commitment

Creating the vision is one part of getting your workers to buy in. However, just because they have bought in doesn't mean they are sold forever. Actually, in most cases, people need support to keep the commitment. This is why it is important to continue to communicate the vision you originally sold your workers on.

Once the vision has been created, write it down, so you don't forget exactly what you said that sold your workers, suppliers, and upper management. Then send the written version to everyone. Post it on the bulletin boards at work. Repeat it often to those with whom you talk. When you are in meetings, restate it again and again. Remind others during discussions, and check to verify that everyone knows it.

Discuss often the impact of your project on other areas of work. Continually update everyone on the progress being made. Use frequent short announcements. Create lots of little celebrations and milestones. Give away little mementos and keepsakes.

■ ■ ■

Jerry offered, "Yeah, my manager on a plant project I remember was a nut about that stuff—status updates in the division's weekly staff meetings and monthly operations review. He posted pictures of the site at each stage of completion around the cafeteria walls of the mother plant and published short write-ups in the company newsletters. Announcing every little milestone, capital appropriation approval, site selection, land purchase, foundation. This was such a big deal to him that one employee commented, 'You can't break open a pack of mints around here without a celebration!'" Everyone laughed. "But, you know, our whole team worked hard, and had a good attitude."

■ ■ ■

These points are important because people will begin to talk about the goal and accomplishments amongst themselves. Word will travel around, and those who work on the project will begin to feel like they belong to something important. This constant talking and reminding of the project's goal will ensure that everyone knows all about it and no one is left "unsold" on it. Just make sure that if something changes with the project, you start all over and spread the word. This way, everyone knows of the new information.

With inspiring vision and clearly defined goals, you will create focus of effort and encourage commitment to the outcome. With commitment, the end product or job has a good chance of becoming the best possible work, a source of personal and professional satisfaction for you and your team.

Chapter Summary

When you are preparing a project for the start phase, it is imperative for the focus and commitment of the project to be clear to everyone, especially you.

The goal of the project reflects its focus, and is defined along three critical *measurable* dimensions; specification, time, and cost objectives. In addition you must address goal conflicts. Pursue all groups until they are "on-board" and have their various conflicting views, needs, and resources streamlined.

The commitment to the project reflects what's in it for the team. Commitment to the project should be gained from all of the workers involved. It does you no good to have only some, even most, of the workers committed. Everyone has considerable impact on a project's success so it is imperative that all have a desire for the project to be completed successfully. Creating a vision for the team is helpful. A sense of purpose makes everyone feel that much more important, and this will show in the results.

Gaining the commitment is only half the battle; you must also maintain it. Various forms of communication between you and everyone involved will do this. The project name should directly illustrate both the focus and commitment of the project.

Chapter Questions

1. What is the difference between doing things right and doing the right thing?
2. Why is it critical that the goals be measurable? State the three critical dimensions of project goals.
3. How can you relate the "agreed upon" aspect of the goal development process to commitment?
4. Who has to agree to the statement of goals for the project? Why?
5. What effect does resource availability have on time lines?
6. What are three causes of goal conflicts?
7. Why is establishing good professional relationships necessary for project managers?
8. What is the role of vision in maintaining goal commitment?

Project Challenge: Applying What You Know

A. Kitchen Remodeling Project A homeowner's son has agreed to invest some money in materials for the remodeling of his parents' kitchen, if he can decorate the kitchen and the cabinets in vinyl he likes. He and his wife live in the house in a basement apartment, and they use the kitchen quite a lot. The problem is that the owner's son has horrible taste. The owner needs the money, but doesn't want to turn control over to the son. The son feels that since he will use the kitchen a lot and is investing money, he should determine the decorating. Since their tastes are completely different, their goals for the final "look" for the kitchen would be completely different.

1. How do their goals fit our goal conflict guidelines?
2. What are the issues in the conflict between the two?
3. Suggest at least four possible solutions to the conflict.
4. Write the goal statement of the solution that best resolves the conflict.

5. What role might a budget of time and cost play in this situation?
6. How could each party involved secure "buy-in" from the other?

B. Industry-Based Problem For a more challenging, industry-based problem, examine the following situation.

Power Cell, a battery manufacturing company, has been asked to develop a new battery to power electric vehicles. Federal mandates are requiring the manufacture and sale of electric vehicles in California and seem to be moving that way in several other states.

Power Cell is a lead acid battery company, and they feel that a new battery chemistry, such as nickel metal hydride or lithium ion variation, would deliver more power with less weight. This would make these new batteries more suitable for electric vehicles and would give them more driving distance on a charge. The federal government is offering $500,000 in grants to contribute to the development of these batteries. However, it will cost nearly $900,000 to develop the battery.

Marketing sees a great opportunity to enter into a new market for electric vehicles and feels this should be a real goal for the company. Accounting is concerned that the grant will only offset a portion of the cost in an "iffy" market that is just opening up. Engineering has the battery experts to do the research and feels it is important to advance patents just as a matter of keeping up with the changes in the demands of the battery market. Time can be a problem since this is a whole new application of these batteries and will require considerable research and development, testing, and prototyping.

Write what might be legitimate and supportable goal statements for:

1. The Vice President of Marketing
2. The Chief Financial Officer
3. The Vice President of Engineering
4. The Environmental Protection Agency (the supplier of the grant money)

Questions for analysis:

1. What goal conflicts do you see emerging?
2. Why would the goals conflict?
3. How would you manage the conflict?
4. Develop an overall goal statement that all four interests could support.

Interview with an Expert

***Norm Conwill**, Principal, Marinetics*

Question: How is goal setting different for a Project Mgr. than a line manager ?

Conwill: The line manager must set goals that are somewhat perpetual in nature, even though they must continually be analyzed/evaluated, and modified to meet current demands. Whereas, the Project Manager usually is faced with a discrete set of requirements that have a start and finish, and therefore his/her goals are more specific to a given event completed at a given time within a prescribed budget.

The line manager's goals must relate to the needs of a department operating within a company that has many other departments and functional areas of a company whose common goal dictates the goals of each department. Therefore, the line manager's goal-setting philosophy must mesh with the goals of the company and thus the other departments on a continuing basis.

The Project Manager's goals are more like the overall company's goals, in that the Project Manager has a specific goal which is an end in itself and need not mesh with any other event.

Question: How does the receipt of Specifications and Deliverables received from a customer relate to goal setting?

Conwill: Once a Project Manager receives Specs and Deliverables from a customer, goal setting must be his number one priority. The specs, etc. define the customer's requirements and the PM can accomplish nothing until he organizes a team, then defines the project's goals, and establishes a schedule to complete the project. The goals help to determine the team, the resources needed to reach the goals. Within resource groups, will be goals determined by the group that will allow them to meet deliverables for the project?

Question: Is a start-up business set up like a project?

Conwell: So few would-be entrepreneurs understand that that is exactly what a start-up is. Especially if the business will need outside venture capital or bank funding, those with the money want to see the goal of the company with a deliverable of profitability within a definite time limit and with detailed plans for resources. Without a very specific target for profitability and almost a Gantt chart-level of detailed planning showing intermediate goals with timetables and justifications, no investor will touch a proposed venture, no matter how good the concept sounds.

Question: Success Story relating to goal setting.

Conwell: I was part of a group of businessmen who started a company in the computer hardware industry. The group were professionals with diverse personal and professional capabilities that were complementary. One of the first things we did was write a business plan that defined the company's goals, and the operating plan to accomplish those goals exactly as a project manager would do. The company stuck to its goals pursuit, met objectives and grew successfully. Within eight years it was purchased by a major corporation—our goal.

Look at all these e-commerce businesses that just drifted along with funding from outside with no clue or plan how to become profitable. Huge numbers of them will "bite the dust" by the end of 2000.

Question: People set goals in their own lives all the time. How is goal-setting in project management different?

Conwell: That's the problem, people set goals all the time. Most people live by the seat of their pants, day to day, making decisions and setting half-hearted goals. And with no plan to meet those goals. I would say that by definition a goal must be developed with an accompanying set of plans with timetables and deliverables along the way. Otherwise, like a project's goals, personal goals won't be met.

CHAPTER 8

SCHEDULING

CHAPTER PREVIEW

THE PROJECT MANAGEMENT SEMINAR: SESSION 8

Ragdeesh was late. He struggled onto the train in a frenzy, tie slightly askew, fresh coffee stain adorning his wrinkled shirt. His disheveled appearance was highly unusual for this characteristically fastidious man. He plopped down into a seat. It wasn't difficult to find one by this time, since he had missed most of rush hour. There were advantages and disadvantages to having training in your own hometown. The others could just take the elevator downstairs. He had to plan for a commute. Opening his bulging briefcase, he resituated some of the papers whose corners were sticking out.

"There's simply too much to do, " Ragdeesh thought. His son was in bed with a bad flu from which his wife was just recovering. And then the boss called at midnight to tell him that the Berkmar deal was on the brink of falling through, which meant an all-nighter reworking the budget. Now he couldn't even stop by the office to check in on things, because he had this training to attend. "How could I have possibly anticipated this?" he wondered.

The train's brakes squealed as it reached Ragdeesh's stop. "Okay, " he thought, "We'll find out how good this Ralph is. Let's see if he can teach me how to schedule for sniffles and snafus."

By the time Ragdeesh made it to the hotel conference room, George had begun the day's discussion. It was obvious that the trainees had already broken into groups to discuss their concerns about project scheduling. Several questions were spelled out on the flip chart in George's now familiar method for starting class.

- Who sets the schedule?
- How do we set priorities?

- How do we get everyone to agree?
- How do we handle foul-ups?
- Can we really anticipate problems?
- What about changes?

Jerry and Tom sat together at one table, with Hilda, Yury, and Jaime sharing the other. Tracy stood at the back of the room. They all listened intently to what Ralph was saying, as Ragdeesh took his seat, looking at the objectives for the day, listing the steps necessary to develop a project schedule:

- **Determining work breakdown structure**
- **Noting precedence relationships**
- **Using scheduling tools**

1.0 Work Breakdown Structure (WBS)

Work Breakdown Structure
a schedule that shows each step of the project

Imagine that you want to remodel your kitchen. With the exception of a recently purchased refrigerator, stove, and oven, nothing has been done in 22 years. Or perhaps you bought a fixer-upper house built in the 1920s. The "how" is not important. What is important is that you're short on cash. You can't afford to hire someone to remodel the kitchen for you, so you gather a few of your old college buddies and set out to do the job yourself. Remodeling a kitchen is not quite the same thing as painting the Sistine Chapel, but it's no small feat in itself. This project will require some planning. You can't just call your friends over and say, "Let's get to it!" First you're going to have to develop a schedule, to make sure that each step of the project is completed in the appropriate order.

The chart in Figure 8–1 illustrates this.

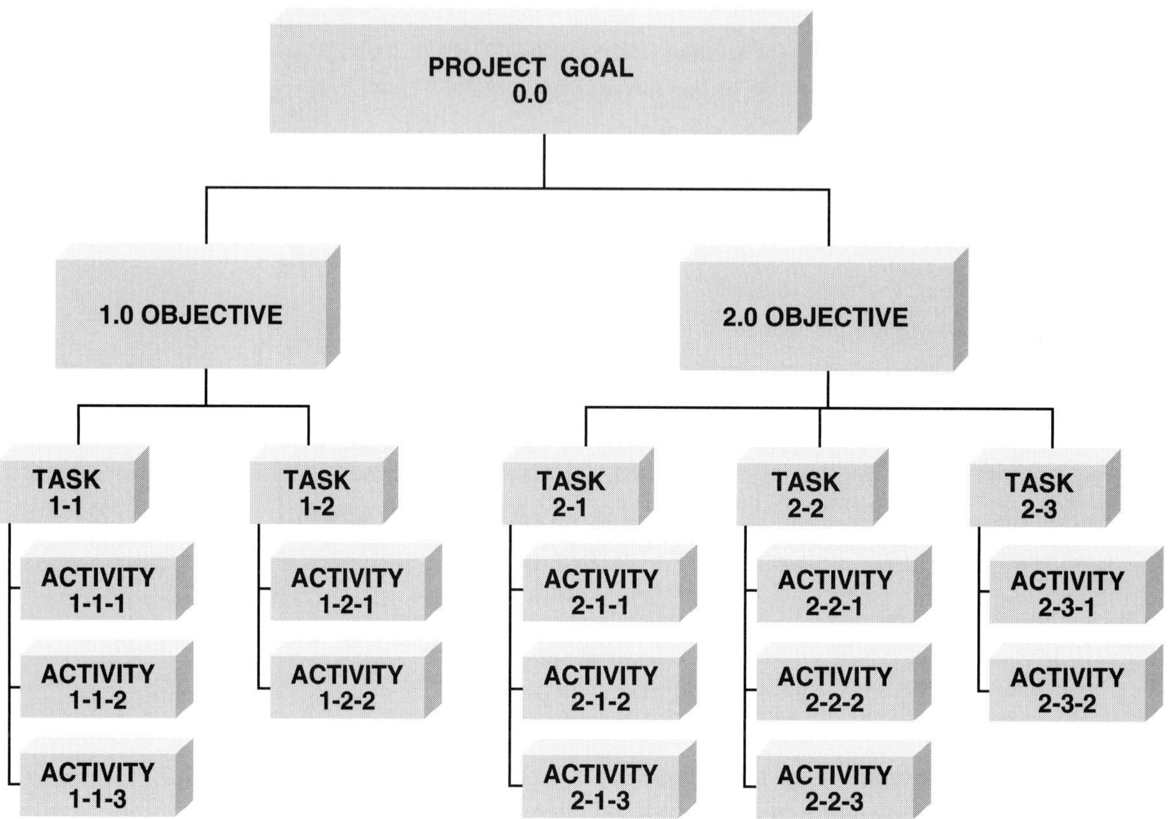

Figure 8–1
Typical Work Breakdown Structure (WBS)

To develop a schedule, the successful project manager must break the project down into small work components. This concept is fairly intuitive. Most people understand that any job is easier to handle when broken into smaller pieces.

The challenge arises when you actually set about breaking the project down. You must be careful to make sure that each piece is neither too big to be competently handled, nor so small as to be a nuisance. Remember when you wrote your first research paper in school? You knew generally how you were supposed to go about doing it, but you needed a little direction. Initially you were overwhelmed because you saw only the entire monstrous project. You calmed down a little and thought it through; things got a little easier when you isolated the objective of research from the writing objective, the objective of the first draft, and the objective of the final product. You further dissected the first draft objective into smaller tasks, such as table of contents, bibliography, abstract, and so on, then divided each of those into manageable activities, each taking just a couple of hours to do. The paper as a project probably became progressively easier as the pieces contributing to it grew smaller. This is where the successful project manager's skills are highly desired.

1.1 Hierarchy of Work

A job must be broken down into objectives, then into tasks, and finally into activities. Using this hierarchy of work simplifies the process of breaking down the project into its smallest components, called activities, and ensures that you don't miss any. The work breakdown structure chart in Figure 8-1 shows how the project goal breaks down into **objectives.** These are big chunks of the project, which, when added together, accomplish the project goal. Further, each objective then breaks down into several tasks. Tasks are sub-objectives, or work packages, each made up of multiple activities.

objectives Big chunks of the project, when added together accomplish the project goal

1.2 Objectives

Remember goals and objectives from the previous chapter? An objective is a combination of tasks that concern specific functional groups, major contractors, major subassemblies, or some other logical division of the total project. Recall our example of an electric vehicle manufacturer. When opening a factory to produce this new technology, decision makers might first design the work-flow and plant layout. These are fairly standard steps in the process of opening a new unit in a business.

But objectives won't always be so well prescribed or apparent for every project. So how do you go about developing objectives? There are several ways. The most common and useful way by far is to consider functional groups. A *functional group* is a team that specializes in a specific discipline, like accounting or research and development. This means that you define objectives around the specialty of each functional group since a functional area has the necessary expertise to deliver realistic and useful plans. This will greatly aid in achieving consensus and agreement about the overall project. Consider the company's structure. Is there a director of operations, one for marketing, and one for finance? These people are already expert in their areas, and their contributions will be vital. The company is structured in that way for a multitude of good reasons. Let the company's organizational chart guide you in the creation of your objectives.

You may not subdivide by functional groups for every project. Other categories by which to define your objectives include:

- **Major subassemblies**—a collection of smaller assemblies that form a logical grouping. The drivetrain on your car is a major subassembly. The body is another.
- **Major parts**—the big parts around which construction of a project might revolve. The user interface might be a major part of a software development project.
- **Skills**—often specific skills required for a project will be a defining element. This may present itself as groups of contractors or segments of work. Program coding may become an objective requiring programmers from various groups.
- **Major resources**—may include a variety of critical resources, such as some critical skills, suppliers, critical materials needed, and/or venture partners.

But what about our kitchen example? One objective might be plans; another could be demolition and clearing, while a third objective may be installation and finishing (see Figure 8–2). What's important is that each objective makes sense and clearly contributes to the completion of your goal.

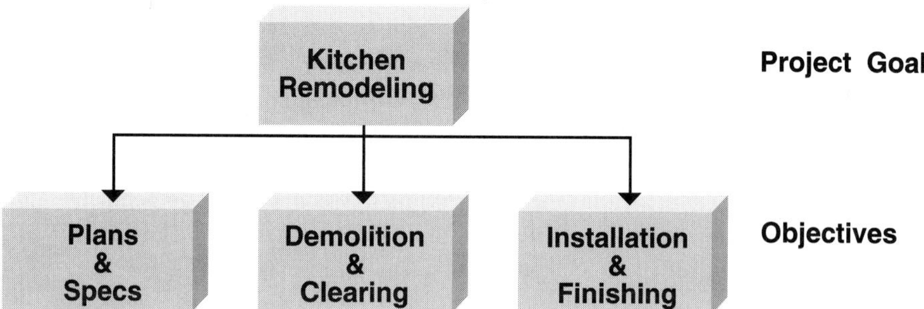

Figure 8–2
Dividing project goal into major objectives.

Remember that objectives are the broad areas of focus that will help to organize the team's thinking and point out activities that may otherwise be overlooked.

The planning up to this point has been preliminary planning—the advance planning that is done with minimal involvement by other participants. In order to engender commitment in your team, it is highly advisable from this point forward to involve the other participants heavily. The remaining planning activities must be generated by them, with your guidance, rather than the other way around. Following is a series of steps to consider:

1. Gather your team for a planning session. Present your preliminary plan to them.
2. Ask them to refine and finalize the objectives, defining each objective along the three critical dimensions: **specs, cost,** and **time.**
3. Mutually distribute responsibility for each objective.
4. Ask each objective owner to formulate the tasks. Have the team discuss the tasks in order to ensure continuity of handoffs. It is also wise to involve the doers (those who will do the actual work) in this stage.
5. Allow the doers to break down tasks into activities. Insist that the activities be small, discrete chunks of work.

specs specifications of what must happen with a project

1.3 Tasks

The next step after establishing your objectives is to divide each one into tasks. A task represents one of several major deliverables towards an objective. Look at Figure 8–3 showing tasks that follow from one of the objectives in our kitchen example. Completion of each task marks a major deliverable of its parent objective.

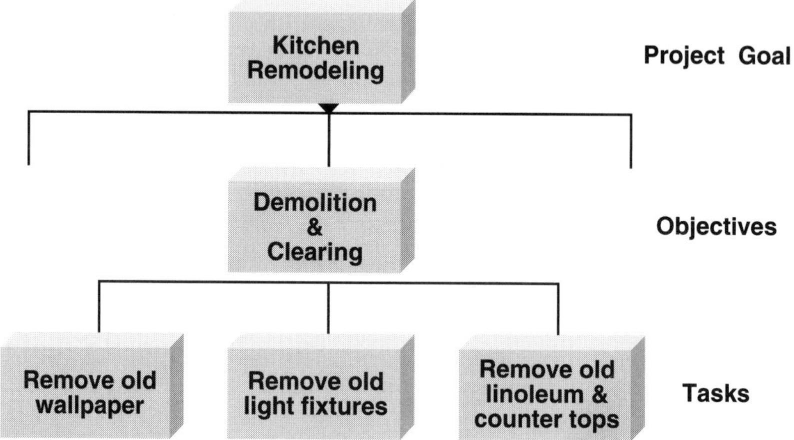

Figure 8–3
Subdividing one objective into tasks.

1.4 Activities

Next, you will further subdivide tasks into **activities.** Activities are the basic building blocks of a project, the individual actions that will be performed one at a time. If a project is a pyramid, then activities are the individual blocks. The task of finding a restaurant might be broken into the activities of asking for a friend's recommendation, then looking in a phone book, and finally looking at a map of the area.

activities the basic building blocks of a project, the individual actions that will be performed one at a time

For our kitchen example we can develop some activities. Notice in Figure 8–4 that the name of each activity is exactly the same as the desired result. This makes it easier for everyone to remember what the activity entailed, as well as for the doer to know when it is complete. It is also important to notice that there is no precedence information here. There is only a list of activities. The main concern here is to compile an exhaustive list of the activities and not to miss any. It is important that you do an effective job of developing your activities.

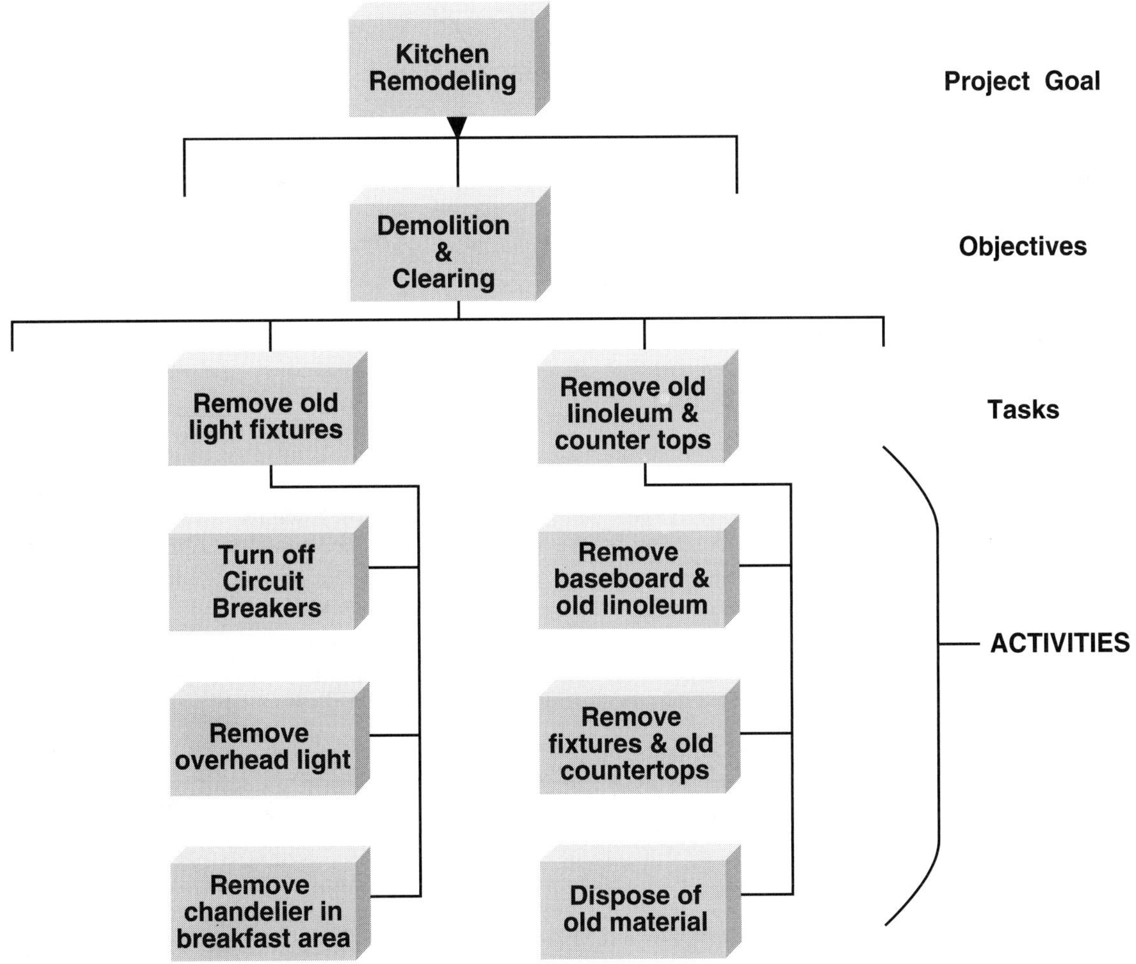

Figure 8–4
Dividing tasks into activities.

Also important is to develop the activities in exactly the right amount of detail. If your divisions are not detailed enough, it becomes easy for work to fall through the cracks. The challenge of the process is in dividing jobs down to a small enough level of detail so that it is easy to see the work involved, and the way the parts fit together—but not too detailed to the point of micromanagement! Obviously, a good activity cutoff is at the point of handoff between team members, but you may still be left with activities that are too big.

duration rule rule that requires you to define activities that will take hours to days to complete, thereby limiting the amount of time during which you have no visibility of progress

A good rule of a thumb is to define activities that will take somewhere between several hours to a couple of days to complete, depending on the circumstances. This **duration rule** limits the amount of time during which you have no visibility of progress. This way, if an activity is stuck or delayed, you will know in a day or two when it becomes overdue, thus allowing sooner intervention. Obviously, bigger activities with longer durations will aggravate this exposure.

Work Breakdown Structure Objective

- Divide and subdivide the project into smaller work packages.
- Organize activities into an organizational chart so that teams can readily identify their responsibilities, and how other teams' work relates to them.

Another challenge is in anticipating where there will be problems. Finer detail is needed in problematic or critical work in order to facilitate resolution and be able to exercise preventive action on a timely basis.

■ ■ ■

Tracy spoke up at this point. "We had to relocate a production facility during a live ramp-up of production. All the prep work was scheduled during the week, but the actual move took place over several weekends. We had a war room set up with schedules displayed all the way around the walls. I remember that the prep work was scheduled in daily chunks, but the critically orchestrated weekend work was scheduled by the hour!"

■ ■ ■

A major element of critical importance here is activity assignments. As activities are being developed and agreed upon, each has to be assigned to someone, preferably a doer or a work-package manager who may assign the specific doer later, in which case the manager's name is assigned. Activity assignments must be treated carefully. Each activity must have one primary responsible person assigned, though many people may collaborate. He/she is in charge of the activity, is the point of contact, initiates and coordinates action, and raises flags when things get off course.

To develop your Work Breakdown Structure:

- Develop the project goal yourself.
- Take a cursory pass at defining the objectives—the preliminary plan.
- Have teams refine the objectives.
- Have teams break down the objectives into tasks.
- Have doers break down tasks into activities.

Project: You are planning an event for your company. The event will include flying in out-of-town guests, catering, entertainment, speaker events, meetings, hotel accommodations, and more. In total, you should have about 16 activities that will fall under the responsibility of the district manager, the administrative assistant, the sales secretary, marketing, and janitorial. Create a Work Breakdown Structure organizational chart that shows at a glance which Work Package Manager is responsible for each activity.

2.0 Precedence Relationships

So you've broken your project down into objectives, tasks, and activities. You're ready to call your buddies over and get cracking, right? Wrong. Just doing the work in serial fashion will (a) take too long, and (b) leave some of your friends idle and getting bored!

Which activity are you going to start with? Which need to wait for the completion of another? Which tasks need to be completed simultaneously? At which points do we really need the various materials we ordered? These are important questions, and how you answer them will determine the success or failure of your project. In other words, you must first determine the **precedence relationships** of the activities—which activities must precede others.

precedence relationships relationships between activities based on when they occur in relation to each other.

There are four main logical categories that will influence the sequencing of your activities:

1. Technical requirements
2. Safety and efficiency considerations
3. Policy or preference decisions
4. Availability of limited resources

2.1 Technical Requirements

When you remodel your kitchen, there are planning questions that should, logically, be asked. "Does the refrigerator have to be moved before the countertops are redone?" "Do you have to do the plumbing before you can install electrical?" These are physical requirements of the job. You can't really do them in any other sequence.

Physical requirements for other types of jobs might include:

Run electrical wiring prior to putting up drywall.

Write before editing; it's physically impossible to edit before writing, and it's mind-boggling to try to edit while writing.

Test before repairing; you'll save yourself a lot of time.

Frame before you pour concrete.

■ ■ ■

Jaime interrupted, "It's kind of like the way the power company is always warning you to call before you dig. Calling first isn't really a technical requirement. You could dig first, and everything might be okay. But if you hit a power line, you'll wish you'd thought about safety."

"Exactly," said Ralph.

■ ■ ■

2.2 Safety and Efficiency

It can be helpful and revealing to think of matters of safety and efficiency as separate from technical requirements. The reason for this may not be completely obvious, so consider putting up an old style TV antenna on your roof. Is there any real technical problem with just climbing up and erecting the antenna? Probably not. Safety, however, requires that you secure a ladder and perhaps even a scaffold first. It was once said that there are old pilots and there are daring pilots. But there are no old, daring pilots!

Other safety examples might include:

Check preflight checklist.

Keep lighter fluid away from the grill.

Crash bars on exit doors

Disconnect power before making repairs.

Efficiency concerns are those that make your or your customer's life easier, but don't have direct physical or safety requirements. Consider the relationship between carpeting and painting a room. There is no physical requirement that prevents us from painting a new room after the carpeting is laid down. But unless we want paint on the carpet, there are some additional work items that should be done—like covering the floor with plastic. It would be more efficient to paint first and then lay carpet. Unless we do, we add work to our day, cost to the project, and doubts to the customer's mind.

Some other examples of efficiency concerns are:

Scheduling preventative maintenance

Market testing before product launch

2.3 Policy or Preference

Most companies will have policies in place that will affect the sequencing of your activities. Some policies concern aesthetics. A developer may insist that landscaping of the entrance must precede the opening of the sales office. There is no technical reason to beautify the front prior to selling. It may even be less efficient. But the public is more likely to approve of a condominium complex that has an attractively landscaped front and, therefore, more likely to purchase a unit there.

Other policies regard spending. For instance, you may not have to get approval to take your accountant out to lunch at a fast-food restaurant, but you likely will have to fill out some paperwork before spending $50,000 on computerized analysis equipment for the new water treatment plant. It will likely require several levels of approval and payback analysis, not to mention the need for the purchasing people to shop around!

Policies will have an impact on the sequencing of your activities. They are not physical requirements, but they do affect budget and client satisfaction.

■ ■ ■

"As I toured the plant of one of our top-notch contractors," Ragdeesh put in, "I noticed several people sitting idly chatting at their work stations, with plenty of unfinished work available on the stations," said Ragdeesh. "Surprised, I asked if this laxity is tolerated. Turns out that team was working on a military contract which requires inspections by the client at each stage of production and they usually had to wait for the late inspectors."

"Perfect example of policy decision by the client, even if it seems counterproductive to the project," said Ralph.

■ ■ ■

Some other examples of policy might be:

Vendor certification prior to contract

Bidding procedures

Legal requirement that can differ by region within the same company

Preference to minority contractors

2.4 Availability of Resources

The final category, which will heavily influence scheduling, is the abundance or scarcity of **resources.** Resources can be anything: money, computer equipment, even technical expertise. Your critical resources will determine which activities are given precedence in the sequence.

resources money, computer equipment, technical expertise, or anything that you may need to accomplish the goal

If the company is short on cash, you may not be able to commit major expenditures until revenue is realized or credit is obtained. Or you may not be able to hire outside experts in some fields, and have to do it with in-house teams, when they become available. Maybe you need your networking wiz, and he is working on a more critical project. You may have only one paving crew or one 400-ton crane between several different projects. These are restrictions that must be paid attention to.

A word of caution here. Precedence adds time. As you add in precedence, you are serializing steps, and that series turns into time. Make sure there is a good reason for each and every one that is created. Fewer precedence steps result in more parallel activities (more on that in a bit), and that will result in a shorter project. Test each precedence and question its necessity. Be thorough and creative. The later stages of the project are the most difficult and potentially the most expensive to alter, and unfortunately, a mistake in precedence relationships will show up there.

But how do you deal with the unexpected? The only real way to cope with the unexpected is to have all the expected eventualities planned for, and then you can add some elbow room to cope with the remaining unexpected problems. In the following section you will see how all these things relate to each other, to get a better idea of how to put together a viable schedule.

3.0 Scheduling Tools

Charts are wonderful inventions. They simplify our daily lives by laying out in detailed sequence exactly what we need to know in order to complete a project. We should all take a moment now to silently thank the individuals who first decided to put down their plans and activities in the form of a chart. There are two basic options from which to choose when considering scheduling tools—the bar chart and the flow chart. Which one you use will be determined by the requirements of each particular situation. Each type of chart has its strengths and weaknesses.

3.1 Gantt Charts

Gantt chart a bar chart that is a visual representation of the sequencing and duration of activities on any given project

A **Gantt chart** is a bar chart that is a visual representation of the sequencing and duration of activities on any given project. It consists of a list of activities, a time scale, and a bar for each activity. Each activity is assigned a number, and time is plotted along the horizontal axis (see Figure 8–5). This kind of chart was developed by Henry Gantt during World War I.

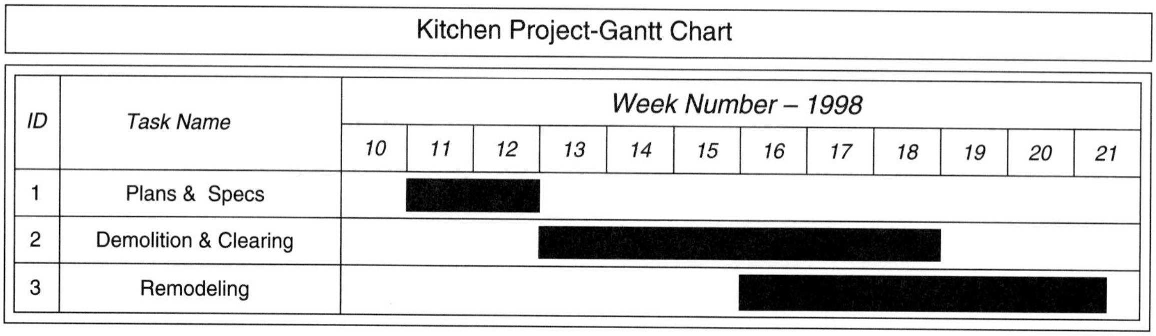

Kitchen Project-Gantt Chart

ID	*Task Name*	*Week Number – 1998*											
		10	*11*	*12*	*13*	*14*	*15*	*16*	*17*	*18*	*19*	*20*	*21*
1	Plans & Specs												
2	Demolition & Clearing												
3	Remodeling												

Figure 8–5
Kitchen Project Gantt Chart

People find Gantt charts useful because:

- They are easy to read.
- They give each team member a quick overview of the project.
- They indicate clearly the status of each activity (when properly updated).
- They allow each individual to track his or her own progress.
- They allow for analysis of what-if situations.
- They can be drawn to show budgets, needed resources, and equipment usage instead of activities.

Actually, Gantt charts are the most widely used tool for projects great and small. But like all other things in life, no tool is perfect. Even Gantt charts have their disadvantages. For instance, precedence relationships are difficult to display on a Gantt chart. In the past, Gantt charts were very tedious to update when changes needed to be made to the schedule, and changes do need to be made if you are doing your job as project manager. However, with modern software available to keep the charts up to date, much of this problem has been removed.

Scenario: DeVry Institute of Technology's audiovisual equipment room schedules audiovisual equipment for class time for teachers and students of the institute. Scheduling is done in 2-hour blocks with no slack time between classes. Currently, DeVry is having a problem with its returns and pickups. Some people want to pick up early for setup, and others are held up by students' questions and return late, which causes a problem in scheduling.

Problem: Equipment can be checked out any time between 8 A.M. and 8 P.M. You have been given the task of master scheduling the equipment such that the problem is alleviated. Create a Gantt chart that will allow a slack time of 15 minutes between scheduled hours, thus creating a scheduling buffer for the audiovisual room. (See Figure 8–6.)

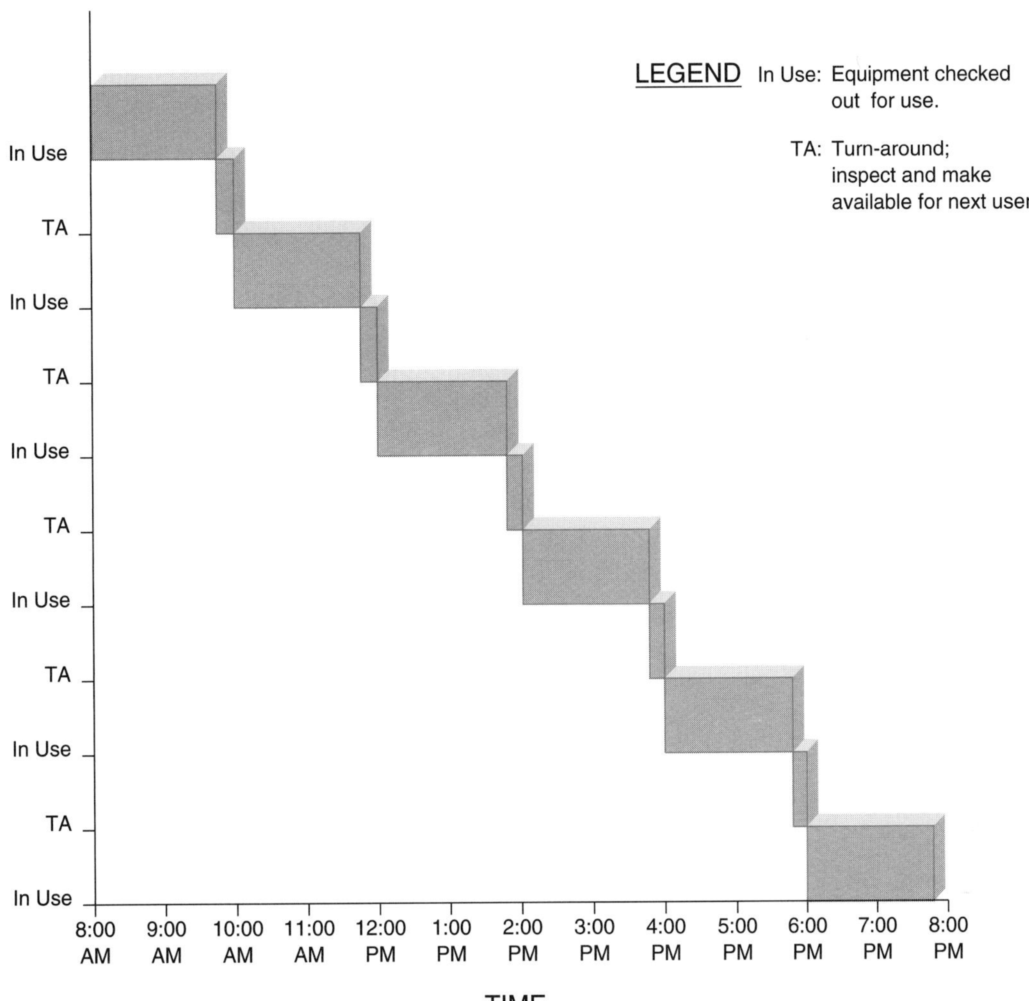

Figure 8–6
Gantt chart for audiovisual equipment at DeVry

3.2 PERT/CPM Networks

PERT/CPM networks examples of flowcharts, sometimes called diagrams

PERT/CPM Networks are examples of flowcharts, and are sometimes called network diagrams. They will be discussed in detail in Chapter 9. This chapter discusses the tools that will be needed to build PERT or CPM charts, which are diagrams consisting of nodes, connected by arrows. They are useful because they are designed to show the flow of work and highlight precedence relationships.

Pert chart diagrams, consisting of nodes connected by arrows, that show the flow of work and highlight precedence relationships

PERT or **CPM charts** can be drawn in one of two ways: the project activities can be represented by the nodes (Activity-on-Node), or they can be represented by the arrows connecting the nodes (Activity-on-Arrow).

3.2.1 Activity-on-Nodes

Activity-on-Node chart each activity is represented by a node or a box

For **Activity-on-Node** (AON) flow charts, each activity is represented by a node or a box. The label in the box can be used to indicate a more complete description of the activity, perhaps on a separate page. Precedence is indicated by the arrows that connect the nodes. Let's look at the basic elements used to create the AON flow chart.

Finish to Start. This means that Activity A must be finished before Activity B can start. An example of this from our kitchen would be to remove the old countertop before installing the new one. It is shown in Figure 8–7.

Figure 8–7
Activity-on-Node, Finish-to-Start Precedence

Start to Start. A must start in order for B to start. You must start writing in order to start typing. Once A has begun, the two activities may proceed concurrently. Figure 8–8 shows how to indicate this type of precedence.

Figure 8–8
Activity-on-Node, Start-to-Start Precedence

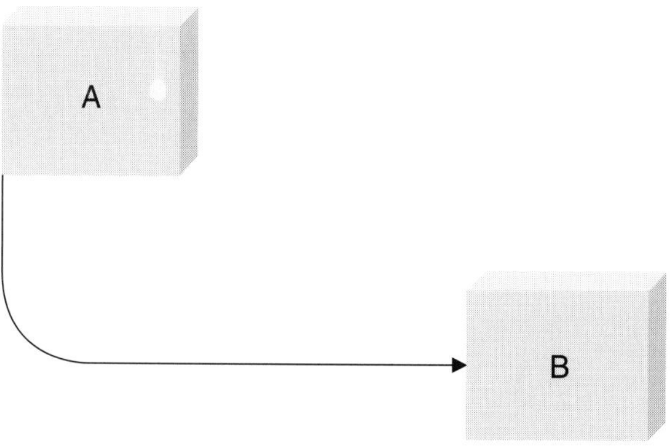

Finish to Finish. A must be finished in order for B to finish, as shown in Figure 8–9.

Figure 8–9
Activity-on-Node, Finish-to-Finish Precedence

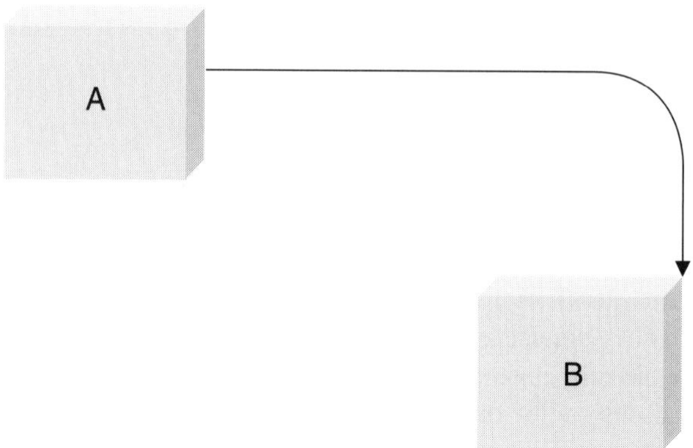

Combinations. Extending the example of writing and typing, since their durations are different, and since typing cannot finish until writing is finished, the relationship can be shown as illustrated in Figure 8–10.

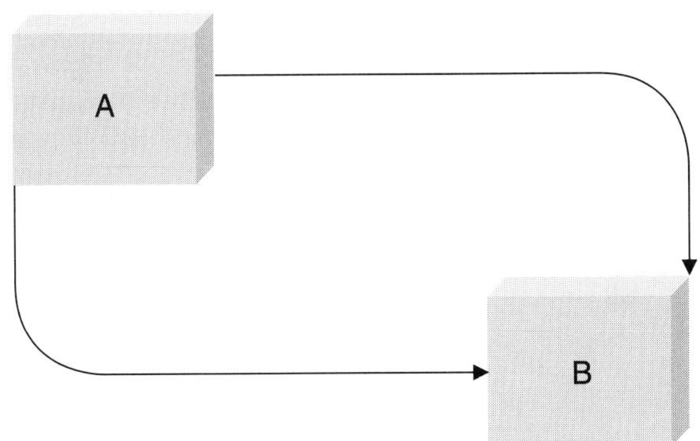

Figure 8–10
Activity-on-Node, Combination Start-to-Start and Finish-to-Finish Precedence

Example: Draw an activity-on-node diagram of the following scenario:

Activity A precedes activities B and C. E cannot start until both B and C are finished. B precedes D. D and E must finish before F can start. G must wait for F to finish. (See Figure 8–11.)

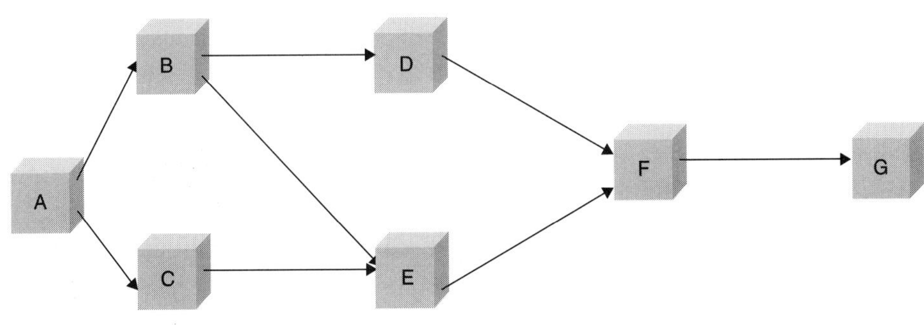

Figure 8–11
Activity-on-Node Diagram for Example

3.2.2 Activity-on-Arrows

The **Activity-on-Arrow** (AOA) technique is very similar to the AON method. AOA has the activities represented by the arrow, or branches. The arrows move from label to label, and you may use the two labels to relate a more detailed description of the activity on a separate sheet. Many people find that it is easier to grasp time information with the AOA network. In an AOA network, one advantage is that the nodes can be used as milestones.

activity-on-arrow
activities are represented by arrows, or branches

Finish to Start. This is straight series planning. Activity A must be complete prior to the starting of B. (See Figure 8–12.)

Figure 8–12
Activity-on-Arrow, Finish-to-Start Precedence

Start to Start. Regular parallel planning. AOA requires the addition of a "Dummy Activity" to keep the precedence correct. It is not an activity per se, but a placeholder in the diagram. A Dummy Activity has a duration of zero and is shown as a dotted line. (See Figure 8–13.)

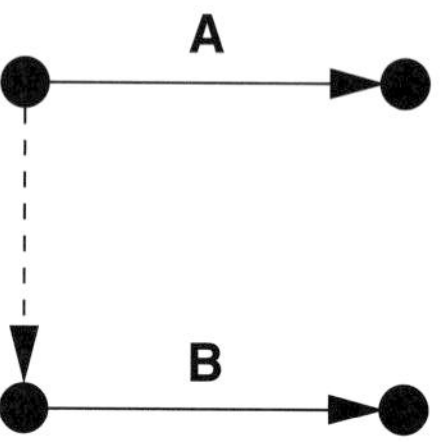

Figure 8–13
Activity-on-Arrow, Start-to-Start Precedence

Finish to Finish. Activity A has to finish before Activity B can be finished (Figure 8–14.)

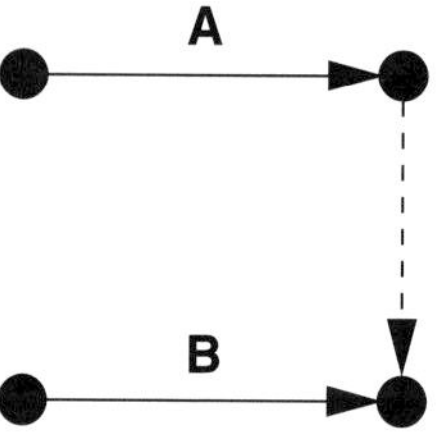

Figure 8–14
Activity-on-Arrow, Finish-to-Finish Precedence

Combination. Start to Start and Finish to Finish combined require two Dummy Activities to keep precedence in order (Figure 8–15.)

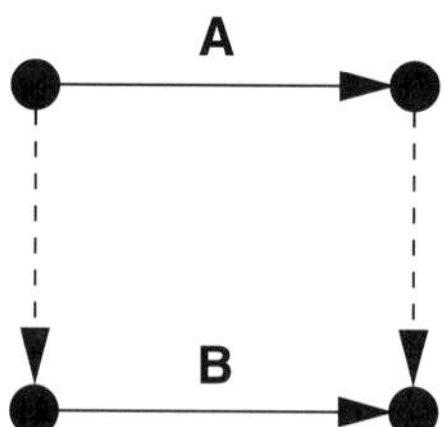

Figure 8–15
Activity-on-Arrow, Combination Start-to-Start and Finish-to-Finish Precedence

Example: Repeat the above example from AON, only use AOA this time. (See Figure 8–16).

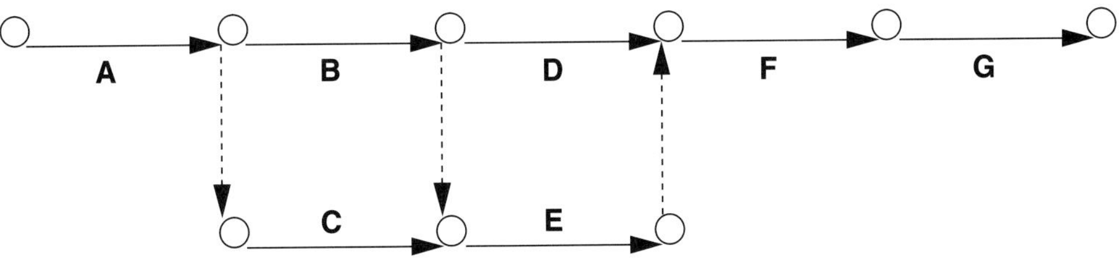

Figure 8–16
Activity-on-Arrow Diagram for Example

Figure 8–16 has exactly the same information as the AON diagram in Figure 8–11. Note the use of dummy activities to keep precedence in order. It is a good idea to verify your diagram's validity by comparing the numbers of activities and precedence from the list to those shown on the network. In addition, the nature of the relationships conveyed by the dummy activities is not readily clear. For example, the dotted arrow on the far left representing finish to start between A and C could also mean start to start between B and C, which is not true in this case.

For these and other reasons, the Activity-on-Node (AON) technique will be used from this point forward.

3.2.3 Application: Surprise Party Cake

In the earlier discussion about scheduling the example used was that of remodeling a kitchen with just the help of a few friends. Before returning to this example, another real-life situation is examined first.

You are standing in the shower one morning, singing a little something from Pavorotti at the top of your lungs, wondering why your significant other was acting extremely friendly upon awakening. Then it hits you—the birthday! You forgot . . . almost. So now, what are you going to do for a present? You haven't done a thing to plan any sort of celebration and now feel extremely guilty, especially after the birthday party thrown for you at the Ritz this year. You decide that the only way out of this sticky situation is to bake a surprise birthday cake. Surely this will get you out of your bind. But how do you get your significant other out of the house long enough to gather supplies and bake the cake? The task seems particularly daunting. But it's really a piece of cake, for a project manager, that is. First you spend some time defining your goal.

Project Goal: Bake a cake from scratch for a surprise birthday party. (See Figures 8–17 and 8–18.)

Project Goal

Focus

S	German Chocolate Cake
M	4-layer 9" round
A	Mother, kids, guests
R	About two boxes of cake mix
T	By noon today, up to $25.00

Commitment

Source		Why they want it done
End Users	Spouse	To know I care
Top Management	Mother-in-Law	Maintain control
Immediate Management "Check Signer"	Self	To not blow week's budget
Peers	Neighbor	Pal around with wife
	Guests	To surprise spouse on birthday
Team Members	Self	Same as above
	Kids	
	Neighbor	

Alternative goal statements

Surprise birthday cake

"I care" birthday cake

"Save the marriage" cake

Final goal statement:

"I care" surprise cake (Project Surprise)

Figure 8–17
Birthday Cake Project Goals—SMART Technique

Preliminary Project Plan - Project Surprise

Project Goal:
I Care Surprise Cake
4 layer German Chocolate, 9" round

Completion Deadline:
Noon today

Purpose of Project:
Keep spouse happy
Avoid embarrassment
Good times for friends and family

Total Budget:
Capital
Expense $25.00

Assumptions:
All utensils and tools available
All materials available
Neighbors and kids will cooperate
Mother-in-law will help

Major Objective:	Responsible Group:
Logistics	Neighbor & Mother-in-law
Prep & Clean-up (Tools)	Kids
Cooking	Self
Decorate & Present	Self & Kids

Check-Point & Significant Dates:
- Spouse leaves the house
- Spouse return time
- Party start time

Figure 8–18
Preliminary Project Plan Worksheet for Birthday Cake Project

Work Breakdown Structure

Next you need to perform your work division. To make things a little easier, assume that you have unlimited resources and all of the supplies you need are already in the house. Since this project is relatively small, the project's goal is your only objective, and you can go directly to the task level. You'll probably come up with three major tasks something along the lines of Find the Tools, Cook, and Decorate. The preliminary plan may look something like Figure 8–19.

Next you need to break the tasks down into activities. Try to list them out randomly without too much thought as to sequence; this way you're less likely to become hung up and forget something. See Figure 8–20.

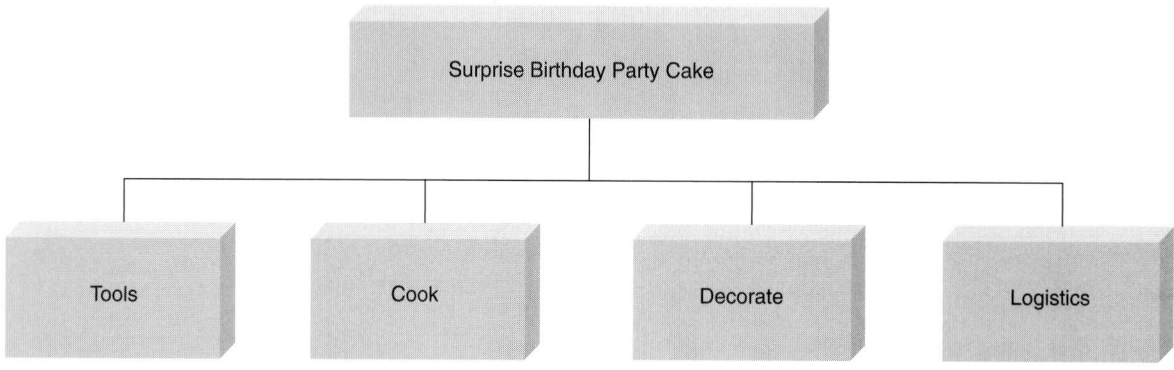

Figure 8–19
Preliminary Plan—Project Surprise

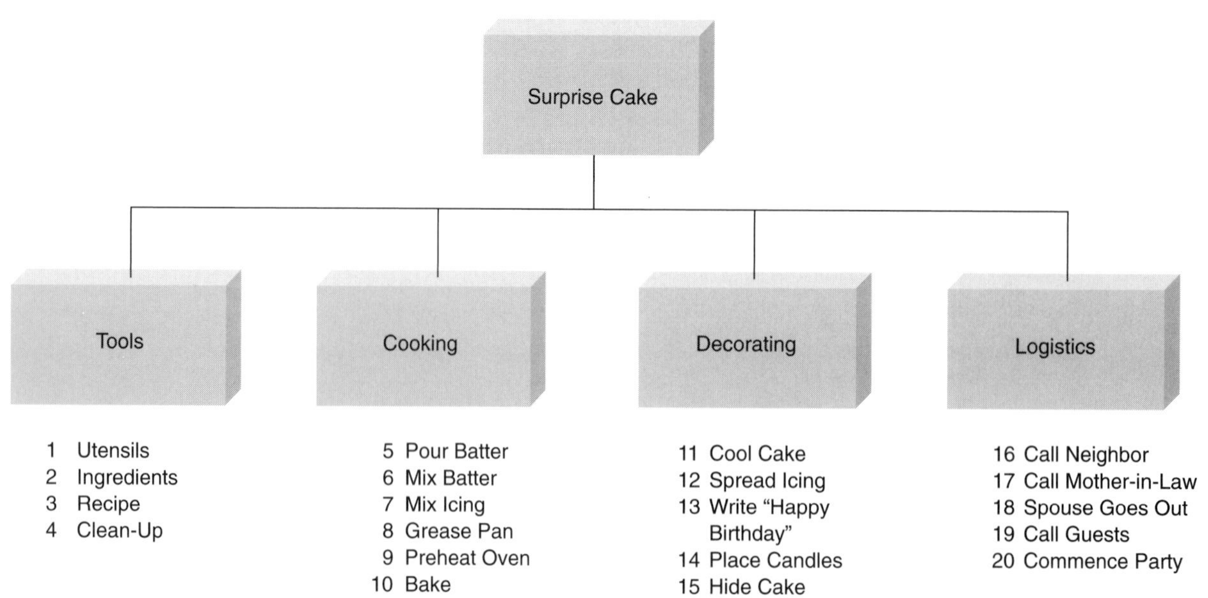

Figure 8–20
Dividing Tasks into Activities for "Project Surprise"

Precedence:
Now that the project has been broken into some tasks and activities, its time to establish the best order in which to complete them. While sorting through activities, you may discover a few that you had forgotten about, like sifting the flower or taking down the cake stand. This is the beauty of project scheduling: it is a reiterative process in which nothing is ever final, until the end.

Finally, the work breakdown structure needs to be effectively rendered in the form of a bar or flow chart.

■ ■ ■

Tracey broke in at this point. "Hey," she said, "I think it's just getting to be time for a break."

"You're right," replied Ralph. "But before I let you all go," he addressed the group, "you know that I'll require something of you. You, as a team, are going to develop a work plan for Project Surprise. I want you to break into three groups. Hilda, I want you and Jerry to list out the tasks associated with the Tools objective. Yury and Tom will work on Cooking, while Ragdeesh and Jaime will be in charge of Decorating."

The diligent trainees set to work. Tracey and Ralph left the room.

After about 10 minutes they returned to see what the group had come up with.

"Is there anything we've forgotten?" Ralph asked. The only response was silence. "Right next to the sink of dirty dishes, your significant other is going to see your beautiful cake, because you forgot to hide it!" Ralph exclaimed. "What category do you suppose 'hiding the cake' would fit under?" he asked.

"Well," said Hilda, "It isn't really a tool, and it isn't part of baking the cake, so I guess the closest objective it would fall under would be "Decorating."

Ralph said, "Not each activity needed to complete a project will fall nicely into one of your objectives. Rather than creating a new objective just for that activity or leaving it to float and possibly get lost with no one to be responsible for it, you as the project manager must be able to determine which objective owner is most suitable, and place it there."

"Good work, everyone," Ralph concluded. "See you back here after lunch."

■ ■ ■

The next step is to finish the activity list. Only activities need be listed here. Some activities may be combined at this stage; you may grease the pan and pour batter at the same time. You could combine spreading the icing and writing "Happy Birthday" under an activity called Decorating. You may refine your list to more accurately reflect reality, say by substituting "Ready for party" in place of "Commence party."

There are a few points worth mentioning here. Note that activities are listed as they come up, without strict observance of any chronological order. This reduces the temptation of serializing the activities and adding unnecessary time to the project. Note also that activities that are combined with others may be skipped in the list (they were listed above for clarity only).

Next, precedence relationships are determined. This is done by placing next to each activity the numbers of any other activities that must precede it. In Table 8–1, Activity 6, Mix batter, is preceded by activities 1 and 2, Set up utensils and Set up ingredients, respectively. Some activities can start any time without precedence. Write "none" under precedence for those.

Table 8–1
Project Surprise Activity Precedence List for Project Surprise

Activity	Precedence
1. Set up utensils	3
2. Set up ingredients	3
3. Get recipe	none
4. Clean up	15
5. Pour batter	6
6. Mix batter	1, 2
7. Mix icing	1, 2
8. See 5.0	–
9. Preheat oven	3
10. Bake cake	9, 5
11. Cool cake	10
12. Decorate	7, 11
13. (see 12.0)	–
14. Place candles	12
15. Hide cake	14
16. Call neighbor	none
17. Call mother-in-law	none
18. Spouse goes out	16
19. Call guests	18, 17
20. Ready for party	4, 19

Once precedence relationships are determined, you are now in a position to construct a network diagram. AON (Activity-on-Node) is used first. Start with activities that have no predecessors. In this case, these are activities 3, 16, and 17. Draw these nodes at the left-hand side of the network to start it off.

Then pick one of these activities, say Activity 3, and scan the precedence list to find where it is listed as preceding another activity. It precedes activities 1, 2, and 9. Draw the activity nodes showing the relationships as illustrated in the example earlier as shown in Figure 8–21.

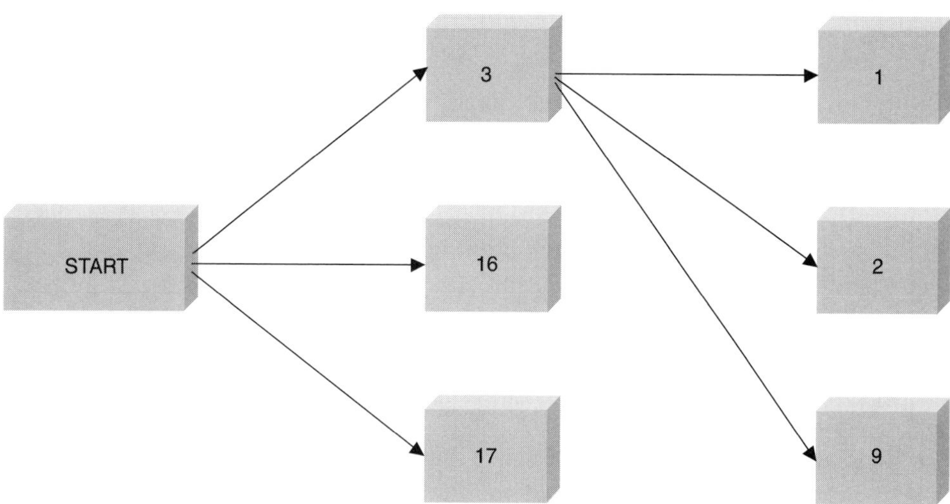

Figure 8–21
Partial AON Network for Project Surprise

Note that activities 3, 16, and 17 are loose at the beginning of the network. To facilitate using the network properly, create a Dummy Activity called "Start," with a duration of zero. If more than one activity were hanging loose at the end of the network, we would create a Dummy "End" activity. These are about the only instances in AON where dummy activities are needed.

Next, the process is repeated with the next initial Activity 16. When its successors are identified and drawn, you can move on to Activity 17, then start with the next layer of activities, say Activity 1, then 2 and so on, until all activities on the list are checked off (Figure 8–22.)

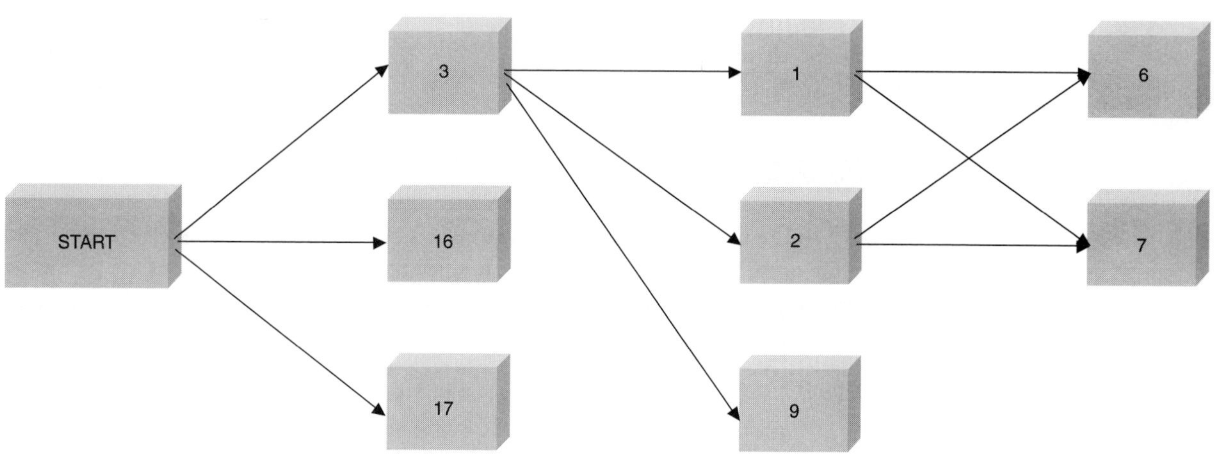

Figure 8–22
Partial AON Network for Project Surprise

The result should look something like Figure 8–23.

Some other points to notice are:

In examining the completed AON, you can see that the Oven is preheating (9) while Setup (1, 2), and Mixing (5, 6) are going on simultaneously. This is an example of parallel activities. Mix icing (7) is free to start early but is not needed until later on, when Decorating (12) is to begin.

A chef may prefer to delay his icing until just before decorating so the icing is fresher. On the other hand, a project manager prefers to do it as soon as possible in order to get things off his or her plate, and to preempt trouble, leaving you with less to do if things were to go wrong later in the project, and extra resources become needed to get back on plan. This is known as being "completion oriented."

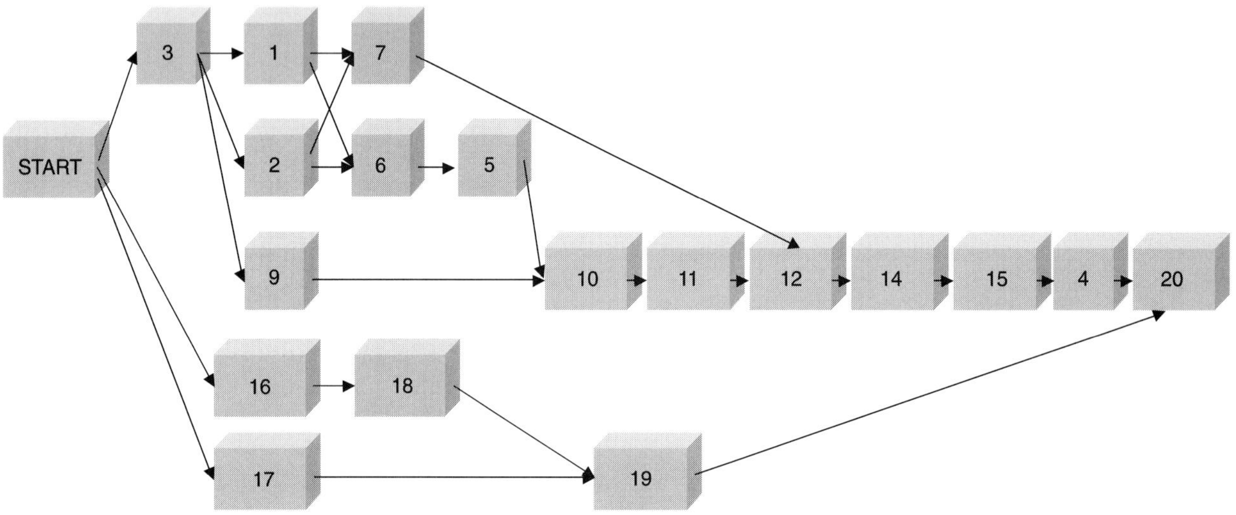

Figure 8–23
Completed AON Network for Project Surprise

To see the full impact of this network, you might redraw it on a larger sheet of paper, with large enough boxes (nodes) so you can write in the names of the activities, rather than the numbers, in each box. Examine the sequence and precedence of the activities to validate the process thus far. Some inconsistencies and/or missing relationships may pop out at this stage. This is a good time to fix them.

Chapter Summary

Scheduling techniques allow the project manager to estimate the project's duration as well as identify concurrent and succeeding activities.

Work Breakdown Structure (WBS) is a systematic technique to break the project down into its smallest work elements (activities), so that it can be planned and managed more easily. WBS uses a hierarchy of Goals, Objectives, Tasks, and Activities, in order to identify all required activities to accomplish the project's goals.

Precedence relationships identify which activities may proceed in parallel, and which must wait for predecessors to be finished. The more activities that can be done in parallel, the shorter the project will be.

PERT and CPM are networking techniques used to express the precedence relationships in visual form in order to facilitate scheduling of activities. CPM tends to be used more often in common commercial, industrial, and residential applications, while PERT is more comprehensive, and is more commonly used for government projects, as well as other applications where risk assessment is paramount. Networks can be constructed using either Activity-on-Arrow, or Activity-on Node techniques. The latter is simpler and is more commonly used.

Gantt charts are another method of displaying the schedule in bar-chart format, which lends itself very well to daily use and management of the schedule.

Chapter Questions

1. What are the different kinds of charts from which a Project Manager can choose? What is the benefit of each?
2. What is the hierarchy into which a project must be broken down? What is it known as?
3. What are three categories that influence the assignment of precedence relationships?
4. Name two different kinds of flowcharts.
5. You're working on an assignment for school that is slated to last the entire quarter. Midway through, you come down with a flu, which knocks you out of commission for a week. What do you do?

Project Challenge: Applying What You Know

For our example of remodeling a kitchen, do the following:

1. Complete a goal definition and preliminary plan.
2. Complete the Work Breakdown Structure to activity level by trade (painting, electrical, and so on).
3. Develop an activity list and set the necessary precedence relationships.
4. Draw the network diagrams for the project, using AON techniques. Verify your work.
5. Repeat the network for the project using AOA techniques. Verify your work.
6. Use Microsoft Project to construct a Gantt chart for the following problem:
   The BIS department has been given the task of developing a system to help Human Resources track employee performance evaluations. The requested development and implementation interval is 20 weeks. A senior member from HR has been assigned to work full time with BIS for the 20 weeks. The activities are as follows:

Activity	*Start Week*	*End Week*
Initial Evaluation	1	2
Systems Design	2	4
Sub-Systems Design	3	6
Programming	5	10
Sub-Systems Test	8	12
BIS Systems Test	12	16
HR Dept Systems test	16	19
Acceptance	19	20
		END

Interview with an Expert

David Brammer, *Senior Project Manager, Enrev Corp.*

Question: You handle scheduling in a new product environment. what particular challenges does that present?

Brammer: Ours is not only new products but actually a new technology. So, we are designing as we go, not just building or organizing something where there are a lot of known time schedules. Also, management often gives us our deliverables date, since there is a potential, or contracted, customer waiting for what we are developing. This prevents us from starting at the bottom and generating a final completion date from input by all members of the team. It becomes instead a process of backing up from the management-required end date of the project and getting each resource group within the team to agree to durations for their part as it contributes to the final product. But the project manager must also give management best and worst-case scenarios, while publishing any updates or slips immediately, as well as being aware of potential bottlenecks that can occur.

Question: What is your basic operating philosophy in scheduling in your situation?

Brammer: The procedure I use is basically: specify, design, then qualify. Two weeks at the front end of the project are devoted to planning—breaking sections and steps out. Time, money, and quality all have an impact on the outcome and are interrelated—management needs to tell us which to prioritize. An important customer might be worth the extra money it takes to speed up the process. But scheduling never works perfectly in new technology development—the schedule has to be a living document.

Question: Can you elaborate on the process a little more?

Brammer: Developing specifications is an interactive process with the customer and all parties concerned. For instance, what is the end product supposed to do? Without a good set of specs, the end result is a moving target. Then, each of the resources for each functional section (the teams that will do the actual work) will develop their own set of specs. Each section has its own steps—prototyping, testing, and so on. Some activities within a resource or functional group (like research and development) have precedence relationships, and some functional groups, in order to complete their part, must have another group's part first. So there are sucessions as well as parallel activities. Finally, the design must include testing to qualify the end result—does it meet customer specs and perform as required?

Question: What is the project manager's role in maintaining the schedule?

Brammer: The project manager is the helmsman—he plots the course and steers the ship, but he doesn't row. Project managers understand what activities may take longer than others and they are also the link between the schedule the engineers say they can meet and the schedule management insists on (not always the same). Eighty percent of the project manager's time is spent going to people and updating the schedule, solving problems, clearing the path, such as getting purchase orders signed or securing equipment and materials so the schedule can be met.

CHAPTER 9

Network Analysis and Duration Estimating

Chapter Preview

The Project Management Seminar: Session 9

Yury looked down at his beeper, frustrated that he had not yet received the important page from his assistant. With every minute that passed, Yury could feel his level of anxiety rising.

Hilda noticed the expression on Yury's face. "Are you all right?" she asked.

"It all depends, " replied Yury.

"On what?" asked Hilda.

"On whether or not I hear from my assistant that this transfer has taken place. We're already behind schedule. If we fall more behind, there's no way we'll get this project completed within budget expectations."

"All I can say is good luck, " Hilda sympathized, giving him a pat on the shoulder. She turned her attention to Ralph, who was ready to begin the day's session.

Ralph addressed the group. "Today, let's look at duration estimating. Since time is such an important element to manage, this is a major concern."

After a few minutes of deliberation, the two discussion groups came up with the following:

- Why is duration estimating so important?
- How do I get my team members to stick to the estimated durations?
- What about when no one will commit to a duration?

- How does duration estimating affect project cost?
- What are the tricks to estimating durations?
- When duration estimates seem out of line, how do I get them adjusted?
- We already have a deadline to meet. Why have duration estimates?

George used these concerns to establish the outline for the day:

- **Laying the groundwork for commitment**
- **Setting duration estimates**
- **Determining the critical path**
- **Meeting external deadlines**

■ ■ ■

1.0 COMMITMENT

1.1 Example—Wiring for a New Plant

Picture this. You have decided that the underground wires for the new plant must be laid by the end of next month. If not, the project doesn't proceed on schedule, and you fall behind budget. What you don't know is that the ground at the new site is frozen and no underground cables will go in until the next good thaw. If you'd checked with the technicians before making your schedule, this problem could have been avoided.

Part of sticking to any **estimated duration** is having commitment from your project team members. If you develop duration estimates on your own and the people who have to perform the activities have no input, it is not likely that they will feel compelled to comply with your deadlines. Further, in a very real sense, you are shooting in the dark. However, you can inspire commitment in your team by consulting them about the durations. They are much more likely to stick to a duration time that they helped to determine.

estimated duration the estimated time needed to finish a project

This is the most important aspect to activity duration estimation. As discussed earlier, the good project manager is constantly asking questions and getting input from his or her team members. Duration estimates are no exception to this rule, and are in fact the best illustration of it.

When consulting your team members, be sure to ask the people who will actually do the work the time-related questions. For example, you would ask an electrician how long it takes to wire a 1,000-square-foot space for 30 cubicles, not the person who orders cable. If you are in Florida, planning a job in Michigan, you should consult with the people in Michigan (remember the frozen ground and the wiring?).

You should also look for the team member with the most experience in any given area. Those who have performed a task many times over know realistically how long an activity will take, and will give you the most accurate estimates. They will also be aware of the hidden factors associated with the job. They will know of any useful and time-saving techniques, tips, and/or equipment. They might even know a particular type of music that makes their crew work more productively. In the case of the frozen ground, someone may come up with a way to string the wire above the ground temporarily so that the project can move forward at once.

Make sure that you are realistic in your expectations of how long various activities will take. Suppose you place an order for some heavy equipment to be delivered from a plant 700 miles away. If you expect that the activity involving the use of this equipment will be completed within 3 days, you have your head in the clouds. Shipment by next-day air for earthmoving equipment is not an option. You cannot expect to inspire commitment from your team members by negotiating duration estimates that are unrealistic. People lose confidence in a leader with irrational expectations. On the other hand, if your crew knows that you are looking out for their time and interests, and you have a track record of setting realistic timetables, they will be much more likely to buy into the project's goal and schedule.

■ ■ ■

Ralph George looked out at the training group with a big smile. "OK, let's take a look at the preliminary scheduling networks you put together for the New Millennium problem. We'll use those for reference for the rest of today's discussion."

What each team produced had been based on a handout supplied the day before. Each team had a copy.

■ ■ ■

1.2 Example—New Millennium Enterprises

The management of New Millennium Enterprises, which is headquartered in Atlanta, has decided to open a new plant in Charlotte, North Carolina. The Industrial Engineering staff will immediately perform a "production requirements analysis" to determine the amounts of equipment, personnel, and floor-space needed based on sales projections for the Charlotte market area. New Millennium's production manager will also immediately begin the process of selecting one of his veteran plant managers to manage the new plant.

As soon as the production requirements analysis is complete, purchase orders will be placed for the necessary equipment. It will take 25 days for all of the equipment to be delivered to a warehouse in the Atlanta headquarters complex. While the equipment is in Atlanta, the Corporate Maintenance department will check it thoroughly and add some safety and quality-control modifications. Also, after the production requirements analysis is complete, a building will be selected and leased for the new plant in Charlotte. The Industrial Engineering staff will then develop an equipment layout for the building, and the layout will be turned over to contractors who will perform the necessary electrical and plumbing work to prepare for the installation of equipment. Moving the plant equipment from Atlanta to Charlotte and the installation at the new plant will require 3 days.

As soon as New Millennium has leased the building, purchase orders will be issued for the initial stock of materials. The materials will be delivered directly to the new plant over a period of 30 days. Once the manager of the new plant has been selected, he will need about 20 days to relocate in Charlotte. Meanwhile, the Corporate Human Resources Department will place help-wanted ads in Charlotte area newspapers for operating personnel based on the production requirements analysis. Once in Charlotte, the plant manager will begin interviewing and selecting plant personnel. After the personnel have been selected, the equipment has been installed, and the materials have been delivered, the plant manager and his assistant will train the personnel. When the training is complete, the plant will be ready to begin operations.

Explanation: Identification of activities required to complete the project, along with their precedence relationships, allows the project manager to construct a project network with Activities-on-Nodes. Once the network is created, the duration estimates given in the example can be recorded in the appropriate places on the network diagram.

The activity list and precedence relationships appear as follows. Once they are established, the final pre-planning step is to draw the preliminary network.

Activity	*Activity*
1. Perform production requirements analysis.	8. Check equipment.
	9. Move/install equipment.
2. Select and lease a building.	10. Develop layout.
3. Select a manager.	11. Secure electrical/plumbing services.
4. Relocate the manager.	12. Order materials.
5. Place advertisements.	13. Receive materials.
6. Order equipment.	14. Interview and select personnel.
7. Receive equipment.	15. Train personnel.

The activity list precedes generating the next list, a precedence list. This is the final requirement to creating the preliminary network.

Activity	*Precedence*
1. Perform production requirements analysis.	—
2. Select and lease a building.	1
3. Select a manager.	—
4. Relocate the manager.	3
5. Place advertisements.	1
6. Order equipment.	1
7. Receive equipment.	6
8. Check equipment.	7
9. Move/install equipment.	8, 11
10. Develop layout.	2

11.	Secure electrical and plumbing services.	10
12.	Order materials.	2
13.	Receive materials.	12
14.	Interview and select personnel.	5, 4
15.	Train personnel.	13, 9, 14

The final preplanning step is to draw out the Preliminary Network, shown in Figure 9–1.

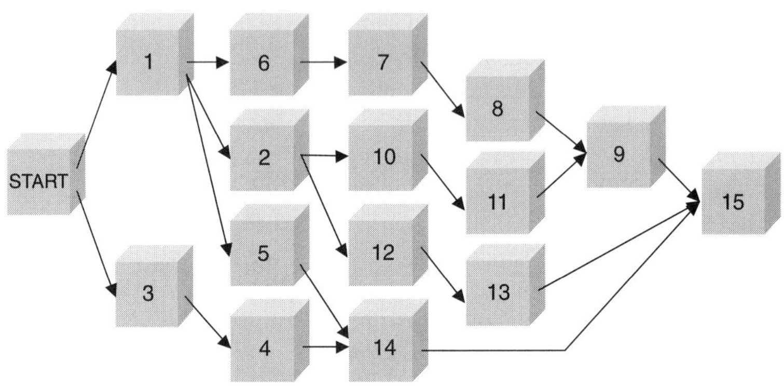

Figure 9–1
Preliminary Network for New Millennium Enterprises

2.0 Duration Estimating

2.1 Duration versus Effort

effort the actual time spent on activity

First of all, it is vital to distinguish between duration and effort. **Effort** is the time one spends performing an activity, once he or she sits down to do it. Most activities require an effort of a few minutes, to a few hours, or even days of solid setup and work, broken up over several sessions. To finish planning the kitchen remodeling problem will probably take us a total of 3 to 4 hours of effort, spent over a week.

duration the elapsed time from the start of an activity until it is finished

The **duration,** however, is the *elapsed time* from the start of an activity until it is finished. This includes the effort, the time spent on other things in between sessions of effort, waiting for results or reports, having meetings, working on other projects, as well as any needed handoff time to the next step. The clock starts running from the time an activity *is available* to be worked on, and stops when the activity is *completed, delivered* to the next party, and is *available* so that the work on the succeeding activity can begin.

In the kitchen remodeling example, the problem was handed out midday Tuesday, and we should be done planning it late Thursday, giving the planning activity a duration of $2\frac{1}{2}$ days.

2.2 Duration Estimating Techniques

As stated earlier, remember to *always* consult with those who will do the task when estimating the duration of activities, as this is your best opportunity to obtain commitment from your team. This bears repeating, since quite often the project manager finds it simpler to do the estimating himself rather than waiting to consult with the team members. This is especially true if the work happens to fall within the project manager's area of expertise. It is imperative to resist the temptation to do it yourself.

There exists only one exception to this rule: that's when you are in the process of putting together a concept for the purpose of preliminary planning. You can make this preliminary plan yourself, but then hand it to the team and have them refine it as they see fit. As you consult with the team, you may suggest to them to use one or more of the following estimating techniques:

1. Experience. The most commonly used estimating technique is to ask someone with experience. Generally speaking, your own team members should be sufficiently experienced in the work required, and will gladly share this knowledge with you. Asking them for their estimate, discussing it with them, and finally accepting the estimate will validate their worth to the team. This validation of worth will serve to form early bonds among the team members, and it will gain their commitment to seeing the task through within the estimate they gave. You should remember, however, that asking for such estimates shouldn't be done in an offhand fashion. Even if you approach the experienced person in a casual setting, it should be taken seriously. Let everyone involved know that you value their time and input. If you don't, you will possibly lose the commitment discussed earlier.

All team members deserve to have their tasks carefully defined and specifically related to the goal of the project. These discussions are normally held when defining and detailing the major objectives of the project, and they help connect team members to the project vision. As a matter of course, using the goal-setting techniques (Chapter 7) in the definition of tasks improves everyone's understanding, sets the correct explanations, and facilitates the duration estimating process.

2. Historical Data. When experience alone is insufficient to arrive at reliable estimates, one must turn to historical data. Historical data for many tasks may be found in a variety of forms, including actual performance information from previous projects, data bases that have been acquired over time, engineering logs, computer logs, accounting records, test records, and so on.

3. Research. When nothing else is available, research will save the day! Nowadays, the problem to overcome is the overabundance of information, rather than the lack of it. The Internet offers a wealth of information, which requires some skill in sifting through. Consulting experts in the field is more difficult (and potentially costly if you have to pay an hourly rate for their information) but often yields more reliable information. Your vendors are an excellent source of information also, but be careful not to create false hopes of a sale or a contract.

Research of a specific estimate should be assigned to the doer of the task, after some group discussion of the resources to explore, and the time this should take.

4. Modeling. Modeling is sometimes possible for tasks of a complex nature or those having stochastic processes. Mathematical models abound for all kinds of processes, and these models can be found through academic and professional institutions. Several are available commercially. Flowcharting, transportation algorithms, linear programs, queuing models, simulations, and so on are examples of mathematical models.

Physical modeling can sometimes be used to validate an estimate of a repetitive process, which can then be extrapolated to the whole task.

5. Experiments. The same idea of physical and/or computer modeling can be extended to include experimentation on a small scale. These small-scale experiments can also be extrapolated to full scale. In preparing a new car to pass crash testing, engineers model the crash on computer simulations until they reach a fairly reliable result. Then they can save the trial-and-error money spent on unscrutinized experiments.

*6. **Breakdown/ Roll-Up.*** A complex or unusual task may be broken down into familiar steps as an aid to estimating the duration. An estimate is then made for the duration of each step. These individual estimates are then "rolled up" to arrive at an estimate for the whole task, with some adjustments for overlap and coordination. This is a helpful technique with new team members who may not have had this type of experience. They probably have a good feel for durations of smaller tasks in their area of expertise, and it is sometimes easier to help them think their estimates out in this way.

*7. **Delphi Method.*** An expensive extension of the research method is the Delphi Method. Here, each of a group of "experts" is asked in isolation to estimate the task duration. Those with extreme (long or short) estimates are asked to justify their differences. This information is made available to all, and another round of estimating is begun. Most projects do not require going through this trouble. Others though, such as estimating the time it takes for a spacecraft to navigate the Asteroid Belt, or for scientists to design a landing system for a Mars Rover, would. Other down-to-earth tasks can do with less exotic techniques.

*8. **Consultants.*** This technique is much less complicated than the Delphi Method. Consultants are abundant, affordable, and come with a lot of experience. They can be utilized for just the scope or time needed.

*9. **Three Outside Estimates.*** Approaching outside contractors for their estimates with quotes for the work is a reliable method. Averaging of three such estimates should be sufficiently accurate. Ethically, though, you should ask for estimates only when you actually intend to contract the work to someone outside your company, or when you are willing to pay for the estimates.

*10. **Ranging.*** When the estimator doesn't have a clue or won't volunteer an estimate, ranging can sometimes extract one. Start by asking if the task would take an unusually long time, when the answer is "of course not", then ask if it would take some unusually short time. Keep flipping back and forth by narrowing the times until you detect a "comfort zone" from the individual.

An example of this is an engineer who is designing "first silicon" for a new and complex chip and is reluctant to guess at the duration of the task. When asked if it would take him 3 months to finish it, he says that there is "no way" it would take that long. When asked if it could be done in a week, he is equally appalled and says that no one could do it in a week. He is then asked if 2 months would be closer, then asked about 2 weeks, and so on. A comfort zone of 5 weeks is eventually detected, and this is used as the estimate.

*11. **Other Techniques.*** Rarely would a situation present itself when one must resort to guesswork, trial and error, and so forth. But, even if you must flip a coin or consult a psychic, do what you have to do in order to get some agreement on an estimate of a task's duration. Your objective is to come as close as possible to the true duration of each and every task on the project, with a healthy level of commitment from the doers.

*12. **Special Cases.*** Anyone who has had to deal with getting a permit or a license knows that this is an activity that can assume a life of its own. The offices can open and close at some unusual times. Lines can be very long. The requirements for successful application can seem to change from person to person. This must be accounted for by the successful project manager.

Inspections can put strains on timeliness. Frequently, the inspectors seem to have criteria that are completely new to even seasoned professionals. Further, an inspection is a hurdle that must be overcome. There is no way to open a new restaurant without a certificate of occupancy. Doing your homework on individual inspectors can allow you to plan for their visits and keep the schedule on track.

Some other examples of special cases that must be accounted for in a complete duration estimate:

- *Deliveries.* These can cause major problems. Often transportation is done by yet-to-be determined third parties, and is subject to external conditions, such as traffic problems, unexpected strikes, and so on.
- *Breakdowns and Repairs.* These are of course inevitable. The instances of breakdown can be reduced by allowing for and insisting on preventive maintenance in the schedule.
- *Approvals.* Securing internal approval is an ongoing requirement in any business, which won't go away for your project. Examples include securing approval from the legal folks, purchasing high-ticket items, and signing off on new layouts. Keeping the approving authority involved, or at least informed about the item's progress, will grease the process and shorten the approval's duration, or at least make it more predictable.

Based on the outcome of the estimating techniques you use, you will be building your budgets, resource plans, staffing plans, and so on and you will be prepared to argue deadlines and be ready to determine the duration of the whole project. At this point, there is no need to push people for tighter estimates since you don't know which activities are driving the project. To do so would create unnecessary stress and may not help the project's duration anyway.

2.3 Normal Duration

Now you know how to inspire commitment from our team members; but how do you actually go about selecting specific duration estimates? Any given activity can have one of several possible durations, depending on several factors: how much of a hurry you're in, how tight the budgets are, what the availability of machinery or technology might be that may accelerate things, and so on.

To reach what is known as "normal duration," our objective is to come up with the most *cost-effective* plan for the project—the plan you would come up with if you were going to bid against competitors for the same project or resources (and indeed most projects are competing, at one level or another). You should always follow three simple steps:

1. Determine the most cost-efficient technical approach. In other words, determine which method will allow you to complete any given activity while spending the least amount of money. If you've found an approach with which you are comfortable, stick with it. This is not the time to take chances with untried methods. Example: if you wish to have a ditch dug in your yard, the high school kid next door will do it in a few days for $50, or you can rent a ditch-witch for $160 and do it in an afternoon. Plan to use the kid, because it's the lowest cost method, but be sure that your liability insurance is current.

2. Make an estimate of how long the most cost-efficient method will take to complete. This is meant to give you an advantage if you are "bidding" for the work. You must be careful not to underestimate durations. Engineers, especially those without a lot of experience, are notoriously optimistic when estimating time, and will often think "effort" rather than "duration." Your team should be using one or more of the estimating techniques discussed above, while you guide the discussion and continuously watch out for unreasonably optimistic estimates. Ignore any external special conditions at this point, such as bad weather or sick leave. Assume that things will go as planned. In the case of the ditch example, the kid will take 5 days to finish it, but you could do it in half a day with the ditch-witch. Plan on 5 days.

3. Selectively adjust your estimate for any activity that is subject to common problems. If you know that while pouring concrete you have a 20% chance of rain, you then adjust the duration of the pour accordingly. If pouring would take 10 days without interruption, then adjust it to 12 days. Likewise, there is a certain probability that, while your software developers are writing programs, the network will go down at some point. At this stage, you are anticipating common problems. These are occurrences that do not necessarily require additional resources, but they will add to the duration of the activity.

Be sure to adjust only those activities subject to common problems. Leave all the other estimates alone.

Back to the ditch example. If you won't allow the kid to dig in the rain, a 20% chance of rain means you change the planned duration from 5 to 6 days! This is the "normal duration" for digging that ditch.

3.0 CPM VERSUS PERT

In the 1950s, the U.S. Navy developed the project management tool known as PERT (Program Evaluation and Review Technique). In the same decade, CPM (Critical Path Method) was developed jointly by engineers at DuPont and Remington Rand. Other organizations and companies were using them by the end of the 1950s, and by the 1960s, it was rare that a manager's office didn't have a PERT chart hanging on the wall. Since the mechanics of the two approaches are so similar, they are now commonly referred to as CPM/PERT. The most obvious difference between the two is that PERT recognizes uncertainty in activity duration by the use of optimistic, pessimistic, and most likely durations, whereas CPM makes only one time estimate for an activity.

PERT requires that you develop *three* duration estimates for each activity. The *most optimistic* duration is how long the activity takes if all went right, without any problems. Next, the *most pessimistic* duration is how long it would take if everything went wrong. And last, the *most likely* duration is what we would expect based on experience of what usually happens. A probability is attached to each estimate, and the final duration is derived from a stochastic formula;

$$D_o.P_o + D_p.P_p + D_e.P_e = \text{final duration}$$

Where: D_o is the most optimistic duration.
P_o is the probability of D_o.
D_p is the most pessimistic duration.
P_p is the probability of D_p.

D_e is the most likely duration.
P_e is the probability of D_e.
The sum of the probabilities adds up to 100%.

CPM is most often used in commercial projects. It differs from PERT only in the duration estimating technique. In CPM, we require only one duration estimate: the *most likely duration,* arrived at by using any of the techniques discussed above. This tends to give results that are just as valid as those of PERT, and sure do save a lot of time and effort. Throughout the remainder of this book, we will use the CPM methodology.

4.0 Calculating Project Duration

"Now let's separate into the original teams and arrive at some kind of consensus about the duration of the New Millennium project," Ralph said.

Hilda, Yury, and Ragdeesh spent the next 20 minutes with the handout and generated the durations.

■ ■ ■

	Activity	*Precedence*	*Duration (days)*
1.	Perform production requirements analysis.	—	3
2.	Select and lease a building.	1	15
3.	Select a manager.	—	5
4.	Relocate the manager.	3	20
5.	Place advertisements.	1	5
6.	Order equipment.	1	1
7.	Receive equipment.	6	25
8.	Check equipment.	7	10
9.	Move/install equipment.	8,11	3
10.	Develop layout.	2	5
11.	Secure electrical and plumbing services.	10	10
12.	Order materials.	2	1
13.	Receive materials.	12	10
14.	Interview and select personnel.	5,4	10
15.	Train personnel.	13, 9,14	10

■ ■ ■

Ralph seemed pleased. "Since the durations of the various activities were given in the handout, there was very little guesswork involved in this particular example. Go ahead, put these durations on your preliminary network, and let's see what we get." (See Figure 9–2.)

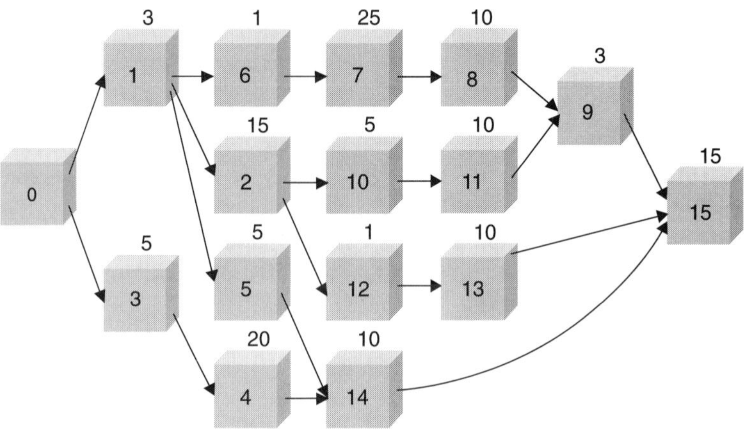

Figure 9–2
New Millennium Enterprises Preliminary Network with Durations Added

Now we are in a position to actually determine the duration of the project.

4.1 The Critical Path

To figure out how long the project will take, It's simple, right? Just add up all the durations and you have it. Wrong! Many people fall into this trap. This would be true if all the activities were in series. Most networks will have parallel activities, meaning that they are happening simultaneously. In the New Millennium manufacturing problem, we have no less than five distinct paths, which are unique sequences of activities done in series leading from the start to the final node. The question really is, Which of these paths is the longest in terms of cumulative duration? This path will determine the length of the project, since all other paths may be complete and waiting. The longest path is called the "Critical Path" (CP).

This path is critical for several reasons:

- Its combined duration (length) determines how long the project will take.
- It has no slack! Each activity must start immediately when its predecessor is finished, and consume no more than its allotted time.
- Delay of *any* critical path activity will delay the completion of the *entire* project.

4.1.1 Forward Pass

forward pass calculation the approach to determine the duration of the whole project

The approach to determine the duration of the whole project is called the **"forward pass" calculation.** This approach defines the start and finish times for each activity in the network, which is needed information for constructing a Gantt chart or any other chart, as well as in managing the project.

First, here are some abbreviations and their meanings:

1. EPS—Earliest Possible Start time for an activity
2. EPF—Earliest Possible Finish time for an activity
3. DUR—Duration, the elapsed time an activity is expected to be finished.

Therefore, EPF = EPS + DUR

Enlarging the node box to accommodate this new information leads to the graphical representation shown in Figure 9–3.

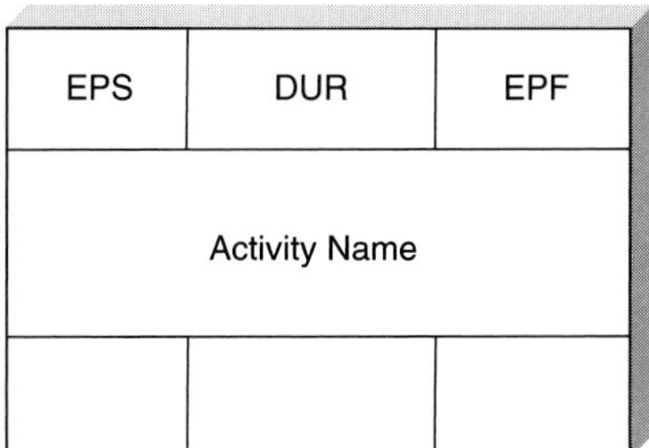

Figure 9–3
Standard Node box notation for AON networks

So, an activity A, which can start no sooner than week 3, and has a duration of 4 weeks, is represented as follows on the network:

EPS = Week 3

DUR = 4 weeks

EPF = EPS + DUR = 3 + 4 = Week 7

And graphically, as shown in Figure 9–4:

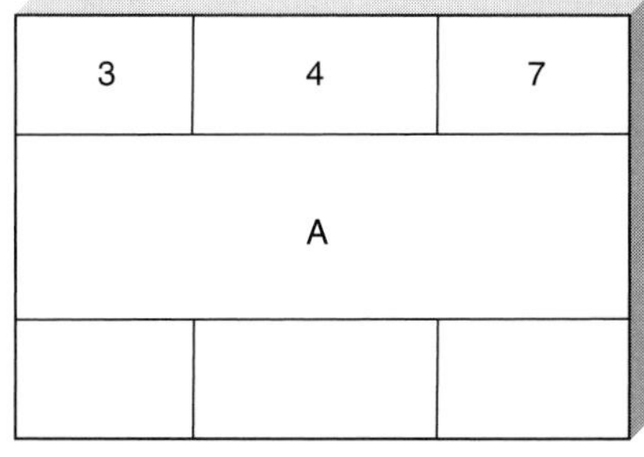

Figure 9–4
Standard Node box showing values

The whole subdivided box represents the node for activity A.

EPS (of activity B) = EPF (of activity A)

Further, if activity A precedes activity B, whose duration is 5 weeks, we find that:

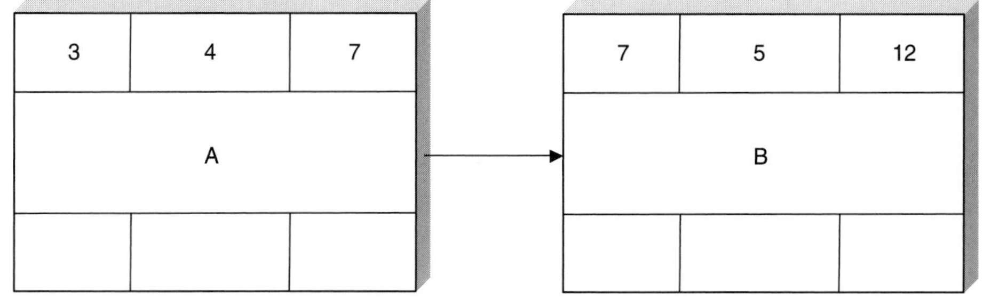

Figure 9–5
Standard Node box of Start-to-Finish precedence showing EPS/EPF calculations

making the EPS of activity B also week 7.

This is because B cannot start until A is finished. This can be represented on the network as shown in Figure 9–5.

End-of-Period Convention. To eliminate any confusion about what is meant by "Week 7," the common convention is that it refers to the *end* of week 7. And since durations express only scheduled work time (e.g., 9 o'clock to 5 o'clock, Monday through Friday) the beginning of one period is the same as the end of the preceding period. So "week 7" means both "the end of activity A," and the "start of activity B."

Special Case. When an activity has several predecessors, it must wait until the latest EPF of all the preceding activities before it can start. Say you must make coffee, boil an egg, and toast bread before sitting down to breakfast. If coffee takes the longest, breakfast won't start until the coffee is ready, even though the egg and toast are done and waiting. See the CPM Network representation in Figure 9–6.

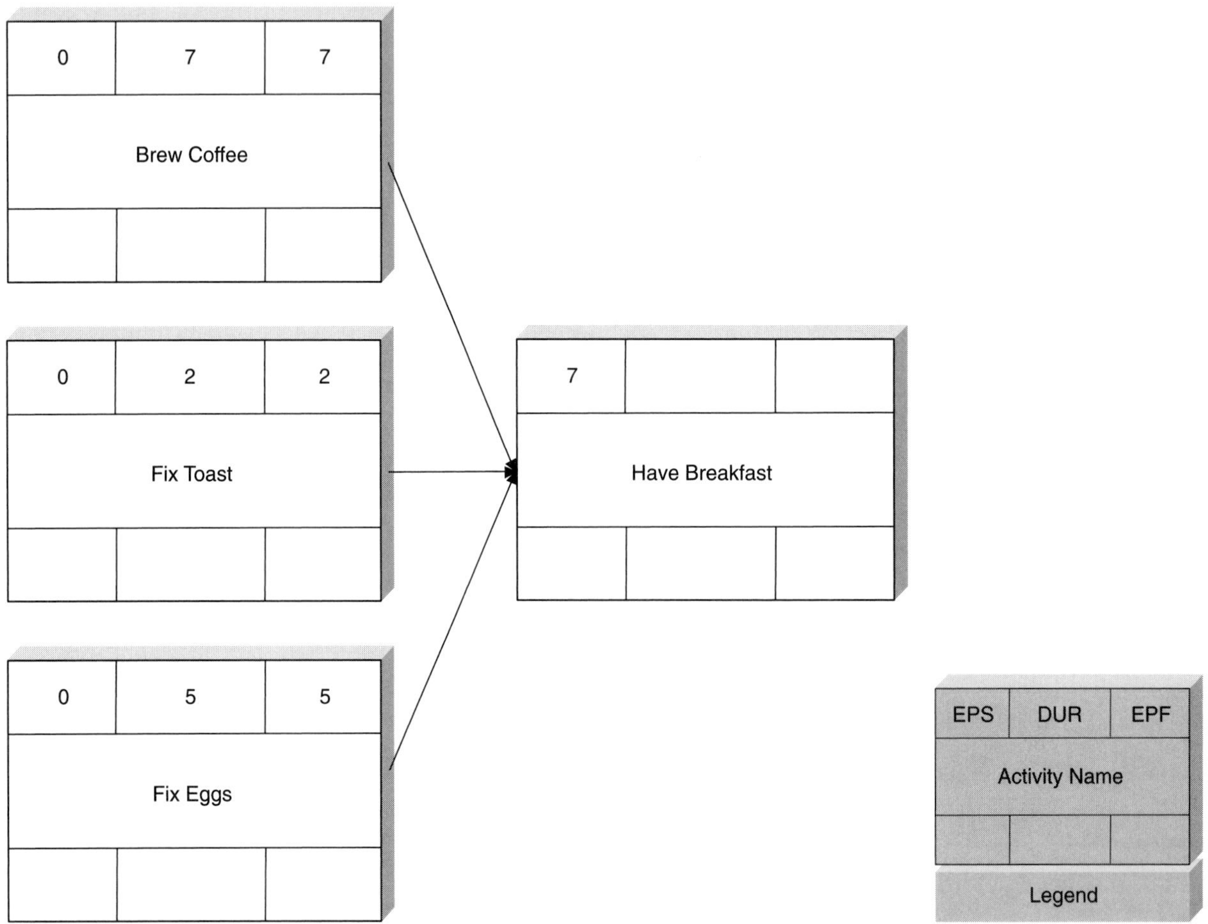

Figure 9–6
Special Case: AON Network showing activity with several predecessors

We can now rewrite the equation:

EPS (activity) = the latest EPF of all its predecessors.

■ ■ ■

"It will be much clearer after we do an example," Ralph assured the group. "Let's add the forward pass calculation to the New Millennium Enterprises problem." As the teams bowed to their task, Ralph and Tracey wandered among them, pointing things out and offering encouragement.

■ ■ ■

Forward pass calculation starts with the first activity. A start time of "period zero" is assigned as its EPS. Add the duration to the EPS to arrive at its EPF period. Do this to all free-starting activities—in this case, activities 1 and 3. This yields EPF periods of days 3 and 5 respectively. We will proceed in "layers" of activities. In other words, we will deal next with activities 6, 2, 5 and 4. Activity 6 can't start until activity 1 is finished. This gives it an EPS of day 3 and, adding its duration of 1 day, yields an EPF of day 4. Similarly, activity 2 gets an EPS of day 3 and EPF of day 18. Activity 5 also gets an EPS of day 3 and EPF of day 8. Activity 4 is driven by the completion of activity 3, giving it an EPS of day 5 and EPF of day 25.

The next layer of activities includes 7, 10, 12, and 14. Activity 14 is a special case, in that it depends on both activities 4 and 5. Activity 4 will drive it since it has the later EPF of the pair, day 25. This gives activity 14 an EPS of day 25 and, with a duration of 10 days, an EPF of day 35. This process continues until we find that the last activity, 15, ends day 52. This is the duration of the entire project: 52 days, and its completion date is projected to be 52 days after whatever start date is chosen.

■ ■ ■

Tom in particular was mystified initially, but became more comfortable as the process went on.

Soon the teams had networks that looked like the illustration in Figure 9–7.

■ ■ ■

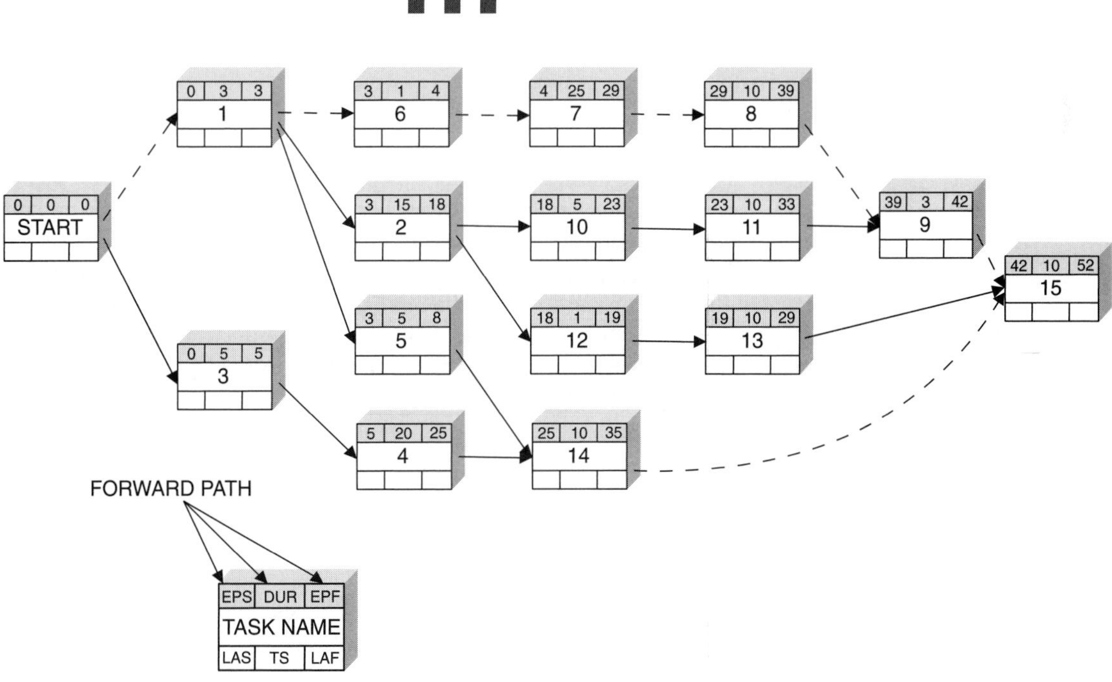

Figure 9–7
Forward Pass Calculation for New Millennium Enterprises Problem

4.1.2 Methods to Identify the Critical Path

Once the CPM network is complete, we have another opportunity at a reality check. Remember that precedence relationships will lengthen the duration of a project, the extreme case being when all activities are in series, and the project's duration equals the sum of all the activity durations. The fewer precedence relationships we have, the more activities that can be done in parallel, thus shortening the total project duration. The extreme case of that would be having no precedence relationships, and all activities can start immediately, and proceed in parallel. In this case, the project duration is simply equal to the longest activity.

As discussed earlier, the duration of the project equals the length of the critical path on the CPM network. It is therefore important to identify it, so that it can be examined for reasonableness.

The simplest approach is to add up the durations of each path, compare the totals, and pick the longest one(s). This is how computers perform the procedure, but it can be tedious for humans, especially if the project has several hundred activities.

backwards pass calculation allows the identification of slack time for each activity

Another technique is known as the **"backwards pass" calculation.** It allows the identification of slack time for each activity. The Critical Path will be the one whose activities show no slack time. This technique requires some effort and will be discussed later on in the following chapters when the need to identify slack arises, such as when leveling resources.

Follow the EPS For now, a simpler technique can be used to identify the Critical Path (CP). Its called "Follow the EPS." Start with the end node, and see which of the links leading to it is driving its EPS to be what it is (the predecessor that took the longest). That is the first link of the CP. Go to that predecessor node, and see which of the links leading to it is in turn driving its EPS. That is the second link of the CP. Continue in that fashion, working towards the start node, finding each link that is driving the EPS of the predecessor activity, identifying the links of the CP one at a time, until you reach the "Start" activity.

The Critical Path is then expressed as a series of the activity names along its path, usually from start to end.

In Figure 9–7, activity 15 is the end activity. Its EPS is day 42. There are three links leading into it, from activities 9, 11, and 13. Their finish dates (EPF) are days 42, 33, and 29, respectively. It should be clear that activity 9 is driving the EPS of day 42 for activity 15. Therefore, we can highlight the link from activity 9 as our first CP link. We can now ignore the other two links, and focus next on activity 9. Activity 9 has an EPS of day 39, and has two links leading to it from activities 8 and 11. Activity 8 is the one driving the EPS of day 39 for activity 9. So we can highlight the link from activity 8 as the second CP link.

Activity 8 has only one link leading into it. It is from activity 7. Therefore this is the third CP link. Similarly, the links from activities 6, 1, and the Start nodes are single links and are the balance of the CP links. Please note that at times, by chance, two or more paths will have equal length, and be the longest. In that case, the network will have two or more Critical Paths. The CP can now be expressed as "1-6-7-8-9-15." Translated back into names, the CP reads as follows:

■ ■ ■

"Perform production requirements analysis–Order equipment–Receive equipment–Check equipment–Move /install equipment–Train personnel."

■ ■ ■

Figure 9–8 shows the network with the critical path highlighted.

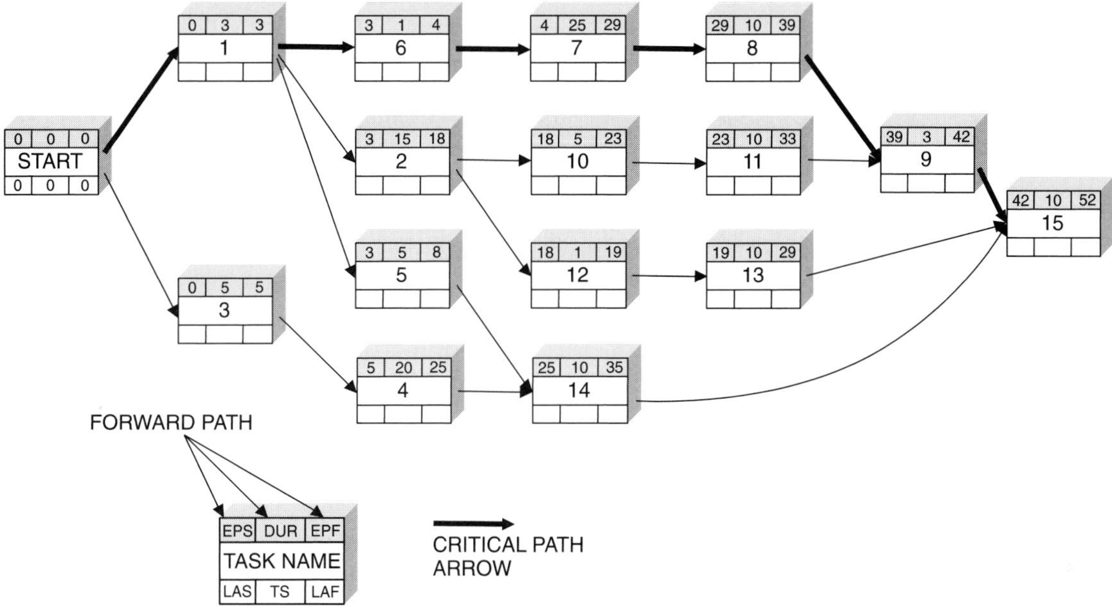

Figure 9–8
Critical Path for New Millennium Enterprises Problem

Examining the CP for a reality check shows it to be in order. The activities in the CP are typically the ones that take the longest. The sequence in which they appear also seems reasonable in that they are valid technical precedence relationships.

Prudent questions to ask during a reality check are:

- Is this a typical duration for this type of project? A 3,000-square-foot house takes about 6 months to build. It takes about 15 months to start a manufacturing plant from scratch. Ask around!
- Are the CP activities truly critical? Do they consume scarce resources? Are high skill levels required? Do you require expensive facilities?
- Look more closely at the duration and precedence estimates along the CP, and across the network with an eye toward completeness and accuracy.
- Reexamine the assumptions made during the planning process. Are they still reasonable? Validate them by checking with the right people.

Once you are comfortable that all seems well, you can move on to optimizing the plan.

5.0 Optimizing the Plan

5.1 The Need to Meet External Deadlines

"What if the total duration significantly exceeds the required project deadline?" Tom queried, looking puzzled.

"Would one of you veterans like to take that one?" Ralph asked.

"If the glass comes up half empty, no one cares why. You'd just better have a plan to fill it," Jerry grinned.

"What about glasses?" Yury looked puzzled now.

"That's an expression we use in business to describe how people view a problem," Ralph explained. "Do they see the situation as half completed or half not completed? Frankly, and you all know this, management doesn't care why you are saying you won't meet the deadline. No answer or explanation you give will matter. The only response, then to your question, Tom, is figure out what it's going to take to bring it in on time. Period."

The group nodded in agreement, but Tom shook his head.

■ ■ ■

Oftentimes, the reason for the project is to meet some customer need or market competition. If this is so, then time allowed will be dictated by outside forces: "Do it by this date or I'll go elsewhere!" However, many project participants tend to overestimate durations in order to bring the project in on time with surety and thoroughness. Marketers, on the other hand, understand that if market-driven deadlines are not met, an opportunity may slip by and the reason for the project will go away. There is always the conflict between timing estimates that we are confident about and those we must meet.

Project managers very likely have to answer the following question on their duration estimates: "What would it cost, require, and so on to complete this project 3 months early?" It is at this point that you as the project manager will have to look at critical issues of your timetable:

- Would bringing more expert talent to bear on this project speed it up?
- Are there changes we could make in the resource procurement process to shorten wait times?
- Would round-the-clock scheduling (such as automated 24-hour testing equipment or night shifts) shorten the project duration?
- If we throw more money at the team, would they work faster?
- Would a different organizational setup speed things up, such as creating a full-time team in a bullpen-style war room?

Finally, the most critical question that every estimator has to face,

- Do we think it will take this long just because it always has, or are there other ways to do this, which we haven't thought of yet, that would shrink the timetable?

■ ■ ■

Jerry said, "I specifically recall a conversation with one of our design engineers whose previous company had gone out of business. He told me that at that company, they weren't given timetables, so if a project took 3 years, it took 3 years. At my company, we have done similar challenges in 3 months. I have to think partly it's because we were told we had to."

Ralph nodded, saying, "This exact case is a central reason as to why good engineering project managers are scarce and valuable; they can size up a situation and determine how much of a duration estimate is conservative self-protection and how much of it is justifiable. In new technology development or new product design, this whole issue becomes even more complicated. You will have to ask your team to give estimates of time for creating something brand new—with no experience base to draw from. And, to make the task more stressful, a customer is going to plan its own business strategies around the date you give that customer for delivery." Ralph George watched the rueful nods of agreement around the room. 'Don't let this scare you!" he said. "We will explore three distinct techniques, which are specifically designed to shrink project durations to meet externally imposed deadlines. I refer to them as our 'Three Lines of Defense.'"

■ ■ ■

To reduce resistance to tighter deadlines:

Have customer explain reasoning to team.

Represent the change as a challenge.

Offer tangible incentives for best ideas, such as dinners, tickets, and so on.

Relate successful project completion to success of the company and the individual success of team members.

Tell the team "Nobody likes these kinds of changes, but let's look at how we can do this."

Show enthusiasm and confidence in the team's successful meeting of a new deadline.

5.2 The First Line of Defense: Relieve the Critical Path

Once you've determined which activities make up the Critical Path, go back and see if any can be taken off the Critical Path. Look at each one and try to view it creatively. Consult with your team members. Can some of the activities be started before their current predecessor is completely finished? Are there opportunities for some start-to-start relationships? Can some be split so that some of the work can be finished sooner? Can some be combined such that the combination affords paralleling some work, thus reducing the net duration? This is the time to really let loose. Remember that creativity reduces stress. In addition, as duration reduction efforts go, this introduces the least stress to the team.

Now, redo the forward pass calculation. Find the New Critical Path and project duration. This is a reiterative process. Do it several times. Use problem-solving techniques such as brainstorming to get the most mileage possible at this stage.

What if we still don't meet the project's deadline? Go on the second line of defense.

5.3 The Second Line of Defense: Sharpen Your Pencil

Now look at the Critical Path again. This is the time to push for tight estimates! Ask the team members involved in each Critical Path activity for a *detailed* breakdown of duration. Usually, when you ask team members to account for each detail of the work, the duration estimate will go down. Fudge factors and rules of thumb will mysteriously disappear from the estimate. It's okay if, after this detailed breakdown, some duration estimates go up. At this point, we're really fine-tuning everything, and you will have averted a future surprise.

Caution! As you continue to shrink the length of the CP, you will start creating other alterations. So be certain to reidentify the CP after each change you make, just to be sure you know when another CP pops up. When this happens, you now need to make two simultaneous reductions, one on each CP, in order to actually shorten the project duration. It will also be useful for you and your team to go back to relieving the new Critical Paths (your first line of defense), since the now new critical activities were not examined in that light before. In the majority of cases, the project's deadline can be met at this stage.

What if this is one of the few projects that still doesn't meet the desired deadline? It's time for the third line of defense.

5.4 The Third Line of Defense: Crashing Activities

At this stage, you have to resort to "crashing," which means spending more money in order to shrink the durations of some activities of the project sufficiently to bring the whole project within deadline. Although some activity crashing is helpful, this will obviously increase the project's cost, aggravate risk, and is probably the most stressful of all duration reduction techniques. It is for these reasons that it is used as a last resort. Crashing is discussed in detail in the following chapter, Resource Management.

In summary, then, to determine the total project duration:

- Construct a CPM network for the project.
- Estimate the normal duration of every activity.
- Perform the forward pass calculations.
- Identify the Critical Path(s).
- Conduct a reality check.
- Optimize your plan to fit the imposed deadlines by using:
- The first line of defense—Relieve the Critical Path.
- The second line of defense—Sharpen your pencil.
- The third line of defense—Crash selected activities.

Chapter Summary

The last chapter began with a preliminary plan, and involved the team in developing the WBS down to activity level, in order to begin to gain their commitment. The team was then further involved in developing the precedence relationships, which led to the first picture of the project—the CPM Network.

In this chapter, the team's commitment is futher cultivated by allowing them to estimate the durations of all the activities. The project is set up for success by using normal durations, which are based on the most cost-efficient approach for each activity. Using these duration estimates, we apply them to the CPM Network in order to arrive at the Critical Path, the total project duration and its projected completion date.

In order to meet often tight externally imposed deadlines for completion, the team further optimizes the plan. This is done using the three lines of defense: 1. Relieve the critical path: 2. Sharpen your pencil; and finally, 3. Crash selected activities. As this is done, more critical paths may emerge and become subject to the optimization techniques.

Chapter Questions

1. List three steps for setting normal duration estimates. Discuss each step in the context of a project in which you may be involved. What is meant by "selectively adjust for common problems"?
2. List the various techniques available for estimating durations and give a brief description of each. Briefly discuss those you or your employer uses, citing some examples.
3. Discuss the similarities and differences between PERT and CPM techniques.
4. Define Critical Path and list its most important characteristics. Discuss the importance of identifying the Critical Path of a project plan. Describe two of the methods used to identify it.
5. What is meant by "reality check" in this chapter, and what are some of the commonly asked questions in this regard?
6. List the three lines of defense used to optimize the project plan and describe each. What are some compelling reasons for optimizing the project plan?

Project Challenge: Applying What You Know

Use Microsoft Project to help you solve the following problems.

Refer to Figure 9–8:

1. How many paths are there?
2. What is the total duration of each path?
3. Which is the Critical Path?
4. Assume that a careful analysis of activity 7 revealed that it could be completed in 18 weeks instead of the original estimate of 25. What is the impact on the project duration? Identify any new Critical Paths created by this change.

Refer to the Kitchen Remodeling Problem (from last chapter):

5. Estimate and assign the most cost-efficient crew size for each activity.
6. Estimate normal activity durations in working hours based on crew sizes.
7. Your in-laws inform you that they will be coming to visit your home sooner than expected. You realize that the remodeling project needs to be completed in 80% of its currently planned duration. Using the three lines of defense, show how you would meet this objective. Illustrate your answer with a modified CPM network.

Interview with an Expert

***Donald "Skip" Hall,** Former Program Manager for Coast Guard Ordnance.*

Scheduling well is a function of two things: securing realistic estimates of durations to begin with, and monitoring the schedule to catch any deviation early. You have to look at all tasks, both within your own company and outside from contractors. With contractors, especially, they need to be told that you are scheduling based on their commitments. After you extract as close to an exact time as they will commit to, then further impose a 2% plus or minus variation on their estimate for a realistic schedule.

With in-house project team members you have to explain Critical Path dependencies. Even then the machinist or the computer coder might answer the question "how long will it take?" with a figure of 1 1/2 times what he or she expects—to cover any eventualities. Supervisors will often tell you 1/2 to 3/4 the time it will actually take—to look good. For your own peace of mind, go one step further and call others who have had experience with contractors and/or suppliers and get their estimate.

A quick formula to use would be:

{Most optimistic + most pessimistic + (most likely X 4)} / 6

For example, if the most optimistic estimate were 4 weeks, the most pessimistic 14 weeks, and the most likely 6 weeks, the answer would be :

(4 x 1 + 6 x 4 + 14 x 1) / 6 = 7 weeks

As you research realistic duration estimates to develop the schedule, be wary of the estimate that is inordinately high or noticeably low. If you don't know the contractors or suppliers well, go to each and ask how the time estimate was arrived at. Don't be afraid to make them explain their logic or formula; it's you who is responsible for the outcome. Investigation might help you out. In one case we had a bid that was several million dollars below the others. When we checked, we found out that the company had no prior experience with the specific application we were using. The implications of that down the road are the material of nightmares. In another case, most of the bidders were between $18,000 and $42,000. One, however, was only $9,800. Instead of throwing it out, we checked with the bidding company, who told us that they were just covering their cost of materials. Apparently, the workers were between jobs and they had to pay them anyway; they felt it was better to keep them working, than to have them off that time. It made sense to us and saved many thousands of dollars.

Make sure all on the project, both internal people and contractors, use the same scheduling software and update regularly. Also, though, you have to publish and circulate the adjustments, to alert you and others to problems before they become unmanageable. The biggest enemy of the schedule, though, is often the customer, whose deadline you are trying to meet. Someone from the customer's crew asks, "Can we get this changed?" or "Can we have this extra?" Then someone from your crew, in an effort to please the customer, says, "Sure." Enough of that will throw your time line off, and it's the customer who will take you to court and sue you for missing the deadline. Just keep in mind, the contract is always right, not the customer. Instruct all your people that any requests or changes *must* come through you and have a contract addendum signed by the customer. Schedule overruns are cost overruns, and somebody has to pay. Don't let it be your budget that pays.

CHAPTER

10 RESOURCE MANAGEMENT

CHAPTER PREVIEW

Resource Management

"Project managers must be resourceful," Tracey said, opening the day's session. Now just what does that term mean for us here? Resourceful."

"In my business it sometimes means duct tape," Jaime laughed as he answered.

"Okay, this sounds like a good one. Go ahead, Jaime."

"Sometimes equipment doesn't work as it should, or wiring gets in the way of an installation, maybe a cover won't stay on. Duct tape handles a lot of situations. Right now it's handling a leak in the water hose in my car." Everyone laughed along with Jaime.

"Yes, resourceful can mean the creative use of materials to solve problems," Tracey agreed, "but it also refers to our being able to accomplish our goals with what we have, even if that is a limited pool to choose from. It means being able to handle contingencies such as scarce resources or changes in price or durations."

"My son is a building contractor," Yury offered. "Last week he had to fire a man. The man left the job with the key to the forklift. They had no forklift for nearly a whole day, and on a tight schedule that cost money. On top of that he is in a union area, and the man was the only certified forklift operator on his crew. It was bad, very bad for him." Yury shook his head.

"What happened? How did he handle it?" Tom inquired.

"First he yelled and banged his fist on his desk." Yury chuckled, as did the others. "He knew a large equipment contractor who rented him another forklift with a driver for a day. That way he didn't lose too much time before he found another key and another man."

"So understanding the impact that each of our resources has on our ability to finish a project is an important part of the project manager's job," Tracey concluded. She wrote the following on the easel:

- How do I compete with everybody else who needs resources?
- Where do I find people when I can't hire new employees?

- What does time cost me in terms of resources?
- How can I make up for missing resources?

Resources include all you have at your disposal, all you can locate, and all you can leverage to carry out your project. Resource management is a huge challenge as it includes not just materials, equipment, and facilities, but also the skills and productive capacity of your people. As stressed in the first chapter, people can be the most difficult to manage, so that is the first topic addressed in this chapter: the human resource. However, planning your budget in a realistic way is a critical element as well, and attention will be paid in the second half of the chapter to managing the money part of the resource picture.

■ ■ ■

1.0 The Human Resource

As a project manager, you know that your most critical resource is people. Remember, the equation for magic is money, time, and people. Of these three, people will demand the most attention. The most important decisions you will make are those associated with people. Your people are your intellectual capital. You have many tools available to you to get the job done, but the most important tools are the people doing the work. An example might be a great computer with super software. Without the right person to use that computer, it is a big, expensive paperweight. Remember, techniques don't manage successful projects, people do!

1.1 The Human Resource Challenge Today

In response to changing conditions and the ensuing constantly changing human resource needs, today's project managers are more and more often turning to contract employees. These employees are screened, paid, and in some cases, managed by the contracting company that supplies them. They purchase benefits and invest in retirement plans with the contracting company and thus create no permanent salary or benefits burden to the project manager's budget. Because your company does not have to pay benefits to the employee, and because the contracting company incurs the expense of securing and managing these employees, the hourly rate of a contractor will be higher than the hourly rate of your regular employees. As we've stated earlier, however, it is still probably more cost- effective than paying a full-timer with benefits. Plus, the costs of hiring are reduced or eliminated.

The use of contractors solves some dilemmas in the management of your human resource, but sometimes creates others. One advantage to using contractors is that they usually are highly expert, often highly motivated people with fresh ideas and solid skills. The moral dilemma of having to fire someone due to slowdown or project end is eliminated, because the contractor fully expects to be temporary. Contractors, temps, and permanent part-timers give you flexibility in your changing human resource needs, both in the areas of skill and time needed. You can thus "rent" talent for as long as you need it without having to purchase it and without adding to "head count," as it is referred to in budget terms. One other added bonus of using temporary employees is that you have a chance to "try out" what could become a full-time employee, if that person fits and the need arises.

There are disadvantages to using contractors as well. One is that contractors are not the total answer in solving human resource challenges. There is a certain amount of company history and continuity that creates the stability needed to do business. Contractors will not have this. Another is the difficulty of "marrying" temporary and permanent employees in close-knit, fully integrated teams. Sometimes there is resentment when contractors "make more money" than full-time employees (discussed above). In other instances, outsider versus insider animosity rears its ugly head.

You will find that some of your long-time people will be suspicious of the level of commitment to be expected from a contractor. Integrating the skill, talent, and interpersonal motivation sets of diverse employees, contract or permanent, involves all the elements outlined in prior chapters. Creating some shared experiences within the group helps in this area. Offices where parties celebrate workplace achievements and where a big laugh might ensue over some prank have high productivity, mostly because these are shared, bonding experiences. Every milestone in a project's rollout is a potential team-solidifying opportunity. The clever project manager learns to lead the team, not worry about who "belongs" and who is just "passing through."

As a quick reminder for managing your human resources, here are some short guidelines.

You must provide:

- Direction
- Guidance
- Support
- Encouragement

1.1.1 Direction

Keep the team focused. There is a real tendency in some employees to be sidetracked by attractive but tangential issues. These absorb the time, money, and energy of the team. Recognize these for what they are and steer your team away from them.

1.1.2 Guidance

Coach your people along. Help the team individually and as a group address their weaknesses and recognize their strengths. Have frequent one-on-one sessions with individual members.

1.1.3 Support

Back your team. Use your resources to help them along and smooth their way. Encourage creative thinking. Your team will respond much better if they are certain that your clout is supporting them and not threatening them.

1.1.4 Encouragement

Some call this cheerleading. There is nothing wrong with a good, effective cheer. Show them the light at the end of the tunnel (make sure they know it's not a train). The proper words of encouragement can go a long way towards making a group come together and making an already cohesive team fly.

1.2 Cost of the Human Resource

Unfortunately, cost-wise, one of your most variable and difficult to manage resources is the human resource. When you add the consideration of wide salary scales and the related indirect costs, you have a potential wildcard element in the initial project cost estimate. You are accountable for project cost estimates to your manager or to the customer. Thus, many elements of the human resource picture must be examined in assessing management of this resource area: salaries, benefits, fees, and time to manage.

1.2.1 Salaries

With up and downsizing, as well as expanding and shrinking projects, management is reluctant to hire "permanent" employees for a variety of reasons. One is the fluctuation of need in the project environment. Projects require a great variety of people skills and a dynamic requirements profile.

Another reason for reluctance is the cost of hiring a full-time person with a specific skill set. A full-time, permanent employee means a long-term commitment to a resource that will cost more each year, much beyond the life of the project, when you may just need those skills for one project. In addition, some projects require highly specialized (and scarce) skill sets that are held by individuals who know fully their value in the market. Paying $80,000 to $100,000 in salary for a high-voltage power supply engineer is a heady expense year after year, especially if you need that person on projects less than all the time. This level of expense makes your planning even more critical. Many managers offer the guideline that you should need one and a half to two people before you hire one.

1.2.2. Benefits

benefits payment or service given to employees in addition to salary, including paid leave, life and health insurance, retirement/investment plans, training and so on

Another cost of the human resource is **benefits**—paid leave, life and health insurance, retirement/investment plans, training, supporting facilities, and so on. Some larger companies with a good benefits package that includes all of the above figure the cost of an employee at 2.5 times salary. Thus, to add an employee full-time to your budget, you must have at least twice the salary of that employee budgeted for the project.

1.2.3. Fees and Cost of Hiring

Initial hiring costs are becoming a huge consideration in the project management environment, because skilled and competent employees seem to be harder and harder to find. However, there is no shortage of people looking for work. Thus, if you place an ad in a newspaper, you may receive as many as 150–400 responses—only 10 or so of which are truly qualified. Recruiters—specialists in locating qualified people in a particular field—can screen candidates prior to referring them to you. This reduces the number you actually have to take the time (your time costs money too) to interview. Recruiters, however, charge a fee, often to the hiring company, instead of the employee. This incurs even more hiring expense, since some companies fly employment candidates and their families in, put them up at a nice hotel, and treat them to meals and entertainment. Then, every member of the "team" takes time out from his or her own work (more cost incurred for their time) to interview the candidate. This could happen with as many as 30 to 100 candidates a year in high-growth companies with the accompanying downtime for interviews. You can see why paying recruiters to screen applicants could actually save your company money.

1.2.4. Time to Manage

high-maintenance employee requires excessive amounts of the project manager's time

Talented people, as already noted, are sometimes hard to come by. So, managers will occasionally compromise on interpersonal skill requirements in order to secure desperately needed technical expertise. What happens then is that these employees become **high maintenance** and require excessive amounts of the project manager's time, not only in managing them, but also in managing the fallout that occurs with other employees. Project teams, as discussed in an earlier chapter, are intimate relationships of a sort, and a toxic individual can make life miserable for all involved.

Project managers often have to weigh the plusses and minuses of individual employees' contributions and make tough decisions. Technically talented engineers have been fired because they couldn't get along with the other team members. It does happen, because productivity is based in large part on the effectiveness of the team's interactions.

2.0 THE CAPITAL RESOURCE

Everything costs something. Your people cost, their offices cost, and the materials they use cost. However, the unwary can be caught by surprise by some costs. Awareness of the relationship of all elements of your project to their potential costs will go a long way toward improving the credibility of your estimates.

2.1 Elements of Cost

Let's examine the different categories of cost involved in project management. Accountants, for various reasons, classify costs in two general categories: direct cost, also known as variable cost, and indirect cost, sometimes referred to as fixed cost.

2.1.1. Direct Cost

The more volume you're trying to produce, the more wages you'll end up paying and the more materials you'll need. This is direct cost. **Direct costs** are those that vary directly with the volume of your output. If you were manufacturing paper, and you wished to increase production by 50%, one of the first things you would notice is that the amount of money you were spending on wood pulp would also increase by about 50%. Direct costs may be reduced by some other means. Buying better technology will often cut down direct costs but you have to pay for the machinery, which fits under another category of costs.

direct costs costs that vary directly with your volume of output, including labor wages, overtime premium, materials, and sales tax

Direct costs include the following:

- Labor wages
- Overtime premium
- Materials
- Subcontractors
- Freight
- Sales tax

2.1.2 Indirect (Fixed) Cost

Indirect costs are fixed periodic costs. These don't change with the amount of product created. The indirect cost, however, accumulates over time. The longer a project goes, the longer you pay indirect costs. Rental of equipment is a good example. As long as you keep the equipment, it doesn't matter what you do with it.

indirect costs fixed periodic costs, including insurance, start-up, overhead utilities, and security

- Insurance
- Start-up
- Overhead utilities (HVAC, lighting, etc.)
- Security
- Marketing
- Goodwill
- Opportunity for problems

■ ■ ■

2.2 Duration and Cost

Jaime Martinez was concerned. "Many times, when surprises come up, I must decide which is the greater evil between extending the time line, and maybe costing dollars in penalties or lost sales, or bringing in more resources, also costing more."

Ralph nodded in sympathy. "This is a difficult issue. Can anybody offer a suggestion?"

Hilda answered, "Sometimes this is a decision that must be made by upper management, not necessarily the project manager. Cost may be a relative issue, but the project manager may not know all the elements involved in the issue to make such decisions. So, it is important not to second-guess management."

"That's right," Ralph said, "the priority may be getting to market first with a new design, with the ensuing market share dominance and profitability justification enough for the added cost. Therefore, cost may not be an object. We have actually seen this situation in research and development environments. By the same token, there may be a point where completing a project that has had multiple duration problems may not be cost-effective. Either way, upper management must be made aware of the situation. But, let's look at how you as the project manager might go about analyzing the issue of activity crashing."

■ ■ ■

Consider the following situation in a project of relocating an office complex. It was found that the duration for erecting the movable partitions and their attachments varied as the number of workers assigned was increased from 2 to 8 workers. Table 10–1 shows the resulting durations and costs in man-hours.

Table 10–1
Resources and Costs Involved in Relocating Office Complex

Workers Assigned	Duration (hours)	Direct Cost (man-hours)	
2	25	50	
3	14	42	
4	10	40	N
5	9	45	
6	8	48	C
7	8	56	
8	8	64	

Now, identify the Normal Point look for the line with the lowest direct cost (i.e., 40 man-hours corresponding to four workers assigned). This is highlighted by the N. Normally there is a limit to how much time can be saved by adding workers, mostly due to increased coordination effort required, communication, and just plain getting in each other's way.

Next it is necessary to identify the "Fully Crashed" point for this activity by looking for the line with the least duration in hours. This will be 8 hours, corresponding to six workers assigned, since incurring more cost doesn't improve the duration further! This is noted by the capital C. Plotting these points on a Cost/Duration Graph (Figure 10–1) shows the effect of crashing an activity on the direct cost of the activity. Both cost and duration rise as resources are added beyond the Crash Point of an activity, or if resources are decreased below the Normal Point for the activity. An example of the latter would be making up a bed in the morning. Two people can make a bed in a short time because they can work on opposite sides of the bed; whereas, one person would have to keep walking around the bed to attend to both sides of the bed. The one-person job would obviously take longer than twice the time that it takes two people!

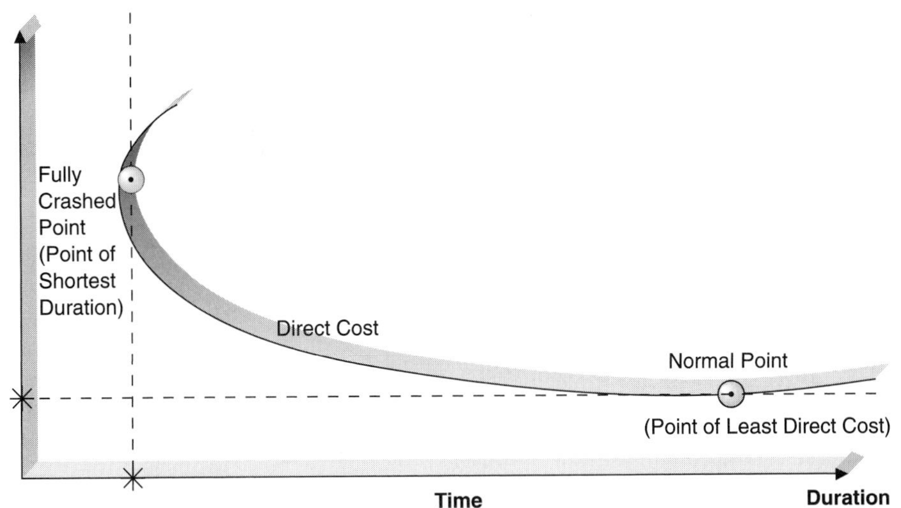

Figure 10–1
Cost/Duration Graph

2.2.1 Activity Crashing

"I got this note from the new V.P. of Marketing attached to a copy of a project plan, which I sent for his review," said Jerry. "The note said that every activity on this project needed to be shortened by 15%, because the project is too long."

"So what was your response?" Ralph asked.

"I was stunned! I thought senior managers like him would know enough about project management not to make such statements," responded Jerry. "Most activities already had slack and spending money to shorten them only buys more slack!"

"Exactly!"said Ralph. Hilda then suggested that they discuss how to choose the best activities to crash.

■ ■ ■

2.2.2 Criteria for Selecting Activities to Crash

There are several characteristics that mark or highlight an activity that exists on the Critical Path as a better candidate for crashing.

1. ***Must be on the Critical Path.*** As Jerry stated, crashing noncritical activities that already have slack only buys more slack and doesn't shorten the project duration any! Only Critical Path activities drive the project and crashing them will shorten the project duration.

2. ***Precedes multiple activities.*** When an activity bottlenecks numerous succeeding activities, it is a great candidate to shorten. Once this activity is shortened, it allows the multiple activities to begin.

3. Long duration. An activity that has a long duration offers more potential time gain from crashing it.

4. Lower cost per period gained. Activities that cost less to crash are preferred. These include those requiring lower paid, lower skilled workers or other resources that are otherwise sitting idle.

the Sunshine Rule If it is early in the project and you fail in crashing the activity, you still have recovery time, and demand on resources is usually low early in the project.

5. Early in the project **(the Sunshine Rule).** If you fail in crashing the activity and it takes longer than planned, it is still early in the project. Thus you still have recovery time. Also, typically demand on resources early in the project is lower than other times, and they should be readily available (so you can make hay while the sun shines!).

6. Labor-intensive. When an activity is low-skill labor intensive, it is easy to add people to help complete the project early. When an activity requires high skills to complete, it may be hard to find qualified individuals who are capable of completing the task.

7. Subject to common problems. Try to pick activities that are subject to higher probability of common problems. Shortening the duration lowers the exposure time and lessens the chances of having a problem!

2.2.3 Time/ Cost Tradeoff Analysis

Until now, the discussion has centered on how direct cost changes as duration changes. At this point the indirect costs are introduced into the equation.

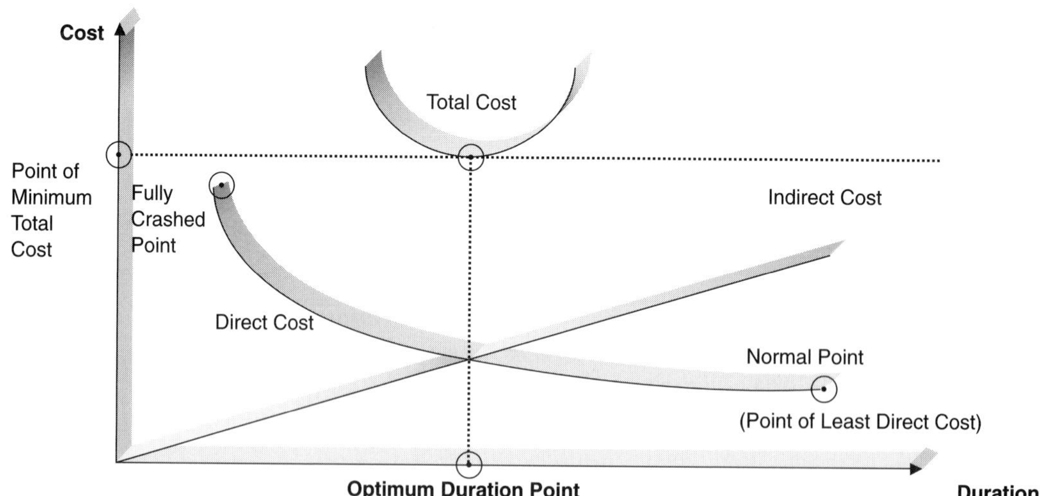

Figure 10–2
Cost/Duration Graph showing Time-Cost Tradeoffs and Optimum Duration Point

Figure 10–2 is an example of how a project's total cost varies with duration. The curve marked Total Cost is the point-by-point total of the Indirect and Direct Cost lines. One should note that the indirect cost line is a straight line because indirect cost is a direct function of time. As the duration of a project increases, the project's indirect cost also increases. The direct cost curve starts at its lowest with the Normal Point, then slopes upwards as duration decreases towards the Fully Crashed Point. This is due to the fact that more resources are needed as you begin to crash an activity closer to the Fully Crashed Point.

2.2.4 Optimum Duration

The purpose of graphing the total cost curve is to determine the Minimum Total Cost and the corresponding Optimum Duration Point. The Minimum Total Cost Point is easily spotted because it is at the bottom of the Total Cost curve. Once this value is found, drop down to the Duration axis (the x-axis) and this is the Optimum Duration for the activity.

The Optimum Duration point is usually shorter than the Normal Duration, that is it involves some level of crashing. In other words, it's where the savings in indirect costs exceed the added direct costs of crashing.

Recall the formula for magic? Magic happens when you have the right amount of money, people, and time. Change any one of these and the other two greatly increase. Using the ditch example from last chapter, if you ran out of time and had to have the ditch dug in half a day instead of 5, you may have to resort to using the ditch-witch instead of the kid next door. Your direct cost will go from $50, the kid's fee, to the $160 it takes to rent the ditch-witch. This corresponds to the fully crashed point, since paying even more for bigger machines won't reduce the duration any further.

If the indirect costs associated with keeping the lawn torn up are $10 per day, then the total cost in this case would be $160 (machine rental) + $5 (indirect cost for $\frac{1}{2}$ day) = $165, versus total cost at the Normal Duration of using the kid at $50 (kid's fee) + $50 (indirect cost for 5 days) = $100. Now, say the kid would take a $10 bonus to finish in 3 days. This is a partial crashing of the activity. The new total cost would be $60 (kid's fee and bonus) + $30 (indirect cost for 3 days) = $90. Cheaper than the original agreement at the Normal Duration, saving $20 in indirect costs outweighs the $10 extra bonus costs and you're money ahead.

Unless planned at the Optimum Duration level, further crashing of activities adds to their total cost (overtime, special shipping, etc.), which may defeat the reason you got the bid in the first place: cost. Crashing activities also adds to your team's stress level, which increases the chance of failure. Since you as the project manager are obligated to lead your projects to profitable completions, you must become expert at figuring the Optimum Duration for your project, and still stay within manageable stress levels. As you can see now, starting with accurate duration estimates will really help in this regard, and avoid the need to further crash activities due to surprises.

Remember the Third Line of Defense from earlier? When having to crash activities to meet an external deadline, it is an opportunity to reach for the Optimum Duration and actually reduce total cost as you reduce duration.

3.0 MANAGING THE RESOURCE PROFILE

A project's resource profile describes the rate at which resources are consumed over time. It would be great if the project used resources at a nice even pace, giving you a level profile. In reality the resource requirements of a project may resemble the graph in Figure 10–3.

Figure 10–3
Typical Project Resource Profile

The variations in the graph show that at different times along the project's duration, drastically more or fewer resources are needed. In this case, a lot of the resources are due at the beginning of the project. The danger in such a profile is that the peaks represent resource levels much higher than what's available in an organization, and may not be achievable without considerable expense and risk of delays.

A bad side effect of wide fluctuations in resource requirements is "hurry up and wait," which is demoralizing to the team and undermines management's credibility. Other undesirable side effects include excessive expenses due to overtime, training, and hiring/firing; and frequent assignment and priority changes for team members. All of these increase overall project cost, and add stress for the project team. It is important to do everything possible to level the resource profile.

Some typical resources that exhibit erratic profiles are:

- Staffing levels
- Consumption of funds
- Equipment use
- The need for travel

3.1 Profile Management Tools

The key to leveling resource profiles is to shift work from the peaks to the valleys by rescheduling activities. To accomplish this, you need to take a look at tools for managing the resource profile, which will include slack and float and time-scaled networks.

Finding Scarce Resources

Maintain good contacts inside company
Network with others in industry

Keep an alternate suppliers list

Treat team members and suppliers well (so they will work for you again)

Borrow skills and/or equipment

Reward innovative alternative ideas from teams members

3.1.1 Slack and Float

Having gone to considerable trouble to shorten the project duration in order to meet the customer's deadline, you must find ways to shift work around the schedule without impacting the project completion date, or the dates of critical milestones within the project. You do this by avoiding any changes to activities on the Critical Paths. Activities not on the Critical Path afford us our only real opportunity to level resource requirements, since they have some slack. We can selectively slide noncritical activities within their slack, in order to move work away from the peaks of the profile. For this reason, we must be able to figure out which activities have which kind of slack. (See Figure10–4.)

3.1.2 Backwards Pass

This technique is needed to calculate slack (or float) in activities or paths in the project network. The backwards pass method is performed on the project's CPM network. Following are more definitions:

LAS = Latest Acceptable Start time. This is the latest date on which an activity must start without delaying the project's finish date.

LAF = Latest Acceptable Finish time. This is the latest date on which an activity must finish without delaying the project's finish date. This means that an activity's LAF must equal the succeeding activity's LAS.

Again,
LAF = LAS + Duration, and
LAS = LAF – Duration
TS = Total Slack

To apply this to the CPM network, we will agree on another convention. We'll show the LAS and LAF times on the activity node in the bottom squares as shown in Figure 10–4.

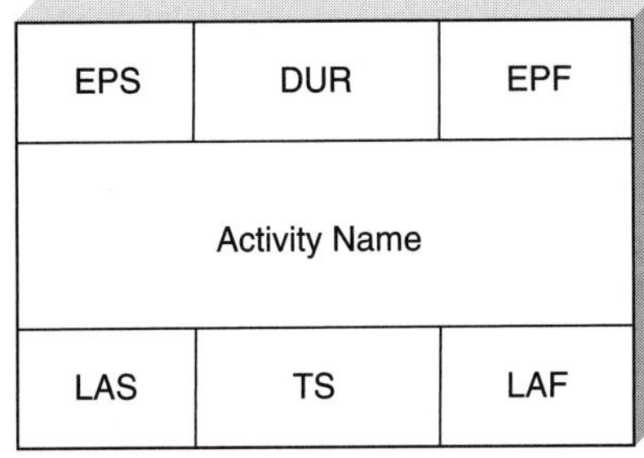

Figure 10–4
Completed Standard Node Box Notation with Backwards Pass Information

Figure 10–5 shows an attempt to discover the LAS and LAF times of each activity.

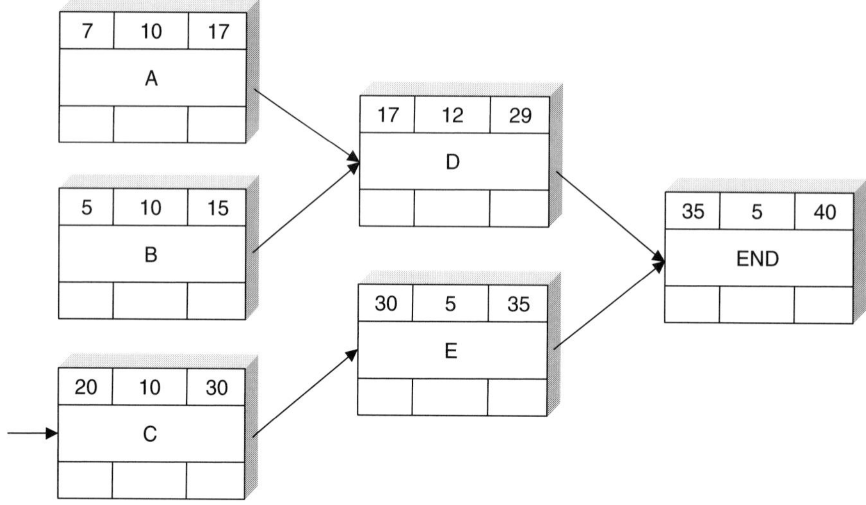

Figure 10–5
Partial AON Network

Notice that the LAF of the end activity is the same as its EPF, Earliest Possible Finish. This is true because that EPF represents the deadline agreed upon for the project. This also gives us our starting point for the Backwards Pass calculation.

Calculation Steps for the Backward Pass

1. Start with the end activity, where LAF equals EPF.
2. Use the formula LAS = LAF–Duration to determine its LAS (40–5 = 35). Fill it in.
3. LAF of the preceding activities must equal the LAS of this activity; that is, the LAF of both D and E is also 35. Fill them in.
4. Now calculate the LAS for each of D and E:

$$\text{LAS (D)} = 35 - 12 = 23$$

$$\text{LAS (E)} = 35 - 5 = 30$$

5. Similarly, the LAF for A and B equals the LAS of D (23) and the LAF for C equals the LAS of E (30).
6. Again, calculate the LAS for each of A, B, and C:

$$\text{LAS (A)} = 23 - 10 = 13$$

$$\text{LAS (B)} = 23 - 10 = 13$$

$$\text{LAS (C)} = 30 - 10 = 20$$

This is the Backwards Pass! Completed, the above example looks as shown in Figure 10–6.

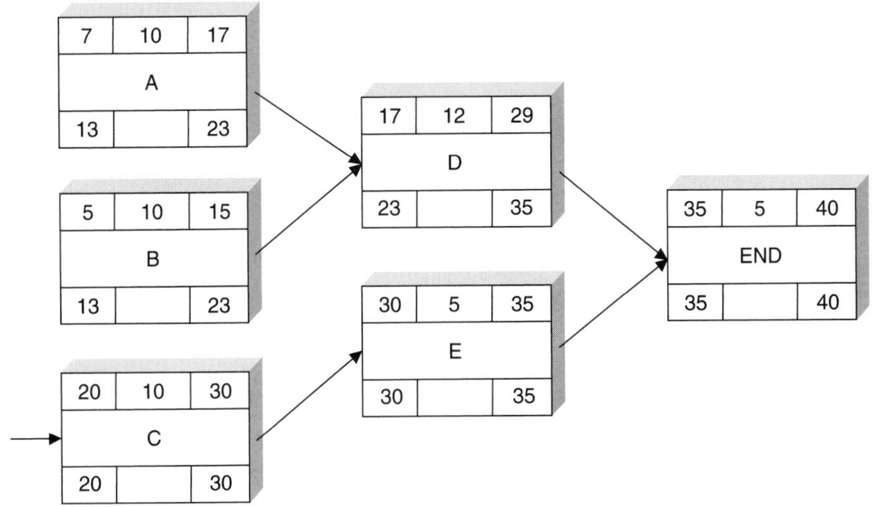

Figure 10–6
Partial AON Network Showing Backwards Pass Calculations Completed

You will notice that for activities C, E, and END, the earliest and latest times are equal. That is because they have no slack, which means they must be a Critical Path. This is the other technique for finding the Critical Paths of a network, which was mentioned in an earlier chapter. Non-Critical Path activities, however, do have slack, since they can start and finish at later times than their EPS and EPF indicate.

As discussed in Chapter 9, there are two kinds of slack:

1. **Total slack** (TS) is the amount of time an activity can be delayed without delaying the finish date of the project.

total slack (TS) the amount of time an activity can be delayed without delaying the finish date of the project

TS = LAF – EPF of the same activity.

For activities A, B, and D, total slack is calculated to be:

NODE	LAF	–	EAF	=	TS
A:	23	–	17	=	6
B:	23	–	15	=	8
D:	35	–	29	=	6

2. **Free slack** (FS) is the amount of time an activity can be delayed without delaying its successor tasks.

free slack (FS) the amount of time an activity can be delayed without delaying its successor tasks

FS = EPS of the following activity – EPF of this one

Free slack for the same activities is:

NODE	EPS (following activity)		–	EPF	=	FS
A:	17	17	–	=	0	
B:	17	15	–	=	2	
C:	35	29	–	=	6	

Note that even though A has a total slack of 6, it has no free slack. The reason is that Total Slack actually belongs to the path, and not the activity. It is actually a dangerous kind of slack. To illustrate, assume that the person responsible for activity A decided to use the total slack of 6 periods to go hunting, and started the activity upon his return on the LAS, in period 13. Consequently, he then finished on the LAF in period 23.

When the person responsible for D's turn came, he too decided to use the activity's total slack of 6 periods to go fishing. When he returned in period 29 (23 + 6), the activity was started and was finished after the duration of 12 periods in period 41, thus holding up the end activity and delaying the project!

The total slack belongs to the entire path; it can be distributed among activities on the path, but can't be used over and over again! Free slack, however, belongs to the activity itself. In the above scenario, A cannot be delayed since it has no free slack, but D can slip by 6 periods without impacting the LAS of the END activity.

In any case, it is a good rule to consider that slack of any kind belongs to the project manager, to be used in resource leveling, as we will see below. Team members are to stick to *earliest start and finish dates* as a matter of routine.

When applying these techniques to the New Millennium Problem, the results will look as illustrated in Figure 10–7.

3.1.3 Time-Scaled Networks

Another tool you will need in resource management is the time-scaled network. It is a hybrid of a Gantt Chart and a CPM Network, sometimes known as "Plannet" Chart. (This is the name used by the American Management Association.)

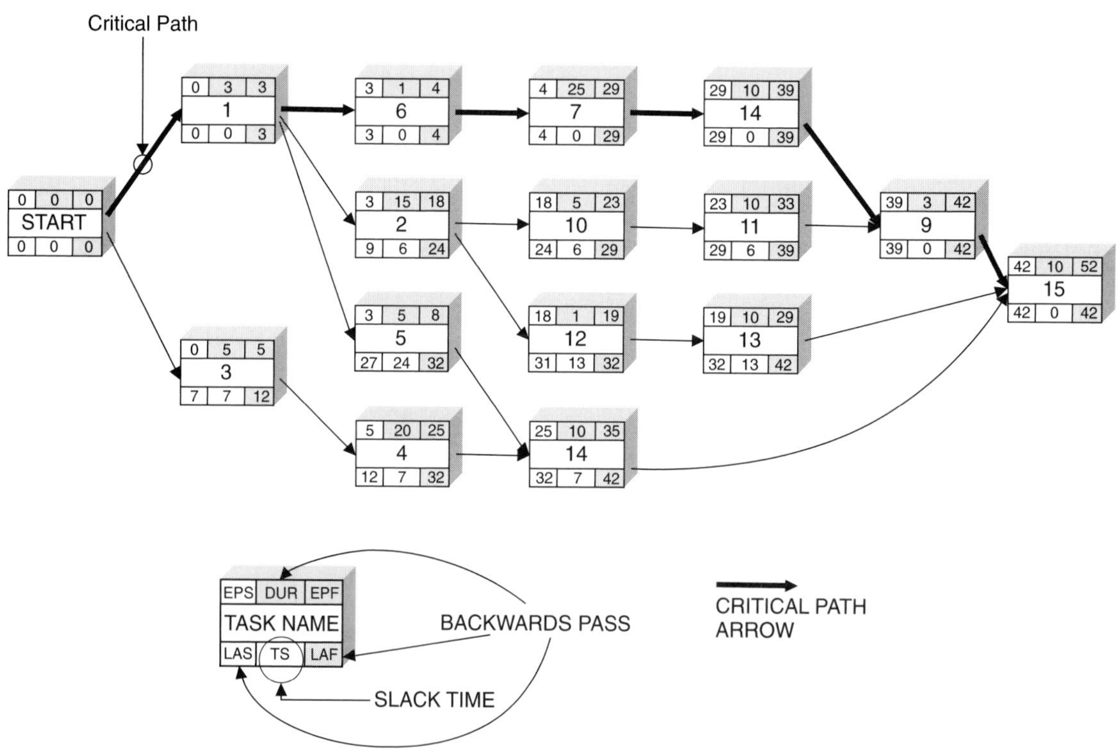

Figure 10–7
Backwards Path Calculation with Critical Path; New Millennium Problem

Starting with a horizontal time scale, activities are shown as blocks stretching between their EPS and EPF times, as in a Gantt Chart. But, like in a network, they are lined up next to each other, and the precedent relationship arrows are shown. In Figure 10–8, a time-scaled network is developed for the example we used in Figure 10–6 for the Backwards Pass calculation.

First, plot the critical path activities along one line near the center of the chart. Notice they butt up against each other, since they have no slack.

Next, plot the noncritical activities, starting from the end, backwards, in rows above and below the Critical Path, using the earliest possible start and finish dates. See Figure 10–9.

This is followed by showing the precedence arrows between the interconnected activities, and lastly, showing in brackets the amount of resource tied up by each activity, expressed in a common unit. In this case, the number of people is used. This can be the number of machines, hours or percent of bottleneck capacity, capital expenditures, credit required, or any other resource you wish to level. This is shown in Figure 10–10 in the completed time-scaled network.

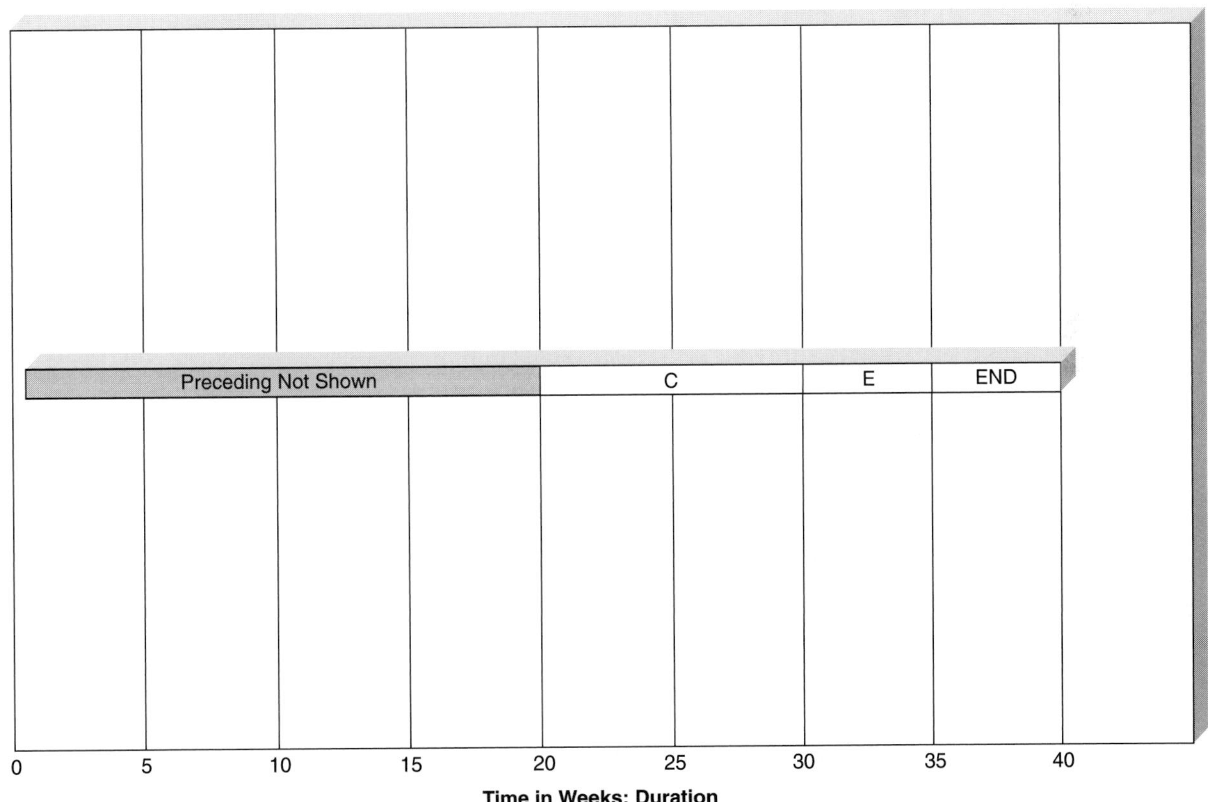

Figure 10–8
Time-Scaled Network Showing Critical Path Activities

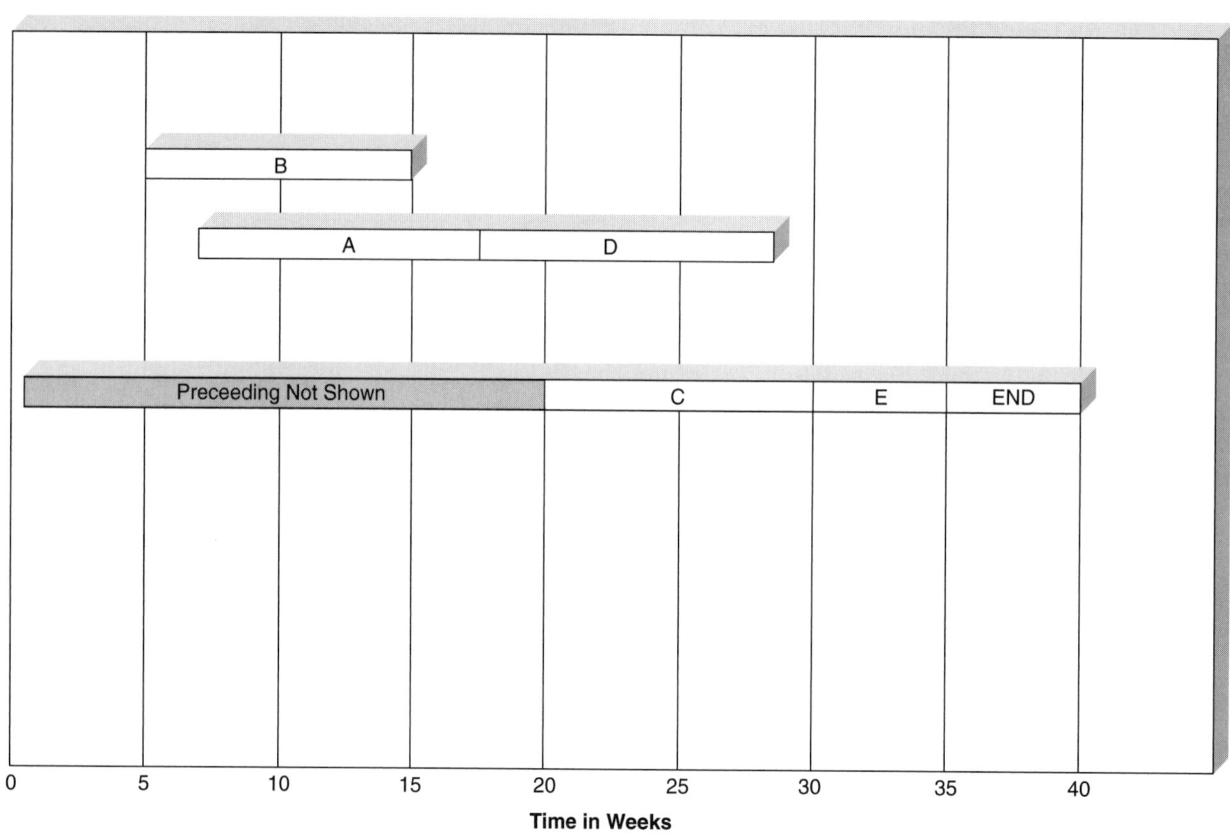

Figure 10–9
Time Scaled Network Showing Noncritical path Activities

Note how Free Slack is highlighted by the precedence arrows, which is represented by the horizontal portion of the arrows. Compare these lengths with the FS calculated in the table on page 213.

3.2 Resource Leveling Methods

"One Hat Method"
Used to develop a project's aggregate resources

The **"One Hat Method"** is widely used to level a project's aggregate resources. It applies well to capabilities of production facilities, people in general, space usage, and so on. Building on the time-scaled network, a graph is aligned on top of it showing the cumulative resource used for each time period. Known as the Resource Profile, this is shown in Figure 10–11. It shows that up until period 5, only the preceding critical activities (X) are going on, tying up 3 people. Starting at period 5, activity B starts, adding 8 people to the profile, so the total jumps to 11. At period 7, activity A joins in with 5 more people, pushing the profile up to 16. At period 15, activity B ends, freeing up 8 people, so the profile drops down to the 8 still tied up by D and X. Then at period 20, X stops and C starts, dropping 3 but adding 4 people. The profile now shows the sum of C and D of 9 people occupied, and so on.

This profile clearly shows a very uneven utilization of people, peaking at 16 people between periods 5 and 15 and bottoming out at 2 people towards the end of the project. Some of the disadvantages of operating with such an uneven resource

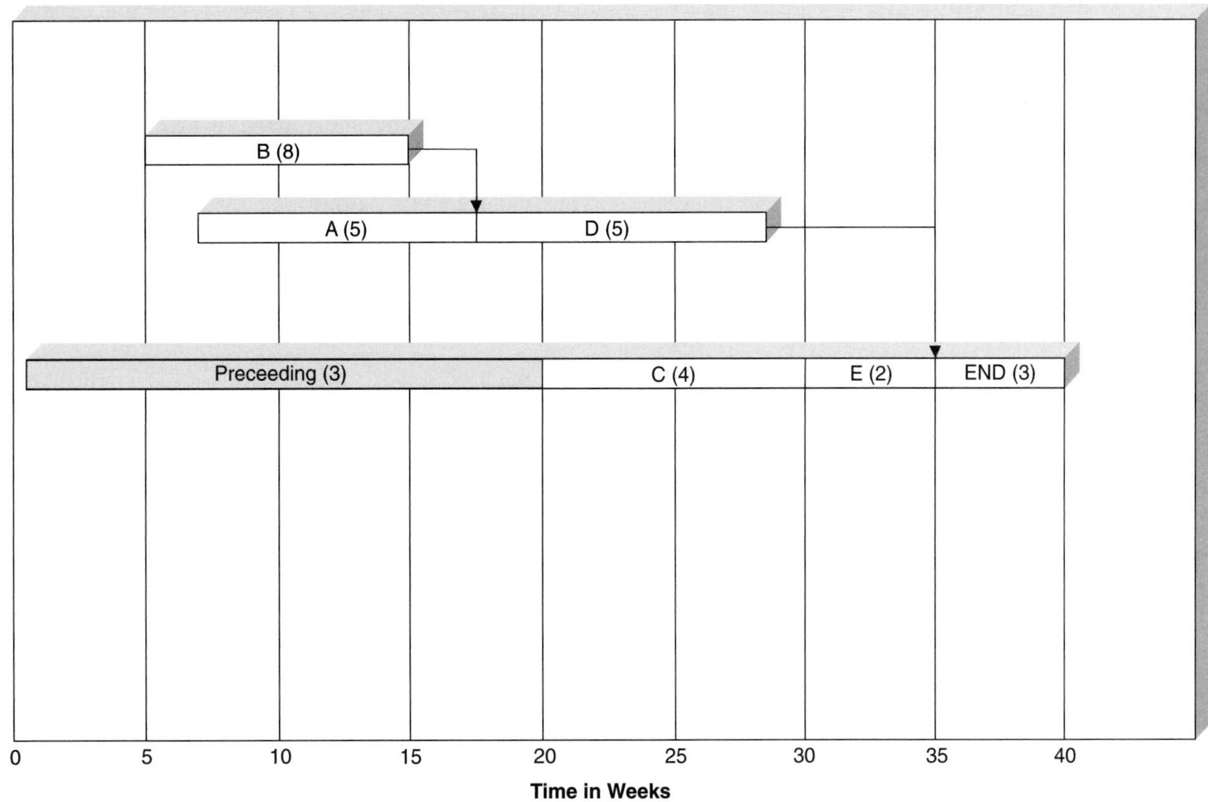

Figure 10–10
Completed Time-Scaled Network Showing Precedence Arrows and Amounts of Resources for Each Activity

profile were mentioned earlier. In order to reduce the effects, an attempt will be made to level this resource.

Again, the idea is to move the peaks into the valleys. Use slack time to do this by moving some of the activities with slack from the peak periods, forward in time into the low periods. Start at the end of the project and work backwards, moving activities with slack from higher periods into the low periods. This has the advantage of making room for preceding activities to move forward also, if necessary.

First move D as far forward as possible, that is, to its LAS and LAF time of 23 and 35, and then replot the profile. Figure 10–12 illustrates this.

Next, you could move either A or B. It's a good idea to move B (since it will have more impact, being labor-intensive) to its latest start, and replot the profile. The results are shown in Figure 10–13. Although the result is more desirable than the original profile, because it rises and declines more gradually, a peak of 16 people still remains.

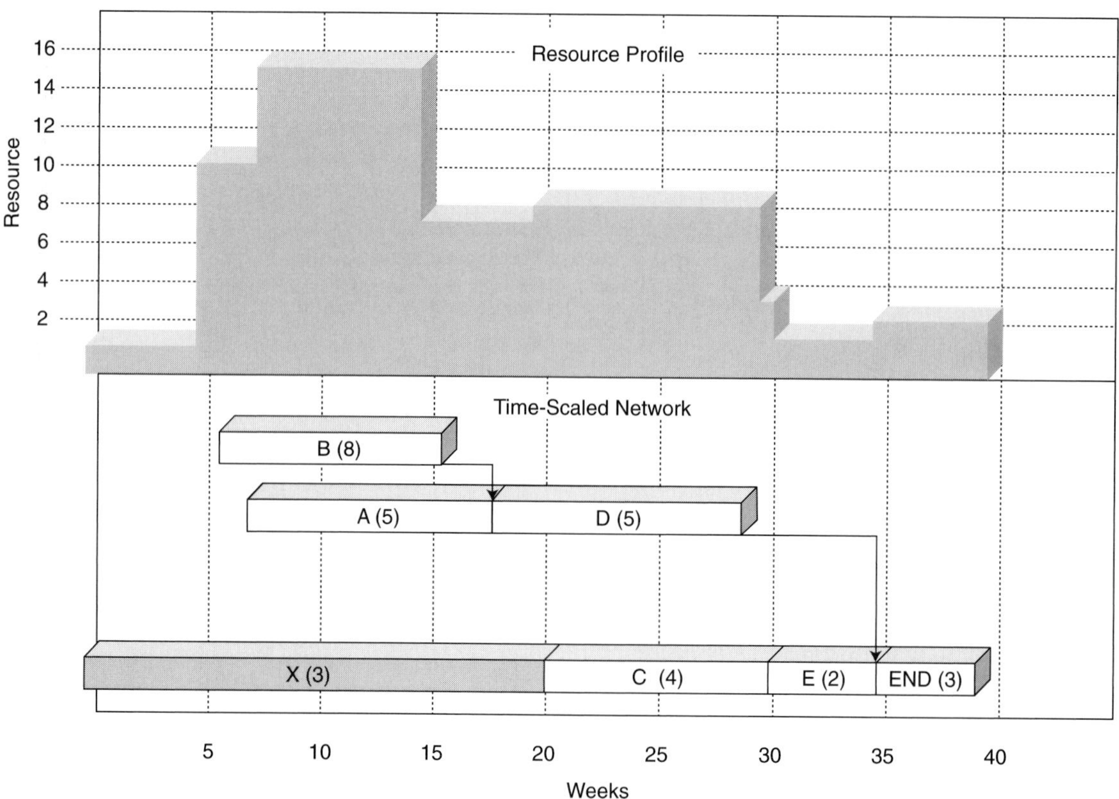

Figure 10–11
Resource Profile

■ ■ ■

Hilda interrupted, "There aren't 16 people in my part of the world with the specialized talent required. Also, our equipment is fairly unique. It's not like we can just buy or rent more if we need to meet this peak. I see how this works, in principle, but what happens if the peak is still too high?"

"Yes," Jerry agreed. "My projects are all done using people and equipment that my company owns and shares internally among the projects. We have to look at shared resources, and sometimes another project pulls people or machinery off mine, depending on the company's priority for projects. What do we do in this case?" he asked.

Ralph smiled, saying, "You guys are great. You give me the perfect lead-ins. We can use two approaches—additional crashing to eliminate overlaps, or stretching certain activities to reduce resources needed at one time."

■ ■ ■

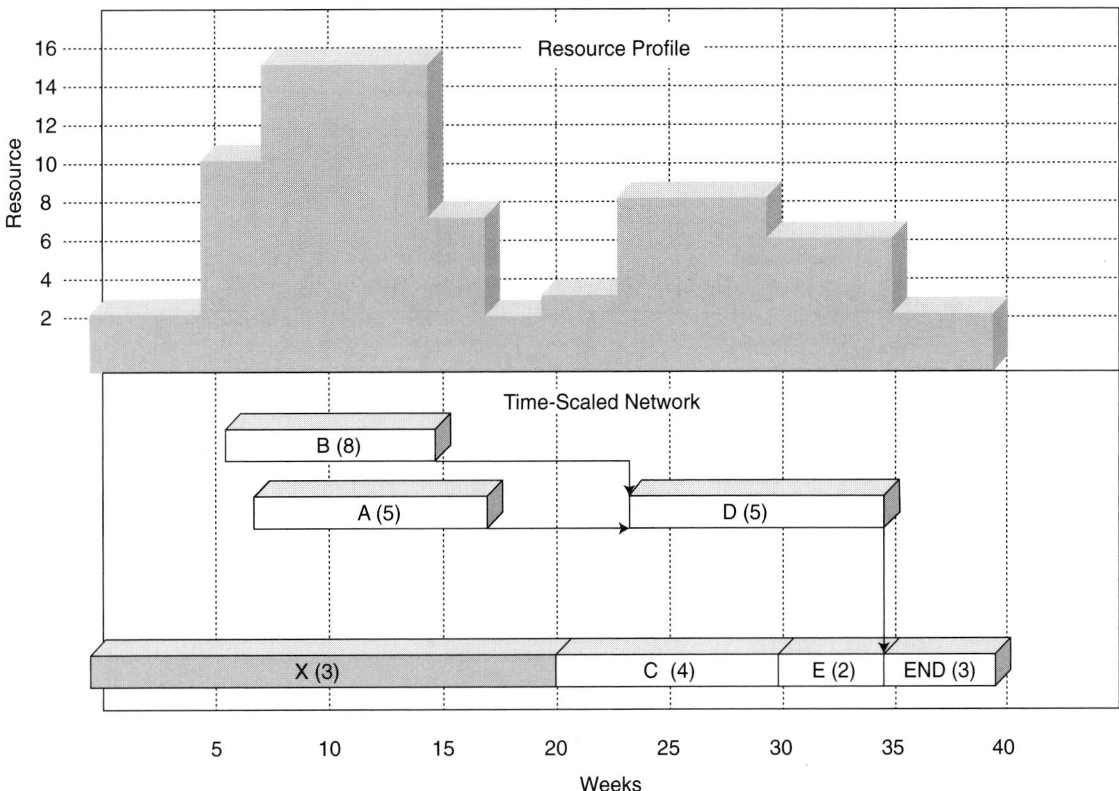

Figure 10–12
Resource Profile Showing Effect of Moving Activity D to Its LPS/LPF

To reduce the peak further, consider some alternatives:

1. Crash activity D sufficiently to allow B to move forward far enough not to overlap with A. This assumes that D can be crashed that far. It will also cause D to require more resources and more cost, hopefully not enough to cause another peak. Figure 10–14 shows the effect of this, where D now requires 7 people instead of 5 people to implement the crashed duration. The results are much better, since both the peak and the slopes are lowered.
2. Another alternative is to stretch activities A and B to reduce the number of people needed by either one, thus reducing the peak. This will have the effect of increasing cost, perhaps significantly, since the durations will be below the Normal Points. This ends up calling for higher direct costs, and may be even fixed costs, since the duration will be longer. The latter may not be significant if all they need is to share the project's overhead in general, since the project's duration has not been increased.

Assume you can stretch both to start on their respective EPS and end on their LAF. Assume that B now requires 5 people while A requires 3 over the longer duration. The resulting profile is shown in Figure 10–15, with attractive results.

Although it is rare to be able to achieve an **ideal level profile,** as you can see, it is possible to improve it significantly by exercising imaginative options. The same techniques can be applied to unique or scarce resources, which may need to be monitored individually, such as bottleneck facilities (e.g., a semiconductor foundry or a testing lab).

ideal level profile
is possible to improve by excersizing imaginative options

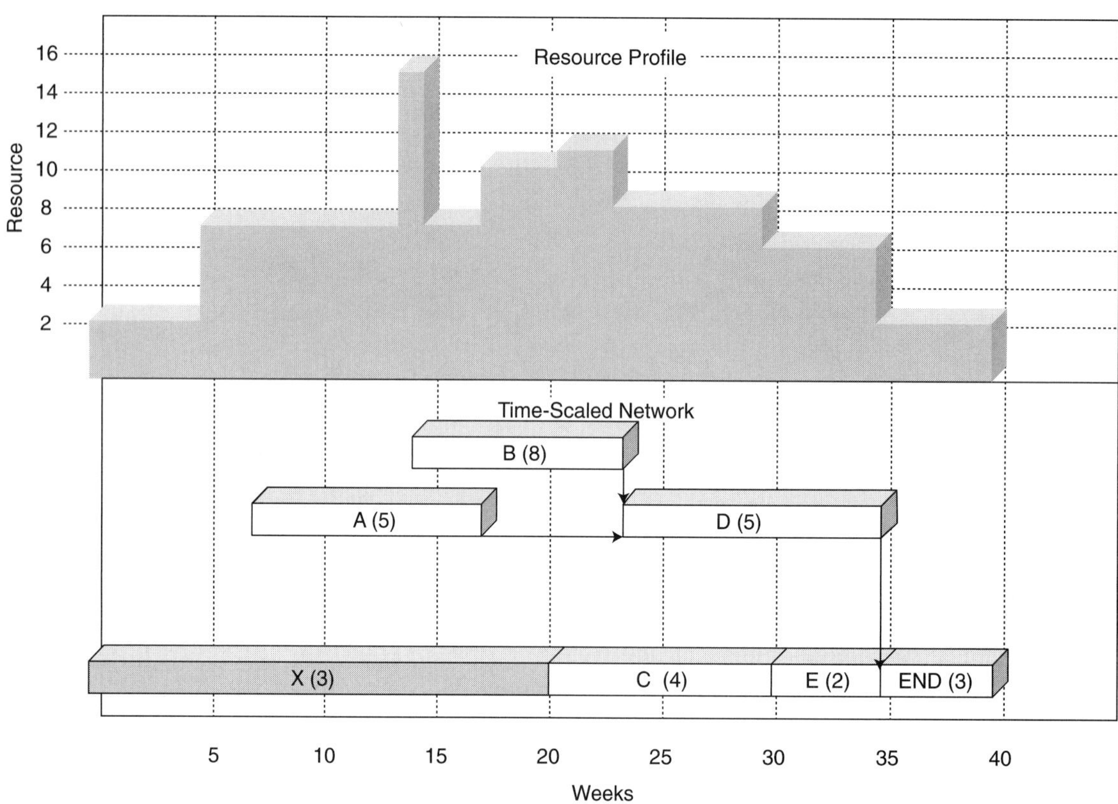

Figure 10–13
Resource Profile Showing Effect of Moving Activity B to Its LPS/LPF

■ ■ ■

"Of course," Ralph said, "Hilda's comment about specialized talent is often pertinent. There are many cases where carpentry work must be done by carpenters, bricklaying by masons, and so on. Still, in many cases, people are flexible enough to perform many varied tasks where the skill requirements are not too specialized," said George.

■ ■ ■

It is also a good idea to look at the load profiles of individual team members, to make sure none is overloaded, or scheduled through pre-arranged off time, such as vacation time. These same resource leveling techniques are used to detect and resolve anticipated problems as well as surprises as the project progresses!

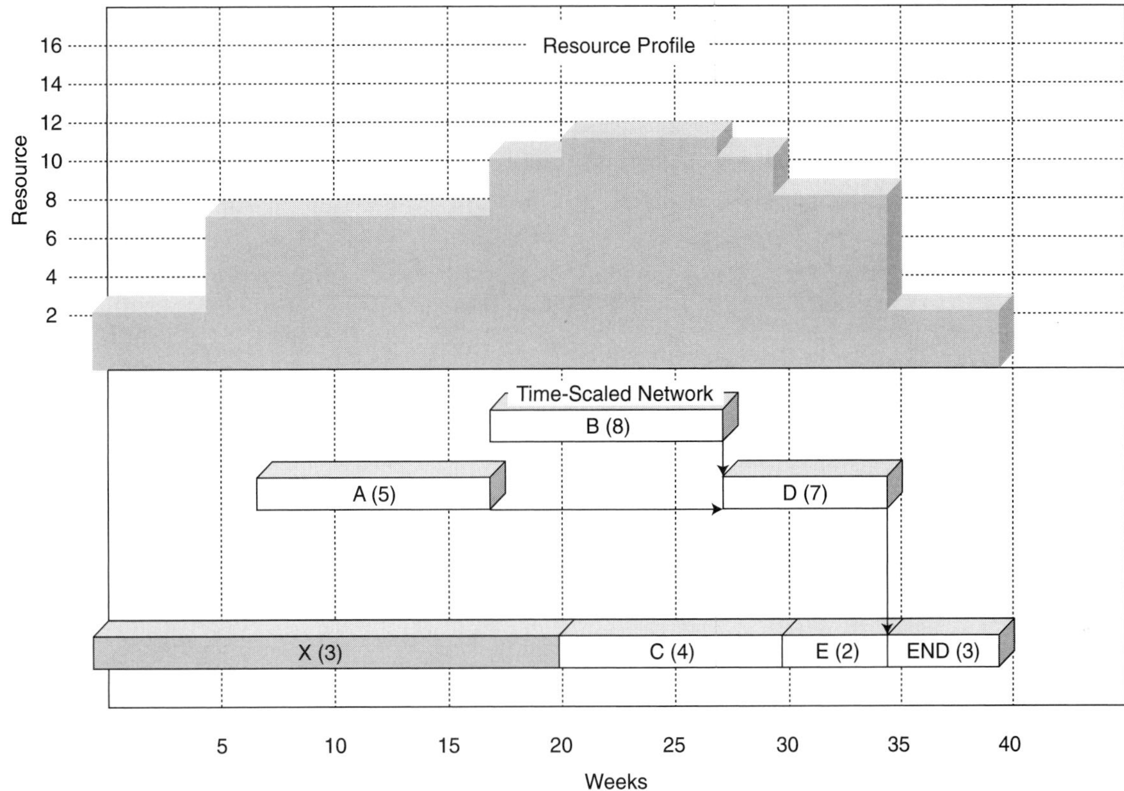

Figure 10–14
Resource Profile Showing Effect of Crashing Activity D and Moving Activity B Forward to Avoid Overlap with Activity A

4.0 THE FINAL PLAN

Resource leveling should be performed after the necessary "lines of defense" have been exercised, the optimum durations found, and the project's duration is brought within th expected deadlines. Once resources are satisfactorily leveled, the CPM network is to be redone, and both forward and backwards pass calculations performed.

One last review for reasonableness is performed before the plan is considered firm, and is presented for final approval. It is based on this firm plan that final budgets are developed, as well as staffing plans, cash flow requests, facility schedules, contracts drawn, and so on. After all of these are done, the planning phase of the project is now complete.

To finalize your plan:

- Use the three lines of defense to meet the customer's deadline.
- Find the optimum duration for the project.
- Level the critical resources:
    - People
    - Bottleneck facilities
- Perform a last reality check.

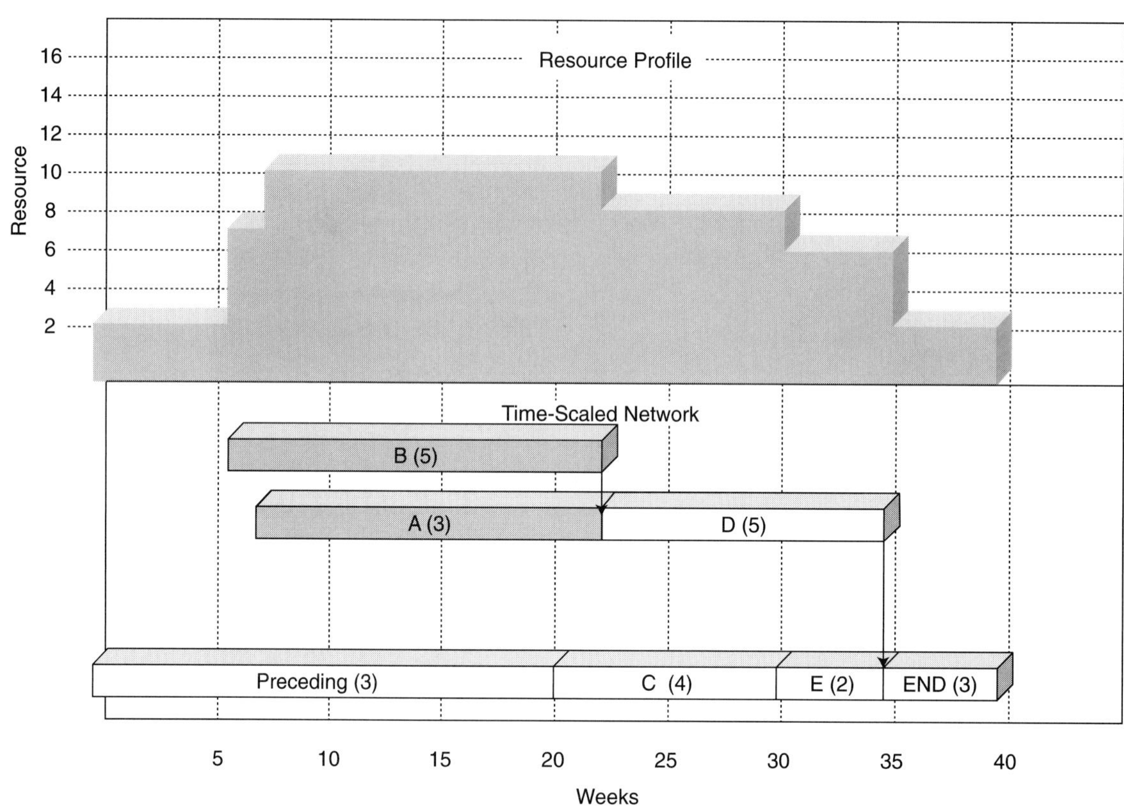

Figure 10–15
Resource Profile Showing Effect of Stretching Activities A and B to Reduce Resource Level

To level resources:

- Find Slack and Float, using backwards pass.
- Construct Time-Scaled Network.
- Plot the resource profile.
- Start from the end; work to the front.
- Move activities with slack into valleys.
- Replot profile.

Chapter Summary

To complete the planning of the project, the project manager must consider all the resources that will be needed for a successful completion of the project's goal. This includes resources such as people, equipment, capital, facilities, subcontractors, vendors, and more. This chapter deals with the people and capital resources.

People are arguably the most critical and challenging of all resources. Weighing the pros and cons of arranging for temporary/contractor help as needed versus attracting full-time employees involves cost issues, both direct and overhead, team interaction issues, and management attention time, as well as timeliness of their availability. Resource leveling is introduced using staffing as the example because it tends to have the most problems with the typically erratic resource profiles of a project environment. Slack and float, calculated using the backwards pass, allows the project manager to level resources without lengthening the project duration. Time-scaled networks are a hybrid of Gantt charts and CPM networks, and are a powerful tool when used to level resources.

Capital considerations relate to time/cost tradeoffs. Although Normal Duration is a means to cost-competitive projects based on direct cost, when total cost is considered, including indirect costs, some activity crashing below the normal duration level leads to further reduction of the activity's total cost! This is true because savings of indirect costs resulting from the shorter duration often outweigh the increases in direct cost needed for the crashing. This is referred to as Optimum Duration.

Crashing activities requires careful consideration if it is going to lead to the desired objectives of shorter project duration and possibly lower total cost. Only those on the Critical Paths need be considered. Crashing activities must be done incrementally while recalculating the network since additional Critical Paths will emerge, complicating further reduction of time. Other intuitive rules apply to the selection of the most advantageous activities to crash, such as early in the project, labor-intensive, low cost to crash, and bottlenecks.

Chapter Questions

1. Of the two main resources (human and capital), which is probably the most challenging to manage? Why?
2. Why are contract employees desirable for project managers? Could you receive some of these same benefits using "loaned" internal company employees? Why or why not? What are the negatives to using contractors?
3. What is the relationship between time and duration?
4. Explain the difference between direct and indirect costs.
5. What is the goal of the "one hat" method of managing the resource profile?
6. What are the advantages and disadvantages to activity crashing for managing projects?
7. Under what conditions can slack and float present problems?
8. Why is it desirable (and often absolutely necessary) to level resources?
9. Use Microsoft Project to evaluate the recommendations made by the group for Figures 10–11 through 10–15. How do the two solutions compare?

Project Challenge: Applying What You Know

You have been assigned a new project: to develop a manufacturing/production prototype of a high-efficiency automobile climate control system that has been given to you as a design/research and development prototype. Your assessment of the situation and the requirements of the project have revealed the relationships shown in Table 10–2.

Table 10–2
Project Activity Relationships

Indirect cost $1,200/wk				*Direct cost $800/man-wk*	
Step	**Precedence**	**Normal Duration**	**Normal Staffing**	**Crashed Duration**	**Crashing Cost**
		(wks)	(Head count)	(wks)	($/wk)
A	—	6	3	4	$1,500
B	—	8	4	5	$2,000
C	—	2	4	1	$2,000
D	A	4	2	3	$1,000
E	A, B	6	2	5	$1,000
F	C	2	3	1	$1,500
G	D, E, F	4	2	3	$1,000
H	F	2	2	1	$1,000
J	G, H	2	1	1	$500

1. Use Microsoft Project to calculate the Normal Duration, Normal Cost, and the corresponding total cost for the above project.
2. Determine the minimum economical project duration (Optimum Duration) and the minimum total cost of the above project.
3. Perform the "backwards pass" calculations to determine free and total slack.
4. Construct a resource profile for the optimum project duration using a time-scaled network.
5. Perform resource leveling for this project assuming resources are interchangeable. (Use the "one hat" method.)

Interview with an Expert

Stan Jarvis, *owner Goucher Contracting. (Note: Goucher is a masonry subcontracting company in the commercial building industry.)*

I have to tell you about the other side of this project management activity. See, the estimator on a project has a tough job. He has to figure out exactly what everything will cost and how long it should take. But, a lot of times there's something that throws the budget off. Now I know it's his job, but when this happens, the project manager starts squeezing the subcontractors—either to do it faster than originally contracted, or to wait for payment. The customer expects the contract to cost the same at the end as it was signed for in the beginning. So if the estimator made a mistake, the project manager is more likely to go outside his operation to the subcontractors to fix it.

I have a good business, but bringing in more guys to speed up a job or waiting for my money because something's off somewhere cuts into my pocket. I have to pay my people whether I get paid or not. We have to bid close in order to get the jobs, so there isn't any slack in a subcontractor's bid. I know the project manager has to hang on to his company's money as long as possible, but a subcontractor may be asked to float $20,000 to $30,000 for maybe several months and still hold to the time schedule. It would be nice if project managers treated subcontractors more fairly. We're a resource too, and we save them a lot of headaches since they don't have to manage the employees, equipment, and materials we use for our jobs.

CHAPTER

11 PROJECT CONTROL

CHAPTER PREVIEW

Project Control

Tom snapped his laptop shut and breathed a sigh of relief. "I'm glad that's finally taken care of. It's smooth sailing from here on out," he said, taking a sip of lukewarm coffee. He had just checked his E-mail and discovered that an important contract had at last come through.

Tom was interrupted in his musing by the sound of Jerry Benjamin entering the break room, just off the phone from one of his hourly office check-in calls. "Why are you looking so chipper today?" he questioned, grumbling.

" I just checked my E-mail," Tom replied. "The contracts are signed and the expansion plans are underway. Now all I have to do is sit back, relax, and watch the Southwest profits grow. It's a big load off my shoulders. I've been working on this deal for months now, and my other regions have really suffered. I'm glad I can move on to more pressing business."

Jerry laughed wryly. "This is your first big project, isn't it? " he asked.

"Well, actually, it is," Tom admitted sheepishly. He was quite insecure about his youth and lack of experience compared to the others in the training. "Why do you ask?"

"Tom, my man, " Jerry responded with his usual world-weary air, "lesson number one: the work never ends with the signing of the contracts. "

Just then, Yury Tomicovic entered the room. Overhearing Jerry's comment, Yury joined in. "That is the truth," he said. "I just always hope nothing goes wrong."

The crestfallen look on Tom's face was enough to remind Jerry of his own days just starting out. Jerry patted Tom on the shoulder. "Come on buddy," he said, "training's about to start. Maybe you'll pick up something useful today. "

After everyone had seated in for the session, with plenty of coffee and donuts at hand, the group considered the day's topic, Project Control. Ralph asked them to come up with some concerns of their own:

- How do I spot problems?
- What do I do once I find them?
- How do I stay on track?

- What happened to my plan?
- How do I stay flexible?
- How do I keep the focus?

Ralph and Tracey reviewed the suggestions and adjusted the day's outline as follows:

- **Project Control—What is it?**
- **Philosophies of Project Control—different approaches for different situations**
- **Project Control Process—Managing the beast**

Many executives and project managers become fixated on their initial plan much like young Tom with his contracts. You spend most of your time planning a project. But what happens after the plan is approved? Most people have experienced situations in which a plan went terribly awry. How can this type of situation be avoided? The key is that it can't always be avoided, and that's where project control comes in.

1.0 Project Control—What Is It?

As comfortable as it is to plan, there comes a point in time when you have to stop full-time planning and actually start doing something. Depending on time constraints, you often have to take the plunge and start "doing" almost immediately while still in the planning phase. Usually this involves some long-lead items that everybody recognizes to be needed.

It's true, your plan may be good enough to go off without a hitch, but that probably will happen only once in a lifetime. And it has more to do with luck than with the quality of your plan. Why? Because some things just happen, period. But understanding that your plan may hit a few rough spots along the way can be the key to making it go more smoothly in the long run.

This is not to say that you can do without planning. Your plan is crucial to the success of the project. However, the way in which you control its implementation determines whether your project succeeds. Keep in mind that planning will probably require less than 10% of the time on any project, while control and execution will comprise over 90% of your time. This is why ongoing project control is so important. It is your opportunity to exercise your chances for success.

To sum it up, project control is the process of overseeing the implementation of the project plan. It involves monitoring progress, anticipating, discovering and resolving problems, and replanning to get back on track.

1.1 Purposes of Project Control

So now that you know what project control is and why it is so important, the next step is to understand the goals, or purposes, of project control. What are your goals as a project manager? Obviously, these include getting the job done on time and within budget. Knowing exactly how that is done is what separates the good project managers from those who have gone bald by pulling their hair out.

You have three main goals while overseeing the execution of your project:

- Identify problems.
- Solve problems.
- Get the project back on track as soon as possible after the problem has been identified.

1.1.1 Identify Problems

The reward of diligent project control is that when problems do occur, you'll know about them right away. The fastest way to get off schedule and over budget is to leave a problem alone. Problems left alone generally will do one of two things—feed or breed. They feed off themselves and grow bigger and more problematic, or they get lonely and breed new problems to keep them company. Or worse, a combination of the two will occur. A problem solved quickly and effectively is almost as good as money in the bank. Money or time saved—or at least not squandered—is what makes your client or company happy.

Problems tend to come in two varieties. Both can be discovered and solved as long as you keep your eyes open. The first type is the anticipated problem. You can usually spot these potential difficulties during the planning phase and develop a contingency plan for dealing with them. The second type is the surprise; this kind can occur in even the tightest of plans. Surprises require astute problem definition and solid problem-solving techniques.

Anticipated Problems

At this point Ralph turned to the group. "Can anyone tell us about a problem you found during the planning phase?" he queried.

After a few moments of silence, Jaime spoke up. "Last year," he began, "I worked on a project that required shipping some machinery out of Chile during the month of July. This was excellent quality machinery at a much lower cost than any competitor could provide."

"Good for your budget," Ralph interjected.

"Yes," agreed Jaime. "However, after I was assigned to oversee the project, I pointed out to them that in July, while we're having our summer, Chile is having winter weather. If there is bad weather, this excellent, inexpensive equipment could be snowed in just when we needed it.

Hilda spoke up, "But at least you were discovering this in December, while you were still planning, rather than finding out on the first of July."

"Exactly my point," said Ralph. "So Jaime, what did you do with the seasonal discrepancy between your two hemispheres?"

"Well, " said Jaime, "We located some other high-quality equipment in Phoenix, but it would cost more. We knew that this manufacturer had many extra and that the machinery would be available if we needed it."

"It's always good to have a little something in reserve," cut in Jerry.

"Now why didn't you just order the machinery from Phoenix to begin with?" asked Ralph.

"Because the Chilean equipment was just as good, and cheaper," explained Jaime. "It would bring the project to completion on time and far under budget. But we knew that if we did have to spend the extra money on the equipment from Phoenix, it would still be better than putting the project behind schedule."

At this point Tom, who had been listening intently, joined in. "So," he concluded, "it would have been nice to save a few bucks on the Chilean equipment, which is why you figured it into your plan in the first place. But you anticipated the fact that the problem might occur, and had a contingency plan in place that wouldn't put too much of a crunch on your budget either."

"Exactly," said Ralph.

■ ■ ■

Many project managers intuitively attempt to anticipate problems during the planning phase. However, they usually don't know that this is an important project control technique, and therefore tend not to do it all the time, or only do it halfheartedly. Every industry has its anticipated problems, and they will be different for each, both in likelihood of occurrence and in impact. Simple statistical analysis of past problems in your industry and the frequency of their occurrence will help you to anticipate certain types of problems.

If in the planning phase you have done a good job of anticipating best- and worst-case scenarios, and ascertained what areas are likely to cause problems, your job in the monitoring phase then becomes looking for symptoms. In strategic planning, managers call these symptoms "trigger points." They are the little alarms that alert you to a problem of a type you have seen before. For example, if you live in an area where the rain almost always comes from the east, you might see clouds in the eastern sky and know with a high degree of certainty that rain is coming. The **anticipated problem** is called just that—*anticipated*—because you can guess with a good probability of being correct that it will occur. If shipments from component Manufacturer A are late as much as a week 30% of the time, you might try to determine if a possible pattern exists. For example, are shipments late more often in the fall or in orders placed at the end of the year? If you discover that parts shipped in the fall are late 80% of the time, then you can anticipate with near certainty that a project requiring parts from Manufacturer A will have a delay if it requires ordering in the fall. In this way information from other experiences can help you.

anticipated problem
problems that can be predicted

Old-timers like to make you think that there is some sort of mysterious intuition to this that can only be found after years of experience. Delivery histories are not mysterious and the math requires little or no intuition. Don't be afraid to tackle these types of prediction situations. Understanding the factors that contribute to progress or hindrance of your project will put you light years ahead in being able to anticipate problems and correct for them.

Thus, with the anticipated problem you have likely thought out a contingency plan to either prevent it or to manage its effect when it occurs. You now only have to be able to recognize the first signs of trouble by knowing what they are and by being on the watch for them.

Surprise Problems

surprise problem
a problem that will not arise during planning

The second type of problem is the surprise. A **surprise problem** will not be apparent during planning, so spotting them is a little trickier. A surprise problem can be anything from a natural disaster—Canadian forest fires in December—to unanticipated changes among your team members or co-workers. For example, your head of procurement's son becomes ill and she must take a 3-week leave of absence. Sometimes it's the seemingly minor computer glitches that turn into major pains in the neck; suddenly a bug develops that prevents you from processing essential data, putting you 2 weeks behind schedule.

These problems require that you be observant and ask many questions of everyone on your team. You may be able to spot these problems coming a mile away or they may just jump up and slap you in the face. You must be prepared for either possibility and remember that the earlier a problem is detected, the less expensive it is to solve.

■ ■ ■

*Ragdeesh spoke up at this point. "So basically what you're saying is that these problems are going to occur, and there is **nothing** I can do to prevent them. Well, that doesn't put me any farther ahead than I was when I started this training," he said frowning.*

"I think that you're missing the point," countered Ralph. "Most project managers and planners tend to have your point of view–that things will go wrong and there's nothing you can do to stop them. But good project managers understand that problems will occur, and they use all of their communications resources to make sure that they are the first ones to know about them, not the last. Time is the key when it comes to fixing a problem. Remember the saying: Any problem can be solved given enough time! And the less the time, the costlier the solution!"

Ralph drew the graph shown in Figure 11–1 on the flip chart:

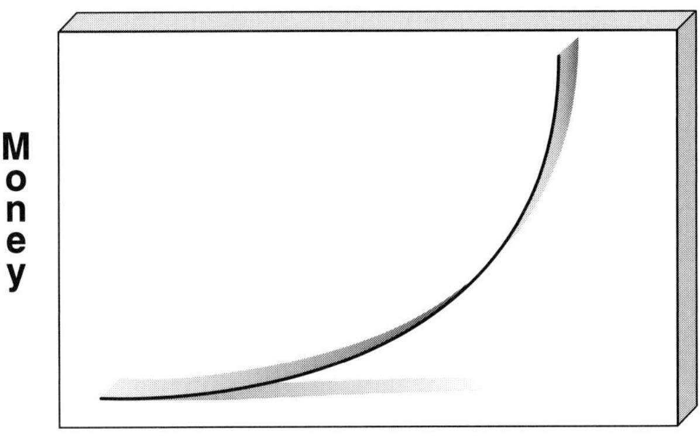

Figure 11–1
Relationship between delay time before action to resolve a problem, and cost of resolving it

■ ■ ■

"It may sound deceptively simple, " said Ralph, "but there is usually a direct correlation between how long you wait to take action on an issue, and how much it will cost to fix the problem."

■ ■ ■

1.2 Detecting Problems

So now you understand the need for discovering problems early. But how do you actually find them? Mostly by keeping your eyes and ears open. Don't rely solely on E-mail messages from your team about what they're up to. Certainly, don't just assume that things are getting done because that's what your schedule says. You need to be active. Talk to people both in- and out-of-house. Pay attention to what is going on; get regular updates from your team about how they're progressing, walk around often. Stay visible and accessible. Look for early warning signals.

Ways to ensure timely problem reporting

- Rewards for problems reported
- Acknowledgement of solutions and their authors
- Anonymous path for problem alerts
- Clear management commitment to "never shoot the messenger"

1.3 Solving Problems

If you're doing a good job, you've planned your project, begun implementation, and now a few (but hopefully not too many) problems have arisen. You've spotted the problems early and are ready to solve them. Just as in spotting problems, communication is essential to solving them. This is where you need your team. If you've selected them carefully, they will help bail you out. Get their input and look for creative solutions.

It is vital that you view problems as momentary distractions, rather than disasters bound to derail the entire project. Your team will feed off your attitude. If you take a creative attitude toward problem solving, so will they. Remember that several heads are always better than one, especially when brainstorming solutions. Never forget your team. The following guidelines walk you through a method for handling these problem-solving sessions with your teams.

1.3.1 Guidelines for Problem Solving in Groups

Please note that whole books are written on problem solving, so this is by no means exhaustive. It is, however, a brief guide to get you started with a solid approach for tackling particularly sticky problems that threaten to divide your team.

Problem-solving teams thrive in a diverse environment. Males approach problems differently than females; African Americans and Caucasian Americans may have alternative views. And Asian or European team members will bring still more breadth to the process. Fact and detail people should be included as well as vision and results-oriented members. Although this much diversity may breed a great deal of disagreement sometimes, it improves the quality of the ultimate solution because few facets are left unexplored with everyone looking from a different angle. If group members are oriented to value both conventional and unconventional ideas, then true synthesis for the betterment of the process will occur.

First: Everyone must play by the rules.

1. The problem will not be considered solved until all implications (as far as can be reasonably determined) have been explored.
2. Supportive communication will be used at all times. This means that issues will be the focus, not blame or personalities.
3. The goal of all will be the best solution, not just the "okay for the time being" solution. (One rule of thumb is that this "best" solution will be closer to being the 27th solution you come up with than the 3rd. If only three attempts could solve the problem, it probably wasn't a serious problem to begin with. Complex problems require complex solutions, and those don't come right away.)
4. Everyone must agree to persist in the activity until all can either be committed to the solution or can "live with it." If there is hesitation on anyone's part, the problem will not stay solved for long.
5. Input from all is required, including those not directly affected by the problem. (Sometimes those on the outside have a clearer view.)
6. No solution will be evaluated, officially or subtly (snickers or rolling eyes) until all are given out. Outlandish or especially creative suggestions that might indeed solve the problem should be affirmed whether they appear doable or not. (Remember, the police "stun gun" grew out of the need to shoot fleeing suspected felons without shooting them—a seemingly impossible notion.)

Second: Have each member state his or her view of the problem for one minute.

No one else speaks during that minute. No comment is allowed on anyone else's view until all have been heard.

1. Allow people to give their input in writing if they are uncomfortable with speaking to a group. Be certain to count the number of suggestions to ensure complete participation.
2. Record all views on a master chart or board.
3. Start with a definition of what the problem really is as follows:
    a. Define the reasons the situation is problematic and implications if the problem remains unsolved.
    b. Decide for whom this is a problem. (If it's not generally agreed to be a problem, then the one who proposed it may need to overlook the situation. Not all individual irritations are team or project problems.)
    c. Record and submit for group approval a statement of the problem to be solved.

Third: Develop alternatives in "waves."

1. If group is larger than eight, divide into smaller groups of four to five. Have each group discuss and develop 10 possible alternative solutions.
2. When each group has finished, ask them their top three that would solve the problem, and their most creative alternative. Record these visibly (chart or board).
3. Have groups exchange alternatives, so no group has the ones originally developed by it.
4. Instruct each group to come up with at least three new or expanded ideas related to each of the four they now have to work with (three best plus the one most creative).
5. After these have been recorded (now up to 20 or more depending on the number of groups you are using), instruct each group to choose 3 and discuss how each of them might realistically be implemented. Caution must be observed here. Research into whether an alternative is possible or not may be required to move beyond the information or perceptions of the group. Things change, and what was impossible just last week may be indeed doable this week.

Fourth: Identify the top three solutions that would appear to solve the problem for all concerned, and get the group to choose the best one.

1. Narrow options down by asking who can commit to support each solution.
2. Work toward a commitment to the solution by all members. If total agreement can't be reached, then ask, "Those of you who aren't enthusiastic about this, can you live with this solution?"
3. Ask those who are affected most directly again, "Does this solve it in a way that is helpful to you?"
4. Repeat this until the top solution emerges.

Fifth: Develop an implementation plan for the solution chosen by asking the group.
Write names of group members beside parts of the implementation plan and ask for their commitment to the action item. Provide the due date and primary name for completion of action.

Sixth: Implement the solution, keeping the top two other solutions on file as "Plan B" or "Plan C."

This will reduce recovery and redirection time if Plan A doesn't actually solve the problem.

Seventh: Follow-up.

Return to the group most directly affected by the problem and elicit an evaluation of the results.

Eighth: If Plan A doesn't work, determine why and move immediately to Plan B (or Plan C if it seems to fit better).

Generally, the surprise problems will require the most creative solutions.

1.4 Getting Back on Track

The most important part of solving a problem is getting the project back on track as soon as possible afterwards. This means showing how the original project completion date will be met.

In order to do this, you'll have to update your plan. Consider how this event affects the rest of your schedule and your cost predictions.

Everyone involved in the project, including the client, needs to receive a copy of the new information, including updated schedule and cost projections, Make sure that everyone knows how any changes affect their activities. This way you can be sure that everyone is headed in the same direction.

When issuing version after version of updated schedules, the most important thing is to make sure that everyone is using the same version. Things can get difficult if operations is using the current schedule, but someone in marketing is still working with the one from 2 weeks ago. If everyone is on the same computer network, simply update the master worksheet/schedule to which they refer. If you are stuck with using paper, it's important to have some sort of issue numbering system in order to differentiate current schedule versions from obsolete ones. You might consider reissuing new schedules every Monday, whether they are changed or not, with the date clearly indicated.

■ ■ ■

Yury interjected: "In a tough plant start-up a few years ago, we had engineering changes to the product every day, while we hired new people every week. Instruction booklets for operators had to be updated every week. To keep control, we had a young industrial engineer take away every booklet from every operator on Friday afternoon to update over the weekend, then give back on Monday morning. No old books could stay out. We had them all numbered and checked off."

"Whatever works, I guess!" said Hilda.

■ ■ ■

2.0 Approaches to Project Control

Consider two project managers, Dan and Lucy.

2.1 Dogmatic Approach

Dan is also known as Dogmatic Dan. To Dan, the plan is sacred. Otherwise, why would he have spent so much time developing it? He will stick to activity deadlines at all costs and tolerate no variance. Dan's projects are usually completed on time, but his teams resent him and the job is done usually over projected cost.

2.2 Laid-Back Approach

Lucy's team calls her Laid-back Lucy. Lucy's plan is amorphous and constantly changing. Lucy accepts changes to the plan like someone might accept a free sample in a grocery store—without a second thought. She has no problem with preplanning numerous times during the course of a project, allowing for bad planning and surprises. She tries very hard to make up for lost time in other activities, but isn't always successful. Her projects are usually completed within budget but grossly miss projected deadlines.

2.3 Pragmatic Approach—A Healthy Blend

Which of these project managers do you want to be? Neither, of course. In order for a project to be truly successful, you will have to develop your own philosophy that works for you. It should contain a healthy mix of Dan's and Lucy's styles, along with the following keys for effective control:

- You absolutely must be completion oriented. This does not mean that you have to be unwaveringly dedicated to the plan like Dan. But you cannot be as willing to accept deviation as Lucy is. If an activity can be done now, see to it that it gets done now!
- Have a healthy respect for deadlines. This means that if something can be finished on time, go ahead and insist on it, even if it takes some extra effort.
- When you ask team members for a completion date, expect a specific date, and don't accept fuzzy answers.
- Require completion dates to be the earliest possible (EPF). When left on its own, human nature tends to work toward the latest possible deadline. This is where valuable time and money are lost, not to mention room to help with unanticipated problems. Team members will rise to your level of expectation. You must make your expectations clear early, and set them high.
- Develop the ability to tell which problems are legitimately unanticipated from those that are due to complacency, lack of commitment, or incompetence. Deal with the legitimate situations in the most cost-efficient manner possible while not compromising the project completion date. This may require replanning a portion of the project and crashing some activities to get back on track as soon as possible. Problems that are not legitimately unanticipated must be recovered at the expense of the cause.

■ ■ ■

At this point Tom spoke up. "But what about me?" he asked. "I don't have a team working for me. I work with shippers and suppliers with bosses of their own. There's really nothing I can do to influence how or when they work."

"I think you underestimate your position, Tom," said Ralph.

" I agree," added Hilda. "I understand where you're coming from, Tom. But you need to understand that your shippers and suppliers need you as much as you need them. It really is a symbiotic relationship. And once you understand that, it's much easier to confidently demand that deadlines be met, because everyone really is working toward a common goal "

"Exactly," said Ralph. "The common goal is success. Success for the team or success for the different companies—the shippers and the department store, in Tom's case. Usually just knowing that you hold them responsible for their activities is enough to motivate your team members. Which brings us nicely to the last key for effective control, accountability."

■ ■ ■

2.4 Accountability—Different Strokes

When developing your own personal project management philosophy, you must consider accountability. Team members must feel that they are a vital link to the successful completion of the project and will be held accountable for their actions.

You will inevitably encounter two types of individuals when putting together a team. The first kind will do the job they say they'll do. These individuals take pride in their work and understand how it affects the outcome of the project. You must be sure to give these people the recognition they deserve. All too often, good work goes unrewarded because, of course, it's what you expect of all team members. You'd be amazed what wonders a small reward will do. On a big-money project, a reward dinner for meeting an important deadline won't take a huge bite out of your budget, but it will increase the **camaraderie** and motivation of your team.

camaraderie friendly relationships between members of a team

The second type you'll run into is the excuse maker. The excuse makers don't follow through with what they say they'll do, and it's never their fault. These people, too, need a little motivation, but they also need a lot more supervision and follow-up. Their activities must have clearly defined objectives, be broken into smaller bites and deadlines down to the hour. As a result, the excuse maker won't work well with a project manager like Dan, and they are absolutely disastrous for Lucy's projects. Make sure these types have the necessary tools to perform their job sufficiently, providing you with some security against the "But I couldn't because. . ." excuse. Review their progress constantly, documenting everything, and quickly deliver short-term consequences for both good and bad performance.

Peer pressure is also an effective tool to use against the excuse maker. Make sure that others know that this individual failed the plan in some way. The flimsiness of the excuse will quickly become clear to others, and they will begin to exert pressure on your excuse maker. If all else fails, get them off your team! You are better off working shorthanded, with solid team members. Excuse makers are a net liability and will ultimately cost you the success of the project. In rare situations, you may not have a say in getting excuse makers off your team. In those cases treat them as an anticipated problem, expose them at every level, keep them out of Critical Path activities, and lobby forcefully to avoid having them on your next project!

3.0 Project Control Process

Once you've developed your own personal style of management, you're going to need a few weapons in your arsenal that are essential for the successful project manager. Learn these lessons, incorporate them into your style, and require them of your team. You don't even need a permit to carry these weapons!

Weapons

- Communication
- Participation
- Analysis
- Action
- Commitment

3.1 Communication

Your first weapon is communication. Remember that you, as the project manager, are the central facilitator of communication for everyone working on your project. Think about how helpless you feel when your E-mail is down. You send messages, and you know somewhere out there someone is sending important information to you, but somehow the connection isn't being made. This is how your team would feel without continuous communication with you and among themselves.

Every successful project is run by a team that communicates. Without communication you won't be able to find or solve problems, update your schedule, or generally disseminate information to everyone involved in the plan. Communication can be good or bad. For communication to be good, it must be concise and relevant to the person with whom you're trying to communicate. The best way to do this is to make your interactions with team members and co-workers face-to-face. Then always follow up face-to-face talks with some form of written confirmation. This way there is little chance for misunderstanding.

However, face-to-face communication isn't always possible, especially if you're overseeing an interstate or international project. Video-conferencing is the next best thing. If that is not feasible, E-mail is an excellent option. It allows you to send frequent, short messages. An added benefit is that E-mail gives everyone a record of communication that has taken place during the project.

■ ■ ■

"This is a biggie," Ralph said, "Most trainees I work with cite communication as one of the biggest problems in their workplace. Ragdeesh, you look like you want to say something."

"I just don't know how much more I can do," Ragdeesh responded. "I provide team members with an open forum for communication, and all of the tools necessary, and we still fall out of touch with each other during projects. It's very frustrating."

"Well," Ralph said, "oftentimes just providing the tools isn't enough. That's one of the most common mistakes a project manager can make. Along with the tools for communication, you have to inspire the commitment for communication, which brings us to the second weapon of any successful project manager."

■ ■ ■

3.2 Participation

Your second weapon is the ability to inspire your team to active participation in the project. Have you ever worked on a job where no one wanted to commit to any particular activity?

If so, you understand how vital participation is for a successful project. Remember the discussion about how critical it is to assign activities in the planning phase? Assignments are to be taken very seriously and not shifted around lightly. Remember that resource leveling was done around the specific assignments, and casual changes will cause problems.

Typically however, some assignment changes are necessary. Certainly during negotiations to resolve a problem or to bring the project back on track, some reassignments are necessary. Also when team members leave the team for various reasons, reassignments are mandatory. But in all cases, you should never assign tasks to absentees. Assignments must be made carefully and with the full consent and support of all involved.

Typically, either you'll have team members who wholeheartedly participate and give their all, providing suggestions on how to improve the project, or you'll have wallflowers. Don't let the wallflowers just sit and bloom; require full cooperation of all members. Go directly to the members who are shying away and ask, "What do you think, what's your opinion about this?" Maybe in other workplaces, the opinions of these people were not valued, or they were merely expected to follow orders, rather than provide input.

Make sure you treat in-house and outside members equally. Be careful to require participation of the decision makers and doers involved in any particular activity. Don't waste your time with unempowered delegates, stand-ins, or sidekicks. Go to the source.

3.3 Analysis

Your job is to constantly assess the impact of current activities on the project completion schedule and budget. Once mastered, analysis will become a valuable weapon. Any time a problem is discovered or anticipated, you must ask yourself "What if?" and prepare a response to the potential problems. Explore the potential impact on the completion dates of dependent activities, resource usage profiles, exposure to common problems, cost projections, and certainly on the ability to meet the quality requirements of the project.

3.4 Action

In order for any project to come to successful fruition, you must take and demand action, the fourth element of successful project control. Time is your enemy; waffling and considering and reconsidering the solution to a problem cost you time and, therefore, money. Whenever you see the indication of a problem, consider it a gift. Deal with the situation aggressively and act to resolve it.

■ ■ ■

"Where will these last two weapons, analysis and action, come in handy?" Ralph queried the group.

After a few moments of consideration Tom replied hesitatingly, "Well, it seems like the two combined would be necessary for solving problems."

"But how? " asked Ralph.

"You need to be able to quickly analyze any given problem and decide upon an appropriate solution," Tom replied. "Without good analysis skills you're likely to over- or underestimate the gravity of a problem. You're also less likely to develop a good solution. Ill-considered solutions will have undesirable side effects that can surface later and be costlier than the original problem!"

"And what about action, why is it so important, Ragdeesh?" Ralph asked.

"Without taking action, your solution will never be implemented," Ragdeesh, replied confidently.

"Exactly," said Ralph.

■ ■ ■

3.5 Commitment

The final weapon at your disposal for the project control process is commitment, which comes in three levels. The first two may seem obvious—commitment to the goal and commitment to the schedule. In order for the project to be a success, your team must understand what it is they are working toward, and respect the deadlines they helped set.

The third level of commitment may not be as readily apparent, but it is still essential. Everyone must have commitment to the project management concepts you establish. This means that they respect you and your opinions, since you are their fearless leader. You should hold an initial meeting for everyone on your team in which you make sure that everyone is thinking on the same level. This means communicating your expectations about everything from the way subteams are established to the software standards you require. Everyone must be committed to using the same tools and techniques in order for any of them to work.

■ ■ ■

"That almost brings us to the lunch break today," said Ralph. "But before I let you go, let's talk about an activity in which you can apply some of your newfound project control skills." Ralph put a slide showing Figure 11–2 on the overhead.

■ ■ ■

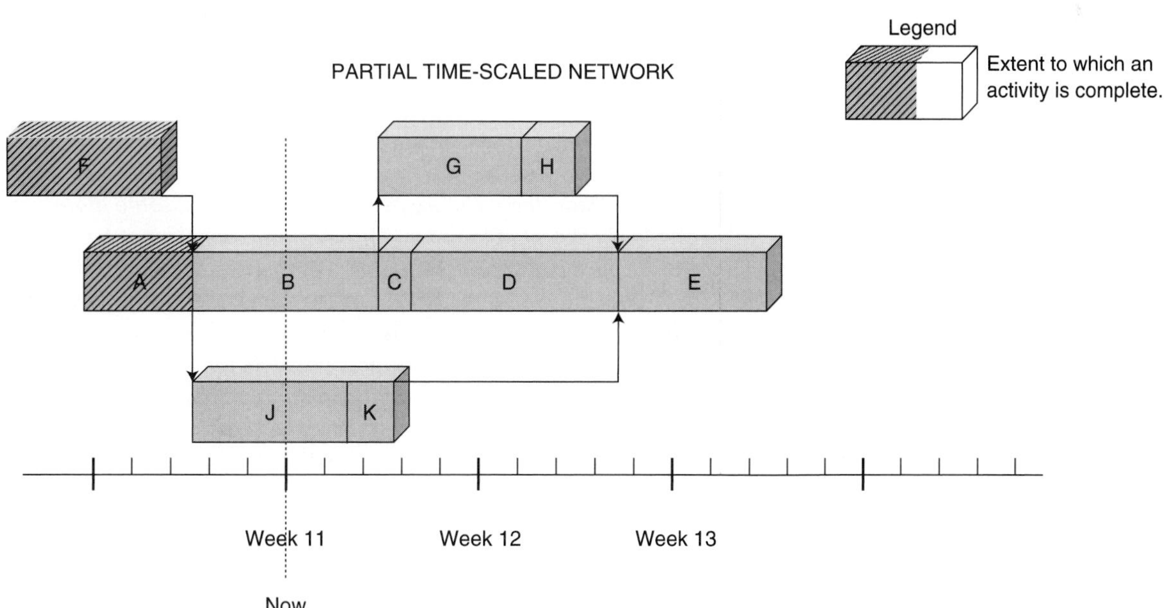

11–2
Partial Time-Scaled Network Used for Project Review Meeting

"The diagram," Ralph explained, "represents a partial project and some of its components. The project team is having its regular meeting at the end of week. You can see that activities A and F are complete. Activities B and J, however, have just started because A was 2 days late on completion. Also, it has been determined that activity H will take 2 days longer. The final thing to keep in mind is that activity B would be very expensive to crash."

4.0 EXAMPLE—RESOLVING A PROJECT PROBLEM

"Now, I want you to break into two groups," said Ralph. Jerry and Ragdeesh, the most contentious and vocal of the group, threw in with Jaime, who was much more easygoing, leaving Hilda and Yury with the novice, Tom.

"Jerry," said Ralph, "I want you, Ragdeesh, and Jamie to take 15 minutes and come up with a good description of what may be going wrong with this project. Hilda, I want you, Yury, and Tom to take on the task of making two recommendations about how to get the project back on track. Any questions? No? OK, lets get cracking. Lunch will be your reward! "

When Ralph returned, he found that all of the trainees were engaged in lively discussion. He could only hope it applied to the topic at hand.

"Are you ready to wow me with your outstanding project control skills?" asked Ralph.

"Yes Sir, " replied Jerry in a mock military tone.

"Then let's start with your group, Jerry. What is going wrong here?"

"Well," Jerry began, "first of all, it seems like this team has a serious lack of communication."

"And why is this?" asked Ralph, smiling.

"Obviously, if activity A slipped by for 2 days without the project manager finding out and taking action, something is going wrong in terms of communication."

"Good," said Ralph. "What else is wrong here, Ragdeesh?"

"If the team working on activity A was falling so far behind, and team B was depending so heavily on A's completion to begin their work, why didn't team B say something?" Ragdeesh asked. They must not be very committed to the successful completion of the project."

"Exactly, " said Ralph. "Okay, there's more here. Anyone else see some more problems?" Ralph let the silence sit in the room for a few moments before he continued. "Did anyone notice activity H? We're in the 11th week here, activity H isn't scheduled to start until the end of week 12, and we know already that it will take 2 days longer than planned. Someone grossly underestimated the time requirement for this activity. Now, this kind of error is possible, but it also indicates that undue pressure was placed during the planning phase to shorten activities. While you should always require that activities be completed in the shortest possible time, pressure of this kind should never be used, least of all on a noncritical path activity like H."

Ralph then turned to Jerry's group and said, "Good work, team." "How about you, guys?" he asked, pointing to the second group. "How did you do with your task?"

"We did came up with some suggestions, and we redrew the time-scaled network to show our primary suggestion," said Hilda. "Why don't you start, Tom?"

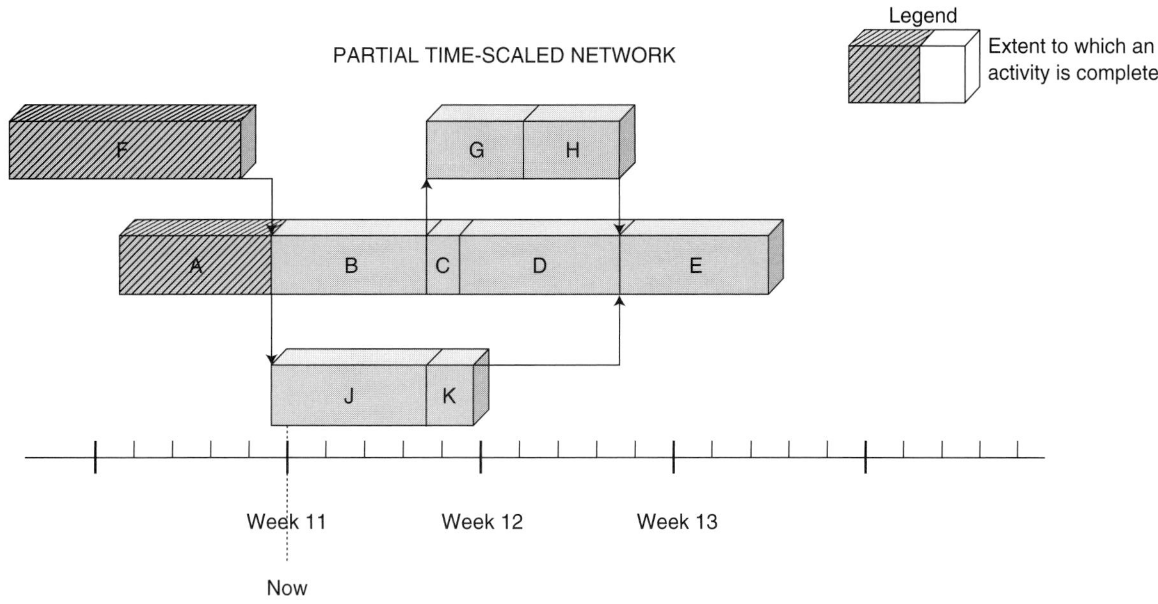

Figure 11–3
Time-scaled network showing revisions of crashing activities B, G, H, and D, as well as true completion date of activity A

■ ■ ■

"OK," said Tom, "As things stand now, the project will be delayed 3 days—2 days from activity A and 1 from activity H, since it had only 1 day of slack built in. Now, G and H will be on the Critical Path, instead of C and D. So first of all, we'd try to fully crash G and H, and then crash activity B by the remainder, if necessary, absorbing the 3-day delay."

"What's the benefit of that?" asked Ralph.

"This solution gives an early resolution at a manageable cost, " replied Tom.

"Also," continued Hilda, "you could crash E instead of B, since you said B was very expensive to crash. Now, this would be less desirable since it delays your resolution because E occurs so much later than B. This increases the risk that other critical delays could pop up in the meantime, and you may miss deadlines."

"Good," said Ralph, "The only other points I would add is that, by crashing E instead of B, you still incur delays in starting C, D, and E, which could upset resource leveling. Another option is to divert some resources from the other activities with lots of slack: J and K, to help with the crashing. This should be less upsetting to the resource leveling." He paused and looked around the room. "But speaking of being upset, Jerry looks a little upset that he hasn't had anything to eat since this morning, so we should probably break for now."

Chapter Summary

With a plan and the project proceeding, the project manager must maintain control. The purpose of control is to maintain the three critical dimensions of the project goal: completion date, outcome specifications, and approved budget.

The project manager must learn to find and resolve each problem that arises, in such a way as to get the project back on track. Constant communication with the project team and all other stakeholders is the foundation of project control.

Anticipating, uncovering, and solving problems are what project managers do most of the time. It is what occurs over 90% of the project duration. They constitute some of the most critical contributions to the project and therefore are the most critical skills of a successful project manager.

Chapter Questions

1. What is the relationship between the time available to take action on an issue and its cost?
2. What are the techniques of effective project control?
3. What are the weapons available to you in the project control process?
4. Explain why a "dogmatic Dan" project manager can be both a good and a bad approach.
5. Is it necessary for all team members to have good problem-solving skills? Why or why not?
6. What would you do with an employee who was committed to action, but had poor analysis skills?

Project Challenge: Applying What You Know

1. Use Microsoft Project to evaluate the impact on the project of each of Tom and Hilda's recommendations.
2. Use Microsoft Project to evaluate Jerry's and Ragdeesh's analysis. Cite some examples from your experience of similar situations, and the impact they had on the projects.

Interview with an Expert

Ron Grob, *Managing Partner, Connection Solutions, Inc.*

When managing multiple projects, there are several key elements to successful, on-time completion. Element one is the project charter. This is a combination of the what, why, and how of the project. It summarizes the strategic reasoning behind the project, whether it is an internal one for management or an external one for a client. This lets everyone involved know what the project is and why it is important. It also outlines the scope of the project—exactly what is to be accomplished, by when, and by whom. Finally, it should include budget considerations. That is, where is the money going to come from to pay for the tasks required?

Element two is the political backing within the organization. Who needs this done as opposed to who has been told to do it? A project can fail quickly with the best plan if the necessary people are not either assigned or freed up (time-wise) to complete their role. I don't know how many times I've heard, "Yes, I know your project is important, but my manager expects me to do his job first, then yours if I have time." A manager or even a vice president can be enthusiastic about a project, but if the people who actually manage the bulk of the skilled people on your team do not place the priority on that project, little will happen. You should study the organizational chart—both the official one and the unofficial one. Look at formal reporting structures but also try to gain an understanding of how things "really" work in the organization. Then, look for a power person to back your project.

Element three is tracking. There is a lot of sophisticated software out there now that can monitor all deadlines and milestones of multiple projects. Of course, you have to have set specific and measurable milestones for this purpose. The key is to require that all leaders of project teams use the same software to report. This saves you reworking reports from pieces of paper or trying to import an incompatible document into your project plan. You can actually set up the project-reporting format to give you a statement as to the status of each milestone and red flag any that are not on target as soon as you open the software. Missed milestones are the first symptom that something is wrong, possibly that something is terribly wrong.

Element four is follow-up. Different project managers have different styles, though, so follow-up is different with each. Sometimes groups of engineers are very jealous of their projects and refuse to release information on status until the prototype is operational. If you know the group and their method of meeting deadlines, you might be able to get enough information in casual conversation to be comfortable with their milestones. Others will send you reports on time, so you will never have to question them. Important, though, is substantiation. If the milestone calls for 300 lines of code or a working prototype, then you should probably physically look at what is being presented. You may have to shuttle it off to the expert at the next stage of the project process to verify if what you have been given is indeed what the milestone stated, but knowing that you are going to follow through might prevent some from trying to throw up a smoke screen.

A final element is to support progress. Never underestimate the value of buying someone coffee or lunch when a major milestone is reached or a particularly tricky portion of the project plan has been worked through. People rarely work just for money; they appreciate your acknowledging their hard work, which is frequently over and above their regular job responsibilities. Especially on large projects that may be a full year or more before completion, team members need some kind of closure at shorter intervals. Very few people can stay motivated for months at a time towards some future resolution and/or reward. Defining progress is a motivator in itself.

CHAPTER

12 PROJECT CONTROL TECHNIQUES

Chapter Preview

Project Control Techniques

It was 1 o'clock before Jaime arrived at class. He was dressed in a suit and tie, which was not his usual attire, and was red-faced and sweating. Everyone stared at him as he sat down.

"What's going on? You look like you've been to a funeral." Tom said.

"I've been in court all morning," Jaime responded, still obviously stressed from the ordeal. We had a contract and went over bid and time because their people messed up."

"So what happened? Did you get nailed?" Jerry queried.

Jaime's demeanor suddenly changed to a smile with just a touch of smugness around the edges. "No, because I had my project logs."

"Logs? You keep more than one set of records?" Jerry asked, accusingly.

"Yes, I do. There is the official log that says things like 'customer agrees to cost and time increase due to damaged components.' My personal log noted that on August 1st on a visit to the loading site I saw a dock worker, who was their employee, drop a critical component off a fork lift load, breaking the housing and damaging the controller system inside. Since it was a custom piece, the whole thing had to go back to the design people for a new build. After I told them that and showed the change order, signed by them, the attorney just looked pitiful. It was beautiful."

Ralph George congratulated Jaime. "Great! You'll especially appreciate today's session on control techniques and tools. It feels good to have all the answers in the case of a suit like that, doesn't it?"

"Yeah, I used to resent all that tracking follow-up, but now I document everything," Jaime responded. Tracey wrote down responses on the flip chart while Ralph solicited input on the group's concerns.

- How do we tell when something's off?
- What reports do we need to keep and to whom do we send them?
- Solving problems?

- How do we get a handle on spending?
- Where do I find time to do all this monitoring stuff?
- How do I stay within budget?

The objectives for the day rolled out:

- **Using periodic control techniques including meetings and reports**
- **Applying preventive control techniques**
- **Implementing the keys to cost control**

1.0 PERODIC CONTROL TECHNIQUES

To get the project underway, the project manager must begin applying the concepts of project control. Fortunately, there are many tools and techniques to help you with this. In this regard, keeping detailed track of everything to do with the project is a necessity.

Because others have an interest in the progress of your project, you will need to use this information to report on the progress and other indicators. It is also very helpful if you can keep this information at your fingertips. You never know who might walk into your office and want a status report as of that moment. The tools covered here will be both for your own use and for others who will need to stay abreast of your progress. This section includes a discussion of the control/tracking meeting, along with the other tools: the project log and the project-tracking chart.

1.1 The Project Meeting—Tracking and Control

Chapter 1 covered the basic principles for designing and running good meetings. Provided here is a more detailed guideline, however, for the project tracking and control meeting specifically. Chronically, people try to avoid project meetings. This can render the meetings ineffective because critical players and decision makers are absent. People avoid meetings mainly for two reasons; they drag on for too long, way beyond people's attention span, and they lack focus and clear, useful purpose. This situation must be remedied if the project is to benefit from this expensive investment of resources. First and foremost, absolutely do away with the "general purpose" project meeting. Discussed here is one specific type of project meeting; others will be discussed later. Never mix them!

The project tracking and control meeting is *not* a status review meeting. Those are discussed later in the reporting section. The purpose of this meeting, as the name implies, is to solve problems! This meeting provides a reliable time and place for problems to be raised, discussed, resolved, and the project put back on track with the participation of all the critical players.

Time Horizon You don't want to discuss the entire project in one meeting. The core horizon for discussion ought to be the activities for the period between the last meeting and the next one (i.e., the two periods that straddle this meeting). Add to that all overdue items, and any imminent significant milestones. Red flag items need their own dedicated meeting as soon as they come up.

Invite Only Those Who Must Contribute Those who were, are, or will be working on any of the activities to be discussed in the meeting *need to be there,* along with the corresponding decision makers. No one else! No spectators, guests, or curious parties. The smaller the group, the more effective the meeting.

Distribute Agenda in Advance The agenda that you have prepared for the meeting should go to each participant in advance of the event. This gives all a chance to prepare the information they will need for this specific meeting. Attach to the agenda a relevant time-scaled network that is up-to- date and covers the time span involved in the discussion. This will focus the discussion on the element of time.

Start and Finish Exactly on Time Those who are punctual will appreciate it, and those who are not will get the message. The meeting should last 30 to 45 minutes, no more. If more time is needed, then the meeting's horizon was set too far. Schedule a follow-up meeting, and next time, shrink the horizon a little.

Keep Meeting Focused This meeting should be short and snappy. Don't allow tangents and deviations. Table for other meetings non-agenda issues that come up. Sidelines should be resolved outside of meeting time. Use the time-scaled network as the centerpiece for discussion.

Get Updates First Address Critical Path activities first, in order of due date. Next, deal with the activities that have float and slack. Keep the time-scaled network out and visible. An overhead projector could be very handy here. Don't attempt to solve problems at this point! You don't yet have the whole picture until you have all the updates. Updates should be simple: "complete," "on-track," "ahead of schedule by x days," "behind schedule by x days." Reflect updates on the time-scaled network.

Press for Critical Path Solutions Deal with the hottest problems first. The problem activity on the Critical Path with the earliest due date gets the most attention. Start with clear technical definitions of the problems prior to discussion. Get agreement on a solution that will recover the schedule. Get specific commitment from each decision maker (specific finish date, specific resource, etc.) for the solution. Reconcile these specifics with the schedule and achieve commitment from all affected players. Reflect the solution on the time-scaled network. Go on to the next Critical Path issue.

Once all Critical Path issues have been resolved, quickly go down the list of any issues with slack, identifying the problems to make sure they will not become critical. Note here that no technical discussion of non–Critical Path items should be allowed in the meeting, since these problems can, and should, be dealt with off-line by the interested parties. Do get commitments as to who will deal with which problem, and when the resolution is to be expected.

Assign Action Items Record all Critical Path issues with the specific action items and attach a name and due date to each. Be certain to document every one of those tasks, who agreed to which task and when the task is to be completed. Further, you must take responsibility for ensuring that everyone receives a written copy of the action list. This list must go out immediately.

Document Record what happens in each meeting in the form of minutes. A scribe who is involved in the process is often better than a clerk or secretary who merely records what happens and doesn't know what is important about the items. Give a copy of this record to each participant as soon as possible. Be sure to include updates from the last meeting as they relate to action items from this meeting. This record should go out next.

Close the Meeting Go around the table asking for any recommendations, anticipated problems, and/or issues. Summarize action items and agreed-upon solutions. Set up additional outside or small-group meetings as appropriate. Set the date for the next project tracking and control meeting. Compliment all for their hard work, contribution, patience, or whatever is true and positive. Find something to note as an achievement, especially when things are going rough. Adjourn the meeting.

If the above guidelines are followed faithfully, your meetings will be effective, short, and people will actually look forward to them.

There is a great deal to keep up with in managing large and long-term projects, but there are many tools, such as those that follow, that will help keep you moving and up-to-date.

1.2 The "Offical" Project Log

As you saw in the opening dialog with the trainee, a project log can be the most important control tool you use. A well-experienced project manager on multimillion-dollar military projects, Skip Hall, explains one aspect of the project log: "In some cases your project team, engineers, or whoever, will be so anxious to please the customer that they give away the store [offer many extras that will cost the company money]. To prevent this, any change or discussions relating to the project should be noted in the project log with a date posted."

change order a document that is completed when a customer changes a specification, delivery method or place, and so on, whose purpose is to record changes that would affect the project's remaining true to the original contract

An example of such an entry in the project log would be a **change order.** This is completed any time that a customer changes a specification, a delivery method or place, personnel assigned to the task, or time of completion. Its purpose is to document anything that would affect the outcome of the project from the original contract. As Hall further notes, "The customer isn't always right; the contract is." So it is absolutely necessary to document all changes *and* be certain the customer or a designated representative signs the change order.

Effects the change will have on the final project deliverables and budget should be noted on the change order, as this is an official amendment of the contract. Just as amendments to the Constitution legally define changes to the original, change orders redefine some detail of the agreed-upon project parameters and protect your company from possible lawsuits after the fact.

Other items in the project log include meetings with dates and people present, limitations of availability of raw materials or resources as they occur, corrective actions, schedule on-times, late or early completions, and so on. You may keep the project log in note form, but it should be readable (a word-processed version is preferred).

In addition to the above entries and a general tracking log, any delays, cost overruns, or problems, along with their implications and solutions, should be documented. This is especially helpful when you are planning future projects, as it allows you to have a record of typical durations and of recurring problem areas. In short, it documents experience when memory might fail.

1.3 The Personal Project Log

Different project managers handle the personal project log in various ways. Generally, the content of the personal project log is your "notes to myself" comments. In this log would go anything you observe that appears out of the ordinary, any tone or conflict in a meeting you think is significant. It's your personal diary of the project in your own words and generally for your eyes only. What it will do for you is to retain events in written form, whether they seem significant at the time or not, in case those events led to some action or problem to the project later. (Some project managers, however, use personal voice recordings for this purpose.)

People have fallible memories, especially for details. The personal log would give you a comeback when the customer says, "But I told you in our phone conversation that we wouldn't be ready on time." If you had recorded the conversation in some way, your notes would allow you to say with confidence, "No, you didn't tell me; maybe you told someone else, but not me. In our conversation that day we discussed the specs on the equipment, not site preparation. I have it here in my notes."

Also, when you are managing multiple projects, you will not be able to keep all the details in your head, no matter how smart or experienced you are. This bears repeating, as it is a recurring source of trouble for experienced project managers: you will not be able to keep all details in your head, no matter how smart or experienced you are. Use your log!

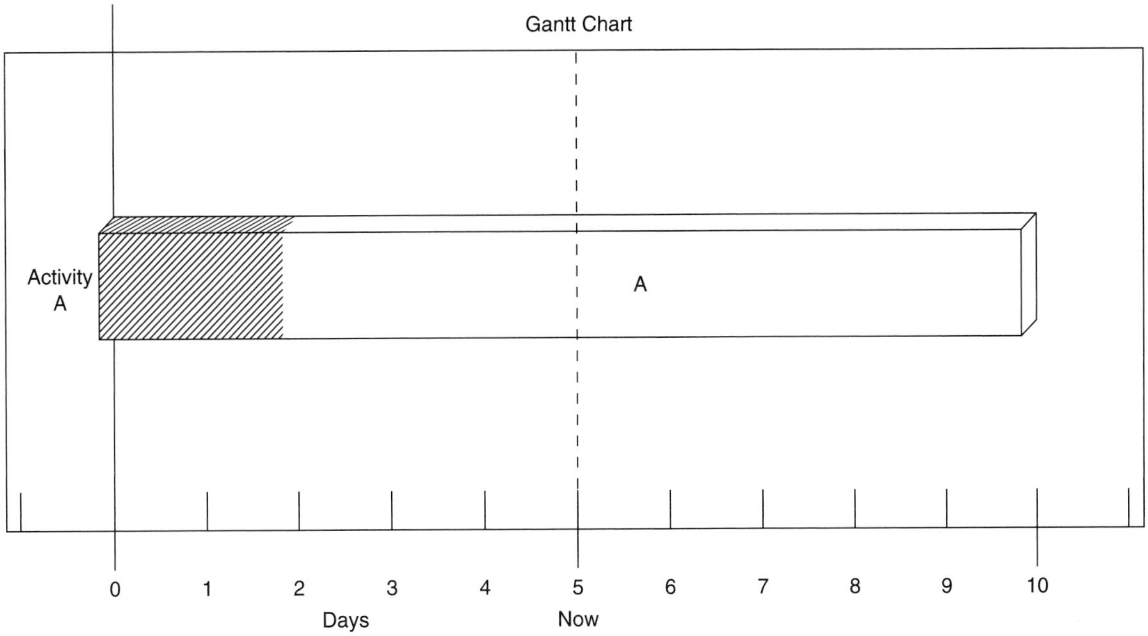

Figure 12–1
Illustration of Time Remaining to Complete an Activity versus Work Completed

1.4 Tracking Charts

Project managers are known for the wall-size charts they have posted of their projects. Many of these are generated by computer from a piece of project management software and have to be printed on plotters because of their size. Some have actually taken up an entire wall of an office.

Gantt charts and other scheduling and tracking diagrams were discussed earlier, but here simplicity is the key. Sometimes a simple time line or other hand-drawn representation of the project is the easiest to size up at a glance. Some managers use colors to denote on-time tasks (green), possible problem areas (yellow) and serious glitches (red). A quick look at the chart tells the story.

For example, one construction general contractor posts a blueprint of a Gantt Chart on the site trailer wall. He pins a string down the chart to show the current date. Every night before going home, he highlights in some fluorescent color the extent to which each activity is complete. When the highlight falls short of the string, it's behind! If it crosses the string, it's ahead. Anyone entering the trailer can tell at a glance the status of things. Subcontractors who belong to the late activities just better be planning to work the weekend and bring extra crew to catch up!

A dry-erase board that allows you to easily change colors or details to be posted can be helpful. Just remember, the most sophisticated control methods known to engineering science are of no help if not used. Whatever your method, be certain to document and track religiously. It is your only hope of identifying problems as early as possible and of having the most time to resolve them.

1.5 Project Reporting

Good project reporting can save you a lot of time, primarily time in meetings. If you are aware of progress at all times, and the rest of the team is also aware of progress (or lack of it), then face-to-face meetings can be fewer. In addition to reducing the need for and length of meetings, reporting serves several functions:

1. Informing stakeholders of project status and projections
2. Assisting team members in staying on track
3. Confirming action items as a result of agreements and changes
4. Supporting requests for changes in resources, time, and/or scope
5. Fulfilling contractual obligations
6. Keeping the flow of funding

Each one of these requires a treatise of its own, but only the most commonly needed forms of project reporting are discussed here.

1.5.1 Informing Stakeholders

This usually consists of some detail and a summary page. The level of detail depends entirely on the level of the stakeholders and *their* needs for reporting to others.

- Identify the stakeholders. Refer to Chapter 7 in which this was discussed this for the purpose of defining the project goal.
- Determine from each stakeholder his/her reporting needs:

  Which information (cost, percent complete, resource usage, etc.)

  What level of detail (activity, task or objective)

  What format is required, if any

  How often (weekly, monthly, quarterly, etc.)

- Work out the lowest common denominator of the various reporting cycles. This will be your reporting cycle. It is usually a weekly cycle and sometimes more often, such as Mondays and Thursdays!
- Tabulate the information requested. Doing so, in addition to providing what you will need to control the project, leads to the list of data streams you need to collect on your reporting cycle.
- Determine the lowest level of detail needed for each of the data streams. Remember that you will need to answer questions about the information you report so be sure to collect one level of detail lower than reported, if possible. This will allow you to successfully verify and "defend" your facts!
- Determine the format in which you need to manage this level of data. The format should make it easy to "roll-up" the information to the higher levels needed by others. (See Figure 12–2 for an example of a cost data sheet, which will allow roll-up of the various cost categories by functional area or team, major task, objective, and capital versus expense.) Similar formats can be used to report days of labor, hours of overtime, hours of usage of a critical resource (such as a high-tech test shop), and so on.

Incurred Cost Report

WSB Objective	Task	Activity	Description	Functions Design Engineering	Custom Shop	Production	Contractor	etc.	Activity Total	Task Total	Objective Total
			Functional Totals								

Total Capital ________

Total Expense ________

Figure 12–2
Sample Cost Detail Sheet for Roll-up

Identify the sources of each of the data streams and any manipulation required. Define the mechanism through which this data will be collected from those sources and then manipulated to result in the various reports required. Sometimes it's as simple as providing a form to your sources to fill in and return so you can roll the data up yourself. Other times you may need a spreadsheet to have the data entered and rolled up. Data may be collected electronically on a network or via E-mail, or even on a disk! Your project management software package may have sufficient capabilities to accept the inputs online, then perform the roll-up required.

Finally, you may have to consult with the MIS (management information systems) department for help in more complex situations, such as government reporting (the earlier, the better).

1.5.2 Creating Gantt Charts

Gantt charts are extremely useful for reporting activity completion progress, current plan versus original plan, and a variety of other information, that can be portrayed graphically. Gantt charts also allow you to roll up the information to higher levels of detail (i.e., fewer details) for reporting to higher levels of management.

Figure 12–3 (page 253) shows a basic Gantt chart in full detail. Note the dark bars showing the extent of completion for each item. This format is typically used to inform doers and first line of supervision.

Figure 12–4 (page 254) shows a Gantt chart rolled up to the task level. It also shows original plan versus current plan for each item. This format is generally used for operational managers.

Figure 12–5 (page 255) shows a fully rolled-up Gantt chart, right up to objective level. This format provides an overview at a glance and is usually sufficient for upper management, until they ask for more detail about a specific area.

1.5.3 Summary Reports

A uniform summary report to go with more-detailed or specific-aspect reports is very useful in ensuring that everyone is aware of the same big picture. It contains top-level information relating to the three performance measures of a project: schedule, cost, and quality. It also relates this report to the previous issue, to provide continuity.

Figure 12–6, on page 256, shows a sample summary, or Project Report. It has several parts labeled to allow you to scan and size up the situation quickly.

red flag items problems that were unable to be solved

It starts with **red flag items.** Under this heading, it should normally say "NONE." It is reserved for problems you could not resolve, which are showstoppers! Nothing here should be a surprise to persons named for action; you should have already discussed it with them.

The next sections provide a high-level overview of the project status:

- *Summary Status* of schedule and cost of the entire project. It reflects your current best estimate of when the project will be complete and compares it to your last estimate and to the original plan. Wild swings in this estimate will undermine your credibility and that of your team. If there are valid business reasons for such swings, they need to be brought to the attention of all stakeholders as soon as possible.
- The *Significant Occurrences* segment addresses the quality aspect of the project. It should convey the direction the project is taking and the state it is in, as well as a sense of the level of competence of the team members.

RG | CRT Phaseout Plan | Fri 4/14 11:43 PM

ID	Task Name	% Compl	Duration	Start	Finish	Predeces	Resource
2	***MATERIAL MANAGEMENT***	***52%***	***52 days***	***Fri 11/5***	***Mon 1/17***		
4	***Material Planning Issues***	***98%***	***35 days***	***Fri 11/5***	***Thu 12/23***		
8	Suspend Item Balance files on unique items	0%	1 day	Thu 12/23	**Thu 12/23**		KC
9	***Purchasing Issues***	***61%***	***10 days***	***Thu 12/2***	***Wed 12/15***		
12	Restart EDI	0%	1 day	Wed 12/15	**Wed 12/15**	11	RM
14	Ask Westerville if they will build whole 14" monitors	50%	5 days	Thu 12/2	**Wed 12/8**		RH
15	***Inventory Issues***	***16%***	***51 days***	***Mon 11/8***	***Mon 1/17***		
18	Overview Table: by size, by wrap package; show O/H, Sch Rcpt:	0%	14 days	Mon 11/22	**Thu 12/9**	17	KC
19	Determine repair inventory needs by major subassy (CRTs, Boa	0%	15 days	Thu 12/2	**Wed 12/22**		Darrel
20	Determine service inventory needs (estimate leftover & advise)	0%	1 day	Thu 12/23	**Thu 12/23**	19	RM
21	Inventory obsolescence reserves	0%	17 days	Fri 12/24	**Mon 1/17**	20	JG,RM,sm
22	Advise marketing of limiting quantities (available to sell)	0%	0.5 days	Thu 12/23	**Thu 12/23**	19	RM
23	Advise mktg of older products and qty's available to sell	0%	0.5 days	Thu 12/23	**Thu 12/23**	19	RM
24	Determine qty's to buy not to exceed tube limits	0%	0.5 days	Fri 12/24	**Fri 12/24**	22,1	KC
26	Scrap potential according to forecast	50%	1 day	Fri 12/10	**Fri 12/10**	25	KC,RM
28	Final scrap plan for approval	0%	1 day	Wed 1/5	**Wed 1/5**	24,26	RM
29	***MIS Issues***	***8%***	***101 days***	***Fri 11/5***	***Fri 3/24***		
33	Create "sell from stock" capability	0%	60 days	Mon 1/3	**Fri 3/24**		CR
39	***SPACE MANAGEMENT***	***3%***	***76 days***	***Fri 11/5***	***Fri 2/18***		
41	LYNX plans	0%	44 days	Fri 11/5	**Wed 1/5**		RH
42	RA space needs	0%	15 days	Wed 12/1	**Tue 12/21**		RH
43	Warehouse space	0%	7 days	Thu 1/6	**Fri 1/14**	41	RH
44	Space release timing plan	0%	10 days	Mon 1/17	**Fri 1/28**	43	RH
45	Space block layout	0%	10 days	Mon 1/17	**Fri 1/28**	41,42,43	RH
46	Grand plan proposal	0%	10 days	Mon 2/7	**Fri 2/18**	45FF+15	RH

Page 1

Figure 12–3
Gantt Chart to Lowest Level of Detail

RG CRT Phaseout Plan Fri 4/14 11:44 PM

ID	Task Name	% Compl	Duration	Start	Finish	Predeces	Resource
2	***MATERIAL MANAGEMENT***	***52%***	***52 days***	***Fri 11/5***	***Mon 1/17***		
4	***Material Planning Issues***	***98%***	***35 days***	***Fri 11/5***	***Thu 12/23***		
9	***Purchasing Issues***	***61%***	***10 days***	***Thu 12/2***	***Wed 12/15***		
15	***Inventory Issues***	***16%***	***51 days***	***Mon 11/8***	***Mon 1/17***		
29	***MIS Issues***	***8%***	***101 days***	***Fri 11/5***	***Fri 3/24***		
33	Create "sell from stock" capability	0%	60 days	Mon 1/3	**Fri 3/24**		CR
39	***SPACE MANEGEMENT***	***3%***	***76 days***	***Fri 11/5***	***Fri 2/18***		
41	LYNX plans	0%	44 days	Fri 11/5	**Wed 1/5**		RH
42	RA space needs	0%	15 days	Wed 12/1	**Tue 12/21**		RH
43	Warehouse space	0%	7 days	Thu 1/6	**Fri 1/14**	41	RH
44	Space release timing plan	0%	10 days	Mon 1/17	**Fri 1/28**	43	RH
45	Space Block Layout	0%	10 days	Mon 1/17	**Fri 1/28**	41,42,43	RH
46	Grand plan proposal	0%	10 days	Mon 2/7	**Fri 2/18**	45FF+15	RH

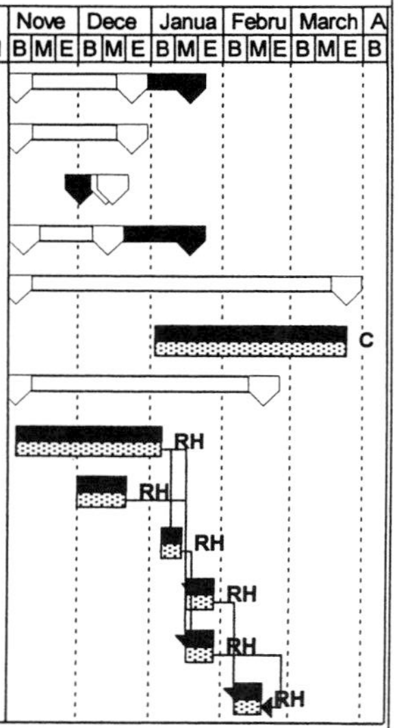

Page 1

Figure 12–4
Gantt Chart Rolled up to Task Level

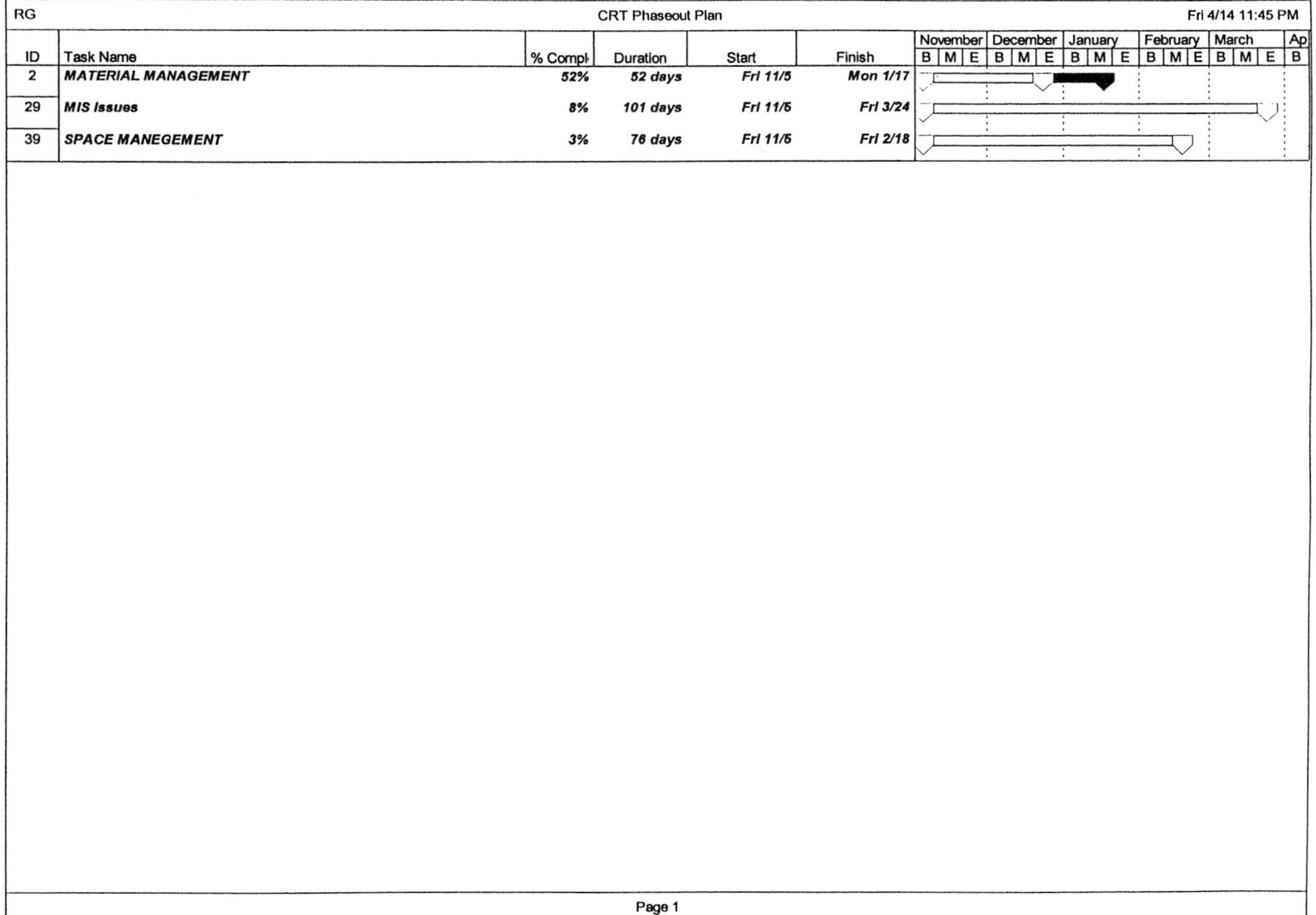
RG CRT Phaseout Plan Fri 4/14 11:45 PM

ID	Task Name	% Compl	Duration	Start	Finish
2	*MATERIAL MANAGEMENT*	52%	52 days	Fri 11/5	Mon 1/17
29	*MIS Issues*	8%	101 days	Fri 11/5	Fri 3/24
39	*SPACE MANEGEMENT*	3%	76 days	Fri 11/5	Fri 2/18

Figure 12–5
Fully Rolled-up Gantt Chart

Project Summary Report

Project Name:______________________ Date:__________________

Red Flag Items:

Summary Status

Date of last report ________________

Estimated completion date last report _____________

–Now _____________

Gain (S ppage) since last report _____________

Estimated total cost: last report $ _____________

–Now $ _____________

Decrease (increase) since last report $ _____________

Significant Occurances

1. ____
2. ____
3. ____

Near Term Schedule

Activity Responsible Resource Start Finnish

1. ____
2. ____
3. ____

Figure 12–6
Summary Report Template

1.5.3 Summary Reports *(continued from page 252)*

- *Near-Term Schedule/Milestones* segment is intended to give the "heads-up" to all concerned about what is expected in the coming days or weeks, the resources you are counting on, and the committed durations. Generally, these will be Critical Path items of the scarce resource kind!

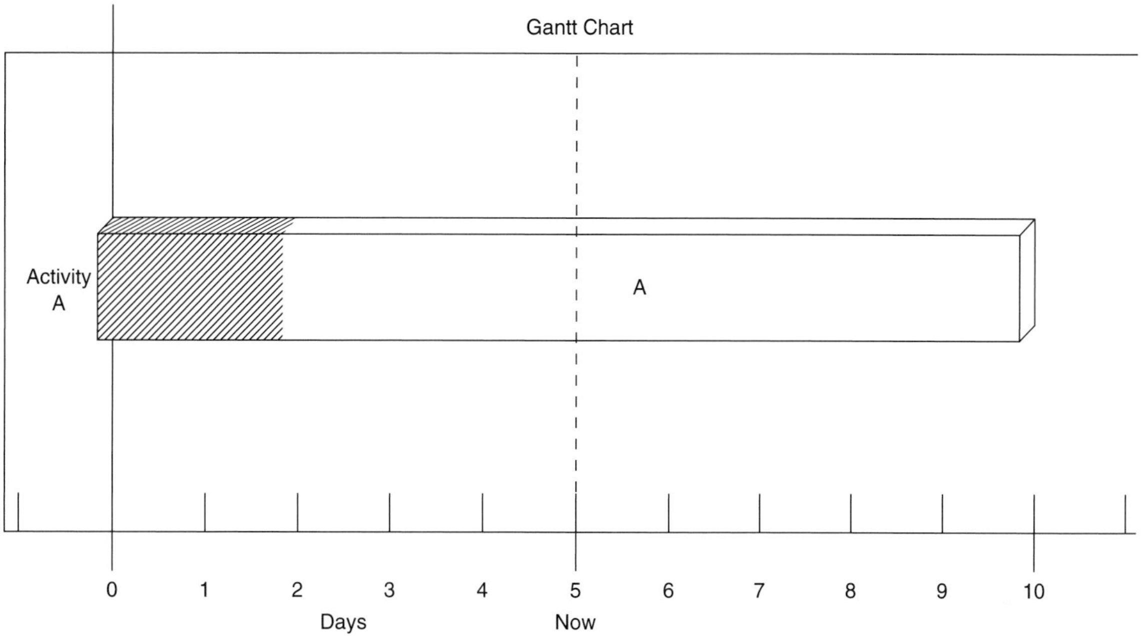

Figure 12–7
Illustration of Time Remaining to Complete an Activity versus Work Completed

■ ■ ■

Ralph sat down and said, "A note here about good and bad ways of reporting completion status. Most people readily report status as percent complete. Can anyone tell me why that is not the best method for project control?"

Jerry was the first to volunteer: "If you're building 10 miles of road and you have the first 5 miles done, you could say that you are 50% complete. But what if the remaining 5 miles have to be blasted out of the side of a hill and cross two ravines! That's gonna take a lot more time and resources to finish than the first straight and level stretch. In this case the 50% would be pretty much a lie!"

"So how should it be reported?" asked Tom.

"Anybody?" inquired Ralph.

After a brief pause, Yury started, "On some military contracts I have worked on, every month we had a Cost-to-Complete report, with time needed to finish for each milestone or job."

"Exactly!" said Ralph. "The best way to report status is to quote Time Remaining! And that is how you would indicate it graphically on a Gantt chart or a time-scaled network. You would color in the completed portion by leaving blank the equivalent length of the time remaining for each activity. Say a 10-day activity reports 8 days' time remaining even though they are on the 5th day, you would color in only 2 days' worth of the activity bar, leaving 8 days' worth not colored. The highlighted part will fall 3 days short of today—the 5th day—and reflect that the activity is 3 days behind schedule." He said this as he drew Figure 12–7 on the board.

■ ■ ■

But what if you are requested to report percent complete? Some projects, such as those done for the government, specify that you report as percent complete. In these cases you would report to the customer or to any stakeholder in the manner requested, but for project control purposes, you must insist on time remaining and cost to complete. These are the most straightforward methods of reporting status because they give a useful picture of the problem and help in making clear how much "solution" you need.

1.5.4 Reports to Help Stay on Track

Reports that help you stay on track are usually action-item oriented reports that help focus people's attention on what they must do immediately, as well as reflect the current changes that have been agreed upon.

Figure 12–8 shows a sample Action Item Report.

- The *Project Title* block shows date, vintage and whom to contact with questions.
- Next come *Red Flag Items,* which must agree with those shown on the summary report.
- Highlighted next are *Past Due Items,* which are any items that are overdue as of the report date. These include mostly items with slack. (You shouldn't allow a Critical Path item to become overdue without prior resolution.) Show original commitment date (strike through) next to the current commitment date. This is intended to turn up the heat on those items. Use italicized type in red if you have color printers. Make it so that no one wants his or her name to show up in this category.
- Next list *Items Due by Next Review.* Here you are reminding people of imminent deadlines, and allowing a last opportunity to flag problems that may delay completion.
- Under *New Action Items* you record those agreements made during the last review, resulting in action items, that were not planned previously.
- Lastly: List any *Items for Discussion,* which are still not agreed upon.

1.5.5 Report Meetings

Report meetings are more commonly known as project review meetings. In these meetings, whatever impression the listener has from that presentation is the impression he or she will pass on to others. Remember, every person to whom you report has to report to someone else and is in some way accountable for your work. So project review meetings should be prepared and orchestrated with care.

On page 259 are some guidelines for presentations. Because a meeting can be 2 people or 20 (and you may not know the number if you are called in on short notice to report), you should follow good presentation procedure regardless.

Action Item Report

Project Title

Today's Date **Report Issue Number** ____________

Date of Last Review **Project Manager** ____________

Functional Coordinators: **Function** **Name**

Next Review Date ____________

Red Flag Items	Resp.	Due
None		

Past Due Items	Resp.	Due
1. *(5-13) Testing first segment of configurator code*	J. Doe	9/18
2.		

Items Due by Next Review	Resp.	Due
1. (5/14) Outline second segment of config. code	P. Smith	(9/20)
2.		

New Action Items	Resp.	Due
1. Coordinate with vendor re new software release	P. Smith	ASAP
2.		

Items for Discussion

1. Training for Configurator users needs to be re-evaluated in light of the new software release.
2. ....

Figure 12–8
Action Item Report Template

Presentation Guidelines and Procedures

1. Determine what the audience expects in the way of oral reporting—formal or informal, using overhead slides, multimedia, handouts, or, "just tell me what's going on." Be wary of the casual presentation, though. No matter where you are or how "relaxed" the atmosphere is, you are expected to do a first-class, professional job. (There are cases where the company president "drops in" on some of these "casual, informal" presentations.)
2. Prepare visuals (charts, graphs, tables, drawings, etc.) in advance. No one wants to watch you write on a board or scribble on a piece of paper to pass around. Even if you use flip charts (large pads of tear-off paper that sit on an easel), you should letter them clearly and professionally in advance. If a multimedia presentation is expected (which is possible on a high-budget, high visibility project), be certain that there are no spelling, numerical, or grammatical errors on slides or graphics. If you do not have skill in developing such a presentation, have someone else create it—either in-house or use an outside contractor.
3. Prepare for "off the wall" questions or criticisms. How you respond to questions has a lot to do with how your information is perceived. If you stammer and appear nervous, the listener thinks you are hiding something, or are winging it and don't really know the real answer. If you become upset or defensive, the listener may believe that things aren't going well. If you don't have a good answer for what the listener thinks is a valid question (whether it is valid in your mind or not is irrelevant), the listener will assume you are incompetent. Again, if you are not good at presentations, find one of your team members who is and go along for questions. Or you can take courses in public speaking to help you.
4. For each slide containing high-level information, have one or two slides containing the details that roll up to it. (Refer to the roll-up feature of your reporting system.) When a question is raised concerning details of a statement you made, answer the first time verbally. If you get one more question about it, flash the detail slide and refer to it. Your credibility should go up a couple of notches immediately. Unfortunately, though, you will then be open for even more contentious questions about the detail if the audience is so inclined.
5. Have a "cut to the chase" version of your presentation. If you've planned for 30 minutes, and the stakeholder receives a phone call and has to leave in 10, you can't afford to stick to your preplanned format. Try to determine what your audience at bare minimum needs to know. (Not what you want to tell them, but what they need or want to know.) One division president's favorite expression was, "Show the last slide. What's the bottom line?"
6. Remember that the purpose of the reporting meeting is to create a feeling of confidence in the audience that things are being expertly handled by you. It's not always necessary to paint a rosy picture (if it's not true), but don't include information in which customers and/or higher-ups in your own organization are not interested. They don't want to know why it's not going well, they want to hear only what you are doing to solve or eliminate any problems. Don't tell them the glass is half empty; tell them your action plan to fill it.

Just a hint here: the better you are at creating confidence in those who are your "customers," the less they will bother you for endless reports and details. All they want is to know that their project is receiving competent attention and that they can count on a positive outcome.

2.0 Preventive Control Techniques

Your project begins its implementation phase after diligent and thorough planning. Contingencies have been anticipated as much as possible, and everyone on your team understands and is fulfilling his or her commitment towards bringing the project in on time and in budget. Now, it is your responsibility to keep everything on track. Your monitoring systems are in place to alert you to problems—time or cost overruns, resource deficiencies, conflicts, and so on. These systems detect problems that have occurred.

Project control meetings and project reports are only one part of the control process. They occur only periodically and leave ample time for hidden problems to develop before detection. To achieve continuous control, however, the key can be summed up in one word: prevention.

As stated before, any problem can be resolved, given enough time and resources. So the key here is that the earlier a problem is detected, the smaller it will be and the fewer resources it will require to solve. Anticipation is the earliest stage of detection, and it is the key to prevention. Essentially, if a project manager waits for problems to be raised or reported, the resolutions will be too expensive, if not too late. Be wary of weaknesses within your team in the ability to realistically size up situations for their problem potential.

Consider the various types of team members who can create disaster on a typical project:

- *Optimists.* They believe everything will go just as planned or better with any luck. When confronted with a problem, they tend to assume that they can take care of it when the time comes. When they finally realize differently, it is usually pretty late in the game!
- *Ostriches.* They hide their heads in the sand and expect the problem to go away. They realize after failing that it didn't go away and bring it up then. It's too late!
- *Machos.* These are the people who will conquer a problem by themselves or "die" trying. When they finally and grudgingly ask for help, the problem is out of control.
- *Timids.* They would rather not bring up any problems since doing so may result in confrontations. They will generally wait until the problem is too obvious, so that someone else brings it up, again, too late.

Of course, not every problem type on the team fits into one of the above categories, but enough of them will. Discover as early as possible who these people are, so you are better able to anticipate them. Conversely, learn whose assessment of the situation you can trust. Just as there are those who are naturally weak in this area, some are quite gifted, even on problems that do not relate directly to their area. Seek the counsel of these people often.

Since prevention is the key to managing problems, here are three points of focus that work together as a basis for a solid prevention effort:

1. Find potential problem areas.
2. Resolve problems on the spot.
3. Keep the commitment alive.

2.1 Find Potential Problems

Your life will be much better if you are clever enough to uncover potential problems before they find you, because they most assuredly will! Assume that, like Murphy's Law, "if it can go wrong, it most likely will!" There are many ways to do this.

Following are some tried-and-true methods.

- **Get out of the office.** Go where the action is. Look in on people engaged in critical activities. Ask how things are going. Ask if they anticipate any difficulties. Ask how you can be of help. Observe progress first hand. Request frequent updates. Make it clear that you are not prying but sincerely trying to help.
- **Listen more closely to people.** If the stress level seems to be rising, things aren't going well. Try to detect previously unexpressed precedence relationships. Encourage people to bring up concerns. Bring up what-ifs and carefully observe the responses. If you ignore these responses, they will soon cease.
- **Snap a string across your Gantt chart.** See which activities should be starting soon. Ask team members directly if they expect any holdups or have any concerns about being able to start or finish tasks on time.
- **Read your CC: messages.** These are copies you receive for your information of E-mails or memos sent to other team members or others related to the project. Sometimes they are disguised cries for help. They present opportunities to ask questions and stimulate anticipatory thinking.
- **Reinforce team members' accountability.** Doing so raises concerns and anticipates problems, one of the differences between a good team and a great one. Treat concerns as gold nuggets rather than a bother, or worse yet, a vote of nonconfidence. When problems are discovered, question people on how they could (or should) have been anticipated. Point out the missed opportunities for earlier resolution. Do this in "training" mode—not blaming, but showing team members what to look for in the way of problem detecting.
- **Be inquisitive and encourage everyone else to do the same.** In short, ask, ask, and ask some more.
- **Resolve problems on the spot.** Potential problems can become very real very quickly. Deal with them as such.
- **Facilitate resolution at the source,** where the problems would develop. This affords the best chances for quick resolutions or work-arounds!
- **Raise flags to all concerned,** to those whose activities will be affected and whose resources will be involved. Remember to include those who may be tapped for help.
- **Hold immediate tête-à-têtes** with those concerned. Have mini-standup meetings. Get quick consensus on approach and responsibility for action. Many decisions are made on the fly, but it is imperative that they be communicated to all parties. The project meeting presents a good opportunity to communicate them.
- **Involve technical experts** in the selection of work-around action.
- **Ask:** Where will the extra time needed be found? Where will the extra resources be found?
- **Negotiate the tradeoffs.** Act as intermediary facilitator. Provide recommendations based on your unique view of the project status.
- **Close the loop.** Inform affected parties of the decision made and the changes needed or anticipated.

- **Keep a running schedule daily.** Continuously reflect progress in your version of the schedule. Keep a copy with you to use in problem solving.
- When decisions are made that affect the schedule, **supply all concerned with the new schedule!**

2.2 Keep the Commitment Alive

People who are committed to the project goal are more concerned with getting there and are less intimidated by obstacles. Stay focused on the goal. As the project leader, you must carry the torch if you expect everyone to work towards it. Resist being pulled in a different direction.

Remind everyone of the goal, often! Team members are naturally focused primarily on their own work. After a time it may loom as a larger priority than the ultimate project goal. They might occasionally need to be reminded that their part goes into something larger. When nonconstructive conflicts arise, remind people that they have the project goal in common. Find ways to constantly bring the project goal to the forefront. You have worked so hard to get commitment to the goal from everyone initially, don't let it slip.

Differentiate between what is a high priority for the project and what is an immediate, but not so high priority, demand. Help your team members do the same. Always ask questions that will clarify a task's relationship to the project goal. Priorities come from the needs of the whole project, not the needs of the individual team member at any given time. Uphold the priorities vehemently. Once you have established that a request is not essential to the primary goals, don't allow any time or resources to be wasted on it!

In summary, continuous control stems from the fact that your primary function is to keep the project on track. You do this by finding or anticipating problems and resolving them and by inspiring your team to do the same.

2.3 Manage Your Time

Finally, you have all the tools you need to get a project planned, scheduled, agreed upon, and under control. You are familiar with the techniques that will allow you to get the necessary information to the people who need it. You can communicate. So when do you sleep? Time management techniques will allow you to get done the things that need doing. This includes having time to have a life. Remember that whoever controls your time controls your life. Good time management techniques reduce stress in the middle of conflicting priorities and cascading problems.

2.3.1 Set Priorities

It seems most people are conditioned to respond to the immediate demands on their time, without regard to the significance of these demands in relation to their own goals or larger accountabilities. While attending a meeting dealing with a top-priority item, you would normally drop what you are doing and get up to respond if paged over the PA, only to find out it's someone who wants to go to lunch with you! Similarly, if the phone rings in the middle of an important task, you pick it up without a second thought, having no idea regarding the relative importance of the call. Following are a few ways to set priorities:

- **Identify what contributes to the goal.** First you need to identify what is truly significant with regard to the goals of the projects in which you are currently involved. Add to this list any "regular job" that which your employer expects you to achieve. These should be your priority items at work. Post these where you can see them.

- **Determine a task's or task request's relation to the goal!** When a task presents itself to you, ignore its immediacy demands long enough to examine its contribution potential to your posted goals. If it is only in your face, but not a goal-related task, promptly drop it; move it to file 13, or bounce it back to the source. If, however, you think it is important to your goals, then list it and assign it a relative priority from the list of goal-supporting tasks.
- **Do It Now!** Two types of time demands fall into this category:

  1. Top-priority items with regard to your planned goals and schedule.
  2. Crisis items that, if ignored, will most definitely affect the project negatively.

Begin the top priority item immediately. Don't move on until it is done, then move on to the next highest priority, then the next, and so on; you have already decided that they are critical to your primary goals. One exception to this rule is to tend to tasks that have a predetermined deadline, such as a report or a presentation. As time goes on, you should find that you have fewer crisis demand tasks and more planned goal-supporting tasks. This is a sign of good judgment and a sure indicator of project success.

2.3.2. Avoid Time Killers

Following are time killers and ways to avoid or minimize them:

- *Procrastination.* Worst offender! Books have been written about this, so we won't elaborate much beyond saying *DO IT NOW!* A word about this area is helpful. Procrastination is often a euphemism for improper prioritizing. People do what they want or feel the need to do. So, in many cases people (you included) will spend time on the more pleasant or immediately rewarding tasks. Be very clear about the reasoning behind the priorities and do a double check to ensure all on the team agree not only on the task, but on the importance of each task and the benefits of completing it on time.
- *The Phone.* The phone rings until you answer it regardless of what else you are doing. If you are involved in top-priority item discussion/meeting, put the phone on hold so you don't hear it ring. (Remember to take it back off when the meeting is done.) Otherwise, use a "Caller ID" feature so that you know who is calling, allowing to take important calls and let the others go to your voice mail. Or, have an administrative assistant or secretary intercept your calls. Dedicate a period of time each day to return your calls—about a half an hour is usually sufficient.

  Avoid phone tag if possible. Also, you will want to avoid engaging in technical discussions or negotiations over the phone. These belong in a face-to-face meeting. Make a quick evaluation of the caller's priority, and respond accordingly. For "bad" cases—callers who can't ever seem to end a conversation—respond by E-mail.
- *The Drop-ins.* By now you have become well-known and well-respected, if not popular. Others find it pleasant to drop by for a casual chat, usually when you need it least. Arrange your office furniture so that when you are deeply involved in a task or on the computer, your back is towards the door. This will discourage

most casual drop-ins. For persistent ones, be pleasantly frank about the deadline and promise to stop by later to pick up the conversation.

A polite way to handle these without curtly dismissing them is, "I'm sorry, I'm involved in this right now and it's taking my full attention. Can I see you at 3 o'clock so I can listen without being distracted?" Remember that it is disrespectful (and will later cause credibility problems) if you don't show that person the courtesy of actually showing up at 3 o'clock.

Finally, close your door (if you have one) during urgent discussions or put up a sign such as "Meeting in Progress—Please Come Back Later."

- *The Hall Hangout.* Hall hangouts are people who circulate around the office, hoping to catch someone they would not otherwise get to see. They can trap you as you manage by walking around. Walk purposefully and quickly. Return greetings without slowing down (It's hard to stop a "train.") If your boss or client is one of "them," find another route.

2.3.3. Delegate

Delegation is a powerful tool. If you are in a position to delegate, it should be your first inclination. Delegating allows tasks to proceed concurrently and to meet multiple tight deadlines. It promotes commitment and helps in training subordinates. Delegate an A-item if (a) you have enough time to correct and redo parts of it, or (b) you have a trained, reliable resource to do it. Delegate a B-item any time you have one, as long as sufficient resources are available. Otherwise, they wait until A-items are done.

In the rare event that all A and B items are done, you may spend some time on C items. Remember first to check again with the source to see if the request is still valid!

3.0 Cost Control

Every company has its own way of controlling cost with a wide variety of record keeping, terminology, and approaches.

3.1 Key to Cost Control

Project cost control systems should be designed to highlight potential problem areas. If you anticipate that some functions or contractors may have cost overruns, then track cost by function or contractor. Conversely if you anticipate certain tasks or objectives to be the source of cost problems, then design the system to track cost by task. Other possibilities include tracking cost by resource type, by work category, by trade, and by activity.

3.1.1. Methodology

Hilda interrupted. "Have I got a story that goes right along with this! It happened over a month ago and we're still trying to straighten out the mess.

"A young project manager started to use accounting reports to keep track of cost. He requested and got special reports from accounting, which provided the breakdowns he needed. He would receive the reports showing accruals and spending, compare them to his budgets and figure out any variances. As the project progressed, the variances became more and more favorable. He began entertaining and approving unbudgeted items that were asked of him, as long as they did not exceed the "surplus " of funds as reported by accounting. When the project was complete, and the final cost accounting was done, he found, to his

total surprise, that he had large cost overruns in almost every area. Enraged, he demanded a thorough audit, which confirmed the overruns."

"What do you think caused the project manager to behave so irresponsibly? " Tracey challenged the group.

"Well, he didn't think he was being irresponsible. There wasn't anything to warn him that there was a problem. " Tom observed "I mean, at worst he's guilty of a lack of experience."

"Good point," Tracey noted. "But the company still suffered. What was missing in the procedures so that he didn't know a problem was developing? "

"He didn't take into account variable completion and billing schedules," Hilda explained. "He was looking strictly at the immediate status of the money. It's a good idea to accuer expenses that you know will occur."

"What happened to the guy?" Jaime's concern was apparent. Tom looked worried.

"First we realized that monthly accounting and project management accounting are two different sets of procedures, so we began to look at the life cycle of the project and flagged intervals where we would do an overall audit. And we sent the guy to training because we'd already invested thousands of dollars in his development and figured we'd finish the job. I don't think he'll make the same mistake again," Hilda laughed. Tom, the youngest of the group and most likely to make that kind of mistake, looked relieved.

■ ■ ■

In order to understand what happened to that project, let's examine the **life-cycle** of the cost of a project item as a series of events.

3.2 Phases of Cost

Event	*Cost Phase*
1. Estimate the item's cost during planning.	1. Budgeted cost
2. Approve contract or purchase requisition.	2. Contracted cost
3. Issue purchase order to Vendor/Contractor.	3. Committed cost
4. Work progress	4. Earned value
5. Receive of invoice.	5. Invoiced cost (accrued cost)
6. Issue payment.	6. Incurred cost

At the outset of the project and during the planning stage, cost items are identified and estimates are made of their cost. These are then rolled up into a budget for the project. These items vary from cost of labor, contractors, equipment rental, communications, insurance, security services, accounting, material, outsourced work, supplies, capital items, and so on. This is the **Budgeted Cost Phase.**

As the implementation phase begins to unfold, purchase requisitions are presented for the items budgeted, contracts are negotiated, and so forth. As these are signed and processed internally, the items have risen to the **Contracted Cost Phase.** At this point, it is still possible to stop the process and reallocate the funds to other uses without any loss.

As processing proceeds, these requisitions are converted to purchase orders, and the signed contracts are delivered, giving the vendors notice to proceed. This brings the items to the **Committed Cost Phase.** Now, in order to change your mind and reallocate the funds to other uses, significant cancellation costs, nonrefundable charges, and even legal cost will be incurred. If accounting does not accrue these costs, they may be committed to some other use. This is a very significant level, at which funds are "irrevocably" allocated for specific items, and are no longer available for other uses.

When work begins on the items ordered by the vendor or by contractors against the contracts, they begin to accumulate **Earned Phase.** In other words, these funds now "belong" to the vendors who "earned" them through the execution of the work. The funds no longer belong to the project manager.

Eventually, items ordered are delivered, and work is completed by contractors. An invoice is then presented for payment according to the vendor's billing cycle, which may be a monthly one. This brings these costs up to the **Invoiced Cost Phase.**

Most companies have standard payment terms, which may vary from 30 to 180 days from receipt of invoice. Payment is then issued against the invoice according to these terms. Only then does the item reach the **Incurred Cost Phase,** which happens anywhere from 2 to 4 months *after* reaching the contracted cost level, obviously too late for project cost control.

The young project manager was watching the invoiced and incurred costs, forgetting that there are 2 to 4 month's worth of contracted costs in the pipeline that were invisible to him. At the end of the project, these eventually matured into incurred costs and caused the overruns. Experienced project managers **track *contracted and committed* costs.** Because these are not normally available from any standing systems, they must keep the project's own books.

3.3 Control of Spending

Even though the project manager is responsible for the total project budget, this budget is made up of a collection of items, assigned to various team members to spend. These team members do not have visibility of the total budget and are usually spending in isolation. In addition, the timing and the amount actually spent on a budgeted item will vary from the budget, causing item variances. These variances can be insignificant or quite large, for a variety of reasons. The sum total of these variances needs to cancel out or be within the budget tolerances. This *never* happens by itself. In order to exercise effective control on spending, you need insight into the behavior of spending.

Most items are spent over a period of time. Each time another expenditure towards this item is needed, a request is raised, approved, and processed, turning an increasing portion of the *budgeted cost* into contracted cost. This portion is called *cumulative cost-to-date.* What is left is called *item balance.* Please note that:

item balance = budgeted cost–cumulative cost-to-date

Your objective is to have a zero or positive item balance when this item is complete. An easy way to keep track is to keep a running balance per item, except that you don't know at which point the big variances may hit. Fortunately, as you get deeper into the implementation of an item, you also get better visibility of its true cost requirements. In other words, you can better estimate how much more will it take to complete this item, which is known as *projected cost to complete.*

Now, armed with this knowledge, you can forecast with improving accuracy how much this item will end up costing us, known as *projected total cost.* Please note:

projected total cost = cumulative cost-to-date + projected cost to complete

Contracted Cost Log

WBS #	Item Description	Budgeted Cost (1)	Requested Item	Requested Cost (2)	Cumulative Requested Cost (3) (Sum of (2))	Balance (1) - (3)
26 - 91	Functional Test Set	$ 180,000	1. Processor	$ 20,000	$ 20,000	$ 160,000
			2. Spec. Analysis	82,100	102,100	77,900
			3. Fixtures	16,500	118,600	61,400
			4. Software	35,000	153,600	26,400

Figure 12–9
Sample Cost Control Log

By comparing this projected total cost with the budgeted cost, we can anticipate the ultimate variance for this item, known as *projected variance.* This is calculated as follows:

projected variance = budgeted cost–projected total cost

Keeping this projected variance at zero or positive becomes the responsibility of the item "owner." In addition, if individual owners anticipate a negative projected balance, it is their responsibility to negotiate with other owners to find the excess elsewhere in the budget. When control is kept at the item level, the total budget will remain in control!

EXAMPLE

Given the following data for an important project item, calculate (a) the item balance, (b) the projected total cost, and (c) the projected variance:

cumulative cost-to-date = $532,000

budgeted cost = $700,000

projected cost to complete = $200,000

(a) item balance = budgeted cost–cumulative cost-to-date
= $700,000–$532,000 = $168,000

(b) projected total cost = cumulative cost-to-date + projected cost to complete
$532,000 + $200,000 = $732,000

(c) projected vaiance = budgeted cost–projected total cost
= $700,000–$732,000 = –$32,000 or ($32,000)

It is obvious that this item will overrun the budget if action is not taken to get it back in budget. First, the project manager must determine the reason for the impending overrun. Next, the item owner becomes the person to negotiate a resolution to the deficit.

When I started plants for Northern Telecom, I gave my assistant a set of books that showed in detail every budgeted item, its budgeted cost, and time it was expected to be used. I then required that all spending requests should go first to the assistant to be logged against the budgeted items and running balances maintained. Before I would approve an item for processing, with it came a note from my assistant showing whether the item was in the budget, the budgeted cost, the cumulative cost-to-date, the item balance, the current projected total cost and the projected variance for the item. I then made a decision on how to handle the request based on that information. This allowed the visibility to anticipate the expected variance *before* the items were contracted.

Figures 12–9 and 12–10 show a sample log and a sample request note. It was the responsibility of the requester to provide an up-to-date projected cost to complete along with the request. In addition, a negative projected variance required that the requesters negotiate with owners of other budget items with projected excess, identify these items to the assistant, who "debited" against the excess and transferred the allocation.

The assistant also verified that all were in agreement with the change. When an approved request was cancelled for any reason, the assistant reversed the entry and showed the funds available again.

Cost controls demand vigilance and a high level of discipline carried out at the contracted or committed cost level of each item, by the entire team, including the project manager.

All elements of the control process require attention and diligence, and the more the project manager can prepare team members to pursue excellence in this area individually, the less stressful it will be for the project manger. However, responsibility for monitoring all the elements of the project goals and parameters is ultimately yours, as project manager. Practice and experience will teach you to know almost intuitively when a problem will occur, but do not make the mistake of relying on this cultivated intuition. Just as even the most experienced pilot goes through a structured preflight checklist to ensure passenger safety, the project manager must observe the rules and practices of good project management. Being responsible for a client's or your company's multimillion dollar project makes "winging it" not an option for you. By using the people and process skills you have accumulated, you are on your way to low-stress project management.

■ ■ ■

With the final few hours of the 2-week training session coming to an end, the group planned a practical joke to play on their two facilitators.

"So how are we going to catch them in this?" Hilda asked, her enthusiasm for the group's prank growing.

"It'll take some planning, but if we all do our parts, this should go off great." Jerry, the main perpetrator, led the discussion.

"My office is going to call me at 10 tomorrow morning, and I'll go out then to set everything in place." Ragdeesh said, his creativity beginning to shine. "While I'm out, I'll get the balloons delivered and arrange to have the rooms moved."

"You know, I can guess that there could be a hitch with getting the room filled while they're gone," Jaime interjected. "Does anyone have a backup plan?"

"Yes," said Jerry, "We're going to have the hotel blow up the balloons with their helium tank, but if that falls through, there's a local company that will deliver as many as we want if we reserve them today." He looked at his checklist, and turned to Jaime. "Okay, Jaime, do you have the schedule for the interruptions?"

"Yes. Every 20 minutes someone will come in. Phone calls for each of us will be every hour; the meal planner will come in at 11:00; the hotel clerk will be there at 11:20 about checkout; the bell captain at 11:40 with a question about bags. Ralph's assistant will call at 12:00 and get him out of lunch, and the afternoon is even better than that."

Spending Request Note

Budget Item: (#26-9-1) Functional Test Set **Budgeted Amount:** $180,000

Requested Item: (1.4) Software

Requested Cost:	$25,000
Cumulative cost-to-date, this budget item:	$140,000
Projected cost-to-complete (beyond this request):	$23,600

Total projected cost:	$188,000
Projected variance from budget: fav./(unfav.)	$ (8,600)

Adjustments to Balance Variance:	**Item No.**	**Projected Variance**
	(18.10.2	$ 1,600
	(62.29.16)	$ 7,000

Total Projected Cost Summary:

Original Budget:	$3,467,800
Current Projection:	$3,450,000

Requestor's Initials: ____________________ Date: ______________

Initials for Adjustments:

Approval: ____________________ Date: ______________

Figure 12–10
Sample Request Note

"Well, what happens if the time is off on any one of them?" Tom questioned.

"All the better. Two at one time ought to blow them away," Jerry laughed.

"What about Tracey?"

Yury, who had been quiet up to now, broke in. "She's supposed to be the crisis expert. Let's cancel her flight and have the hotel lose her bags."

"Oh, Yury, when you come up with one, it's really devious. My hat's off to you." Tom bowed ceremoniously to Yury, who cracked a bit of a smile.

"Let's see, we've got times, cost, events, expected outcomes, contingency plans. I think that about does it." Jerry looked one more time at his checklist.

"Do you guys realize we did this just like they've been teaching us this week?" Ragdeesh observed. The group looked at each other and all burst into laughter.

At that time the two instructors walked into the room.

"What's going on?" Tracey asked.

"Um, Yury just told a funny joke." Tom snickered as he answered.

"Yury? You guys have definitely been at this too long." Tracey rolled her eyes and Ralph shook his head as he went to the flip chart.

■ ■ ■

Chapter Summary

This chapter covers two major categories of project control techniques: periodic and preventive. Periodic techniques have the advantage of being formal and regular in nature. They consist mainly of regularly scheduled meetings and reports. The main disadvantage of periodic control is that it occurs after most problems arise. Meetings must have a specific purpose and be short and focused. One meeting should be dedicated to Critical Path problem solving, another dedicated to progress review, and so on. Reports must be designed to serve the information needs of the stakeholders. The design should result in continuous streams of data into a "database" which can be rolled up into the various reports.

Preventive control techniques fill the gaps between periodic control events, and provide the ability to anticipate problems, therefore affording the greatest opportunity for early resolution or even avoidance. Preventive techniques are less formal and ad hoc in nature. They are as varied as there are project teams, but they all share a common foundation of continuous communication among all participants. The difference between a good project team and a great one is in the mastery of preventive control.

Effective cost control cannot depend on standard accounting reporting. Instead, a project manager must set up the project's own cost tracking "books" in order to capture cost as it is being committed, which is typically much earlier that when accounting will capture it. In order to keep team members accountable for their assigned items, cost control needs to be maintained at the item level. The project's cost tracking mechanism must progressively compare an item's projected cost to its budgeted cost, so that it is kept within budget. Discipline must be exercised in negotiating the excesses in balance with the deficits. Of course, the ultimate solution to the problem is an accounting system that keeps all these items current, but in most cases, that is a long-range solution.

Chapter Questions

1. In the case of the young project manager who overran his budget due to unexpected charges, was the fault totally his? What could accounting have done to prevent this kind of overrun? Would an actual system that anticipates future expenditures have helped? Could the MIS department have helped if they had been consulted?
2. Your manager needs your assistance on a major project. He is worried that he will lose control of the project if it is not tightly managed. He has asked you to set up a plan to keep him up-to-date on the status of the project. Based on what you have learned in this chapter, how would you proceed?
3. Explain the differences in meaning and implication for cost control of each of the following:

   Incurred costs

   Committed costs

   Accrued costs
4. Compare and contrast the role of the personal project log with the role of official project log.
5. Write an E-mail to your team members requesting information for a status meeting to a panel of client representatives and upper management. Specify what role you would like each to play in the actual presentation. Suggest ways they should prepare for their actual speaking task.
6. Why is reporting not a substitute for monitoring?

Project Challenge: Applying What You Know

You are a manager at a manufacturing location of a large multinational corporation. About 6 months ago, one of your colleagues (and close friends) was assigned the task of managing the installation of a Local Area Network (LAN) in your plant, a 2-year project. This was a large undertaking, since there were more 700 high-speed and lower-speed terminals connected to several different computers inside and outside the plant. At this point, the engineering is almost complete, but very little of the physical installation has been started. Recently, the project manager was transferred (and promoted) to another company location.

The general manager of the plant, who is also your immediate supervisor, has picked you to become the new project manager. In the process of getting yourself up to speed on the project, you have heard several presentations by managers of the various subprojects (major objectives).

You learn that the transmission medium that has been selected is coaxial cable. Because of your intimate knowledge of the facilities in the plant, and also of transmission requirements between computers and terminals that operate at extremely high speeds, you are certain that coax is too slow; you believe strongly that optical fiber is required.

The problem is that a group of very talented engineers have spent 6 months designing the system for coax, and they are obviously committed to it. Your job is to convince them that you are right, and at the same time to get them on your team. Time is important, because 6 months of the project's duration is gone.

Based on meetings with your subproject managers, the major project steps are as follows:

1. Evaluate present and near-term terminal requirements. (Complete)
2. Evaluate present network cabling plan. (Complete)
3. Evaluate present host computers. (Complete)
4. Identify slow-speed terminals where present twisted-pair will suffice. (Complete)
5. Develop new cabling plan. (Unfortunately, already completed for coax)
6. Plan to consolidate all terminals on in-house computers. Plan acquisition of new computers if necessary.
7. Submit new cabling plan to contractors.
8. Plan and install new computers.
9. Begin installation of new cable network.
10. Begin moving users to new computers, if required.
11. Test system.
12. Implement system.

What do you do first? How do you get the engineers and subproject managers on your side? Then how do you manage a project that now has only 18 months of its interval remaining, rather than the original 24? How do you handle the possibility that fiber is more expensive than coax and still be conscious that you are operating under budget constraints? You will need to use the resources of *all* 12 chapters in this book. This is an exercise in applying what you have learned.

Interview with an Expert

Richard Beggs, *Technical Staff (Senior Engineer), Lucent Technologies*

Managing projects on multiple continents

One of the difficult things for project managers to accept is that products must roll out at the designated date. If not, then there is full customer involvement with your problems.

There is a right way and a wrong way to manage a complex project. Just because you manage it well, doesn't mean something can't go wrong. But a well-managed project can recover from problems. Although there are numerous steps along the way, there are general stages a successful project goes through:

1. Identify the need—not just the final product specifications, but end-to-end documentation—everything it will take to turn out the final product. This is the product map. Use face-to-face meetings, phone calls, E-mail, whatever it takes to define each step to the final result. Clarity reduces wasted effort. Even if you have different manufacturing locations or teams in different time zones, make sure everyone is face-to-face regularly and communicates often by some method or other.
2. Develop attributes that will achieve objectives. Design experiments for testing. This is a complex process. At this point develop a prototype with identifiable variables to be tested.
3. Keep shop engineers (production engineers) informed about possible pitfalls. Engineering change orders should include any new testing requirements and rejection points. At the end of this stage you should be at the RTM—ready to manufacture—point.

This is also the point where problems will show up, especially if you have different test equipment at different locations run by different people. Even if the manufacturing equipment matches, the test equipment may not be calibrated exactly the same, so results will vary. Also, the materials tested in the lab might not be identical to the final material—for instance, fire-retardant coating required for final product, but test product might not have that.

Other hitches that often come up on projects:

- Lack of dedicated resources. Some project members may view this as a "side" job and have to manage it with other duties.
- Time needed to reach consensus. Maybe 60% of time is spent this way, but it helps to stem problems later.
- Too much management "help" or interference.

When faced with a problem or "hitch":

- Meet problems with a "solutions" approach, not a blaming one
- Invoke the Theory of Constraint—items in the critical chain cannot be deviated from. All others are dropped until that one is back on track.
- Identify ownership of all activities and tasks related to solutions.

4. Conduct a design review—an auditor links all data to physical performance and claims made to customer.
5. Roll out product on time, to customer requirements, gain dominant market share, and guarantee your and your company's future.

In the well-run project you will begin to see that although individual parts of the team perform nominally, put together they achieve even better than expected results. The collective system yield is impressive.

EPILOGUE

A great project team is the key to a successful project! So is a great project manager! However, great project teams and great project managers don't just happen.

A typical new project team is assembled from people who come from a variety of experience backgrounds, which presents initial challenges unrelated to the particulars of the project.

A plethora of project management techniques exist across companies, varying from the simple to the most sophisticated, causing team members to be either overwhelmed or feel deprived by whichever techniques you choose to employ.

Project management terminology varies widely from industry to industry, which contributes to communications difficulties among team members. Even project management itself carries different names, definitions, and conventions, adding to the ambiguity of objectives, roles, and responsibilities.

Additionally, team members possess various degrees of mastery—even basic awareness—of the principles of project management. These variables and others present pitfalls that will exasperate start-up efforts of a project, and magnify the effects of normal project difficulties, to the detriment of project success.

Training, in a word, is the most effective remedy for all of these difficulties.

Whether a new team is trained together, or a mature team is given refresher training at the outset of a project, several benefits arise:

- The importance of the project is emphasized.
- The value of using the techniques is reinforced.
- Respect for schedules is heightened.
- Common language and terminology is mastered.
- Mastery of using the techniques is more uniform.
- Information gathering for managing and reporting is facilitated.
- Team building is accelerated.
- Initiation of the project is smoother.

This work has been presented with training in mind. Because people skills are so important in the success of a project, critical people skills were presented first, as well as the tools to apply them in the project management environment. Next, the particular project management techniques explored were selected for practicality, ease of use, and applicability to a wide variety of projects.

The authors hope that the readers found this text to be entertaining and easy to read, the techniques to be applicable in their projects, the terminology to be intuitive, and the total experience to have helped them become more effective project managers.

May your work be free of stress, your project teams enthusiastic, your solutions creative, and your projects completed on time, at specs, and within budget.

Here's to your bright project management future!

REFERENCES

APPENDIX

Alcorn, Paul. *Social Issues in Technology: A Format for Investigation.* Upper Saddle River, NJ: Prentice Hall, 2000.

Bennis, W. G., and P. E. Slater, *The Temporary Society.* New York: Harper and Row, 1968.

Bijur, Peter, "Changing the Corporate Culture: A Competitive Imperative." [On-line]. *www.worldenergysource.com/texart.html* (1998).

Block, Julia Chang, "Diversity in the Workplace." [On-line]. Internet: *www.execed.com/diverse.html* Spring 1992

Cameron, Julia. *The Artist's Way.* New York: Jeremy P. Tarcher/Putnam, 1992.

Carr-Ruffino, Norma. *Managing Diversity.* International Thompson Publishing, 1996.

Clarke, Clifford C., and G. Douglas Lipp. "Conflict Resolution for Contrasting Cultures." *Training and Development* 52, no. 2 (February 1998): 20–27.

Cornell University. (1994). *Managing Diversity and Glass Ceiling Initiatives.* [On-line]. Internet: *http://www.ilir.cornell.edu/library/e_archive/GlassCeiling/5/5front.html*

Dinsmore, Paul C., *The AMA Handbook of Project Management,* New York: Amacom (American Management Association), 1993.

Flamholtz, Eric, and Yvonne Randle. *The Inner Game of Management.* New York: Amacom, 1987.

A Guide to the Project Management Body of Knowledge, Newton Square, PA: Project Management Institute, 1996.

James, W. B., and M. W. Galbraith. Perceptual Learning Styles: Implications and Techniques for the Practitioner. *Lifelong Learning: An Omnibus of Practice and Research* (1985): 20–23.

Kemper, Cynthia L. "Global Training's Success Factors." *Training and Development* 52, no. 2 (February 1998): 20–27.

Kenton, Sherron B., and Deborah Valentine. *Crosstalk: Communicating in a multicultural workplace.* Upper Saddle River, NJ: Prentice Hall, 1997.

Kinney, Susan T, and Raymond Panko. (1997). "Project Teams: Profiles and Member Perceptions." [On-line]. Internet: www.cba.hawaii.edu/PANKO/research.html

Kolbe, Kathy. *The Conative Connection: Uncovering the Link between Who You Are and How You Perform.* Reading, MS: Addison-Wesley, 1990.

Lewis, James. *The Project Manager's Desk Reference,* New York: McGraw-Hill, 1995.

Mager, Roger, and Peter Pipe. *Analyzing Performance Problems or "You really oughta wanna."* Belmont, California: Fearon Publishers, 1970.

Martin, Paula and Karen Tate. Project Management Memory Jogger™, Methuen, MA, GOAL/QPC, 1997.

Smith, Michael H. "Cultural Diversity in the Workplace." [On-Line]. Internet: *www.mit.edu/~penfield/pubs/diversity/html,* Spring 1992.

Walters, Brenda, and Sandra McKee. *Life Management: Skills for Busy People.* Upper Saddle River, NJ: Prentice Hall, 1997.

Whetton, David A., and Kim S. Cameron. *Developing Management Skills.* 4th ed. Boston: Addison Wesley, 1998.

Yukl, Gary. *Leadership in Organizations.* Upper Saddle River, NJ: Prentice Hall, 1998.

APPENDIX B

SOFTWARE PACKAGES FOR PROJECT MANAGEMENT

Microsoft Project is included with this textbook material in a time-limited demonstration format. However, to secure information on the full business version, go to:

www.microsoft.com

Although Microsoft Project seems to dominate the market, there are many software packages for specific applications, and each industry has a preferred tool. Other packages and their related websites for more information are:

Primavera Project Planner *www.primavera.com*

Primavera SureTrak *www.primavera.com*

Microsoft Excel *www.microsoft.com/office/excel*

ABT Workbench *www.abtcorp.net*

Timeline (no web site)

CA Super Project *www.superproject.com*

Scitor Corp Project Scheduler *www.scitor.com/products*

Artemis Views *www.artemispm.com*

PROJECT MANAGEMENT ORGANIZATIONS

APPENDIX C

International Project Management Association
P.O. Box 30, Monmouth NP25 4YZ, United Kingdom
Tel: +44 1594 531007;
Fax: +44 1594 531008
E-mail: ipma(a)-btinternet.com
The International Project Management Association (IPMA) is a nonprofit, Swiss registered Organization, with a secretarial office based in the United Kingdom. Its function is to be the prime promoter of project management internationally, through its membership network of national project management associations around the world. Additionally, it has many individual members, people and companies, as well as cooperative agreements with related organizations worldwide, to give it a truly worldwide influence.

The Association for Project Management
Thornton House
150 West Wycombe Road
High Wycombe Buckinghamshire
HP12 3AE, United Kingdom
Tel: 01494 440090
Fax: 01494 528937
E-mail: *secretarial@2om-uk.demon.co.uk* Please ensure your full postal address is included on any request for further information.

CIPPM: Center for International Project & Program Management
(CIPPM, Ethics, Membership, Affiliation, Sponsorship, Certification Information)

Project Management Institute (PMI): *Building Professionalism in Project Management*—Since its founding in 1969, Project Management Institute (PMI) has grown to be the organization of choice for project management professions. With over 50,000 members worldwide, PMI is the leading nonprofit professional association in the area of Project Management. *http://www.pmi.org/*

PMI, Dallas Chapter: Building professionalism in project management. This is the PMI Dallas Chapter website. The purpose of this website is to share information with current and future chapter members. *http://www.pmidallas.org/index.html*

Phoenix PMI: *Home Page*—Request for help from PMI members and Technology Expo invitation go to the What's New page for information.
http://www.goodnet.coml-pmiphxlindex.htm

PMISA WesternCape: Any comments, suggestions? Want to change your contact details? Want to know more about PMISA membership? See how you can benefit from the PMISA in the Western Cape. *http://pmisawo.hypermart.nettindex.htm*

Project Management Institute, Northern Utah Chapter: *Home Page*—The Project Management Institute, Northern Utah Chapter. Information about project management training, certification, publications, events, and PMI membership.
http://www.projectmanager.org

American Production and Inventory Control Society (APICS): APICS is another related organization that looks at resource management, among other areas. Many processes in manufacturing are similar to those in project management. *www.apics.org*

Young, Clark, and Associates: Project Management trainers
2336 Westeria Drive
Snellville, GA 30078

Council for Logistics Management (CLM): CLM represents one of the most rapidly-growing industries in the world—that of logistics. Project management skills are an integral part of logistics management.

American Management Association (AMA): AMA offers basic and advanced training in project management to novices and professionals alike.

SUGGESTED READINGS

APPENDIX

Angus, Robert, and Norman Gundersen. *Planning, Performing, and Controlling Projects, Principles and Applications,* Prentice Hall, 1997.
This text maintains that the use of a systematic approach to project design and management can lead to an efficient, useful, and cost-effective product, process, or service. The authors use extensive conceptual diagramming to illustrate complex concepts.

Moder, Joseph, Cecil Philips, and Edward Davis. *Project Management with CPM, PERT and Precedence Diagramming*, 3rd ed., Van Nostrand Reinhold, 1983.
The authors offer a treatise of the scheduling of activities under constraints on resource availabilities.

Schwalbe, Kathy. *Information Technology Project Management*, Course Technology, 1999.
This book focuses on the nuances of applying project management knowledge areas—project integration, scope, time, cost, quality, human resources, communications, risk, and procurement management—and project management process groups—initiating, planning, executing, and closing—to information technology projects. It is organized by areas of management skills utilized.

Smith, Preston and Donald Reinertsen. *Developing Products in Half the Time*, Van Nostrand Reinhold, 1995.
This book offers 14 specific techniques that will contribute to the reduction of the cycle time of new product introduction projects, each of which can be a stand-alone technique yielding some improvement. Together, 50% to 60% improvements are typical.

Additional Suggested Readings

The following readings are referenced from the bibliography of *Planning, Performing, and Controlling Projects; Principles and Applications* by R. Angus and N. Gunderson, Prentice Hall, 1997.

Archibald, R. D. *Managing High-Technology Programs and Projects*. New York: Johns, 1992.

Badiru, A. B. *Project Management Tools for Engineering and Management Professionals*. Norcross, GA: Institute of Industrial Engineers, 1991.

Badiru, A. B., and Whitehouse, G. E. *Computer Tools, Models, and Techniques for Project Management.* Blue Ridge Summit, PA: TAB Books, 1989.

Banios, E. W. "An Engineering Practices Course." *IEEE Transactions on Education*, 35, no. 4 (November 1992): 286–293.

Boff, K. R., and Lincoln, J. E., eds. *Engineering Data Compendium: Human Perception and Performance*. Wright-Patterson Air Force Base, OH: Henry G. Armstrong Aerospace Medical Laboratory, 1988.

Bransford, J. D., and Stein, B. S. *The Ideal Problem Solver.* New York: W. H. Freeman, 1993.

Francks, P. L., Testa, S. M., and Winegardner, D. L. *Principles of Technical Consulting and Project Management.* Chelsea, MI: Lewis Publishers, 1992.

Graham, R. J. *Project Management: Combining Technical and Behavioral Approaches for Effective Implementation.* New York: Van Nostrand Reinhold Co., 1985.

Kim, S. H. *Essence of Creativity.* New York: Oxford University Press, 1990.

Lewis, J. P. *Project Planning, Scheduling, and Control.* Chicago: Probus Publishing Company, 1991.

Lumsdaine, E., and Lumsdaine, M. *Creative Problem Solving.* New York: McGraw-Hill, 1990.

Mager, R. R. *The New Mager Six-Pack,* Belmont, CA: Lake Publishers, 1984.

The following captioned readings are referenced from *Information Technology Project Management* by K. Schwalbe, Course Technology, 1999.

Abel-Hamid, Tarek K. "Investigating the Cost/Schedule Trade-off in Software Development," *IEEE Software* (1990).
Hamid analyzes current models for estimating the effect of schedule compression on total project cost. He then presents his own system-dynamics model to illustrate the integrated nature of projects by including subsystems related to software production, planning, control, and human resource management.

Boehm, Barry W. "Software Risk Management: Principles and Practices," *IEEE Software* (January 1991).
Boehm describes detailed approaches for several risk management techniques including risk identification checklists, risk prioritization, risk management planning, and risk monitoring. This article includes an example of Top IO Risk Item Tracking.

Bolton, Bart. "IS Leadership," *Computer World* (May 19, 1997).
http.llwww2.computerworld.comlhomelptint9497.nsfIAIIISL9705lead
Bolton emphasizes that project success depends more on leadership than creating PERT charts. This article includes questionnaires to determine personal and organizational leadership scores.

Brandon, Daniel M., Jr. "Implementing Earned Value Easily and Effectively," *Project Management Journal 29*, no. 2 (June 1998): 11–18.
Brandon describes the benefits of using earned value analysis and the reasons why more organizations do not use it. This paper provides suggestions for overcoming some of the problems associated with this technique.

Bylinksky, Gene. "How to Bring Out Better Products Faster," *Fortune* (November 23, 1998): 238 [B].
This article describes how companies like Xerox, Hewlett-Packard, Ford Motor Company, and Goodyear have developed outstanding new products by using Taguchi's Robust Design method. This method goes directly to the basic physics and thermodynamics of product design—torque, electrical charge, heat flux, and so on—that are causing trouble, and solves the problem during the early design phase.

Covey, Stephen. *The 7 Habits of Highly Effective People*, New York: Simon & Schuster, 1990.
Stephen Covey is famous for his books, audiotapes, videotapes, and seminars on improving effectiveness. This book continues to be a business bestseller with more than 10 million copies sold.

Gates, Bill. *Business @ The Speed of Thought. Using a Digital Nervous System,* Warner Books, 1999.
The main premise of the Microsoft CEO's 1999 book is that the speed of business is accelerating at an ever-increasing rate, and to survive, organizations must develop a "digital nervous system" that allows for rapid movement of information. Gates suggests that how organizations gather, manage, and use information to empower people will determine whether they win or lose in the competitive business environment.

Goldratt, Eliyahu. *The Critical Chain*, North River Press, 1997.

This book shows you how to use project management to deliver information systems on time, without sacrificing quality. Goldratt emphasizes three simple steps—limit multitasking, end procrastination, and plan for dependencies—to improve your delivery time.

Goldratt, Eliyahu and Jeff Cox. *The Goal: A Process of Ongoing Improvement*, North River Press, 1994.

In this book Goldratt uses a fictional story to illustrate the fundamentals of running a business. He describes several problem-solving techniques for managers who lead organizations through change and improvement, which are inevitable in any industry.

Ireland, Lewis R. *Quality Management for Projects and Programs*, Project Management Institute, 1991.

This PMI publication includes seven chapters and several appendices with information on project quality management. Lew Ireland is well known for his expertise in quality and project management and his contributions to PMI. In 1999 he served as the president of PMI.

King, Julia, "Post-Y2K: Project Management Key," *Computer World Web Site* **(*www.computerworld.com*)** (January 18, 1999).

Now that Year 2000 projects have wound down, many companies are focusing on a more rigorous approach to managing information technology projects. This short article provides some statistics and examples of how companies are increasing their use of project management.

Kirchof, Nicki S. and John R. Adams. *Conflict Management for Project Managers*, Project Management Institute, 1989.

This 53-page booklet contains information on the theory of conflict management, conflict in project organizations, conflict management and the project manager, and two-party conflict management. It also provides more information on Blake and Mouton's five basic modes for handling conflict and many references on the subject of conflict management.

Knutson, Joan. "From Making Sense to Making Cents: Measuring Project Management ROI-Part I," *PM Network* (January 1999).

This is the first part of a two-part article related to measuring the financial value of project management. It explains return on investment (ROI) calculations and provides examples of costs and benefits of using project management in organizations. Part of this article appears in the February issue of PM Network.

Kouzes, James M. and Barry Z. Posner. *The Leadership Challenge*, San Francisco, CA, Jossey-Bass, 1990.

Kouzes and Posner show that leadership is not the private preserve of a few charismatic people, but a learnable set of practices that virtually anyone can master They suggest that leadership involves five basic practices—challenge the process, inspire a shared vision, enable others to act, model the way, and encourage the heart.

Levesque, Paul. *Breakaway Planning*. Amacom Books, a Division of AMA, 1998.

This book walks readers through the entire planning process, from creating a compelling vision to making that vision a reality. Levesque describes eight important questions to address in planning, such as: How do we spread the word internally? How will we make things better for employees? How do we measure success?

Maguire, Steve. "Getting Your Team Off on the Right Foot," *Software Development* (May 1997): pp. 37–44.

A former Microsoft project manager offers advice for planning and managing project teams. He suggests stressing that project team members can create high-quality products, the work can be done on time, team members are not required to put in long hours or seven-day workweeks, and people should be excited about the work.

McConnell, Steve. "How to Defend an Unpopular Schedule," *IEEE Software* (May 1996).

This article emphasizes the fact that it is just as important, if not more so, to defend project schedule estimates as it is to create them. Most software developers must learn to defend their schedule estimates by practicing good negotiation techniques.

Mellon University, September 1992.
This report summarizes risk management for software projects. The Software Engineering Institute (SEI) provides this and several other publications on the topic of risk management and other subjects related to software development. Their Website is www.seicmu.edu.

Nuller, John G. *Personal Accountability*, Denver Press, 1998.
The first part of this book explains the Question Behind the Question, a tool to help eliminate blame, victim thinking, and procrastination from people's lives. The second part explores the Pillar Principles, which includes ideas such as courage, excellence, ownership, trust, and integrity.

Peters, Tom. *Thriving on Chaos*, Harper Collins, 1991. (Also, see other books by the same author.)
Peters, the co-author of In Search of Excellence *and* A Passion for Excellence, *provides readers with a book that describes fifty specific courses of action essential to corporate survival in today's turbulent world.*

Project Management Institute. *PM Network*, February 1998.
The entire issue of this magazine focuses on managing risk in projects. Topics of articles include analyzing risk decisions, using risk-based scheduling and analysis, and encouraging team-based risk assessment.

Ross, Douglas. "Applying Covey's Seven Habits to a Project Management Career," *PM Network*, Project Management Institute (April 1996): pp. 26–30.
Ross summarizes key points from Covey's seven habits and relates them to improving effectiveness in project management This article helps project managers translate Covey's principles to their own teams, projects, and personal lives.

The Standish Group, "Unfinished Voyages" (1996). ***(www.standishgroup.com/voyages.html).***
The Standish Group used the project success criteria from the 1995 CHAOS research to create a weighted scoring model for estimating information technology project success potential. The most important success criteria, user involvement, was given 19 success points while the least important, hard-working, focused staff, was given 3 success points. You can use this checklist to decide whether a project is worth starting or continuing.

Stuckenbruck, Linn C. "The Job of the Project Manager: Systems Integration," *The Implementation of Project Management. The Professional's Handbook*, pp. 141–155. Reading, MA: Addison-Wesley Publishing Company, Inc. (1996).
This chapter of Stuckenbruck's book provides more details on how project managers perform the integration management function. She stresses the need for maintaining communication links across the organizational interfaces.

Tausworthe, Robert C. "The Work Breakdown Structure in Software Project Management," *The Journal of Systems and Software* (1980).
This paper advocates and summarizes the use of the work breakdown structure (WBS) in software projects. It identifies some of the problems people have in generating WBS and the need for standard checklist items to be included in a WBS for software projects.

The, Lee. "IS-Friendly Project Management," *Datamation* (April 1, 1996).
http:llwww.datamation.com
This article mentions the unique nature of many information systems (I.S.) projects and offers suggestions on features needed in project management software for I.S. projects. The author also states that understanding project management in general is an important prerequisite to using project management software.

Van Scoy, Roger L. "Software Development Risk: Opportunity, Not Problem," *Technical Report CMUISEI-92-TR-30*, Software Engineering Institute, Carnegie Mellon University, September 1992.
This report summarizes risk management for software projects. The Software Engineering Institute (SEI) provides this and several other publications on the topic of risk management and other subjects related to software development. Their Website is ***www.seicmu.edu***

Ward, James. "Productivity Through Project Management: Controlling the Project Variables," *Information Systems Management* (Winter 1994).
Ward suggests that effectively planning and controlling three project variables—work, resources, and time—is what ensures a project's success. This article describes the typical problems and opportunities associated with project control and the dynamics and interrelationships of work, resources, and time.

Wideman, R. M. "Total Project Management of Complex Projects, Improving Performance with Modem Techniques," *Consultancy Development Centre*, New Delhi, India (January 1990).
This article provides more details on the framework for project integration management. It emphasizes that project integration management, particularly project control, must be applied to each and every other knowledge area throughout the entire project life cycle.

Wideman, R. Max (editor) and Rodney J. Dawson. *Project & Program Risk Management. A Guide to Managing Project Risks and Opportunities*, Project Management Institute, 1998.
Wideman has written several books and articles on project risk management. This textbook includes practical advice for managing project risks and opportunities.

Wiegers, Karl. "Software Process Improvement: 10 Traps to Avoid," *Software Development* (May 1996).
This article lists ten common traps that can undermine software process improvement programs. Lack of management commitment and unrealistic expectations are the top two.

Yilmaz, R. R. and Sangit. "Deming and the Quality of Software Development," *Business Horizons*, Foundation for the School of Business at Indiana University, 40, No. 6 (November-December 1997): 51(8).
This article discusses how Deming's philosophy can facilitate the continuous improvement of software quality. It also describes the Software Quality Function Deployment and Capability Maturity Models for improving software development.

Yourdon, Ed, "Surviving a Death March Project," *Software Development* (July 1997).
Ed Yourdon is famous for his books on software development, including a 1997 text entitled Death March. *Yourdon offers practical advice on how to handle software projects that are plagued with problems from the start. He describes the importance of a project manager being able to negotiate schedules, budgets, and other aspects of a project, with users, managers, and other stakeholders.*

INDEX

Harness the power and flexibility of Microsoft Project 2000 to plan and track projects and meet your business needs!

Visit http://support.Microsoft.com/support for online help for this product. (For all other technical support or to report a problem with the CD packaged with this book, please contact Prentice Hall.)

- To get started, simply insert the CD-ROM packaged with this text into your CD drive and click on "Multimedia Demo" for a guided tour of Microsoft Project 2000.
- Click on "Install Trial Software" to begin using the 120-day free evaluation software packaged with your textbook.
- System Requirements are provided under the "Pricing and Upgrade" button on the opening menu.

Visit the free companion website for *Practical Project Management* at http://www.prenhall.com/ghattas

This text-specific website provides students with an abundance of tutorials, quizzes, and web resources–helping to facilitate a greater understanding of course material.

Prentice Hall is proud to partner with many of the leading course management system providers on the market today. These partnerships enable Prentice Hall to combine our market-leading online content with the powerful course management tools of such respected companies as Blackboard, WebCT, and eCollege.com.

Online course materials for *Practical Project Management* are available in

 WebCT,

Blackboard, and

eCollege.com eCollege environments.